THE PRECIOUS SUMMARY

The Precious Summary

A History of the Mongols from Chinggis Khan to the Qing Dynasty

Sagang Sechen

Translated by Johan Elverskog

Columbia University Press New York

GEISS HSU
FOUNDATION
This publication was made possible in part by an award from the James P. Geiss and Margaret Y. Hsu Foundation.

Columbia University Press
Publishers Since 1893
New York Chichester, West Sussex
cup.columbia.edu

Library of Congress Cataloging-in-Publication Data
Names: Sagan Setsen, Khungtaij, 1604–approximately 1662, author. | Elverskog, Johan, translator.
Title: The precious summary : a history of the Mongols from Chinggis Khan to the Qing dynasty / Sagang Sechen ; translated by Johan Elverskog.
Other titles: Erdeni-yin tobči. English
Description: New York : Columbia University Press, [2023] | Includes bibliographical references and index.
Identifiers: LCCN 2022026534 (print) | LCCN 2022026535 (ebook) | ISBN 9780231206945 (hardback) | ISBN 9780231206952 (trade paperback) | ISBN 9780231556736 (ebook)
Subjects: LCSH: Mongols—History—Sources. | Sagan Setsen, Khungtaij, 1604–approximately 1662. Erdeni-yin tobci.
Classification: LCC DS19 .S5913 2023 (print) | LCC DS19 (ebook) | DDC 950/.2—dc23/eng/20220616
LC record available at https://lccn.loc.gov/2022026534
LC ebook record available at https://lccn.loc.gov/2022026535

Cover design: Chang Jae Lee
Cover image: Urga manuscript of *Erdeni-yin Tobči*

In memory of my teacher
György Kara (1935–2022)

Contents

Introduction

The Mongols are famous on account of Chinggis Khan and the empire they built and ruled in the thirteenth and fourteenth centuries. Moreover, as much recent research has revealed, the Mongols were not simply a marauding horde that destroyed surrounding civilizations; rather, the Mongols and their empire created institutions, trading networks, economic systems, and intellectual and technological exchanges that would come to shape and define the early modern world.[1] In short, the Mongols are crucial to our understanding of world history.

Yet, what became of the Mongols after the glories of the empire? This history is less well known, and is often presented as one of general collapse. In 1368 the Mongols lost China to Zhu Yuanzhang and his Ming dynasty (1368–1644). Forced to flee back to the steppe, they supposedly devolved into endless civil wars and Buddhist obscurantism before being conquered by the Manchu Qing dynasty (1644–1911). In other words, the postempire Mongols experienced centuries of upheaval and discord that in many tellings was only overcome by the nationalist and communist revolutions of the early twentieth century. Only then could the Mongols finally throw off the imperial yoke, secure their independence, and start modernizing and developing into a respected nation-state on the world stage.[2] While such an account does have some truth to it, like all histories, it also leaves many details on the cutting-room floor. So, what did happen to the Mongols in the postimperial period?

This is the history that Sagang Sechen relates in the *Precious Summary*, a work second in importance only to the famous *Secret History of the Mongols*. Yet unlike the mid-thirteenth-century *Secret History*, Sagang Sechen's history was written in 1662, shortly after the Mongols' submission to the Manchu Qing dynasty (1644–1912). His main focus is thus less on the glories of Chinggis Khan and the Mongol empire and more on the often overlooked three-hundred-year period from the fall of the Yuan dynasty in China (1272–1368) through the Mongol-Oirat wars and the revival of Mongol power during the reign of Dayan Khan in the sixteenth century. Indeed, to appreciate Sagang Sechen's telling of this important history it is valuable to recall what happened in Inner Asia from the late fourteenth century to the founding of the Qing dynasty in the early seventeenth century.

THE RETURN TO THE STEPPE

Shortly after defeating his rivals Khubilai Khan founded the Yuan dynasty and began building the imperial capital of Daidu (present-day Beijing). In 1279 he defeated the Song dynasty in the south and thereby consolidated Mongol rule of China. After his death in 1294, however, the Yuan dynasty was beset by political feuds and weak rulers that all came to a head during the reign of Toghan Temür (1320–1370). Not only was his regime beset by political and ideological feuds; the dynasty as a whole was also challenged by massive environmental problems, including famines resulting from the flooding of the Yellow River and outbreaks of disease that killed enormous numbers of the population in the 1350s. These disasters gravely affected the economy, and the government tried to solve the problem by printing money, which drove up inflation and only made the situation worse. The inevitable response to this perfect storm of political paralysis, environmental disaster, and economic collapse was revolution, and as was often the case in China, it was framed in apocalyptic religious terms. Fired up with Buddhist messianic visions, groups like the Red Turbans rose up against the Yuan. Ultimately, however, they merged with other rebel movements under the able leadership of Zhu Yuanzhang, a former Buddhist monk and devotee of Maitreya, who led the revolutionaries on a northward march to expel the Mongol rulers. On September 10, 1368, they were victorious, and Zhu Yuanzhang (r. 1368–98) was declared emperor of the Ming dynasty.

Toghan Temür and his Mongol followers fled north and founded the Northern Yuan dynasty, which continued to be recognized across Eurasia as the rightful heirs of Chinggis Khan, so much so that for several decades the surrounding peoples—from Korea to Central Asia to Yunnan—all continued to recognize the Mongol ruler as the Great Khan. They continued to pay taxes to the Mongols, accepted their seals and titles of investiture, and even used the Northern Yuan calendar as their own. On account of this power Zhu Yuanzhang recognized that outside of China proper, many people in eastern Eurasia saw him and his dynasty as illegitimate usurpers of the Mongol legacy.[3]

Even so, the power of the Northern Yuan was not assured, not least from the continued fighting with the Ming in the south and also from non-Chinggisid Mongols in the north, the Oirats, who had taken control over the Mongolian plateau as the Mongols became more and more embroiled in the affairs of China during the Yuan dynasty. Indeed, on account of the Oirats, when the Mongols fled Beijing, they were not able to return to their homeland. Instead they established themselves in the area between the Great Wall and the Gobi Desert, what is now known as Inner Mongolia in the People's Republic of China. Moreover, two years after his people arrived as refugees in this environmentally and politically marginal buffer zone, the last Yuan emperor, Toghan Temür, died of dysentery.

While Toghan Temür's death may symbolize well the waning fortunes of the Mongols in the post-Yuan period, they were far from powerless. In addition to being recognized as the rightful heirs of Chinggis Khan by the surrounding peoples, they had economic power due to their control of the trade in Central Asian horses, which were essential for both the Ming military and its larger economy. Without them the Ming would quite literally have ground to a halt, since Chinese soil lacks selenium, a vital mineral for the raising of strong horses.[4] The volume of this trade was immense: annually the Ming bought nearly two million horses from the Mongols.[5] Of course, for the Ming court it was intolerable that their economy and national security were in the fickle hands of their enemies. At first they tried invasion and conquest, but the campaigns of both the

Hongwu (r. 1368–1398) and Yongle emperors (r. 1402–1424) could not entirely break the power of the Mongols.

In response to these failures the Ming court adopted a two-pronged strategy. The first was to find another source of horses, which they did by reestablishing the tea-for-horses trading network with Tibet.[6] The second was to keep trading with the Mongols, but on their own terms. Their plan was to funnel all this trade through the small independent city-state of Hami in Gansu province, which in 1406 had been brought into the Ming system of frontier garrisons.[7]

The Mongol Khan Gülichi (r. 1402–1408), however, did not agree with these terms and poisoned the prince of Hami, who had made the deal with the Chinese. At this turn of events the Ming court was bewildered, but they still hoped to salvage the negotiations. When their envoys were executed at the command of the new Mongol ruler, Punyashri (r. 1408–1411), the Ming court finally decided to circumvent the Mongols entirely. They therefore made contact with the Mongols' rivals, the Oirats, and not only bestowed titles and privileges upon them but also opened up direct trade relations. The immediate consequence was that any power the Mongols had over the Ming evaporated, and both their wealth and regional strength started to wane; in their place rose the Oirats. Their power would reach its apogee during the reign of Esen (d. 1455), who in 1449 even captured the Yingzhong emperor at Tumu Fort, fifty miles northwest of Beijing, an event that profoundly rattled the Ming court but emboldened Esen.[8] He thus proclaimed himself khan and the rightful ruler of all the Mongols in 1453. While the Ming court hesitantly approved, the Mongols saw this action as a gross violation of the Chinggisid principle since Esen was an Oirat, and only direct descendants of Chinggis Khan could ever become a true khan and hold the Mongol throne. The Mongols therefore violently resisted, and after Esen's death in 1455, the Oirats were weakened.

In their place rose the Mongols. Yet how they were able to rally themselves at this particular point in time is little understood. One factor in their favor was the environment. Chinese sources record that on account of poor climatic conditions north China suffered severe famine during the 1450s and '60s.[9] The same conditions clearly must have affected both the Mongols and the Oirats. Yet since the Oirats controlled the Mongolian plateau (roughly the territory of the present-day country of Mongolia), which has far greater weather extremes than Inner Mongolia (in today's China), it is very likely that they were much worse off during these decades than the Mongols. Moreover, being closer to China, the Mongols could not only trade with the Chinese but also, if need be, raid over the border. Regardless, it was during this time that the Mongol ruler Manduulun became khan and reigned briefly in the late 1470s. Upon his death, Bayan Möngke became khan, and upon his death in 1484, his seven-year-old son—the last remaining direct descendant of the Chinggisid line of Great Khans—was married to Manduulun Khan's widow, which enabled him to be recognized as the rightful ruler of all the Mongols.

Once the fortunes of the Mongols began to turn under this young ruler's direction, he became famous as Dayan Khan (r. 1480?–1517?). His meteoric rise to power began with his consolidation of the Mongols living in eastern Inner Mongolia and reorganization of them into the Three Eastern Tümen (Chakhar, Khalkha, and Uriyangkhan). Next came his greatest military achievement, the conquest of the Mongols of Ordos, who had taken advantage of the Tumu incident to occupy the area within the great bend of the Yellow River.[10] Having thus only recently moved into and taken over this territory, the Ordos Mongols did not initially want to ally themselves with Dayan Khan and violently resisted his project of unification. Ultimately, however, Dayan was victorious, and the Ordos Mongols were then organized into the Three Western Tümen (Ordos, Tümed, and Yüngshiyebü).[11] And it was through this organizational reformulation into the Six Tümen under the authority of the Chinggisid ruler Dayan Khan that the Mongols were able to reassert their power against the Oirats. While military prowess, marriage alliances, and shrewd politics certainly held this new sociopolitical structure together, it was also ideologically reinforced by the concept of a return to proper Chinggisid rule and a reaffirmation of the Mongol legacy.

Over the course of the sixteenth century, however, this ideal vision of unified Mongol rule began to fray. Thus while the idea of the Mongols being ruled by the direct descendants of Dayan Khan was maintained in theory (as well evidenced in the *Precious Summary*), the reality is that other Dayan Khanid princes were beginning to assert their own power locally. The most notable was Altan Khan (1507–1586), who over the course of his life became the most powerful ruler among the Mongols. He pushed the recognized ruler, Daraisun (r. 1548–1557), out of his ancestral lands; defeated the Oirat and Muslim rulers of Central Asia; made a peace deal with the Ming dynasty in 1571; and in 1578 famously met the Dalai Lama and became a Buddhist.

These developments set in motion a cycle of events whereby other Mongol princes emulated Altan Khan and began to assert their own autonomy. By the time of Ligdan Khan (d. 1634)—the last recognized ruler of the Mongols—there was a civil war raging among these competing descendants of Dayan Khan. Some made alliances with the Manchus and fought against Ligdan Khan. Others, like the princes of the Khalkha, sought independence from both Ligdan Khan and the Manchus. Still others became involved in Tibet's civil war by aligning with Buddhist orders challenging the power of the Dalai Lama and his Gelukpa government. The early decades of the seventeenth century in northeast Asia were defined by political fragmentation, economic collapse, religious feuds, and social discord. And the most common solution for the Mongol princes grappling with this chaotic situation was to seek peace and stability in the rising power of the Manchu state. Sagang Sechen, for example, advised his local ruler—Rinchen Jinong of the Ordos—to do so in 1635. The other fifty or so Dayan Khanid princes followed suit and in short order were reorganized into the Mongol nobility ruling the Forty-Nine Banners of the Qing empire's Inner Mongolia.

MONGOL POLITICAL THEORY

Sagang Sechen wrote the *Precious Summary* in 1662, twenty-seven years after the Ordos Mongols had joined forces with the Manchus. Therefore, to better understand his presentation of these events—and the entire history of the Mongols—it is necessary to comprehend some of the factors shaping Mongol society at the time. The most important, as noted above, was the Chinggisid legacy, which defined political legitimacy in post-Mongol Eurasia from Anatolia to China and held that a ruler—especially one who took the title khan—had to be a direct descendant of Chinggis Khan. If they were not—as with the Oirats on the Mongolian steppe—they had to circumvent this genealogical problem through various strategies. One tactic was to put a weak Mongol princeling on the throne, who was simply a puppet of the Oirat leader. While this charade perpetuated the ideal of the Chinggisid principle—as is well captured in the *Precious Summary*—it also belied the political tensions among the Ming, the Mongols, and the Oirats that defined the first half of the fifteenth century. Those tensions came to a head when the Oirat leader Esen declared himself khan in 1453, which set in motion the scramble for Mongol political authority that was only resolved with the rise of Dayan Khan in the early sixteenth century.

Upon Dayan Khan's death the Chinggisid legacy lived on among his direct descendants. In particular, the recognized ruler of the Mongols was his direct heir and ruled the Chakhar Tümen, but all of his other descendants—the grandsons and great-grandsons—over time came to be the recognized nobility that governed distinctive territories known as *otog*. Across the Six Tümen there were about fifty of these entities, which functioned as fiefs or appanages, each a defined territory and people assigned to the hereditary jurisdiction of a particular nobleman and his descendants. The *otog* and the nobility were the basic building blocks of Mongol society at this time; however, by the beginning of the seventeenth century "the number of descendants of Dayan Khan vastly exceeded the number of *otogs*."[12]

While the *otog* and the numerous descendants of Dayan Khan controlling them were a recent development, this expansion of Chinggisid rulers and its inherent devolution of power was premised on the second major factor of Mongol political life: the theory of *ulus* and *törö*. The term *ulus* means "community" and *törö* means "state," and these two concepts defined Mongol communal conceptualizations and notions of political authority in the post-Yuan period. Within this system, the community, or *ulus*, was understood as a particular group of people with a recognized ruler inhabiting a natural unit of geography. The state was the governmental apparatus represented by a leader (khan, emperor, sultan) who ruled a community, or several of them, by means of a particular form of governance, or "customs of state" (*törö yosun*). Moreover, within this system, while states and their customs could change, so too could the imagined community of the *ulus*: it could expand to the larger category of the *tümen*—and the Mongols as a whole—but also telescope down to the local *otog* depending on context.

The framework defining this conceptualization is well captured in the description of Chinggis Khan's conquest of the Jurchen Jin dynasty found in the *Precious Summary*:

> Thereupon nine generations ensued, and from the Wu Dog year [1058] it was one hundred and thirty-seven years to the Jia Tiger year [1194], when Chinggis Khan of the Mongols expelled and drove out the Manchu Altan Khan of China, seizing his state. And in the Jia Tiger year (1194), at the age of thirty-three, he brought under his power the fifteen provinces of China, the Red Nation of eighty Tümen, and became famed as the Dai Ming, Blessed, Holy Chinggis Khan.

In this description, Chinggis Khan's conquest of the Jurchen's Jin state did not entail the destruction of China. The "Red Ulus" and its fifteen provinces survived, albeit under the Mongol state.[13] Similarly, in describing the fall of the Yuan, Mongol histories of the seventeenth century present the Ming reconquest as the Chinese taking back the "Great State."[14] Contrary to what we might imagine, the Ming conquest is presented as justified in Mongol histories, since the Mongol leaders had lost their ability to hold the state together, which is the sine qua non of any legitimate ruler. In fact, as Sagang Sechen makes clear regarding the Qing dynasty, it too was legitimate because the last Mongol ruler, Ligdan Khan (d. 1634), had also lost control of the various Mongol communities. This breakdown was only set right when the same Mongol groups and their leaders allied themselves with the Manchus, whose state could provide peace and stability.

What is important in all these cases, however, is that all of the new states—the Yuan, Ming, and Qing—did not destroy the various communities under their authority. Thus the Mongol "Great State" did not destroy "China"; it had only ruled the Chinese.[15] Similarly, the Ming reconquest and the Mongol loss of the "Great State" did not entail the disappearance of the Mongols; nor did the Manchu Qing destroy the Mongols, since, according to Mongol political theory, a state could be conquered and its community or peoples subsumed under another state, but it was assumed that these variously incorporated communities—and especially their rulers—would maintain their authority and coherency.

In Mongol histories of the seventeenth century this concept of *ulus* and *törö* did not only refer to the Yuan, Ming, and Qing. It also referred to the Mongols themselves, especially in the wake of Dayan Khan's restoration of Mongol power. Thus, in these works Dayan Khan is often presented as a second Chinggis Khan, since he was the leader who, after the chaos of the Mongol-Oirat wars, once again unified and reorganized the Mongols. At the same time, these works also make it clear that he did not unite the Mongols into a recognized holistic entity—"the Mongols"—as we like to think about it today. Rather, Dayan Khan brought the disparate and pre-existing Mongol communities into his new state and reorganized them into the Six Tümen.

This conception undergirds all the seventeenth-century Mongol histories, including the *Precious Summary*.[16] By referring to the Mongol communities as the "Six Great Ulus" or the interchangable "Six Tümen," these histories argue that Dayan Khan succeeded in securing their acquiescence precisely because he was understood to be the one who could restore order among the divided groups. Moreover, he was a direct descendant of Chinggis Khan and thus fulfilled the mandate of the Mongol legacy. This was precisely why the nobility of the disparate Mongol communities recognized the legitimate right of Dayan Khan's state to restore order and rule over them. The leaders of the Three Western Tümen, for example, came to Dayan Khan and requested that he send one of his sons to rule over them as *jinong*, or viceroy. In doing so, they ceded some of their own authority to Dayan Khan and agreed to pay taxes to the new state. In return they were recognized as the local representatives of this new regime. At the same time, of course, it was readily understood that the new Dayan Khanid state would not dismantle these communities under its control.

Nevertheless, according to the theory of *ulus* and *törö*, if the state were to fall apart, these separate communities would again be able to go their own way. In particular, the descendants of Dayan Khan who ruled their own recognized appanages could begin to assert their independence. This was possible because each group was ruled by a descendant of Dayan Khan, who could thus claim legitimacy not only within the political model of *ulus-törö* but also in relation to the Chinggisid legacy. As legitimate heirs of Chinggis Khan, they all could assert control of their inherited territory and its people.

The most successful of these independent-minded Mongol noblemen was Altan Khan. He was the second son of Dayan Khan's third son, and thus on account of the Chinggisid principle of primogeniture he had no legitimate claim to the Mongol throne. He was simply the lord of his recognized appanage: the Tümed in Ordos. But he was also an astute military and political leader and quickly became the most powerful ruler on the steppe. He even threatened the Ming dynasty. In 1550 Altan Khan launched an audacious attack on China, and by September he had burned down the suburbs of Beijing and forced the Ming court to capitulate to his demands, which included the normalization of relations and the opening of border markets.

These markets were a success, and Altan Khan turned his attention to further securing his position on the Mongolian plateau. In 1558 he marched through Ningxia and Gansu, then turned north into present-day Xinjiang. There he first established relations with the Muslim rulers of Turfan and Hami. Then he campaigned against the Oirats in the Ili Valley and western Mongolia, which eventually resulted in the two sides establishing marriage relations and the Oirat chiefs recognizing Altan as khan. The Ming court also recognized that Altan was then the most powerful ruler among the Mongols and not only gave him an illustrious title but also signed a peace accord with him in 1571.

Even so, Altan Khan could never claim to rule the Mongols. That privilege was reserved for Dayan Khan's direct heirs, who ruled over the Chakhar Tümen. Altan Khan could only claim to be the ruler of his hereditary appanage of the Tümed, which was legitimate according to the theory of *ulus* and *törö*. But rather than abiding by this traditional model of Mongol rule that would have hobbled his larger vision, Altan Khan turned to another form of political legitimacy: Buddhism.

In particular, he drew upon the history of Khubilai Khan, who by being initiated into tantric Buddhist practice by the Tibetan Pakpa Lama had made Buddhism an important element of Mongol political ideology. This theory of rule drew upon the Buddhist political theory of "Two Realms," the religious and the political, represented by a ruler and a Buddhist leader who in a symbiotic relationship oversee the proper functioning of a Buddhist state.[17] It was this model of religiopolitical rule that Altan Khan invoked when he met with the Third Dalai Lama in 1578. Altan Khan therefore not only amplified his legitimacy among the reigning

Dayan Khanid nobility but also revived the very idea of Buddhist rule in Mongolia. Thus, Buddhism became another facet of Mongol political theory above and beyond the Chinggisid legacy and the *ulus-törö* model. By having a Tibetan Buddhist lama recognize his political authority, Altan Khan overcame his inferior position within the post-Dayan Khanid political order. He not only put an end to the Chinggisid principle of one Mongol ruler enshrined by his grandfather Dayan Khan but also made it possible for any other descendant of Dayan Khan to do the same. By allying themselves with a Tibetan lama, they too could be recognized as the rightful ruler of their recognized territory and its people.

This development set in motion a civil war among the Mongols, and since these competing descendants of Dayan Khan allied themselves with different Tibetan Buddhist orders, they were drawn into competing sides in Tibet's civil war. Chogtu Taiji of the Khalkha, for example, allied himself with the Karmapa and his Kagyü lineage and launched an invasion of Tibet against the Dalai Lama and his Tümed allies. Amid these competing religious and political alliances—compounded by the worsening financial conditions due to trade with the Ming collapsing—the situation among the Mongols quickly spun out of control.[18] In written records from the period Mongol leaders boast about killing hundreds of soldiers from other Mongol groups, and of "chopping to pieces the women and children and burning their homes and livestock."[19]

It was in this context of political fragmentation and social mayhem that the Manchus appeared, offering a solution that fit into the existing Mongol political theory. They were blessed by Heaven as Chinggis Khan had been, as evidenced by their repeated victories in battle, and ruled in accord with the theory of *ulus* and *törö*. Their powerful new state could bring peace to the fractious Mongols. The Manchus had also embraced Buddhism. Nurhaci (1559–1626), the founder of the Manchu state, had already received tantric initiation and appointed Olug Darkhan Nangso as the Buddhist lama of the Manchu realm in 1621. Nurhaci had seven large monasteries built near his residence of Hetu Ala in the 1620s.[20] His successor, Hong Taiji (1592–1643), had the famous Mahakala Temple constructed in 1635; it was a paragon of the Manchu appropriation of Buddhism and the Mongol legacy. The temple was to house a copy of the Buddhist canon in Mongolian and even the remains of Ligdan Khan and his teacher, Sharba Khutugtu. Most important, it would hold the famous Mahakala statue that Khubilai Khan had given to Pakpa Lama during the Yuan dynasty, which Ligdan Khan's family presented as tribute when they submitted to the Manchus. This statue, with its historical linkages and ritual significations, was profoundly important for the Manchu claim to be the rightful heirs of Mongol Buddhist rule; therefore, in 1643 Hong Taiji initiated an extension of this important temple complex. In 1645 the project was complete, with four temples and adjoining stupas having been built to encircle the Mahakala Temple, the imperial palace, and the Manchu capital of Mukden within a mandala.[21] In other words, the Mongols understood the Manchus to be Heaven-blessed Buddhist rulers who could restore peace and order through their new Qing state.

SAGANG SECHEN AND HIS WORLD

Sagang Sechen was born in 1604 into an important aristocratic family in Ordos in what is now the southwest part of Inner Mongolia.[22] He was the great-grandson of Khutugtai Sechen Khung Taiji (1540–1586), who had played an important role at the court of Altan Khan and in the Buddhist conversion of the Mongols. Moreover, both his grandfather and his father had continued this family tradition and distinguished themselves in military and bureaucratic service with the subsequent rulers of Ordos. As the *Precious Summary* makes clear, Sagang Sechen was seen in the same light, so much so that when he was only eleven years old he was given the title of his great-grandfather: Sechen Khung Taiji (wise crown prince). Then at the age of seventeen he became a minister at the court of Boshogtu Sechen Jinong (1565–1624), the ruler of the Ordos Mongols. Upon his passing, Sagang Sechen promoted Boshogtu Sechen Jinong's second son, Rinchen, to take his father's throne. The relationship between these two was further solidified when Sagang Sechen helped Rinchen Jinong resist the last Mongol ruler, Ligdan Khan, who had invaded Ordos in a last-ditch effort to rally the Mongols against the Manchus.

Yet, as noted above, Ligdan's actions only alienated the various Mongol leaders, and they instead allied themselves with the Manchus. Some of these alliances were forged already in the first decade of the seventeenth century; others came later. Rinchen Jinong, for example, and forty-eight other Mongol leaders allied with the Manchus in 1635. For his role in facilitating this Sagang Sechen was granted the title Erke Sechen Khung Taiji (beloved wise crown prince), and given the right to be the vanguard in the army and the leader of large battue hunts. After his involvement with these political developments, little is known about Sagang Sechen's life. At some point he moved from his ancestral lands in southern Üüshin Banner to an area in its northern reaches—where he is buried—and he wrote the *Precious Summary* over several months in the first half of 1662.[23]

In taking up pen and paper to write the history of the Mongols at this time, Sagang Sechen was not alone. His work was part and parcel of a literary flowering that occurred among the Mongols in the wake of the Manchu conquest. Although all of these works were similar in terms of narrative structure and thematic issues, Sagang Sechen's volume came to be recognized as the masterpiece. Manuscript copies spread far and wide among the Mongols.[24] Its importance was eventually recognized by scholars in Beijing, whereby the Qianlong emperor had a blockprint version prepared in 1777. This imperially commissioned version became in turn the basis for Chinese and Manchu translations, which only further increased the circulation and impact of the *Precious Summary*.[25] This dynamic increased exponentially when the *Precious Summary* became the first Mongolian work translated into a European language in 1829.[26]

But before Sagang Sechen's work became famous in eighteenth-century Beijing—and then later in nineteenth-century Europe—it was obviously written in a very different time and place: 1662 Ordos. Indeed, we need to begin within that context in order to understand Sagang Sechen's history and what it entails. The *Precious Summary* is many things: a Buddhist cosmological history of the universe and proper rule, a history of Chinggis Khan, a history of the post-Yuan Mongols, a history of China, and also a history of the Mongols' Buddhist conversion. It is also a work trying to make sense of the new Manchu state. The *Precious Summary* therefore builds its narrative around the three political principles outlined above: the Chinggisid legacy, the *ulus-törö* model, and Buddhism. In particular, it fuses them by asserting that proper rule is reserved for righteous Buddhist rulers ("Holy Ones"), who are blessed by Heaven as was Chinggis Khan. In this vision of religiopolitical order, only such rulers can provide both peace and salvation.[27]

Thus although we do not know much about Sagang Sechen's life, based on his presentation of East Asian history, we can readily surmise that he was a Buddhist. In fact, he was an educated Buddhist who knew Tibetan and could thus engage with issues of historiographical debate (such as the dates of the Buddha's life) and directly cite passages from canonical Buddhist texts to bolster his argument.[28] Moreover, as an educated Mongol of the seventeenth century, Sagang Sechen was familiar with the Chinese historical tradition as well.[29]

Yet, for writing the *Precious Summary*, Sagang Sechen's most important historical sources were the corpus of Mongolian works that had developed during the tumultuous postimperial period. Although the famous thirteenth-century *Secret History of the Mongols* had been preserved among the Mongols, Sagang Sechen only used a very small portion of it in his presentation of Chinggis Khan's life and rise to power.[30] He drew instead upon the new legends and stories about Chinggis Khan that had developed during the upheavals of the fourteenth and fifteenth centuries, as well as histories about the Mongol-Oirat wars, both of which were intertwined with the subsequent revival of Mongol power and the conversion of the Mongols to Buddhism.[31] By stitching these disparate sources together Sagang Sechen was able to present a coherent narrative of Mongol history from the creation of the universe up to the reign of the Kangxi emperor (1654–1722).

SCHOLARSHIP AND TRANSLATION

This comprehensiveness—as well as Sagang Sechen's literary prowess—made the *Precious Summary* become recognized as a masterpiece.[32] Prior to the scholarly rediscovery of the *Secret History of the Mongols* in the nineteenth and twentieth centuries, the *Precious Summary* was recognized as *the* premier history of the Mongols. It was a key source for Qing dynasty historians—be they Mongol, Tibetan, or Chinese—and on account of the high esteem in which they held it, for Western scholars as well. As Europeans began investigating Buddhism, the history of Asia, and the Mongols' role in shaping it, they came to recognize the *Precious Summary* as an invaluable source. Sagang Sechen's presentation of Asian, Buddhist, Tibetan, Mongol, and Chinese history would shape scholarship in the West for more than a century.[33] Indeed, the importance of the *Precious Summary* as a source for both understanding early modern East Asian history and the modern discipline of Asian studies cannot be underestimated.

It is for these reasons that I have prepared the following translation of the famous Urga manuscript preserved in Ulaanbaatar: to make an Asian classic available to as many readers as possible.[34] Of course, making a seventeenth-century Mongolian history both readable and comprehensible to twenty-first-century readers is no easy task. It involves not only the basic task of translating but also trying to explain the complicated historical context that shapes the narrative. In terms of the former, while being loyal to the text, I have also tried to provide as smooth and literary a translation as possible. Similarly, since much of the history explored in the *Precious Summary* may be obscure to many, I have provided extensive notes to make the work comprehensible even for the uninitiated.[35] Finally, along these same lines I have divided the work into chapters and provided each with an introductory summation.[36] The hope is that this readable and informative translation will inspire further thought and scholarship, just as Sagang Sechen's original *Precious Summary* has done for the past three hundred and sixty years.

THE PRECIOUS SUMMARY

CHAPTER ONE

History of the Universe, the Buddha, and India

Sagang Sechen begins his history with a Buddhist creation story. By so doing he not only addresses the existential question of why we are here but also lays the groundwork for why Buddhist rule is necessary for human flourishing. According to the Buddha, humans are afflicted with "three poisons"—ignorance, desire, and anger—that drive us to seek riches and power and thereby generate conflict with others. This is the central philosophical idea that propels Sagang Sechen's historical narrative, because the only way to hold in check these destructive instincts and thereby create a stable and just society—as well as make salvation possible—is through proper Buddhist rule. In the Inner Asian historical tradition this genealogy of righteous rule began in India, but on account of human avarice and stupidity it all fell apart. Buddhist rule was then established in Tibet, but the Tibetan empire also collapsed. Thus it was the Mongols who in turn reestablished righteous Buddhist government. Yet, as Sagang Sechen's history makes clear, when the Mongols were defeated by the Ming, they too lost their claim to proper Buddhist leadership. It therefore eventually fell upon the Manchu emperors, emanations of the Bodhisattva Manjusri, to take up the task of bringing back peace and justice to the world—and the possibility of nirvana—by means of the Buddhist Qing dynasty.

I bow down before the Three Refuges, which are the rare and sublime
Three Jewels,[1]
The Three Supreme Bodies of the Conquerors[2] of the Three Times;[3]
The Sixth Vajradhara[4] of the Three Realms,[5] the Three Perfect Ones;[6]
The three beginnings that are the three benevolent lamas.[7]

I will explain how the world system, the external material world, was
established;
How the widely supporting inner descendants and beings were
formed;
How the bodhisattvas who guide beings were born; and
How the Holy Ones who make all greatly rejoice have developed.[8]

I shall relate, comparing the many texts of old, and summarizing
herewith,
How the three countries of ancient India, Tibet, and Mongolia
Have developed since ancient times,
From King Mahasammata of yore to the present.[9]

Now, on the establishment of the external universe, the main support of everything, from the celestial sphere that generally supports the internal beings: if we discuss the establishment of the very first of these, the external material world, it was established by three sorts of mandalas.[10] In particular, these three mandalas were the mandala creating wind, the mandala of billowing water, and the mandala supporting earth. The first of these three, the mandala of wind: because of the colliding together and the moving this way and that way of the great winds from the ten directions in the primordial emptiness of the celestial sphere, there was established a mandala of wind, indestructible and having a bluish color termed "delicate" (i.e., the sky).

As for the second, the water mandala: owing to the warmth of that wind, a great cloud called the Aggregate of Jewels accumulated. Then, because a heavy rain fell constantly, the limitless great sea called the Salty Sea came into being and the water mandala [2v] was established.

As for the third, the earth mandala: above this water, a molecular dust called Having a Golden Heart became fixed like the skim on milk. Thereupon, this very fine dust became larger, each being successively seven times greater than its precedent: an atom; a particle of iron dust; a particle of water; a particle of dust on the hair of a hare; a particle of dust on the hair of a sheep; a particle of dust on the hair of a cow; a mote floating on a sunbeam; a nit; a louse; a grain of barley. Seven barley grains make one inch; twenty-four inches make one cubit; four cubits make one fathom; five hundred fathoms is the distance that the sound of a conch [trumpet] can be heard; eight trumpet blasts make one league. In that way the thick great immensity of the earth mandala, called the Very Mighty Golden World, was formed. And in its middle there simultaneously appeared the majestic Mount Sumeru,[11] the King of Mountains, which is surrounded by seven golden mountains and seven seas, as well the four great continents and the eight lesser continents.[12]

Next, if one discusses the inner one, the establishment of beings: a god of the first level of concentration descended and, by being born in the land of men, gradually propagated. There came into existence different beings [in the various worlds]: in the material world there were seventeen; in the immaterial world, four; in the world of desire, twenty; and in the three worlds, sixteen. Of these beings, if one discusses particularly the people of the four continents, they were in general manifestations of gods, and they lived to an incalculable age. Moreover, when living in this material world they did not travel by foot on the ground; rather, they went flying through the sky. When they ate, they did not eat the impure food that was on the ground, [2v] they ate the pure food of meditative absorption. Since prior to being born there were no men and women, they were not born from the womb, but were born as incarnations. And since prior to being seen there was no sun and moon, they saw by the light emanating from their own bodies. At that time there was no term for "people" and instead the general term "beings" was used.

At a later time, one being who was passionate for tasty things found and ate a food called fat of the land. Then because everyone else also consumed it, the former food of meditative absorption vanished. And because they ate this fat of the land, they lost their ability to travel through the sky and fell to earth. The light emanating from their bodies disappeared, and because it had become night and grown dark, the first [of the three poisons] arose: ignorance. Thereupon, by meritorious outcome of the deeds of beings in general, the sun, the moon, and the stars arose and illumination came to be their light.

After this, another being, again passionate for tasty things, found and ate a food called verdant vegetation. Everyone else consumed it as well, and because they had to constantly eat the impure food of the ground, the distinguishing features of men and women then emerged. And as a result of their lusting for one another, which caused sons and daughters to be born, the second [of the three poisons] arose: desire.

After this, at another time, a being yearning for yet another tasty thing found a grain called self-risen *salu*. "What sort of food is this? Whatever it may be, let me try to taste it," he said and ate that wild rice. In consequence of everyone eating it that former food disappeared, and this rice became what there was to eat. Then, as they continued to eat this rice, always gathering it for eating, [3r] one lazy being took and laid aside today the food intended for tomorrow, whereby that rice started to become scarce. Which is how [the third of the three poisons] arose: greed.

Then, when that sown rice was being eaten, because of eating such impure food of the lower world, the complexion of those who ate a lot grew poor and the complexion of those who ate little was fine. As a result, they ridiculed each other, saying, "My complexion is fine, but your complexion is bad." Then they seized each other's land to grow that rice, and a great quarrel arose whereby they killed one another. The evil tendency of anger originated at that time.

Then again, from the ones who had eaten a lot of this rice and concealed it from those who had eaten only a little there arose the evil tendency of avarice.

Then a fair and handsome, very pure-hearted, bright and intelligent being came forth favoring right action and punishing wrong deeds. Whereupon, since he divided the farmland equally and nurtured all in the same way, then by one and all it was said:

> "Let us not transgress your orders,
> Let us elevate you as our ruler!"

And all promising together, they elevated him to rule, calling him in Sanskrit, Mahasammata Raja; in Tibetan, Mangpo Kurbé Gyelpo; and if we say it in Mongolian, Khan Elevated by the Many. [3v]

It was in this manner that at the time when the Buddha Samantabhadra was teaching,[13] the cakravartin khan, who makes the golden wheel revolve on the four continents, became renowned.[14] The name of that era was the Very First Kalpa When Time Passed in Original Perfection.

Then, through the destiny of beings, the sun, the moon, and the stars appeared in the sky and illuminated the four continents with their light. [Khan Elevated by the Many's] son was King Beautiful Light, his son was King Virtuous, his son King Supreme Virtue, his son King Abundant Defender and Nurturing One Born from the Crown of the Head, and his son King Nurturing Us. They became famous as the first six wheel-turning kings. After that time, up to the present day, there took place the naming of people.

Then the lifespan of human beings gradually decreased. When one calculates time, generally, the shortest time is a single *ksana* (moment); a hundred *ksana* are a single second; sixty seconds are a single minute; thirty minutes are a single quarter; sixty quarters are a single hour; twelve hours are a single day; thirty days are a single month, and twelve months are one year. Calculating by increasing and decreasing the number of years, a kalpa comes into being.

As to the so-called kalpas, there are six: the Kalpa of Establishment, the Abiding Kalpa, the Intermediate Kalpa, the Kalpa of Destruction, the Kalpa of Emptiness, and the Great Kalpa. Of these six, the first, the Kalpa of Establishment, extends from the establishment of the first-created mandala of wind up to the birth of Hell beings without release. [4r] The second, the Abiding Kalpa, extends from when the people of Jambudvipa[15] lived to be an incalculable age down to their living to the age of ten. As to the third, the Intermediate Kalpa: at the end of living to the age of ten, the sons and daughters of Slayers of Life, increasing from having lived to be twenty, then lived up to an age of 80,000 years. The fourth, the Kalpa of Destruction, extends from the destruction by the sword to the destruction by water. As to the fifth, the Kalpa of Emptiness: after the completion of the destruction by water, it extends to the beginning of establishing once again the creative mandala of wind. The sixth, the Great Kalpa, extends from the establishment of that very first creative mandala of wind up to the end of the Kalpa of Emptiness. In this way, by increase and decrease, from the onset of the Kalpa of One Thousand Buddhas of the Good Time, it is said in general that seven buddhas, including Sikhin and Visvabhu, will have passed away.[16]

Now, having regard for this tradition, in the vajra land of Magadha [in India], where the twelve deeds [of the Buddha][17] were displayed in the Kalpa of One Thousand Buddhas, the very first people of Jambudvipa lived for 40,000 years during the time of the Buddha Krakucchanda. During the time of the Buddha Kanakamuni they lived 30,000 years, and they lived 20,000 years during Buddha Kasyapa. It is said that now four buddhas have passed away, counting the present Sakyamuni, (during whose time) people lived to be one hundred.

Thus, in the opinion of Jowo Atisa,[18] it is said that the Vanquishing Sakyamuni [Buddha] was born in the Yi 乙 Ox year.[19] In the Jia 甲 Monkey year,[20] at the age of eighty, he revealed the nature of nirvana (i.e., passed away). In the opinion of the *Wheel of Time* astrologers,[21] [4v] the Vanquishing Sakyamuni was born in the Ding 丁 Sheep year and revealed the nature of nirvana in the Bing 丙 Tiger year at the age of eighty. In the opinion of Sakya Pandita,[22] it is said that the Vanquishing Sakyamuni was born in the Wu 戊 Dragon year and in the Ding Pig year, at the age of eighty, revealed the nature of nirvana. Thus, the opinions of wise men of various languages, including Indian and Tibetan, are many. As for that, as it is said in the supreme *Golden Beam Sutra*:[23]

> The Buddha does not completely pass away in nirvana;
> No destruction occurs to the doctrine of the Holy Ones.
> For the sake of perfecting existing beings,
> He has demonstrated the truth of nirvana to all.
>
> The extent of the age of the Omnipotent One
> No one is able to calculate.
> Although the spiritual, manifest, and physical body may pass on,
> There is no similar death for the illuminating true body of the
> Dharma.[24]

In this regard the holy Sakya Pandita has compared the following four works: Panchen Sakya Sri's *The Numbers of Religion Sutra*, composed and compared with the splendid *Wheel of Time*; the holy Buddha Kirtidhvaja's ancient text, the *Sutra of the Leader Who Revealed a Prophecy to the Maiden Called "Immaculate"*; the story called *The Bouquet of Flowers (That Is) to Be Extraordinarily Revealed*, composed by the becalmed Aksapada, perfected in wisdom; and *The Red Annals*, composed by Sengge Sribhadra, perfected in great wisdom.

In accordance with what these four have written, and similarly in accordance with the opinion of Sakya Pandita, who attained the limits of the realms of comprehension in the teaching of the Mighty Powerful One (i.e., the Buddha), which has survived until now: [5r] if one were to describe the dispersal, among the very first people of India, of the lineage of kings: in the Sakya clan of the aforementioned Khan Elevated by the Many, from King Nurture Us up to when King Lion-Jawed was born in the vajra land of Magadha one *asamkya* had passed, meaning 74,506 generations.

[King Lion-Jawed] had four sons and four daughters. His four sons were Having Pure Food, Having White Food, Having Delicious Food, and Drinking Nectar. The four daughters were Pure, the White One, the Charming One, and Amrta.

If one now mentions his grandchildren: Having Pure Food's two were the One Who Fulfills All Aims and beautiful Nanda; Having White Food's two were Victorious Siddha and Perfected Good; Having Delicious Food's two were Having a Great Name and Unrestrained; and Drinking Nectar's two were Ananda and Devadatta.

* * *

Of his daughters' children: Pure's son was He Who Comprehends Well, White One's son was Having a Rosary, Charming One's son was Batira, and Amrta's son was Vaisalya.

Furthermore, as to the son of King Having Pure Food—the noble prince Who Accomplished Everything (i.e., the Buddha)—on the twenty-second of the month of Asvini of the Bing Tiger year he took rebirth in [Tusita heaven] as Dampa Togkar.[25] From Tusita he descended to the land of Magadha in Jambudvipa in the shape of the elephant called Airavata[26] and in the night of the full moon of the month of Purvasadhha in the Ding Rabbit year [5v], in the city of Rajagrha, entered the womb of Queen Mahamaya in the form of a five-colored light beam. At sunrise, during the full moon of the month of Uttaraphalguni in the Wu Dragon year, the Supreme Body was born in Lumbini Park.[27]

At the age of seven, from the Jia Dog year onward, he completely perfected himself in all the skills of men. At the age of sixteen, in the Gui 癸 Sheep year, in the city of Kapilavastu,[28] he took as his wife Bhumika, the daughter of Having a Bracelet on His Arm. He [continued to] look after the king's state. At the age of twenty-nine, in the Bing Monkey year, he himself became a monk before the stupa called Surely Purified.

For six years he practiced asceticism on the bank of the Nairanjana River. At the age of thirty-five, on the eighth day of the month of Vishaka in the Ren 壬 Tiger year,[29] he tranquilly engaged in meditation at the base of the Bodhi tree. After seven days and seven nights, on the fourteenth night of the month he conquered [Mara's] demons in the city of Rajagrha. The next day, at sunrise of the fifteenth day, seated on the vajra throne of Magadha, he attained the sanctity of a surpassing Buddha called Sakyamuni, the Vanquishing Powerful One.

Thereupon, at the age of thirty-six, from the first of the last month of winter of the Gui Rabbit year until the (day of the) full moon, he performed the Great Miracle[30] at the Jetavana Park and other places.[31] Beginning from the fourth day of the month of Sravana of the same year, he turned the wheel of the Three Doctrines,[32] leading and perfecting all beings of the Three Realms in general. At the age of eighty, on the fifteenth night of the Vishaka month in the Ding Pig year he found the sanctity of nirvana through the conventional material body, for the purpose of making known to beings that composite things are impermanent.

Similarly, six days and nights after she had given birth to the Prince Who Accomplished Everything [6r], his mother, Queen Mahamaya, attained nirvana. Later, when he was thirty-five and had attained the sanctity of buddhahood in the Ren Tiger year, then six years passed and in the Ding Sheep year, when he perceived with the eye of wisdom that his mother, Queen Mahamaya, had been reborn in the Abode of the Thirty-Three Gods, he ascended [to that heaven] in order to lead her to buddhahood.

While he was preaching the Dharma there for ninety days and nights, the King of India named Udayana,[33] being of troubled heart, told [the Buddha's disciple] Maha Maudgalyayana,[34] "Come and make an image of Buddha, so as to appease my troubled mind." Maudgalyayana, going by means of magical transformation to the Abode of the Thirty-Three [Gods], from a sandalwood tree called Elephant's Head, fashioned an image identical to the Buddha, hands spread in a mudra gesture of preaching the doctrine. He straightaway brought it from the Abode of the Gods, and it greatly delighted the king's mind.[35]

Then, when the Buddha arose and returned from the Abode of the Gods and when that sandalwood Jowo [statue] was itself kneeling before the Buddha, the Buddha declared:

> "After I have attained nirvana, this sandalwood Jowo,
> A thousand years hence,
> At that time, proceeding to the land of the Black Chinese,[36]
> It will perform great, vast benefit in the eastern region."

[After the Buddha] proclaimed this prophecy he explained: "Side by side with the noble, powerful, and Mighty One (i.e., Buddha) were King Heart of Aggregate,[37] lord of the city of Varanasi in the land of Magadha,[38] the son of Great Lotus of the Sakyas; King Salgyal, lord of the city of Vaisali in the land of Kosala,[39] [6v] son of Brahmadatta, 'given by Brahma'; King Greatly Luminous in the land of Padsala, the son of Limitless; and King Sharba in the land of Kausambi,[40] the son of Having a Hundred Soldiers." In these thirty-two lands, these four great kings who ruled were born in sequence. It is said that they proclaimed the wisdom of the Buddha and defended the religion.

Now, after the Buddha had entered nirvana, the later kings (were these): Jewel Moon was the son of King Heart of Aggregate; his son was Maskisra Who Maintains Peace; his son was Lion; and his son was Having Ten Chariots.

If we discuss that son, the years after that Ding Pig year when the Buddha entered nirvana, beginning from the Wu Rat year, in the customary manner of reckoning, from that very Wu Rat year were one hundred and ten. In the Ding Rooster year the Lord of Magadha, the grandson of King Heart of Aggregate, King Maskisra, became almsmaster.[41] In the land of Vimala-jang Vina Köndi,[42] the Buddha's three main disciples—Ananda,[43] the Important One,[44] and Kasyapa[45]—heading five hundred arhats assembled and collected the words of the wheel of the Dharma, which revealed the Four Truths,[46] for the first time.[47]

In the Ding Ox year, one hundred and ten years from that same Wu Rat year, the son of Having Ten Chariots, the Dharmaraja called

Sorrowless One (i.e., Asoka[48]) became the almsmaster in the great city of Vaisali. He assembled seven hundred arhats headed by He Who Has Perfectly Pacified, in order to collect the words of the wheel of Dharma on the central philosophy of emptiness.[49] The Dharmaraja Sorrowless One then established an innumerable [7r] number of stupas of the Conqueror's body, speech, and mind.[50]

In the Ding Pig year, three hundred years from that Wu Rat year, the ruler of Kashmir was King Kaniska,[51] who became almsmaster. At the temple of Zalandara in the area of Kashmir called Günesene, there was born an incarnation of an evil spirit who became a monk named Mahadeva. When he persecuted the religion by means of magical transformation, Vasumitra, using this as a pretext, assembled the five hundred bodhisattvas, five hundred arhats, and five hundred panditas and collected the words of the Wheel of the Dharma well preached unto the end.[52]

Then in succession were born the seven Chandra kings: Raksachandra, Harichandra, Srichandra, Aksachandra, Dharmachandra, Vimalachandra, and Gopichandra.[53] Then seven Pala kings: Gopala, Dharmapala, Vigrapala, Ramapala, Dimapala, Mahapala, and Neyepala;[54] and four Sena kings: Palasena, Kesasena, Andasena, and Lakamsena.[55] It is said that they defended the religion of the Buddha. Since the spread [of the Dharma] was so inconceivable [during this time], it has not been written about here.

CHAPTER TWO

History of Tibet

Sagang Sechen's chapter on Tibet draws upon the Tibetan historical tradition that developed in the eleventh and twelfth centuries, when Buddhism was becoming a fundamental component of Tibetan culture. At that time Tibetans needed to explain this top-to-bottom religious and political reordering of society by presenting a coherent narrative that explained the new reality, not only placing Buddhism at the center of the story but also situating it in relation to the Sino-Tibetan conflicts of the empire period (618–842). As with all ethnoreligious and national histories, the historians took certain liberties telling the tale. Indeed, as detailed in the notes to this chapter, modern scholars have made it abundantly clear that many of these stories were simply later fabrications. In reading this Buddhist presentation of early Tibetan history one should keep in mind the comment of a leading scholar: "No evidence, it must be stressed, of these tales is to be found in pre-twelfth-century documents."[1] Rather, what the history in the *Precious Summary* tells us is how Tibetan Buddhists from the thirteenth century on imagined their past.

Now, if we discuss how the family of kings spread out at the foot of the vast Snow Mountain, it is as follows: In the sutra called *The Commentary on the Buddha's Praise of Those Who Became the Descendants [of Mahasammata]*, as taught by the teacher Armor of Wisdom, it says that there were three kings named Great Sakya, Sakya Licchavi, and Sakya

Mountain Rover.[2] In the family of the third, the king named Protector Lion, who was the son of King Manduulchi, had five sons. When he was defeated after fighting a wicked enemy with an army of 18,000, his youngest son, named Rupati, fled to the foot of Snow Mountain [7v] and founded the Yarlung lineage of Tibet.

At that time there was born to King He Who Makes Grow of the Vatsala people[3] a son endowed with the distinguishing marks of a Great Man:[4] turquoise hair; teeth like white shells; the digits of his hands and feet webbed like those of a goose; and eyes that blinked from the bottom upward, like those of a bird. Brahmans were summoned to evaluate these signs and said:

"This son will be a disaster to his father,
Thus it is appropriate to kill him!"

Then, because his father the king ordered his ministers to kill the child, the ministers, to slay him in accordance with the king's command, hacked at him with all kinds of swords. But it was all to no avail. They therefore put him in a copper casket and cast him into the Ganges River.[5]

Then, in the neighboring city of Vaisali,[6] while an old farmer was working his fields by the side of the river, he saw the casket emitting a flash. When he got hold of it, opened it, and looked, there was a beautiful boy inside. As it was, the old man had no children, so he thought, *Let me see if I can rear him*, and concealing him from the king, placed him at the foot of a tree and nurtured him. Different birds came, having gathered fresh fruit for him, and all the wild animals brought fresh meat; thus they reared him jointly.

Then, after he had begun to talk, he inquired, asking, "Who am I? What is my name?" When the old man told him fully the circumstances of what had happened, the boy seemed fearful and departed on a journey to the Land of Snows in the east. He then arrived at the High Bounded Mountain of Heaven. Descending from the Exultant Mountain of Heaven by the nine holy terraces, [8r] he arrived at the four-gated stupa on the righteous Yarlung plain. Here, when he met with Tübsin Bonpo of Heaven and Jang Bonpo of Earth and others, they asked him, "You are a son of which land? What are you called?" Emitting no sound whatsoever, he pointed toward Heaven with his right index finger. To which they said, "Ah! You surely must be a son of Heaven. You are not like ordinary men!" He replied, "I am indeed a son of Heaven. My father is of the golden lineage of King Elevated by the Many!"

When he told them fully the circumstances of what had happened, they said to one another, "First, his not dying in the water, and second, his being befriended and reared by various birds and wild animals, and a person, mean that he surely is a son of Heaven." Making a throne from wood and seating him on it, they bore him on their necks and went to snowy Mount Shampo.[7] By all peaceably agreeing and proclaiming him prince, he ascended the throne in the Wu Monkey year, which was 1,821 years after the Wu Rat year [when the Buddha passed away], and he became famous as a ruler named King Having a Throne of Necks.[8] He then conquered the Four Foreigners and became the lord of the 88,000 Tibetans.

* * *

His son was Mutri Tsenpo, King of the Human Throne; his son was Dingtri Tsenpo, Khiya Varbo of the Bird Throne; his son was Güri Külüg of the Crystal Throne; his son was Mertri Tsenpo, Ai Tulga of the Barley Throne; his son was Siptri Tsenpo, [8v] Gün Sobin of the River Throne; his son was Drigum Tsenpo, Dalai Sobin Aru of the Golden Throne. In all they were called the seven heavenly enthroned kings. When all of these kings passed away, they went up to heaven by means of a path of light called the "Rope of Sanctity," which penetrated upward from their feet and emerged from the top of their head, turning into a rainbow. Their corpses were buried in the land of the gods.

* * *

The minister Longam slew King Dalai Sobin Aru of the Golden Throne by means of a ruse. When the minister ascended the royal throne, the eldest of the king's three sons, Sibuuchu (Birdman), fled to the land of Ningbo; the middle one, Borachu (Grayling), to the land of Popo; and the youngest, Börte Chinua (Blue-Gray Wolf), to the land of Kongpo.[9] Then, for the half-year that the minister Longam reigned on the throne, many of the former king's ministers took his queen and fled. By stratagem, they caused foreign peoples to be greatly agitated and, drawing them in as friends, they slew that Prince Longam.

Now, being in agreement they declared, "It is necessary to invite one of the three sons [to reclaim the throne]." Their mother, the queen, said:

"One night long ago, before Borachu was born
After dreaming that I slept with a white-colored man,
An egg was born.
When this egg hatched,
It was this boy, Borachu.
Therefore, is he not my son of destiny?
Let him be made to come!"

Being thus commanded, they went and brought Borachu from the land of Popo and placed him on the throne. He became famous as King Pude Gunggyal. [9r]

* * *

His son was Esho Lek; his son was Desho Lek; his son was Trongzhi Lek; his son was Guru Lek; his son Isho Lek. In all, they were called the six good kings of the earth. Since their corpses were interred in the earth, after that the corpses of later kings were interred in the earth.

[Isho Lek's] son was Detrul Namshung; his son Denöl Podé; his son Denöl Po; his son Serednam; his son Suua; his son Tringyal Tsen; his son Tongri Tongtsen; these seven kings were called the propagators of the royal lineage.

* * *

His son was Trinam Tsen; his son Togtri Togtsen; his son Lhato Tori was born in the Wu Monkey year, 2,481 years from that very former Wu Rat year. In the Ding Rabbit year, when he was twenty, he ascended the throne.

Then one day, while he was ruling in the palace called Yumbu Lhakang,[10] there descended from heaven the *Mudras of Pangkong*,[11] a one-cubit-high golden stupa, a bejeweled casket inscribed with the original six syllables,[12] and the *Zamatog Sutra*;[13] all four descended together onto the golden pavilion of that great *vimana* palace.[14]

[The king], comprehending nothing of either Bon[15] or the Dharma, did not know what they were and thus concealed them in the treasury. Yet, after they were put underground, the king's fortunes declined: when children were born among the people, they were born eyeless and blind; crops did not grow; famine, calamities, epidemics, and plagues became widespread; and unendurable sufferings grew numerous.

Then, forty years later, in the Ding Sheep year when that king was sixty, [9v] one night, in the king's dream, five nobles with troubled faces appeared and said, "Oh, great king! Why have you concealed this great and powerful secret in the treasury?" and then straightaway vanished.

When the king and his ministers discussed this dream, they had those four objects brought out from the treasury and, festooning them with banners, worshipped them respectfully in various ways. Because they did so, the king's life, fortune, and merit increased; and when children were born they were fair and beautiful; the crops multiplied; the famine, calamities, epidemics, and plagues disappeared; and they had much joy. Thereupon, the *Collected Precepts of Mani*[16] were recited and the religion was initially established there. From that point begins what is called the first transmission of the religion.

On account of this good deed his lifespan increased another sixty years, so King [Lha]to Tori lived to be a hundred and twenty; and then in the Ding Sheep year he became a god. His son Trinyen Zungtsen, his son Tagri Nyansig, and his son Namri Songtsen, and [King Lhato Tori] himself were called the seven kings mighty in word.

* * *

When his son, a handsome and remarkable boy, endowed with the distinguishing marks and with the visage of Buddha Amitabha[17] on his brow,[18] was born from his queen, Mother Zatri Thodkar, in the Ding Ox year [617], the 2,750th year from that former Wu Rat year, they said:

> "What sort of son is this?
> It has been said, 'In former times, when our King Seger Sandalitu's son
> of a different sort was born,
> Not understanding, they cast him into the Ganges River.'
> Now, [10r] be that as it may, he is our offspring."

They gave him his very first intimate name, Tridé Songtsen, and by wrapping him with a red cloth concealed the Amitabha visage on his brow. When he was thirteen, in the Ji 己 Ox year, [629] he ascended the throne and subjected the numerous petty princes of the border to his power. At the age of sixteen, in the Ren Dragon year, [632] he dispatched Prince Thonmi Sambhota, the son of Thonmi Anu, together with sixteen comrades to India, to learn writing.[19]

From the Indian pandita Lion of Heaven's Intellect, he learned the basis of sounds. Comparing them with the sounds of Tibetan, he attached the thirty consonant letters to the four vowel letters. Then, comparing these with the Kashmiri letters and eliminating eleven of the thirty-four consonant letters, onto the remaining twenty-three he introduced six fundamental Tibetan letters and added A to them, thus constructing and creating the thirty Tibetan letters. He then composed *The Melody of Letters* and eight great treatises. When he returned, the king greatly rejoiced, and then [Tridé Songtsen] sat isolated for four years learning these works completely. He translated the *Zamatog Sutra*, the *Pangkong Mudra Sutra*, and the sutra called *The Cloud of the Three Jewels*, and other items.

* * *

Then, [Tridé Songtsen] introduced the rules of the Dharma, with its stiff penalties, to the people of Tibet and its border regions: if one killed a man, a thousand punishments were to be taken; if one committed thievery, the hands were to be broken; if one told a lie, the tongue was to be cut off; and so on. Punishing with such stern measures, he established his rule; thereby the ten dark evils [10v] were abandoned and the ten rules of virtue were adopted. Thereby, true to his second name, becoming manifest as the all-seeing, powerful, and greatly compassionate one [i.e., the Bodhisattva Avalokitesvara], he became universally renowned in the ten directions as the Supreme Cakravartin ruler, Songtsen Gampo, he who turns the thousand-spoked golden wheel.

Now, thinking that there was a need for a Buddha image as an object of veneration, the king created through magical transformation, out of his own heart, a monk named Karma Tiri—with the visage of Amitabha on his brow, like himself—and addressed him thus:

"In the time of that ancient Buddha Krakucchanda,
The powerful, all-perceiving one with eleven faces[20]
Descended from the land of Akanistha[21]
To the western direction of India,

and on the shores of the Sinhala Sea he plunged under the earth at the base of a snake-heart sandalwood tree. Then, sprouting in the time of Buddha Kanakamuni, it subsequently became a big tree in the time of Buddha Kasyapa. Now, in this time of Buddha Sakyamuni, having spread its beautiful leaves, flowers, seeds, and fruit—at the time when the Buddha passed into nirvana—it fell and was pressed into the sand.

When you have brought it forth, bring this object of faith,
The eleven-faced one.
When you arrive at the shore of the Sinhala Sea,
There a herd of elephants will lie.
In the midst of them there will be one with a red trunk,
A great elephant as big as the one bearing the name Airavata[22]
With the earrings of medicine called *kirqang* in his ears.
When you frighten him and cause him to rise,
And dig the earth beneath,
There will be that snake-heart sandalwood tree."

So commanding, he dispatched him. When that emanated monk, by means of magical power, [11r] arrived at that very place, in truth there was a herd of elephants lying there. When he frightened them and made them rise, not going far, they stood waiting. Thereupon, when he cut the branches of that sandalwood tree, a voice emerged saying: "Cut carefully!" Then from within a spontaneously arisen cleavage there came out a protector, all-seeing and powerful, an eleven-faced self-arisen statue. Thereupon, from beneath the stupa consecrated by Buddha Kasyapa and named the Wheel of Flowers, he reverently brought forth many relics of the Three Buddhas. Then that Airavata-like elephant uttered a wicked prayer:

"Your Transformation Lord forgot me of old
When he was seeking salvation;
Now my cool bed has been disturbed and ruined.
Let me, in a future rebirth, be reborn and
Become a mighty king who will destroy your religion!"

Then, reverently taking that object of veneration, [the monk] presented it to the king and, when he reported what that elephant said,

[Songtsen Gampo] proclaimed: "When I was born in ancient India as a son of the maiden Supreme Peace, I erected a stupa called Wheel of Flowers. When I requested blessings before it, there was an ox bringing earth; but [due to my] forgetting about him, he did not receive any blessing. As a result, that ox grew very wrathful and uttered a wicked prayer. I likewise uttered a prayer as antidote. Now, as for his present rebirth as this elephant, through having lain over this very figure of the protector—all-seeing and powerful—his angry thoughts have become pacified. In the future it will prove easy to render him tame. That adversary who shall render him tame, [11v] I shall become that very one."

Thereupon, when the king thought, *Now the supreme Dharma is needed to aid the beings in the Land of Snow*, he saw two beams of light emerge from the space between the eyelids of that statue which had formed itself.[23] One beam shone on the daughter of Armor of Light, the King of Nepal. Named Princess Tritsün, she was born in the Ga Monkey year [624], and at sixteen she had a white complexion and was endowed with the minor characteristics of a great person. She was not besmirched with matters of the world and was insatiably fair and beautiful to behold. The fragrance of the utpala [lotus] flower issued from her mouth, and she found her might in the *Treasury of Jewels*.[24]

As for the second beam, it reached the daughter of Tang Taisong,[25] the ruler of China. Named Princess Munchang,[26] she was born in the Ga Monkey year [624], and at age sixteen was of a bluish-hued complexion, endowed with the minor characteristics of a great person, beautiful and fair to look at, and not besmirched with matters of the world. The fragrance of sandalwood issued from her mouth, and she found her might in the *Sastra of Intellect*.

Thereupon, dispatching both Prince Thonmi Sambhota and Uran Tanggarig[27] in order to first invite the daughter of Nepal, [Songtsen Gampo] gave them three letters, each one in a separate casket, saying: "When the king of Nepal asks three different challenging questions, give these to him one at a time." When King Armor of Light, accordingly, asked each of the three riddles and when, using the three letters in the boxes, they were answered, he was astonished, frightened, and with irritation gave his own daughter Tritsün, an incarnation of the Wrathful Mother, [in marriage to Songtsen Gampo]. [12r]

With White Tara[28] Queen Tritsün there were brought to Tibet three figures that were self-formed; namely, the Jowo Aksobhya consecrated by Buddha Kasyapa, the Dharma Wheel of the Vajra Maitreya, and the White Tara Mother executed in yellow sandalwood, and other things such as copies of all the books in Nepal without exception. She met the king in the Gi Pig year [639], when he was twenty-three.

In order to invite Princess Munchang, he dispatched three hundred emissaries headed by the three noblemen Driseru Gungthun, Uran Tanggarig, and Thonmi Sambhota, giving them three letters in caskets as before. To ask for [the emperor's] daughter, the princess, in marriage, there also came, one after another, emissaries from the four realms: the Dharmaraja of India, the Persian King of Jewels, the Lord Khan of the assembled Mongols, and Gesar, the King of Warriors. Then her father, the emperor, being mindful of the Dharma, said, "Let us give her to the Dharmaraja." Her mother, the queen, because she delighted in wealth, said, "Let us give her to the King of Jewels." Her elder brother, the prince, because he was partial to heroic men, said, "Let us give her to Lord Khan of the assembled [Mongols]." The daughter, the princess, because she herself loved handsome men, thought of going with the King of Warriors. No one mentioned Tibet.

Meanwhile, Emperor Taisong, because he was very wise, thought, *It has been heard that the king of Tibet is different from ordinary men. Yet, be that as it may, let's hear what the emissaries from the Tibetan king have to say and try to understand them to their very depths.*He thus inquired of the Tibetan emissaries, "Does your king have the three objects of veneration of the Buddha? If so, I will give my daughter, the princess; if he does not, I shall not give her."

Minister Uran [12v] proffered the first casketed letter. The emperor opened it and saw that, like the letter given previously to the king of Nepal, it was written in Chinese characters with gold and jewels upon blue paper. It said: "Emperor Taisong, you have the objects of veneration; I am devoid of the objects of veneration. I will one day send one hundred and eight craftsmen, emanations of my person, and when they build one hundred and eight temples facing the land of China, will this not be a marvelous thing of mine? If you have not given me your daughter by the time I do this, I shall dispatch numerous manifested soldiers and slay you, forcibly steal your daughter, and destroy your lands."

After reading this, [the emperor] said to himself, *Is this true or is this deceit? If it be true, then things will be difficult.*

He then asked, "Does your king have a Buddhist government? If he has, I shall give my daughter; if not, I shall not." To this Minister Uran presented the second letter and said, "We'll go at your majesty's command, but our country is extremely far; therefore, deign to look at this," and presented the second letter. When [the emperor] opened and looked at it, it was written just as before: "Emperor Taisong, you have a Buddhist government; I do not. I will one day make myself by transformation into a thousand-spoked wheel-turning king and create a Buddhist government with the ten virtues.[29] Will that not be a marvelous thing of mine? If you have not given me your daughter by the time I do this, I shall dispatch numerous manifested soldiers and slay you, steal your daughter, and destroy your lands."

Oh now, can this be true? [the emperor] thought. Further, he said, "Does your king possess the pleasure of the five senses? If he does, I shall give my daughter; if he does not, [13r] I shall not give my daughter." Thereupon, Minister Uran took the third letter and said the same as before. When [the emperor] opened it and looked at it, it was written in exactly the same way as before: "Emperor Taisong, you have the pleasure of the five senses; I do not. If you desire happiness and give me your own daughter, I shall produce from my own person five hundred different emanations; and when I produce the joy of a thousand beautiful colors, the like of which has never been seen; a thousand suitable harmonious songs, the like of which have never been heard; fine odors complete in all respects, the like of which have never been smelled; hundreds of tasty foods numbered in the thousands, the like of which have never been tasted; and a thousand delicate garments, the like of which have never been worn, will this not be a marvelous thing of mine? If you have not given me your daughter by the time I do this, I shall dispatch numerous manifested soldiers and slay you, steal your daughter, and destroy your lands."

Thereupon, the emperor thought, *This surely seems to be true,* and although he was afraid, said in the manner of one who was unafraid:

"Tomorrow I shall give a feast to the five hundred emissaries. Come early." The next day, when those emissaries came, he gave a great feast. To every man he gave a big bottle of strong wine and said, "If any one of you, alone and by himself, finishes it, to that one among you I will give you my daughter."

Thereupon, the men of the emissaries each drank a bottle by himself and got drunk before finishing it. Unable to find the houses they dwelt in, they spent the night in the houses of others. But Minister Uran went early in the morning and marked with paint the road [13v] they would take home. Moreover, he first poured the contents of one bottle into small cups for each man. Thus, by drinking them one at a time and in small quantities, they finished all the bottles. And when returning at night, they returned to the house they dwelt in by following the markings on the road they had come by.

The next day, when he said, "We have finished it; give her to us!," the emperor said, "Another test," and gave every man a sheep. "Tomorrow, whichever one of you finishes eating up its flesh and tanning its hide, to him shall I give her."

None of the other emissaries finished eating the meat of a whole sheep and tanning its hide. But Minister Uran had previously killed a sheep, and by flavoring its meat he ate it completely; and as for the hide, he finished tanning it by pegging out the whole sheepskin from head to foot.

When he said, "We were able to do it; give her to us!," then the emperor gave every man a mare and a foal that were separated, and said: "Tomorrow, whichever one of you comes and finds which mare belongs to which foal among these, to that one among you shall I give her." Then the other emissaries, although they joined one mare with one foal by force, did not succeed. Minister Uran spent the night having confined the mares and foals separately, so the next day when they were paired up, each one identified the udder of its own mother. He thus said, "We have identified them; give her to us!"

Again, the emperor gave them five hundred chickens along with chicks and said: "Tomorrow, whichever one of you can distinguish which hen belongs to which chick among these, to that one among you shall I give her."

The other emissaries paired them up by simply taking one big hen and one chick, but it did not work. They all fled and departed en masse. Minister Uran, however, scattered millet on a plain and, when the hens were made to go there, he identified the chicks through their eating, [14r] each one entering and remaining under its own mother's neck. He said, "We were able to identify them; give her to us!"

Then, uniformly cutting five sets of a hundred larch trees, the emperor said: "Whichever one of you who is able to identify the top and base of these logs, to that one among you I shall give her."

The other emissaries were unable to find out which end was which in any way whatsoever. Minister Uran, however, threw the logs into a large body of water and knew which end was which by the tops pointing upward and the bases sinking downward. He said, "We have identified which end is which; give her to us!"

"Now, tomorrow I shall place and set in a row five hundred maidens, in appearance similar to my daughter the princess. Whichever one of you can find her from among them, to that one among you shall I give her," said the emperor.

Thereupon, the next day, the emissaries of the five regions assembled, and when they came to the emperor's royal palace, the princess and the five hundred maidens, having been dressed similarly in garment and adornment, were sitting beside the emperor. Now when the emperor said to the emissaries, to each one according to his seniority, "Arise and identify her!" the other emissaries, in view of their rank, arose in due succession, and each one taking the fair and pretty maidens in pairs, left, saying,

"If it be not the first one, then
It will surely be the second."

Minister Uran, however, had beforehand become the lover of a servant girl of the princess. He asked that woman, "Tomorrow, when they say, 'Whichever one of you can identify the princess from among the five hundred maidens, he may take her!,' how are we to identify her from among such identical ones? Will you carefully indicate to me her appearance and her condition? If so, I will take you as my wife."

When he said this, the woman, because the emperor's regime was strict, said, "If they learn that I have pointed her out, they will certainly kill me." [14v]

"How can anyone know that you did it? Nothing will happen, tell me," he said.

"Because our Chinese numerologists are skilled in numbers, they will know by means of numbers," she said. At once Minister Uran said, "I can manage a way out of this." That very night, digging a nine-fathom hole, he placed a three-legged trivet within it. He then filled a cauldron with water and strewed feathers of different birds on the surface. Placing a big wooden lid on the cauldron, he seated the woman upon it. Covering that woman with an iron net, through the holes of the net he made her hold a nine-fathom copper tube in her mouth whereby, through this tube, he was able to speak to her.

Then, when the woman whispered in the minister's ear by means of the tube, she said as follows:

"As for the princess,
She is no more beautiful and fair than the others;
Her garments and ornaments are no better than the others;
On the whole, she sits in appearance just like the others.
As for the characteristics of hers that are different from the others:
She has a verdant, gleaming face;
When one looks at her, she is incredibly radiant;
Her teeth are pearly white like crystal;
Her eyes are jet black like precious sapphire;
Her hair is black-colored lapis lazuli;
Her throat bears a small necklace.
As to her eyebrows, between them she bears
A mark, the size of a barley grain, of the noble Tara;
From her mouth wafts forth the fragrance of green sandalwood.
Thus is she.
She sits above the six maidens seated at the end."

Thereupon, Minister Uran took an arrow with vulture feathers and a five-colored scarf tied to it, stood up, and said:

"Is this not the daughter of a cloth weaver who sits at the very
end? [15r]
She is adorned with a cloth scarf.
Is the one before her not a woodworker's daughter?
Her blouse is faded.
Is not the one before her a porcelain maker's daughter?
Her hands are chapped.
Is not the one before her an ironworker's daughter?
Her blouse is ragged.
Is not the one before her a painter's daughter?
Her nails are colored.
Is not the one before her a goldsmith's daughter?
She wears a gold ring.
As for the one before her, she has a manner like unto
The incarnated princess!"

When he extended the nock of the arrow to the collar of her garment, the incarnated princess wept and arose, and she went out jointly with the five hundred maidens following.

Thereupon, her father the emperor, greatly grieving on behalf of his daughter, supplied items numbered in the many tens of thousands: a statue of the Jowo Sakyamuni; all the books of the profound and subtle sort; the thirteen sutras that are like the wish-granting Cintamani jewel; and other various necessities, such as jewels, silken goods, and so forth, and material goods, and bestowed them assuredly on his favorite daughter. He then dispatched Queen Gongju to Tibet.

Then, Driseru Gungthun, growing envious, spoke as follows: "Oh great emperor, you have given to our king your only favorite offspring. If now, one of us three ministers were to remain behind, would not the states of China and Tibet become firmly allied?"

When he looked askance at Minister Uran, the emperor declaimed, "You have taken the apple of my eye, my only daughter. Now, because the intelligence of this Minister Uran is so great, if he stays here and supports my state, the two great realms [15v] will firmly rejoice." Minister Uran accepted, and thus he stayed.

Then Emperor Taisong said:

"Go and find the person who indicated,
On behalf of Tibet,
This is my favorite daughter, the princess."

When he uttered this command to his ministers, they were unable to find the person. When they respectfully reported this to the emperor, he said:

"Gather the astrologers and
Let it be solved by astrology!"

The astrologers, casting numbers, said respectfully to the emperor:

"It was not a human who pointed out the emperor's princess.
Under nine levels of earth there lie three great iron mountains;
Over it is a great cast-iron plain;
Upon this has been fixed a great ocean of water;
Dwelling in it are various kinds of birds; and
From this a great sala tree has grown.
Upon it is a being with a nine-fathom copper beak;
Its entire body is filled with eyes;
No such man is it, but
A female demon who has said it!"

The emperor was extremely angry, and when he caused all the numerology books to be burned in a fire, Minister Uran said, "Why have you caused the astrology books taught by Manjusri to be burned? Oh great emperor, because our king is very intelligent, when we came we were to test you in various ways. He had said, 'For this reason I shall therefore give a dream to you. You act in accord with that dream!' That night there came a servant of our king's dharma protector in the shape of such a woman and, in a dream, revealed it all to me."

Upon his saying this, the emperor understood that with the three letters [the Tibetan king] knew things in advance, and said, "If this be true, [16r] it is indeed so," and stopped burning the astrology books.

Thereupon, Minister Uran took Prince Thonmi aside and said, "I will stay here no more than three months. In these circumstances be careful and vigilant as you go."

Then the emperor gave Minister Uran a wife and a house, and had him live there. Then Minister Uran made himself seem sick: he held indigo and vermillion in both his cheeks and thus seemingly spat out pus and blood; moreover, by putting a goatskin under his mattress, he lay there giving off a very bad odor.

Therefore the emperor was worried and said, "Let's send a doctor tomorrow and have his pulse taken." Minister Uran put a cat in his armpit and lay there saying, "My body smells." And because he had tied a string from the cat to his fingers, when he had his pulse taken, the doctor said, "It is no different from the pulse of a lower beast," and departed.

The emperor said, "What does this mean? Tomorrow have another doctor go." Minister Uran lay there and had a chicken squeezed in his armpit. In the morning the herb doctor came, and taking his pulse, said, "It is no different from the pulse of an inferior winged creature," and departed. Then, because the emperor grew very fearful, the next day he arose and came himself. He said, "Oh minister! You are a person of great intelligence yourself. What is this illness of yours? What does it come from? What must one do to cure it?"

The minister, in a subdued voice, spoke as follows: "Oh, emperor! This illness of mine has not arisen from wind; has not arisen from bile; has not arisen from phlegm; nor has it arisen from a complicated derangement of the three humors. It is not an illness caused by the thousand and eighty demons. [16v] It is not an illness caused by the three hundred and sixty spirits. Nor is it an illness caused by evil spirits. But my mind is not at rest. It is as if an arrow has struck my heart, a fever, a disease of the windy humor has occurred. On account of my living here, the Tibetan deities of earth and water have become like demons and are displeased. Consequently, it will be difficult to cure me [in China], and thus it is difficult for me to support the emperor," and acting as if he had gotten sicker, he lay back down.

When the emperor asked, "What will cure you?" [Minister Uran] said, "For it, there is really no help at all. But, if I were to go upon a high mountain, such as one from which the vast snowy mountains on the borders of Tibet can be seen, and venerate the Tibetan [deities of] earth and water, it would do a little good."

When the emperor asked him, "What will be necessary for this?" he said, "Give me a skin bag filled with ashes of silk, a stomach of blood from spleens, three fathoms of charcoal the size of lance shafts, a gray horse with a chestnut head for me, and an exquisite horse to carry fuel and food."

That very night, [Minister Uran] dispatched an envoy with a letter and had him flee in haste. The next day, he said [to the emperor], "A guide of mine, learning I am about to die, has risen against me and departed. If he reaches Tibet, our king may very well mount an army. Let us overtake those tracks of his at once before that happens. I shall go in haste and try to perform the veneration."

Then the emperor declaimed:

"Even if you burn every piece of silk, the ashes will not fill a skin bag;
Even if you slaughter all the sheep, it will not make a stomach full of
spleen blood;
Even if you incinerate the whole forest, it will not make enough
charcoal the size of a whip;
[17r] But we have found a solitary gray horse with a chestnut-colored
head!"

Putting a golden harness onto the gray horse and loading onto the fine stallion various sorts of food and goods, Minister Uran departed. He had previously observed and ascertained that that horse was a strong and swift one. Riding these two fine steeds coupled together, he escaped from his Chinese escorts and fled home.

While this was going on, the emperor had said:

"Oh, minister! You are such an intelligent one;
How should we plant crops for them to be good?"

[Minister Uran] replied, "If you bake the seed and then plant it, it will grow very high and the harvest will be large."

When that envoy who had been sent [by Minister Uran prior to feigning illness] arrived and gave the letter to them [in Tibet], it said:

"The fish cast up on the sand is going back to his own sea;
The stag surrounded in the hunt has been struggling for his own mountain.
Release into, and fill up with two-year-old colts coupled together, a river with no outlet;
Go attach "friends of men" to your loads.

Rays of bright sunlight fall on the hinter mountains;
Cast many revolting things onto the tracks of your feet.
A dark iron lamb lies in the heart;
The moon draws nigh to the sun.

Furling a white flag;
Unfurling a black flag;
Do not consort with the splendid peacocks of distant lands;
But sit in silence, give voice to lament."

Although Prince Thonmi barely understood the letter, when he showed it to Queen Gongju, she understood it fully and explained, "When he said, 'The fish cast up on the sand' and 'the stag surrounded in the hunt,' he meant that he himself is coming back to his own country. When he said, 'fill up with colts . . . a river with no outlet,' and 'attach "friends of men" to your loads,' he meant, [17v] fill your quiver with arrows, prepare your armor and swords, and travel vigilantly. When he said, 'cast many revolting things onto the tracks of your feet,' he meant, go, putting fragments of whips on the road and pieces of spears and lances and horse droppings at every campsite. When he said, 'the moon draws nigh to the sun,' he meant 'I shall overtake you.' When he said, 'furling a white flag, unfurling a black flag,' he meant, 'I lie down by day, and travel by night.' When he said, 'do not consort with the splendid peacocks of distant lands; but sit in silence, give voice to lament,' he meant, 'Do not talk about me or indicate anything to the Tibetan minister [Driseru Gungthun].' When he said, 'A dark iron lamb lies in the heart,' he meant that he, Minister Uran, has done bad things in my Chinese country." So saying, she fully explicated and rightly conveyed [the meaning of the letter].

Thereupon, when the [Chinese] had sent an army headed by a Süngbing[30] to pursue Minister Uran, they saw all the horse droppings, spear pieces, and whip ends at each of the campsites and said, "The Tibetan ruler is very foresighted. He realized the situation, and [Minister Uran] will be met by many soldiers." After saying this [and being scared], they turned back halfway and returned. Then Minister Uran caught up to the advance party and was reunited with the [Tibetan] king in the Ren Ox year [641], when the king was twenty-five.

Whereupon [the king] established, to an incalculable degree, innumerable shrines of body, speech, and mind. Then he had the Dharma of the sutras and *dharanis*[31] translated by Sankgara Birmana, the leading teacher of India; Guru Silamanju of Nepal; Guru Osta of Nepal [18r], Heshang Mahadeva of China; Tibet's translator and prince, Thonmi Sambhota; and his younger brother Dharmakosa, among others.

Abandoning the ten dark sins, he ruled by merging the ruler's state with the Buddhist government of the ten merits. He made the sun of the religion rise over the benighted Tibet. At the age of eighty-two, in the Wu Dog year [698], along with his two Tara queens, Prince Thonmi Sambhota, and Minister Uran, he was absorbed into his tutelary deity[32]—the Eleven-Headed [Avalokitesvara]—thus spreading his supreme eternal name in all directions.

* * *

His eldest son, Mangsong, died during his father's lifetime; thus the younger brother called Gungsong, born in the Bing Dog year [685], ascended the throne in the Gi Pig year [699], at the age of fourteen, and passed on in the Ren Rat year [712], at the age of twenty-seven.[33]

* * *

His son, known as King Magically Incarnated by the Power of Düsong Kei, who was left behind in his mother's womb when his father passed on, was born in the Ren Rat year [712] and was elevated to king in that very first year of his life. He maintained the royal realm for twenty-nine years and passed on in the Ging Dragon year [740].[34]

His son, King Tridé Tsuktsen, was born in the Ging Dragon year [740], became king in the Ren Snake year [741] at the age of two, and passed away in the Sim Horse year [802], at the age of sixty-three.

* * *

As regards his son, in the Ging Horse year [790], the 2,920th from that former Wu Rat year, from Queen Gyimshing Gongju,[35] daughter of Prince Jinde, the younger brother of Emperor Tang Chuchung of China,[36] [18v] was born a son, completely perfect in the signs and marks. He ascended the throne at the age of thirteen, in the Ren Horse year, [802] and at the age of seventeen, in the Bing Dog year [806], approving along with his closest ministers—including the Grand Prince Who Takes Delight in the Doctrine, Sakya Khonpoche, and Mergen Tamana—invited Khenpo Bodhisattva from the land of Zahor.[37]

When he came, the king met and received him at the pass in Mang[yül] Güngtang[38] and thereupon invited him to the royal palace at Haspo Mountain.[39] When [the king] respectfully informed [Santaraksita] of his aim to construct a temple of the Dharma wheel, [the Khenpo] said, "Because I have supportively meditated on bodhicitta my whole life, I am unable to pacify gods and demons. Unless one first pacifies the gods, demons, and earth deities, how will it be possible to construct the temple? In the matter of pacifying them, because Guru Padmasambhava[40] of Uddiyana[41] is one who wields a trove of secret dharanis, he is the one who can enslave and subject the eight realms of wrathful deities, gods, and *raksa* demons as are generally extant in samsara. If that saint comes, he will be able to pacify them."

The king then asked, "How can I invite him?" Thereupon Ubadini Bodhisattva [Santaraksita] said, "There is an ancient vow that makes it possible for him to come. Let me explain: 'In the land of ancient India, there was a daughter of a bird catcher named Amuulang, also known as Supreme Amuulang. She lived with three men of different castes: a bird catcher, a dog handler, and a pig herder, and three sons were born. Then, after their mother had passed away, the three children [19r] erected the stupa called Wheel of Flowers, and each of them expressed an earnest wish as follows: the first, the son a bird catcher, said, "By this meritorious deed, let me become, in my next birth, a mighty cakravartin king, a generous almsmaster to the religion." Presently, that great king is you. The second son, the son of the dog handler, said, "By this meritorious deed, let me become, in my next birth, a great Ubadini, who will maintain the religion." At present, I am that Ubadini. The third, the son of the pig herder, said, "By this meritorious deed, let me become, in my next birth, a great dharani expert who will purge the hindrances of the religion." At present, that great dharani expert is Guru Padmasambhava. His close friend who assisted him then is, presently, Prince Sbimi Gribsi of

Yarlung.' Because there exists such an ancient vow, it is now possible to make him come."

[Hearing this], the king greatly rejoiced, and in the Ding Tiger year [810], when he was twenty-one years old, he dispatched emissaries—headed by Prince Sbimi Gribsi, "Vajra the Demon Slayer"[42]—to invite Guru Padmasambhava from India. In accordance with that earlier pronouncement of the bodhisattva, [Padmasambhava] said:

"As for going now,
When one considers the vow of yore,
Since there is no power for me to dwell here,
Let me now depart without delay.

Hitherto, I have brought about my own benefit in abundance.
Now the time has come for me to render benefit to others.
When the wings of a Garuda bird are full-grown
He departs, flying to the sky.
If one considers the Dharma of deeds,
This is no occasion for repose."

Straightaway he got up and started going, [19v] but when they tried to pass between two mountains a demon came at them in the form of a dark bull. Whereupon the Guru appeared sitting cross-legged in the sky, and though he was afraid, when he swore an oath, drawing on his inner heart, he stated the secret name. And then when a great snowstorm broke out and froze everything solid, the Guru remained exceedingly hot and sweating, and when he struck the bull's forehead with the nine-pronged iron vajra, the bull went fleeing to the mountains, and [at once] the snowstorm cleared up, the mountains grew black, the bluish stones turned blue once more, and luminous sunbeams gleamed upon [Padmasambhava]. Then he fearfully drew on his inner heart again, and laying aside the vajra, swore an oath and named the secret name. Thereupon, he pacified without exception the powerful dragons[43] and deities of the Tibetan land,[44] headed by the Twelve Powerful Mothers.[45] He enslaved and made into servants the gods and demons. He made the King of the Dragons, the dragon king Upananda, friendly with the king of men, Trisong Detsen.

Thereupon, in the Xin 辛 Rabbit year [811], when the king was twenty-two, he had a foundation pounded and erected a *vimana* palace of incomparable vajra quality. He built it in accord with the secret dharanis, in the shape of a mandala; in accord with the Three Baskets [of the canon],[46] like the method of Abhidharma;[47] in accord with the essence of the sutras, like the customs of the rules [i.e., the monastic code]; and he further established it in accordance with the predominant secret spells of the conclaves of inner buddhas.[48]

The lower level [of the monastery] was in Tibetan style, the middle level the Chinese style, and the upper level the Indian style. The lower level, perfect with four great supreme ones, had three gates, [20r] and thus symbolized the One Who Had Vanquished [i.e., the Buddha]. The middle level had one gate and was a symbol of the single body of the Dharma. The upper level had four great portals and was a symbol of the perfection of the Four Immeasurables and the Four Activities.[49] That monastery symbolized the inconceivable nature of the wheel of the Dharma: the central structure with three bases; the four sides with four corners; the four major continents and the eight minor continents;[50] on the threshold, the dwelling of sun and moon deities; on the lintel, *yaksas*;[51] the powerful, mighty four great Yamas;[52] the temple of the eight great Mahakalas;[53] the four great stupas and the stupa of the blazing beam; if one included them all, it was a temple numbering thirty parts. A single great iron cakravartin enclosure surrounded it. Thus did he establish this splendid and inconceivable temple of the wheel of the Dharma, in a manner comparable to the temple called Otantapuri,[54] which is concealed in the Sea of India.

The king finished it in the Güi Rabbit year, [823] when he was thirty-four, and led by the holy Padmasambhava, who knows the three times, the great Ubadini Khenpo Bodhisattva [Santaraksita], and Dharmakirti,[55] who wields the dharanis, he had flowers strewn and thus established it well.[56] After inaugurating the consecration ceremony, he made a universal feast of joyousness for three years.

When the king was twenty-five, in the Ga Horse year [814], the Maharaja with Twenty-Five Retainers, in order to become an initiate of the profound, refined, and secret dharanis, accepted from the holy Padmasambhava the initiation of the 720 buddhas of the mandala of He Who Has the Eight Commandments of the Well-Gone Ones, which was bestowed in accordance with the great essence of the secret dharanis [20v]:

1. Heart of Heaven, the monk who was able to travel on a sunbeam
2. Knowledge Buddha, who was able to drive nails into rock
3. Victorious One of the Sublime Voice, who was able to whinny three times with melodious equine sound
4. Dakini of Vastly Conquering Transcendent Wisdom, who could resuscitate a dead man
5. Triumphant Intellect, who was able to compel service of the Dakini Mothers
6. Splendid Lion, who was able to control deities and raksas
7. Vairocana the Interpreter, who was perfected with the eye of transcendent wisdom
8. Khan, lord of the community, who was able to stabilize the world
9. Yudra Ningpo, who was perfect in the wisdom of the Dharma
10. Jnana Kumara, who displayed great magical power
11. Vajra the Demon Destroyer, who was able to be unimpeded and unhindered like the air
12. Jnana Guhya, who swam in the sky
13. Sri Deva, who was able to seize wild beasts with his hands
14. Jnana, possessor of wisdom, who could fly like a bird
15. Sri Indra, who was able to measure water in fathoms
16. Dharma Risma, who acquired a memory free of forgetfulness
17. Splendidly Multiplied, who knew how to dominate the strength of others
18. Splendid Lion, who was able to make water flowing downstream go upstream
19. Triumphant Intellect, who transformed corpses into gold
20. Chi Chung the Translator, who was able with his hands to catch birds as they flew in the air
21. Sky of Heaven, who was able to ride a wild bull
22. Naga Indra, who was able to plunge into the sea like a fish
23. Maharatna, who ate bricks for food
24. Splendid Vajra, who went running unhindered on mountains and cliffs

25. He who, like a supreme, splendid Jewel, shot thunderbolts like arrows
26. The Vanquishing Bodhisattva, who sat cross-legged in the sky. [21r]

In this way each one was empowered to display some perfected ability. Specifically, the Eight Sons of Thought were the Buddhas of the Eight Commandments: [1] Heart of Heaven was Knowledge Vajrapani,[57] the Buddha of True Thought. [2] Knowledge Buddha was Yamantaka,[58] the body of the Buddha. [3] Supreme Victorious, with the horse voice, was Hayagriva,[59] the speech of the Buddha. [8] Khan, lord of the community, was the Buddha of the Great Sublime Virtue. [4] Dakini of Vastly Conquering Transcendent Wisdom was Vajrakilaya,[60] the Buddha of Deeds. [6] Splendid Lion was the buddha who is repeatedly praised by the inhabitants of the world. [5] Triumphant Intellect was the buddha of the domain of women, who sends fulfillment. [7] Vairocana the Interpreter was the buddha of salvation through wrathful dharanis.

Thereupon, in order to translate the Indian language into Tibetan, Tibetan children studied Indian speech. When not one of the children learned anything, the teacher's mind was greatly troubled. He therefore went looking for a youth able to interpret among the people. When he came to the front of one house, there stood a seven-year-old boy whose parents were gone. When he saw the child, the teacher tarried a moment and said, "Now, I shall have lunch here." Settling down there, he had his white tent set up, sat down, and had that child come over. When he said, "Where did your father go?" the boy said, "He went to seek speech." When he said, "Where did your mother go?" the boy said, "She went to seek eyes."

Then, while they waited, the father came back after getting some alcohol. The child saw him and said, "When I spoke of him saying, 'My father went to seek speech,' I meant, 'when he drinks alcohol, [21v] he says a lot of words.'" Thereafter, his mother came, having bought lamp oil. Then the child said, "When I spoke of her saying, 'My mother went to seek eyes,' I meant that when the lamp is lit, even though it be a dark night, one sees everything." The teacher was very happy and departed straightaway, taking that child with him. Then, when he arrived, he said to the king:

"As regards this child,
He is an incarnation of that Ananda of old.

His present father is the son of Begür Gendun,
He is the one called Begür Vairocana."

When they instructed him in the Indian language, [the boy] learned it without hindrance and became famous as Vairocana the Interpreter, the Sage of Tibet.[61]

Thereupon in the Ga Dragon year [824], when the king was thirty-five, he had all the sutras and dharanis, without exception, translated by the following: Guru Padma, the holy Padmasambhava, the teacher, was in charge; the Indian Vimalamitra;[62] the Nepalese Vikamalasila; the Sage of Tibet, Begür Vairocana the Interpreter; Chogri Lu Gyeltsen; the disciple Jisvasti; Kaua Pelzig; the Chinese Heshang Mahayana; and others.

He became famed in all directions as Trisong Detsen, the middle cakravartin king who turns the thousand-spoked golden wheel, an incarnation of the noble youth Manjusri.[63] And after ruling the state for fifty-seven years, he passed on to nirvana in the Wu Tiger year, [845] when he was sixty-nine.

His eldest son, Muné Tsenpo,[64] passed on due to poison; his middle son, Muruk Tsenpo, was exiled to the border regions;[65] his youngest son, Mutik Tsenpo by name, born in the Bing Dragon year [824], ascended the throne in the Gi Rabbit year, [847] when he was twenty-four years old.[66] He greatly established the three objects of veneration headed by the temple named "Having the Vajra Quality of Karchung."[67] [22r] He maintained the royal state for thirty-one years and became renowned as Ang Jun, the Cakravartin King Who Is Alert and Knows Well.

This king—and India's King Dharmapala,[68] and Emperor Tang Yichung of China[69]—were all born at the very same time. Then, when he was fifty-four, in the Gi Rooster year [877], he passed on to nirvana. He had five sons: Zangma, Darma, Trisong Dé, Lotsai, and Lhündub. The eldest brother, Zangma, became a monk. The second-middle son, Trisong Dé, who was born in the Bing Dog year [866], the 2,999th year from the former Wu Rat year, at the age of thirteen, was approved by all as exceedingly good and was placed on the throne in the Wu Dog year [878].

That Holy One, when he was seventeen years old in the Ren Tiger year [882], campaigned against China and slew Emperor Tang Chuchung.[70]

He took great booty and spoils, and his strength and might were famed to heaven. Thereupon, he founded temples and monasteries by the thousands and had all previously untranslated Dharma books translated by India's Ubadini Jinamitra, Silendra Bodhisattva, Danasila, and Bodhimitra, (and by) Tibet's Ubadini Ratnaraksita, Dharmasila, Chogri Lu Gyeltsen, Khon Palpoche's [son] Khon Lu Wangpo, and others.[71]

He tied one piece of silk to the root of each hair of his head and seated one monk on each piece of silk. He venerated and respected them without end and performed considerable promotion of the Dharma. By his having nurtured and instructed in doctrine those in the Snowy Land in general, [22v] at that time the happiness of the Tibetan people became like that unto the gods. As a result, he became famed as Lord Tri Relpachen,[72] incarnation of the great and powerful Vajrapani,[73] the one who turns the thousand-spoked golden wheel, the Cakravartin King of the End Times, the Hair-Seat King. He sat on the throne for twenty-four years and, at the age of thirty-six, in the Xin Rooster year [901], passed on to nirvana.

From the Ding Sheep year [407], which was the beginning of the former spread of the Dharma in general, down to this final Xin Rooster year [901], 495 years elapsed.

Because [Relpachen] had no sons, his elder brother Darma, born in the Güi Sheep year [863], ascended the throne in the Xin Dog year [902], at the age of forty. Being a rebirth of that former elephant, and thus by reason of the wicked inclination of having taken an evil oath, he spent every day and night for twenty-four years devoted to the black arts, and was famed as Langdarma.[74] Downward from the three upland Ngari provinces and upward from the three low ranges at the foot of Lower Kham, he obliterated all mention of the three objects of veneration and the four groups in general, and the religion was greatly destroyed.

When that sinful king was sixty-three years old, in the Gi Rooster year [925], and when the time came to put into effect that former counteroath, the incarnation of the supreme king Songtsen Gampo, called Lhalung Chogtu Dorjé, dyed a sturdy white horse—thereby turning it into a black horse—and then rode it. He turned his white outer cloak inside out to the black inside, thus making a black cloak, and wore it. He concealed a bow and arrows in the sleeves of his cloak, and came saying,

"Let me pay respect and make obeisance to the king." When first he knelt, [23r] he nocked his arrow; at the second genuflection he drew his bow; and at the third kneeling, he shot the sinful king in the heart and slew him, saying:

"Earth is wafted by wind;
Water is covered by earth;
Fire is quenched by water;
The Garuda bird conquers dragons;
Jewels are bored by diamonds;
Gods defeat asura demons;
Buddha defeats demons;
In such a manner I slew the wicked king."

He then washed his cloak and horse, making them white, dressed himself, rode off, and departed, fleeing to the land of Kham.

Thereupon, the son of Langdarma, named Guarded by Light, born in the Gi Pig year, [915] when his father was fifty-three, ascended the throne in the Gi Rooster year [925] at the age of eleven and maintained the state devoid of Dharma for fifty-three years. He transmigrated in the Ding Ox year [977] at the age of sixty-three.

His son, named Pal Khortsen, was born in the Yi Ox year, [965] when his father was fifty-one, and ascended the throne in the Ding Ox year [977], at the age of thirteen. Because he was inclined toward the inner teachings, he constructed eight grand temples and, desirous of religion, maintained the state for eighteen years. He transmigrated in the Gi Sheep year [995] at the age of thirty-one.

He had two sons: Fortune Multiplied and Chief of the Sun. Fortune Multiplied had three sons, Blazing Dé, Illuminating Dé, and Joyous Dé; they became lords of the Four Central Eternal Lands.[75] The three sons of Chief of the Sun were Majestic Chief, Fortunate Chief, and Ranked Chief, and going to the region of the three districts of Upper Ngari, they became the origin of the Guge kings.[76] [23v]

Now, if one relates the subsequent spread of the religion, it is twofold. Of the two, the dissemination from below [i.e., from Kham] and the dissemination from above [i.e., from Ngari], if one discusses first the dissemination from below, it is as follows: At the time when Langdarma destroyed the religion, ten savants[77]—Silaprajna, Gunaprajna, Silasambhava, Silamati, Jnanamati, Vajrasvara, Prajna Sengge, Asta of Oua, and the elder and younger brothers Ubadini and Sita—went to a land called Lower Dantig.[78] And in the presence of a solitary complete statue of Sakyamuni in the midst of a ruined temple, they took the vows of ordination from the Chinese Heshang Mahayana. Thereupon, going farther, Holy Lhachen made a lay community; they made a teacher of secrets out of Buyan Garugchi, made a teacher of Deeds to Fulfill, and both Mar Sakyamuni and Heshang (and the rest) became monks. They established the religion anew in the Central Eternal Lands.[79]

If one discusses next the spread from above, it is as follows: the middle son of Chief of the Sun was Fortunate Chief, who had two sons, the elder brother being Khore, who was born in the Ging Tiger year [990], the 3,123rd year from that same former Wu Rat year. He became a monk and became famous as Lha Lama Jnanarasmi.[80] Then, in his third year, the Ren Dragon year [992], Lotsawa Rinchen Zangpo of Guge was born.[81] Thereupon, that lama, by the light of wisdom, in the Ga Tiger year [1014] at the age of twenty-five erected a temple named Toling.[82] He dispatched twenty-one men,[83] headed by Lotsawa Good Jewel [i.e., Rinchen Zangpo], to the land of India and invited Pandita Sraddhakaravarma, Padmakaragupta, and others [24r] to come.

He had the vehicle of essential Dharma, the four tantras of secret dharanis, and others translated [into Tibetan] and made into books. He headed the religion, and his younger brother Songnye[84] ascended the throne. His son Phodrang Pacified Beam became a monk and was famed as Tsunpa Beam of the Sakyas.[85] He dispatched Naktso Lotsawa Tsultrim Gyelwa[86] and others to India, to the king called Splendid with Merit, whose son, Dibakara Sri Jnana, was born in the Ga Horse year [994], the 3,127th from that very former Wu Rat year. He invited the teacher, Jowo Atisa, to come, in the Ga Horse year [1054], when he was sixty-one years old. By causing books not formerly translated to be translated, he greatly propagated the religion.

The middle son of Fortune Multiplied was Illuminating Dé, whose son was the king named Tsedé. He invited the Kashmiri Pandita Jnanasri [to Tibet]. And by having both Tsongpo's Striving for the Dharma and

Ngok Lotsawa Completely Wise Prajna translate the scriptures, he greatly disseminated the religion.

* * *

In this way, after the final Xin Rooster year [901] of the first spread of the Dharma, eighty-six years passed from the Ren Dog year [902] up to the Ding Pig year [987]. The later spread of the Dharma began from the Wu Rat year [988].

CHAPTER THREE

History of Chinggis Khan

Just as the Tibetans reimagined their past in the wake of their empire's collapse and the twelfth-century Buddhist revival, so too did the Mongols. Indeed, for Sagang Sechen, who was writing about Chinggis Khan at a remove of more than four hundred and fifty years, much had happened in the interim. Not only had the empire and the Yuan dynasty collapsed, but also the Mongols had gone through the Mongol-Oirat war, readopted Buddhism as the state religion, and most recently allied themselves with the Manchu Qing dynasty. Thus the history of Chinggis Khan as found in the famous mid-thirteenth-century *Secret History of the Mongols* no longer resonated as it earlier had. Even though Sagang Sechen used parts of the *Secret History*, he also used Chinese sources, as well as the more fantastical stories that had developed around Chinggis Khan during the upheavals of the fifteenth and sixteenth centuries. One reason was that these new stories made better sense of the new realities, such as the fact that the post-Yuan Mongol elite no longer ruled from Beijing or their "homeland" on the Mongolian plateau. Rather, they resided in the borderland area now known as Inner Mongolia. It is thus perhaps not surprising that many of the new stories about Chinggis Khan—especially those concerning his death and funeral cortege—take place in this territory.

Now, let us discuss the dispersal of the royal lineage in the land of the Bede Mongols:[1] In the seventh generation from the king of ancient Tibet—the Universal Lord—called Having a Throne of Necks, Minister Longam killed the king called Dalai Sobin Aru of the Golden Throne and ascended the throne. [24v] At that time his three sons, Borachu, Sibuuchu, and Börte Chinua, fled to other lands; the youngest, Börte Chinua, went to the land of Kongpo. Being unable to get accustomed to the people of Kongpo, he took his wife named Maral the Fair and crossing the Tenggis Sea, traveled in an easterly direction. At the edge of Lake Baikal, reaching the mountain called Burkhan Khaldun,[2] he encountered the people called Bede. When these people asked him the reason for his journey, he cited his origins from Khan Elevated by the Many of ancient India and the Universal Lords of Tibet up to the present. The people of Bede all approved, and said to one another, "He is a son of nobility. We are without a lord, thus it would be fitting to elevate him as prince!" Making him their prince, they followed all of his commands.[3]

* * *

He had two sons,[4] Batasgan and White Bata. White Bata's son was Tamachag, his son was Khorichar Mergen; his son was Agujam Buurul, his son Sali Khalchagu; his son Yeke Nidün, his son Sem Sochi; his son Khali Kharchu; his son Borjigidai Mergen. From Borjigidai Mergen's wife, Mongoljin the Fair, was born Torgaljin Bayan. From Torgaljin Bayan's wife, Boragchin the Fair, were born the two brothers: Duua the Blind and Dobun the Wise. Duua the Blind's sons were called Tonoi, Dogsin, Emlig, and Erke and became the Four Oirat clans: the Ö'eled, the Baatud, the Khoid, and the Kerenüüd.[5]

The reason he was called Duua the Blind was that, although there was only a single eye in the middle of his forehead, [25r] he could see to the distance of three nomadic camps. While these two, elder and younger brother, were traveling around Burkhan Khaldun, the elder one said: "From Düireng Garudi [Mountain] a nomadic caravan is approaching downstream along the Clear River. Among them, inside a wagon, is a fair and beautiful woman. Let me try to make her your wife."

When the two went and inquired, they said she was Alan the Fair, who was born while traveling at Pure Water from Bagujin the Fair—wife of Khoritai Mergen of the Khori Tümed. Straightaway, Dobun the Wise discussed this with his younger brother and took her as his wife.[6] Then, after two sons, Belgütei and Begütei, were born, Dobun the Wise passed away.

After this, Alan the Fair had a dream wherein every night a handsome, youthful man came and spent the night sharing the pillow, and in the morning, with the light of dawn, he went out and away. She told her fellow elder-brother's wives about this dream, and the consequence of it all was that she bore three sons, named Bugu Khatagi, Bugu Saljigu, and Bodanchar the Fool.[7]

After the boys had been reared, some nasty-minded people gossiped: "Is it really the custom for a woman who is by herself to give birth? Someone named Makhali of the Bayi'ud used to go to her house. They are surely his." As a result, when both Belgütei and Begütei acted suspiciously toward their own mother, Alan the Fair gave a single shaft to each of her five children, saying, "Please break them." They broke them. Taking yet another five shafts and putting them together, she said, "Try to break them again." All five tried in turn, but were unable. [25v] Thereupon, their mother said: "You, my two grown sons, have been suspicious of me on account of the words of others," and then told them in full the circumstances of those dreams of hers. She said:

"Therefore, these three younger brothers of yours
Are like the sons of Heaven.
Now you five, if you act separately, devoid of harmony,
Like those single shafts in the prior instance,
You will be defeated by a single man.
But if you act jointly,
Like those shafts put together in the latter instance,
You will not be overcome even by the many!"

Thereupon, her sons behaved agreeably,
Yet, when each took his own inherited portion and part,
To Bodanchar
Only a dun-colored horse named Orog Jusag
With a sore in the middle of his back and
With a bald-stub tail
Did they give.

Angered at his four elder brothers,
He departed alone upstream along the Onon River.

Then, seeing a gray female hawk catch and eat black khoro ducks, he caught her in a noose and raised her to maturity. He made her catch many ducks and geese, which he ate, and he spent his nights in a grass hut. He also used to go and drink fermented mare's milk with an isolated group of people living there.

Then when his elder brother, Belgütei, came seeking his younger brother, he asked those people, and they said as follows: "This younger brother of yours comes every day and drinks fermented mare's milk. When he comes, a fine rain falls. You just wait a moment!" Straightaway, as rain began to fall from a cloudless sky, Bodanchar quickly came from the land with no lords. Then the five brothers conversed together. When they subsequently took over those isolated people, Bodanchar seized a pregnant woman and took her to be his wife. Her name was Bodan. Then Bugu Khatagi produced the Khatagin clan, Bugu [26r] Saljigu the Saljigud clan, and Bodanchar the Borjigin clan. The son that was in the womb of Queen Bodan, who had the status of a slave, was called Jajiridai, and he became founder of the Jajiraid clan.

The two sons born to Bodanchar were named Ba'aridai—the one born from the woman he had forcefully taken—and Khabichi Baatur, who was of the noble lineage. Khabichi's son was Bigir Baatur; his son was Makha Tudan; his son Khachi Külüg; his son Bai Singkhor Dogsin; his son Tumbagai Sechen; his son Qabul Khan; and his son was Bartam Baatur, whose four sons were Yisügei Baatur, Nekün Taishi, Menggetü Sechen, and Daritai Odchigin.

Thereupon, Yisügei Baatur took his two younger brothers Nekün and Daritai, and while they were tracking a hare, at the side of a nomad encampment with wagons they saw in the snow a woman's urine. "From that woman, fine sons are to be born," [Yisügei] said. When they followed the track of that encampment and overtook them, Big Chilidü of the Tatars[8] was then returning home, having taken Mother Ö'elün of the Olkhunuds. When [the three brothers] approached, Mother Ö'elün said to Chilidü: "Did you not notice the behavior of the big fellow among those three?" While unbuttoning for him the skirt she wore inside, she yelled, "Run quickly for our sake!" And just when [the three brothers] were to attack, Big Chilidü [and Mother Ö'elün] took flight and escaped. Pursuing them across three rivers, [the brothers] captured Mother Ö'elün, and Yisügei Baatur took her to himself.

The youngest, Daritai, said:

"You have crossed three rivers;
You have traversed three hillocks.
If you look about, there is no trail;
If you look away, there is nothing in the distance;
If you weep, no one will hear you."

Hearing these words, Mother Ö'elün went on in silence.

* * *

In the Ren Horse year [1162], the 3,259th from that Wu Rat year, from these two, the father Yisügei Baatur [26v] and the Queen Mother Ö'elün, was born a son, perfect in the wonderful signs. Then, on account of his birth coinciding with the capture of one named Temüjin Üge of the Tatars, they named him Temüjin, Bestowed by Heaven, and thus that was his very first name.

Having the same mother as this Temüjin were Qasar, Qachigin, and Odchigin,[9] four sons, and born of the mothers Tülmelün Abakhai the Fair and Queen Dagasi were Begter and Belgütei, these two making six.

Later, Yisügei Baatur, seeking an in-law relation for his own son Temüjin, while on the way to the Olkhunuds—his maternal uncles—met Dai Sechen of the Qonggirad.[10] And he said, "Oh, my in-law relative, of Borjigid blood lineage and Kiyod bone lineage, where are you going?"

Thereupon, when Yisügei Baatur said, "I am traveling to seek an in-law relation for my son," Dai Sechen replied: "Just last night I dreamed that a white falcon descended onto my arm. Obviously, this was your Borjigid standard. We, from of old to the present, have made our own beautiful and fair daughters the wives for many Borjigids.

It has been that we have made wives for the destined Borjigid
Of our daughters of fine character.
Now, I have one of mine, named Börte,
She is a single child, aged nine.

Let me give this one of mine to that son of yours."

Although his father said, "She is quite young," his son said, "She will always be a thing of use; if it is to be, let it be!" Then each making (the other) drink liquor, and bestowing a brace of horses, he made Temüjin live there [with them] and then returned home.

En route [Yisügei Baatur] happened upon some Tatars who were holding a feast, and when they said, "This is delicious food, eat!" he said, "As the saying has it: 'One will not escape!'" and stopped and got off. Because they were mindful of their ancient enmities [the Tatars] mixed poison in the food for him, and Yisügei Baatur became sick. [27r] When he arrived home, he said,

"Entering the house of friendly people,
I have eaten tasty food, but
I have done evil to myself and my life.
Fetch my Temüjin!"

They dispatched as courier Menggülig of the Qongqotan.[11] In the meantime, Yisügei Baatur became a god.

* * *

Immediately thereafter, with Queen Dagasi also having passed away, Queen Ö'elün was rearing and caring for the six boys alone. One day the two sons Temüjin and Qasar addressed their mother thus: "Once those two, Begter and Belgütei, stole and ate a fish we had caught; and now, today, they have again taken a lark that Qasar had shot and killed with a horn-point arrow. Let's kill the two of them!"

To which their mother said:

"Like the five sons of Örbei the Fair of the ancient Tayichi'ud,[12]
Why do you say these words?
You have nothing else than your shadow,
No whip other than your horse's tail.
Behave peaceably!
Aren't you supposed to be comrades forever?"

Thrusting the doors apart, they went out, and when the four of them went plotting evil against Begter and Belgütei, Begter said, "If you are going to kill me, then kill me! But don't kill my Belgütei; he is a man who will sometime hence give you his support." Even while he said so, they did not agree and slew Begter.

When they came into their mother's presence, their mother grew very angry and said as follows:

"While I have been going about rejoicing, saying,
'My sons, though reared on wild apples and wild onions,
Are about to become famed noblemen;
My sons, though reared on milk scum and wild fruit,
Are about to become distinguished noblemen,'
Why have you done this, slaying one another?
Henceforth, what else will there be but more killing of one
another? [27v]
Like a salbar bird attacking a cliff,
Like a wolf biting its own womb,
Like a falcon pursuing its own shadow,
Like a kerme fish striking its own fins,
In your case, who would be at all different
From a frog, if he be flat and wide?
From a snake, if he be thin?"

Thus did she scold them.

* * *

Thereupon, the soldiers of the Tayichi'ud came and suddenly assembled, saying, "To all of you, no harm will befall you, if you produce Temüjin for us!" Hearing them, Temüjin nocked his arrow and was on the point of emerging when his mother made him escape secretly, and he went to a cave on the Onon River. Yet they knew the cave and thus they went to guard it. Three days and three nights passed, and as Temüjin was about to emerge, he tugged on his cinch and crupper, and when the saddle slipped off he thought:

When this cinch slipped loose, it really slipped!
But how could this crupper get detached?
This is my father warning me from Heaven!

So he waited another three days and nights. Then, when he was again about to emerge, there was a great white stone covering the opening. Once more he said, "That stone was not there before. Is not my father, Heaven, warning me?," and again he waited three days and nights. Thus having spent nine days and nights, he said, "Now let come what may!," and emerged.

The Tayichi'ud had kept watch, and at once they seized him and carried him off. Dressing him in iron fetters and hobbles, they set guards at each tent. Then on the fifteenth day of the middle month of summer, the Tayichi'ud made a great feast with lots of drinking. When night fell, Temüjin twisted apart the hobbles on his feet and, striking the man who was guarding him with the fetters, he fled.

Thereupon, while the Tayichi'ud were seeking Temüjin hither and yon, he lay concealed in a swift-running river. Yellow Torgan of the Suldus saw him and thought, *He once was nice to my two boys, Chiluun and Chimbai.* He therefore went and said, "O young fellow, it is all right for you to lie there; I'll get help." [28r] Night fell, and saying, "He is a kind-hearted man," Temüjin went to the tent of Yellow Torgan.

Then his two boys, Chiluun and Chimbai, said to each other:

"Inasmuch as a bush is a fold
For a meadowlark come to take refuge,
What will be the golden value
To us, unless we sincerely care for and
Treat well like one of us, him,
The heavenly descended Borjigin,
Who has come choosing us."

Breaking his fetters with an axe, they then concealed him, putting him in a cart of wool. The next day, because the Tayichi'ud kept coming and searching every household, they also investigated Yellow Torgan's tent. Then when they were inspecting the cart, Yellow Torgan's daughter, Silu'uqan Sadaan, wailed, "Why do you torment your own kin in such heat on account of a stranger?" And his wife likewise resisted in this way, saying, "How can one conceal a man in wool in such summer heat? Why do you suspect your own people?" Being thus scolded, they left.

Then Yellow Torgan said, "Temüjin, my son, you all but reduced us to ashes." Then, undoing for him the proper [i.e., left-side] stirrup of a barren white mare of theirs, they made him mount, and slaughtering a lamb that had suckled two ewes, they gave him provisions and sent him on his way. Arriving home, he met his mother and younger brothers and all rejoiced together.

Then, at the age of seventeen in the Wu Dog year [1178], Temüjin took as his wife thirteen-year-old Börte Jüsin, born in the Bing Dog year [1166]. Then the Tayichi'ud came again and took for themselves his eight chestnut geldings and departed. Riding Belgütei's horse named Dargi Qongkhor, Temüjin went tracking them by the bent grass. [28v] He came upon Bo'orchu—son of Nakhu Bayan of the Arlad—who was out herding.[13] When they met he said, "Oh son of the Borjigid blood lineage and of the Kiyod bone lineage, where have you come from?"

[Temüjin] said:

"At the hour of sunrise,
Thievery was committed on my eight chestnut geldings;
Tracking carefully, going by the slant of the grass,
I have come to ask of you, son of Nakhu Bayan."

Then Bo'orchu said:

"I have heard that you were having troubles.
It is not otherwise for the troubles of men;
Now I shall accompany you."

Himself riding his bay horse called Swift Browny, he had Temüjin ride his yellowish horse called Orog Singqula, and they departed together. When they arrived [at the Tayichi'ud camp] it had become dusk, and when they snuck up and took a look, many people were sleeping in a circle. Then when night fell and they were going to take back the horses, the prince said, "I am going in."

Bo'orchu said:

"On a fortunate day did I follow
You, scion of the Borjigin.

What will it avail to flee and
Take flight in your battle?"

So saying, the two of them went into the camp and came out driving the eight chestnut geldings. Then they returned and went to the tent of Nakhu Bayan. When Nakhu Bayan heard the words of his son,

Turning this way he laughed,
Turning that way he wept.
"Man's trouble is ever the same;
Do not forget that deed of yours," he said.

Slaughtering a lamb that had suckled two ewes, [Nakhu Bayan] gave [Temüjin] provisions and made him return. Immediately after this, Bo'orchu said, "Let me establish a friendship with Temüjin," and they acted as friends in deeds both harsh and delicate. [29r]

* * *

Thereupon, Prince Temüjin, at the age of twenty-eight, in the Ji Chicken year [1189], ascended the khan's throne at Kögede Island on the Kerülen River.[14] Prior to that day, at dawn of the three previous days, on a square white stone before his tent, a bird of five colors and like a lark perched, and from its call of "chinggis, chinggis"—his famous middle name—[Temüjin] became famous in all directions as Blessed Holy Chinggis Khan.

Then, from the interior of that stone which had suddenly split apart, there appeared the jade seal called Qasbao,[15] its length and breadth one span; on its back, upon a sturdy tortoise, were two dragons entwined, and its pattern stood forth in relief as if engraved.[16] This seal had stamped a thousand papers just as it should. Then straightaway [Temüjin] erected his white nine-tailed banner, which was implanted and raised at the head of the Onon River, and he erected his black four-tailed banner,[17] which was dispatched and implanted at Delüün Hill, and he became Ruler of the Forty Tümen of Bede people.[18]

The Lord [Chinggis] thereupon declaimed:

"When I, in the midst of hardship, was gathering and assembling the great people, painstakingly driving things together,

This very Bede people of mine, like unto a crystal jewel, they greatly gave their strength, whether in trouble or in joy.
Although they have suffered in hardship, as a consequence having become the nucleus of things in general,
They shall henceforth be called the Blue Mongols, the supreme ones of everything in motion!"

And after he had so proclaimed, they were called the Blue Mongols.

* * *

Then Lord Qasar, uniting with the Seven Qongqotan, moved about fighting, and [Chinggis] put at the head of his army Sübe'etei Baatur and had him pursue them. The Lord proclaimed:

"Like the moon on high,
Like the tassel on a cap, [29v]
Enfolding like a traverse lattice,
A rocklike knot, Oh, my [Forty] Tümen!
Enclosing like a cattle fold,
Ranked like reeds, Oh, my soldiers, hear ye!
In deeds of laughter,
Be exuberant like a two-year-old calf;
In energetic deeds,
Go attacking, like the rabbit hawk.
In deeds of play,
Go grazing like young camel colts;
In deeds of adhering,
Go attacking like the duck hawk."

After he so declaimed and ordered, Sübe'etei Baatur respectfully replied:

"Whether we can or not, we shall try to advance;
The standard of the Lord will determine whether we succeed or not.
Advancing assiduously, we shall try to pursue;
the standard of the Lord will determine whether we
achieve (our objective) easily."

So saying, they went and overtook [Qasar's forces]. Sübe'etei Baatur then said to Lord Qasar:

"When one separates oneself from clan and relatives,
One becomes the prey of an outsider.
It is said, when one quarrels with his kin,
One becomes the booty of other men.
All that moves can be found,
But kith and kin cannot be obtained.
Even a subject people may be found,
But elder and younger brothers cannot be gotten."

When he said this Lord Qasar agreed, and went and united with the Lord, his elder brother.

* * *

Then both Qasar and Belgütei, becoming friendly, said:[19]

"This Lord rules unreasonably, and
Is immoderate in the use of force.
By Qasar's marksmanship,
By Belgütei's strength,
The strangers were destroyed and
The difficulties alleviated.
Now, in undertaking expeditions against the people of Five Colors,[20]
Who indeed other than us two have given support?"

Their saying so—and being proud—was reported to the Lord, who thought, *Unbeknownst to them, let me suppress the pride of these children!*

He thus transformed himself into a humble old man and, as he was roaming the encampments to sell an ox-horn bow, Qasar and Belgütei ran into him and said mockingly, "Oh, old man, what can be done with that bow of yours, [30r] other than to make a spring for a mole trap?" The old man replied:

"You two young fellows,
Why do you despise it

Before you have seen what it will do?
When you have seen, you shall indeed know."

Laughing and chuckling, Belgütei tried to string the bow, but his strength did not suffice. When the old man strung the bow for them, Qasar took it to draw, but he couldn't. Then they saw that the old man had become a stalwart white-haired old man riding a blue-blazed mule, and with a golden eagle-feathered arrow he shot a rock in two with this ox-horn bow.

"Oh, you two young fellows, it is said,
'Although you talk big,
You've bitten off more than you can chew!'
Have you not been bested by an old man about to die?" he said and departed.

These two then said to each other:

"That was no ordinary man;
Was it not a manifestation of the Lord?"

After that, abashed, they behaved properly.

* * *

Then, skillful Chenggüi of the Enggüd,[21] taking the people of thirty-one nomadic camps, initiated warfare; and when the Lord and Qasar pursued and overtook him in person, they fought together back and forth. Qasar rode the Lord's chestnut-colored horse named Good Samujin, and he and Togtungga Baatur's son named [Andun Ching] Taiji led the attack. They pressed their attack together and rained shots until Good Samujin turned a bloody chestnut, and they took the rebel [Chenggüi] into submission. On account of his manual dexterity skillful Chenggüi was saved.[22]

* * *

Then Orochi Sigüsi of the Oirat Buriat, catching a falcon from the great Baikal stream, brought it to the Holy Lord, who made him ruler of the Buriat people.[23] Thereupon, at the age of twenty-nine, in the Geng 庚 Dog year [1190], he departed to hunt with this bird of prey, and traveled from the Olkhui River to the Ula River. [30v]

When Wangzun Khan[24] of the Jurchen fled and moved on, the Lord grew angry and, drawing up an army, went on campaign. The Ula River being impassable without a ford, the son of Togtungga Baatur Taiji, Andun Ching Taiji, linked the reins of a myriad geldings and they went shouting and, crossing the sea, they enclosed the city. The Lord declaimed, "Give us ten thousand swallows and a thousand cats and I shall stop harrassing your city." At once they gave him them in full. Tying a hempen cloth to the tail of every swallow and tying cotton yarn to the tail of every cat, when they set fire to them, the swallows struggled for their nests on the houses and the cats leaped onto the houses' ridgepoles. Since the conflagration gradually set fire to the whole city, they were therefore then able to take it. The Lord took to himself Wangzun Khan's daughter, Yalikhai. Then, during their return, Queen Yalikhai died en route.[25]

* * *

Thereupon, in the same year, when he was thirty-one in the Ren Rat year, [1192] he departed in the direction of the rising sun and set out on a campaign across the Fox River, which was flooding over.[26] Because the Lord was on this side, he dispatched emissaries who said, "Give us tribute; if you do not, we will attack you!" King Chagan of the Koreans was fearful and submitted as a token Qulan the Fair, daughter of Dayir Usun of the Korean Merkids, together with a tent covered with tiger skin, and presented a dowry of two camps of people, the Bukhas and the Solonggos.[27] [Chinggis] thus took into submission three Korean provinces of the White Nation and dwelt in style there for three years.[28]

Queen Börte Jüsin was troubled [by this new wife] and therefore sent Argasun Khorchi. [31r] When he arrived and they inquired after each other's health, he spoke thus respectfully to the Lord:

"Your wife, Queen Börte Jüsin,
Your descendants, the princes and princesses,
Your great jadelike state and administration,
All your great people are well.

The salbar falcon lays its eggs in the sala tree.
While trusting untiringly in its tree,
It lets its nest be destroyed by the sar bird;
It lets its fine eggs and young be consumed.

On the reedy lake swans and geese lay eggs;
While trusting their reeds, seeking the shade,
They let their eggs and young be consumed by the buzzard bird.
Let my Holy Lord be informed of this."

The Ruler, brought to his senses, said, "The statement you have uttered is indeed correct," and he returned from his grand journey. When he reached home, the Lord declaimed:

"She whom I met before my accomplishments,
My great Queen Börte Jüsin,
A wife like my mother,
Who was carried off by my precious father.

It is hard for me when I look upon the face
Of Börte Jüsin, who has sat at home
As a consequence of my having married Qulan
When I went out on the steppe.

When strange foreign persons are present,
It is shameful to get angry with one another
Within the confines of the house, so,
One of you Nine Comrades[29] go in first and speak to Börte Jüsin!"

Muqali[30] of the Jalayir[31] said, "I shall go," and went in first. Paying obeisance to Börte Jüsin, the great queen, he respectfully [conveyed the khan's words]:

"I have not guarded the established state;
I have looked in the direction of a loyal state [i.e., Korea].
I have not accepted the advice of ministers great and small;
I surrendered to the motley colors of a tiger-skin tent.

For the sake of attracting a distant people
Did I make Queen Qulan my wife."

After he had said this, Börte Jüsin, the wise queen, declaimed:

"Is Queen Börte Jüsin content?
Is it the resolve of the immensely great realm?
As for our Lord Khan, there is indeed strength. [31v]
The Lord indeed knows his friends and comrades;
On the reedy lake are verily many swans and geese.

The Lord indeed knows how to shoot until his fingers ache.
There are verily numerous girls and women in the whole nation.
The Ruler indeed knows those who are fated and fortunate among them.
It is said, 'Besides your wife, take (another) household.'
It is said, 'Put a saddle on the back of (your) wild horse.'

It is said in the olden tales:
'There is nothing bad in an abundance of health and heartiness;
There is nothing good in illness, suffering, and want.'

May the golden leash of the Lord Khan be firm!
What is one woman more or less to me?"

Then Muqali went and made it known to him. The Ruler was very happy and approved the building of a golden palace. Then when he got there, one night, Argasun Khorchi had fled with the royal lute. The Lord said to Bo'orchu and Muqali, "Put Argasun Khorchi to death!"

These two made Argasun come in much haste and early in the morning made him bear at his breast two skins of liquor, and when they brought him, the Lord had not yet risen. Thus Bo'orchu reported from outside [the tent]:

"Beams are entering your splendid palace,
The guilty ones and trespassers are assembling outside.
Awaken your illuminated body and rise,
While it is gleaming, deign to give your command.

Refulgence has entered your great jadelike palace.
Deign to open your portal and door,
Condescend to judge the sorrowful guilty ones;
Deign to bestow your beloved command."

So he said, and when the Lord arose they took Argasun Khorchi before him. When the Lord said nothing, Bo'orchu and Muqali nodded their heads, and Argasun said respectfully:

"While the seventy-tongued magpie is crying *tang, tang,* [32r]
When the harshly croaking spread-winged hawk comes to injure and attack,
It forestalls its cry of *jang,* and in like manner it is said,
When the destined Lord grows wrathful,
I am unable to find my customary behavior.

At the age of ten I followed you;
I have not been known to be either playful or evil.
True, I have gone astray with hard liquor,
But I have had no far-reaching wicked intentions.

At the age of twenty I followed you.
I have not been known for squandering evil.
True, I have gone astray with hard liquor,
But I have not adopted wicked ways."

He having spoken so eloquently, the Lord declaimed:

"Oh, my Argasun,
Who stands out by the quality of his mouth [i.e., speech]!
Oh, my Khorchi,
Who stands out by the quality of his beak [i.e., language]!"

and had mercy and spared him.

* * *

Then, Wrestler Chilger of the Tayichi'ud dug a pit in the middle of his tent and covered it with a covering of thick felt.[32] Preparing a grand feast with his elder and younger brothers, Wrestler Chilger came and respectfully invited the Lord as follows:

"When you were small we used to
Fight together, not understanding our respective status.
When one now considers how you have unerringly gone on your way,
Truly, you are a destined Holy One from Heaven!

It is said:
'Anger is the destiny of those who are born;
Submission is the destiny of those who are hasty.
Why should one pursue evil in a weak fashion?'
Come to my humble abode!"

The Lord arose, and Ö'elün, the queen mother, said,

"It is said, 'Let it not be said that evil enemies are few;
Let it not be said that a poisonous snake is inconsequential';
Proceed with caution!"

[Chinggis] replied, "My mother's statement is correct.

Qasar, take your quiver and sit outside;
Belgütei, be the sentry;
Qachigin, watch the horses;
Odchigin, sit by me;
You Nine Comrades, let us enter the tent together;
Let the Night Watch of three hundred and sixty [32v]
Surround [the tent] outside!"

Saying so, he got up.

Then the Ruler arrived and entered the tent, and when he was about to sit in the middle of the felt, clever Odchigin pulled his arm and made him sit at the edge of the felt. Meanwhile, outside, a woman cut [the Ruler's] stirrup off and fled. Wrestler Belgütei saw her and went in pursuit, and when he broke the woman's leg in two, a wrestler named Büri slashed Belgütei's shoulder with his sword. The concealed forces of the Tayichi'ud then emerged and fought with them. Skillful Qasar shot them down, making every arrow count a victim. The Nine Comrades shielded [the Lord's] body, and Belgütei by his left hand alone made the Lord ride off on the barren white mare of Togtungga Taiji of the Khorchin. He himself stayed slashing and fighting, and finally made them submit to his might.

Anger having thus arisen among the Tayichi'ud, the descendants of White Bata of yore,[33] namely, the seven sons of Qabul Khan, had broken with Batsagan's descendants, the ten sons of Ambagai Khan.[34] The ten sons of Ambagai Khan went on campaign and mounted an attack on Qabul Khan's seven sons. When they were fighting each other, six of the elder and younger brothers were killed, and thus they brought into subjugation as booty the eight provinces of the Bede people. Only Bartam Baatur, with three wounds, got out and fled with a party of five. Then the eldest son of that Bartam Baatur, Yisügei Baatur, at the age of thirteen, after putting an arrow through a fully armored man, took and rode off on his horse. Coming out from behind his father, he took his wife named Good Maral Khayag and her three sons, Nekün, Menggetü, and Daritai Odchigin, and got out, escaping on foot, and then they linked up once more. Then they went wandering without [ruling a subject] people. [33r]

And thus by trampling beneath their heels the inimical ones,
And by subduing the jealous ones with their own handsThey arose
and returned to dwell in their own palace.

Then, unexpectedly, from above, down through the smoke hole came descending an extremely delicious beverage called "wine"[35] in a jade bowl.[36] And when it came thus, it landed in the Lord's hand. The Lord took it and was going to drink it all himself, when his four younger brothers said, "Why does the Lord alone consume the blessing of Heaven?" The Lord acquiesced, but when he gave them the bowl the foursome quarreled, and when they tried to drink it they couldn't. Thereupon, the four younger brothers spoke respectfully as follows:

"We mistakenly and jealously discussed how
Your father, the powerful God Qormusta[37]

Has graciously presented this to you, his own son, the Holy Lord,
Putting ambrosia in a precious vessel.
You are indeed our destined Lord;
Henceforth we will follow your commands and orders."

The Lord then proclaimed:

"On account of the commandment given to by me by powerful Heaven[38]
When I sat on the throne of the ancient khans,
Heaven gave me the jade-jewel seal of the underground dragon kings.
Now, having suppressed the jealous and inimical ones,
Heaven has given me the royal ambrosia of the supreme gods.
Therefore, if you think this way, these words will become true."

When he was thirty-two, in the Gui Ox year [1193], he took as his wives the two daughters of Big Chooru of the Tatars, the elder and younger sisters Queen Yisü and Queen Yisügei.

* * *

Thereupon, if we are to explain when he brought the Chinese people into his power, [we need to begin with] the very first emperor of ancient China, who was named Qan Gaochung.[39] In the twelfth generation from him, [33v] his minister named Ang Lang,[40] having taken and robbed the throne of that emperor named Qan Gaochung, ruled eighteen years. Then Emperor Kliü Güngbü[41] came into the royal family and killed Prince Ang Lang and seized the state of his own forebear, Emperor Qan Gaochung. To his son, Emperor Qan Mingdi,[42] came by invitation Lama Tangshing and "Victorious in India" Pandita Zoglam, who loaded Dharma books on white dragon horses. Then, by having these books translated by this pandita, they caused the religion to be disseminated for the very first time [in China].[43]

* * *

The royal lineage after this is as follows: in the twenty-fourth generation the minister named Chau seized the throne from Emperor Qan Qindi.[44] After this, a minister of this same Prince Chau, named Umi, seized the throne. Thereupon, again in this family, Sing Ching Sang, the minister of the emperor called Kei Jing, (he) of the elder and younger brothers named Dung Jing and Kei Jing, seized the throne and became prince.[45]

Afterward, when this lineage was interrupted, to Emperor Sui Yangdai,[46] a royal descendant of the former Qan [dynasty], one named Tang Gaochung[47] became a minister and lived in the city of Tayangbu.[48] He was born in the Bing Rat year [566], and at the age of sixty-three in the Wu Tiger year [618] seized the royal throne of Emperor Sui Yangdai and established anew the realm of his own Qan forebears. He ruled for eight years and died at the age of seventy in the Yi Rooster year [625]. After that the former Qan lineage vanished and the Tang lineage came into being.

* * *

The middle one of Emperor Tang Taisong's[49] three sons was born in the Wu Horse year [598] and ascended the throne in the Bing Dog year [626] at the age of twenty-nine. At that holy time, sixteen arhats appeared and came to China. They performed the Dharma of the Varsa lands. He therefore dispatched to India his younger grandson, the Lotsawa named Tang Jangzang,[50] [34r] who translated Dharma books of sutras and dharanis from India. He learned the essence of the Dharma from an Indian teacher named Suvandu. In this way the religion of the Middle Way was spread. Thus, in his twenty-four years [of rule] he established the Two Realms,[51] and at the age of fifty-two in the Ji Rooster year [649] became a god.

He had two sons, named Tang Ciguuchung and Tang Zochung, and a single daughter, named Munchang.[52] As for Munchang, they commonly called her "the one who emits beams [of light]." The emperor's son Tang [Ciguuchung][53] was born in the Wu Rat year [628] and ascended the throne in the Geng Dog year [650] at the age of twenty-three. He ruled thirty-four years, and died at the age of fifty-six in the Gui Sheep year [683].

* * *

His younger brother, Emperor Tang Zochung,[54] born in the Bing Monkey year [636], ascended the throne in the Jia Monkey year [684] at the age of forty-nine, ruled seven years, and died at the age of fifty-five in the Geng Tiger year [690].

His son, Emperor Yichung,[55] born in the Wu Dog year [638], ascended the throne at the age of fifty-four in the Xin Rabbit year, [691] ruled two years, and died in the Sim Dragon year [692] at the age of fifty-five.

His son, Emperor Qanchung,[56] born in the Jia Rat year [664], ascended the throne when he was thirty-one in the Jia Horse year [694]. At that time people worshipped the relics of the Buddha, and he made priests and priestesses submit to the true Dharma, and thus greatly spread the religion. Therefore, it is said that the religion was spread to the Chinese people three times. After ruling for forty-three years, in the Bing Rat year [736], at the age of seventy-three, he died.

His son, Emperor Tang Zungchung,[57] born in the Xin Rabbit year [691], ascended the throne in the Ding Ox year [737] at the age of forty-seven, ruled six years, and died in the Ren Horse year [742] at the age of fifty-two. At the time of this ruler, the last cakravartin king of Tibet waged war and killed him.[58]

* * *

His son, Emperor Tang Dangchung,[59] born in the Geng Dog year, [710] [34v] ascended the throne in the Gui Sheep year [743] at the age of thirty-four, ruled seventeen years, and died in the Geng Rat year [760] at the age of fifty-one.

* * *

His younger brother, Emperor Tang Dingchung,[60] born in the Xin Rooster year, [721] ascended the throne in the Geng Rat year [760] at the age of forty, ruled twenty-five years, and died in the Jia Rat year [784] at the age of sixty-four.

* * *

His son, Emperor Tang Sünchung,[61] born in the Ji Rabbit year [739], ascended the throne at the age of forty-seven in the Ji Ox year [785], ruled six months and eight days, and died in the same year.

His son, Emperor Tang Qunchung,[62] born in the Jia Horse year [754], ascended the throne in the Bing Tiger year [786] at the age of thirty-three, ruled eleven years, and at the age of forty-three died in the Bing Rat year [796].

* * *

His son, Emperor Tang Muchung,[63] born in the Gui Ox year [773], ascended the throne in the Ding Ox year [797] at the age of twenty-five, ruled thirty years, and at the age of fifty-four in the Bing Horse year [826] died.

* * *

His son, Emperor Tang Juchung,[64] born in the Ji Snake year [789], ascended the throne at the age of thirty-nine in the Ding Sheep year [827], ruled seven years, and at the age of forty-five in the Gui Ox year [833] died.

* * *

His uncle, Emperor Tang Sunchung,[65] born in the Wu Tiger year [798], ascended the throne in the Jia Tiger year [834] at the age of thirty-seven, ruled fourteen years, and died in the Ding Rabbit year [847] at the age of fifty.

His son, Emperor Tang Kyuchung,[66] born in the Gui Snake year [813], ascended the throne at the age of thirty-six in the Wu Dragon year [848] and ruled fourteen years. At the age of forty-nine, in the Xin Snake year [861], he died.

* * *

His son, Emperor Tang Krichung,[67] born in the Wu Monkey year [828], ascended the throne at the age of thirty-five in the Ren Horse Year [862], ruled fifteen years, and died at the age of forty-nine in the Bing Monkey year [876].

* * *

His son, Emperor Tang Yichung,[68] born in the Yi Ox year [845], [35r] ascended the throne in the Ding Rooster year [877] at the age of thirty-three, ruled fourteen years, and died in the Geng Dog year [890] at the age of forty-six.

His uncle, Emperor Tang Jinchung,[69] born in the Geng Dragon year [860], ascended the throne in the Xin Pig year [891] at the age of thirty-two, ruled eleven years, and died at the age of forty-two in the Xin Rooster year [901].

The son of this Tang Jinzung, Emperor Tang Inggeyiding,[70] born in the Ji Ox year, [869] ascended the throne in the Ren Dog year [902] at the age of thirty-four, ruled four years, and when the emperor was thirty-seven in the Yi-Ox year [905], Prince Layang of south China seized the state.[71]

In sum, from the Wu Tiger year [618] of Emperor Gaochung's ascending the throne up to this Ji Ox year [929], nineteen princes reigned, and two hundred eighty-eight years passed. This Layang, having ascended the throne in the Bing Tiger year, [906] ruled fifty years.

In the Yi Rabbit year [955], a Chinese called Joo Wang seized the state, and he ascended the throne in the Bing Dragon year [956].[72] Thereupon six generations ensued, and to the one called Joo Taizu Wang,[73] from the Bing Dragon year [956] to the Ding Rooster year [1057] there were one hundred and two years (in which) the Manchu Khung Wang of China held the state.[74]

Thereupon nine generations ensued, and from the Wu Dog year [1058] it was one hundred thirty-seven years to the Jia Tiger year [1194], when Chinggis Khan of the Mongols expelled and drove out the Manchu Altan Khan of China,[75] seizing his state.[76] And in the Jia Tiger year, at the age of thirty-three, he brought under his power the fifteen provinces of China, the Red Nation of eighty Tümen, and became famed as the Dai Ming,[77] Blessed, Holy Chinggis Khan.

Thereupon, hearing that Chinggis Khan had seized the state of Altan Khan of China, Sidurgu Khan[78] of the Tangut[79] was greatly afraid and dispatched as an emissary the son of Bayan Sartagar, named Dortong, saying, "Let me become your right-hand man and give my tribute."[80] The Lord acquiesced, and bestowing gifts on [Dortong], sent him back. [35v] That ambassador, staying overnight in the tent of Yabuga of the Tayichi'ud, said to him during the evening, "Your khan is truly a son of Heaven, but his queen has no looks. In the light from the face of our queen, Gürbelji the Fair, one does not have to look for lamplight at night."

But the Lord had been taking out to the steppe [i.e., having an affair with] Möngölün the Fair, the wife of Yabuga. Consequently, Yabuga reported to the Lord in secret:[81]

> "As for the wife of Sidurgu Khan, they say
> 'The yellow sun is unable to shine
> In the light of the exquisitely pretty face
> Of Silun Gürbelji the Fair.'
> My powerful Heavenly Lord, by all means
> You should take her!"

After that, the Lord dispatched a messenger to Sidurgu Khan of the Tangut, saying,

"I shall campaign against the Sarta'ul.[82]
Since you are my right hand, will you ride with us?"

Sidurgu Khan replied:

"How can you say, 'I am the khan,'
Before you have finished conquering all the people?
The lion, king of beasts, is strong;
The king of men [i.e., Chinggis] is holy;
What need does either of you have of comrades?"

Thereupon, the Lord was exceedingly angry:

"If ever until I depart this, my life,
If it be that I have let you go unpunished,
May my father Heaven perceive [how best then to punish me]."

So did he promise. Then Vajra Sechen of the Qonggirad said respectfully as follows:

"Oh, my Lord! You should instead have said:
'Until the son who was born has become a man . . .
Until the eyehole of the iron stirrup has been breached . . .'
Why did you swear upon your golden life?

May your golden life be firm!
May jealous enemies be weakened!
May your subject peoples be numerous!
May your fame and name be universal!"

Then in the Yi Rabbit year, [1195] when he was thirty-four years old, he went on campaign against the Sarta'ul, and their ruler, Sultan Jalildun, went to meet them at Sagari Tarbagatai. Kilügen Baatur of the Sönid and Major Khuyilidar of the Manggud [36r] led the charge, and they killed Sultan Jalildun and brought under their power the five provinces of the Yellow Sarta'ul.

* * *

After that, when he was thirty-five in the Bing Dragon year, [1196] he campaigned against Tokmag,[83] and on the Khasulug [River] the ruler of Tokmag, Sultan Menggülig, fought the Holy One. In this, Sübe'etei Baatur of the Jürchid and Chülgitei Baatur of the Jürkin led the battle, and killing Sultan Menggülig, they brought into their power the people of Tokmag.

* * *

Afterward, when he was thirty-seven in the Wu Horse year, [1198] he dispatched an emissary to Ong Khan of the Kereit,[84] who was dispatched to say:

> "Of old, when I married my great Queen Börte Jüsin,
> You were the father who put on my garment,
> The gift of a sable coat.
> Now, combining our laws and peace,
> Let us become like father and son, and be friendly with each other."

Ong Khan did not trust him, and taking many of his Kereit he set out on campaign, and they met and fought together while watering at Kölen Buir on the far reaches of the Onon River. Törölji Taiji of the Oirat and Prince Jalma of the Uriyangkhan, and Dödei Cherbi—son of Kilügen of the Sönid—the three of them led the battle and subdued Ong Khan, and brought the numerous Kereit under their power.

* * *

Then, when he was thirty-nine in the Bing Monkey year, [1200] he campaigned against Tayan Khan of the Naiman.[85] Tayan Khan took his eight clans of Betegin and went to meet him with an army of 80,000, and when they met on the Khakir River, with Prince Buurul of the Üüshin[86] and Ögilen Cherbi—son of Bo'orchu of the Arlad—and Khuchar Taishi of the Olkhunud, the three of them in the lead, they routed and expelled Tayan Khan and brought his eight clans of people under their power.

* * *

Thereupon, at the age of forty-one in the Ren Dog year [1202], he campaigned against the Khorlad, and Narin Khan of the Khorlad took his 20,000 [36v] troops and met (him).[87] They fought upon Keriye Khöbker. Leading the battle were the four blood brothers—Lord Qasar, Vajra

Sechen of the Qonggirad, Tüdekü Türgen of the Enggüd, and Ölei of the Bayuud—who took Narin Khan alive, and thus brought the Khorlad people into their power.

Thereupon [when Chinggis Khan was] forty-three in the Jia Rat year [1204], the ruler of the Kharli'ud, Arslan Khan, was very prideful of his clan:

"As for him, the Holy Lord called Temüjin,
It is said, 'He goes about collecting people here and there';
Thus he won't fail to come to me here.
It is said, 'A man is born at home
But dies on the steppe.' "

Hearing that [Arslan] had set out on campaign and was approaching, the Lord went to meet him on Qara Kekül, accompanied by Prince Muqali of the Jalayir, Sigi Khutug of the Tatar, Chambai Darkhan[88] of the Suldus, Prince Sechen Beki of the Khorlad, and Jamuga of the Jajiraid, five blood brothers in all, and killed Arslan Khan and took the Kharli'ud into his power.

Then, when he was forty-five years of age in the Bing Tiger year [1206], he campaigned toward King Güngle Dorjé of Tibet.[89] The king of Tibet proffered as tribute numerous camels, together with three hundred men headed by Prince Ilukhu, and dispatched his envoy to say, "I shall surrender." He met with the Lord on Chaidam of Achin, and accepting the surrender, the Lord presented great gifts to the king and his ambassadors, then had them return.

The Lord sent back Prince Ilukhu and presented to the lama named Sakya Chag Lotsawa Ananda Garbi[90] gifts and a letter that said, "I was to have invited you, but on account of worldly deeds and affairs being unfinished, I did not do so. Let me support you from here; and you will protect me from there!"[91] Then he subjugated the 88,000 Tibetan commoners of the three provinces[92] from the three regions of Ngari on down.[93]

* * *

Thereupon, in this same way did he campaign against India, and when they were crossing the Chindanarang Pass, there came running a wild animal [37r] with a single horn called the *seru*, which bent the knee three times before the Lord. Everyone marveled about it, and the Lord declaimed:

"As to this so-called Vajra Land of India, it is said,
'It is the place where were born the powerful holy khans,
The sublime buddhas and bodhisattvas of yore.'
Now, this speechless wild beast,
Why does he bow thus like a man?
May it not well be, there will be unfortunate results if I go there?
Can my father, the Supreme Heaven, be warning me?"

Saying this, he wheeled about and turned back.[94]

* * *

Then when he dispatched an emissary to Ambagai Khan of the Sartagchin, saying, "Submit and present tribute to me," [Ambagai] was not pleased, and sent him back, saying:

"Why do you sit at home boasting?
You are making a mistake about Ambagai, who is not to be taken unawares.
You take delight in suddenly overcoming
People who live indifferent to you."

And when he dispatched him so saying, the Lord was furious:

"As the saying goes, 'Instead of (merely) talking big,
Put a big piece in your mouth [i.e., show you can do it]!'
I, through the command of my father, Heaven, have said:
'I shall weaken the twelve kings of men and
Bring happiness upon all by peaceful rule.'
My father, powerful Heaven, make it so,
This mighty utterance I have just now said!"

When he was forty-seven years old, in the Wu Dragon year [1208], he rode out on campaign, and Ambagai Khan took his army of 10,000 and met him at Lake Baikal. They fought one another for three days and nights. The Lord himself was in the lead, along with Prince Bo'orchu of the Arlad, Prince Muqali of the Jalayir, Kilügen Baatur of the Sönid, and Major Khuyilidar of the Manggud. They battled in exemplary fashion until a great rout occurred, and Ambagai Khan was killed, and all the subject people captured. [37v]

Concluding the great campaign against the Sartagchin,
The Holy Lord,
To those who had bestowed their strength,
The Nine Comrades foremost,
So as to govern the state of the great people
He gave rightfully high and mighty titles,
Weighty and grand posts, and with great favor
Bestowing weighty and modest ranks accordingly,
Making princes into centurions, chiliarchs into myriarchs,[95]
And distributed vast treasures to the immensely great people.
But he did not remember Prince Bo'orchu at all.

When he was going in to enjoy a rest where he usually spent the night, his wise inspired Queen Mother Börte Jüsin spoke thus at her bench:

"When you were going about and had difficulties,
Was it not Bo'orchu who
Met you readily, and became a good friend,
Performed hard deeds for you,
Cherishing not life and limb?
You the khan, Lord of men,
Have honored each and every other one;
Have you forgotten your very own 'steed,' Bo'orchu?
He has worn himself out giving his all to you."

The Lord spoke:, "I have not forgotten, but have said that I shall display the merits of Bo'orchu to those who are jealous." A servant came, and [Chinggis Khan] said:

"Hide yourself at [Bo'orchu's] house, [I think] he is not mad at me.
He is surely sitting at home saying nice things."

So saying, he dispatched the house servant, and Bo'orchu's wife, named Tegüsken the Fair, was sitting and saying as follows:

"It was you who first met our Ruler,
Jointly defending the entire realm,
Performing all his deeds for him;
You have given your strength more than all the others.

Forgetting the father who sired you, the mother who bore you,
Casting aside the wife of your bosom, the offspring you reared,
This is what you have said:
'I shall give my strength in ardently pleasing my Lord;
Although I may suffer now, in the end I shall be happy.'
The Holy Lord, in granting favor to his numerous people, [38r]
Has made myriarchs and chiliarchs of those who could and could not,
But did he even mention you, Bo'orchu?
Let those who give their strength to the Borjigin be warned by this!"

So saying did she sit. Bo'orchu thus gave his reply:

"It is said, 'One should not be greedy for a morsel to be chewed in hunger;
But one should give one's strength and go in hunger.'
'One should not be covetous for gifts to be taken actively;
One should give one's strength in long-lasting friendship.'

'A woman's reins are short; her thoughts are narrow.'
Let the golden leash of my Lord be firm;
Although not having attained them now, surely I will attain fruits later,
When his precious great jadelike state is tranquil.

What need be there to hasten and grow wrathful?
I shall give my strength all along again and again.

He has surely considered what people are saying.
Why should my Lord forget me, his own one?
Certainly my Holy Lord has another plan in mind."

Thus did the house servant report in full that they had so spoken to each other.

The Lord said, "Did I not know what was going on? As previously, he has contributed more than the others. And now he fearlessly speaks both openly, as well as privately, of his own trustworthy ability. He has no knowledge at all of the envy of the rank and file. Tomorrow, these merits of Bo'orchu will be heard by all. I shall speak and confer mighty favor," he said.

The next day the great people assembled, and the Lord proclaimed: "Yesterday, when I granted favor to all, I completely forgot Bo'orchu. As a result, while my wife Börte Jüsin sat and reproached me in the evening, a boy went and dropped by Bo'orchu's tent. He told me that Bo'orchu and Tegüsken, the two of them, were sitting and talking to each other as follows." And when he had completely related the words that Bo'orchu and his wife had earlier said to each other, [38v] he declared:

"He who said kind words is my Bo'orchu,
While his horsehide bow case was wearing out;
My Bo'orchu, who was not afraid in mind or heart,
Who befriended me well when I was behaving erratically.

Even though his fur-covered bow case was wearing out,
My Bo'orchu, who had befriended me while we were suffering greatly,
He was my Bo'orchu who did not spare even his life to the point of dying;While we were dying and slaying together, he truly befriended me.

Thus now, my nobles, princes, the Nine Comrades, and all others,
You my general subject peoples, do not be jealous of him.
If one does not show favor abundantly to
A man who has greatly bestowed his strength,
It becomes a deterrent to those who will give strength later.

Therefore, because this Bo'orchu gave his strength when I first met him,
Now, this is my reason for making him more important than the others."

He having made this declaration, the princes and ministers said to one another:

"This ruler shows favor here and there,
How did it happen that he did not remember this Prince Bo'orchu at all?
There surely is another thought in the Lord's mind.

"Obviously, this is so. Why should we thus be jealous of him? Has not this declaration been favorable to us all?" So did they say to one another.

Thereupon, the Ruler proclaimed:

"Protecting my internal great jadelike state,
Ruling my external peoples of the five colors,
My one who guards the trumpet with great sound,
Such a one is Külüg Bo'orchu, prince of nine provinces."

And to his wife, Tegüsken the Fair, he bestowed the title of Bujin Taibujin,[96] and Bo'orchu, becoming the head of the Nine Comrades, was awarded the princedom of nine provinces.

Thereupon, the Lord declaimed:

"By the command of my father, the supreme Qormusta Khan, [39r]
Bringing under my power the twelve great kings of earthly men,
Bringing under my control the petty princes of vain and evil conduct,
I finished collecting, while assembling in hardship, my great vast people.
And I completed and finished the majority of all my deeds.
Now shall I dwell with body and mind at rest."
From the Wu Dragon year [1208] until the Bing Dog year [1226],
Dwelling peacefully for nineteen years,
Ordering and arranging the immensely great people,

Founding the great jadelike state on a firm basis,
All rested in peace, outstretched on the ground.[97]
On that occasion, which pacified the immense great people,
The happiness of the khan and commoners in general,
Grew like unto the happiness of powerful Qormusta of
the gods.

Thereupon the Lord declared:

"On the one hand, I have earlier promised to do it;
On the other, now it is only the Tangut that I have not yet subjugated!"

On the eighteenth day of the third month of the Ding Pig year [1227], while he was campaigning against the Tangut, a hunt was set up on [Mount] Khanggai, and the Lord spoke gently thus: "A fair deer and a brindled wolf will both enter this battue. Capture them alive and do not kill them. A commoner on a blue and gray horse will enter [the battue grounds]; take him alive and come to me."

Thereupon, when both the brindled wolf and fair deer came they were captured, and likewise they seized the commoner and brought him to the Lord. When they came, the lord asked, "Who are you? Why have you come?" [He replied:]

"I am one of Sidurgu Khan's retainers.
Sidurgu Khan sent me to reconnoiter.
Unexcelled among all the Tanguts,
I am called Black Boar.
Am I to lay my poor head down?
While I stood watching, I have been caught.
My bluish horse named Küs Bolad is [39v]
A runner, not to be overtaken by any on foot.
Were his four hooves exhausted by the ground?
He was seized while he stood motionless."

The Lord then said, "If this is correct, then he is a good man," and did not kill him. And later he said, "It is said that your khan is an emanation; what can he transform into?"

[Black Boar] replied,

"Our khan early in the morning changes into a black striped snake.
At midday he changes into a dark striped tiger.
In the evening he transforms into a pale-yellow boy.
It is absolutely impossible to catch him."

Then, while he was traveling [toward the Tangut], the Lord beheld Muna Mountain[98] and declared:

"For a shattered state, this is fine place of refuge,
And for a peaceful state, this is good pastureland,
And for an old man, a good resting place."[99]

Then an owl sitting atop a tree called out, and the Lord became suspicious and said, "Qasar, shoot and kill that evil thing!"[100] Qasar immediately took a shot, but the owl flew up and a magpie flew into the line of fire and was killed. Whereupon the Lord scolded him, "Once before you joined up to fight with the Seven Qongqotan. As for that day when I asked for griffin feathers, you were stingy; and now when I said to kill that evil-tongued owl, you killed a fine-tongued magpie!"

Having Qasar bound, he had him watched by four men. Thereupon, the comrades and princes said respectfully:

"Oh my Lord. It is said:
'The saldar of good is attacked by the sarbug of evil;
The damages of evil ones overcome the virtues of good ones.
The evil of the ill-omened owl
Attacks the good-tongued magpie.'
Can we release our younger brother Qasar?"

The Ruler did not acquiesce, and mindful of the blameful words of other persons previously, he did not release him.

Then, arriving at the Tanguts, they surrounded the city of Dörmegei[101] and encircled it three times.[102] A mean old woman named Black Kengge [40r] came out on the ramparts of the city, and when she tormented them by waving around a black pennant, men and geldings collapsed in droves [on account of her black magic]. Thus Sübe'etei Baatur said to the lord:

"Oh Lord, she intends to finish off the men and geldings of our great army.
Now, you should let Qasar go out and try to shoot her."

When he said so, the Lord acquiesced and let Qasar ride his own horse named Winged Browny so he could go and shoot her. Lord Qasar then felled her by shooting apart the old woman's kneecap and killing her.

Then when Sidurgu Khan transformed into a serpent, the Lord transformed himself into a Garuda, the king of winged creatures. When he became a tiger, the Lord became a lion, the king of wild beasts; when he became a boy, the Lord transformed into Qormusta, lord of the gods, and Sidurgu Khan, having no comparable power, was captured.

Then Sidurgu Khan said, "If you kill me, it will be misfortune for you; if you spare me, it will be misfortune for your future descendants."

The Lord said:

"There will be no misfortune for me;
It will be good for my future descendants!"

Yet when they shot, slashed, and stabbed [Sidurgu Khan], nothing happened.

Sidurgu Khan said: "You cannot kill me with your various swords. In the sole of my boot is a saber of steel called Egyptian [i.e., Damascus steel], forged by being folded three times. If you slash with that, it will work."

Taking out that saber for them, he said: "Now you are going to kill me. If milk issues from my body, it is a bad [sign] for you; if blood issues, it is bad for your future generations." In addition, he said, "If you take to yourself my Gürbelji the Fair, scrutinize her entire body well." Then when they killed him, slashing his neck with that Egyptian sword, from his neck emerged milk.

Thus, having killed Sidurgu Khan [40v] and taken his Queen Gürbelji the Fair, [Chinggis] brought under his control the Tangut people called Miñag.[103] And then he said, "Let us spend the summer on the sunny side of Altagana Mountain at the edge of the Black River."

Then, when the beauty of Queen Gürbelji the Fair was overwhelming everyone, she said:

"This complexion of mine formerly used to be far more beautiful than this.
Now it has been ruined and covered with dust from your army.
If I wash it in water, color and splendor like before will come back.
This being so, let me wash in my own fashion."

Gürbelji the Fair then went to the edge of the river and said, "Let me wash." When she went she seized a bird that had been turning in flight high above her, a domesticated bird of her father's servant. Then she said, "I am ashamed [to bathe] before all of you. Thus please stay here and let me go by myself to wash," and went.

She wrote [a letter, saying]: "I shall plunge into this Black River and die. Do not search for my bones downstream; seek them upstream," and tying it to the bird's neck, she sent it off. And having washed herself, she returned.

Truly her color and complexion had increased [in beauty]. Then when night fell and they had gone to bed, because she caused harm to the Lord's golden body, he became ill. Whereupon Queen Gürbelji the Fair rose, went to the Black River, plunged in, and died. Since then and up until today the Black River is therefore called the Queen Mother.[104]

Then her father, Sechen Wang Ye of the Joo clan of the city of Irgai in China,[105] came in accord with his daughter's words, and seeking her bones, did not find them. They found one of her pearl-adorned stockings, and from every person casting one shovelful of earth on top of it, the hill named Iron Ulkhu was made. [41r]

Thereupon, the Lord's illness became worse, and as it threatened his life, he declared:[106]

"My wise Queen Börte Jüsin, the well-met one;
My three [wives], Qulan, Yisü, and Yisügen, who have been friendly with one another;
My prince, Külüg Bo'orchu, who well befriended me,
My friends, the Nine Comrades, who have been of mutual assistance.

My four younger brothers, like musk deer;
My four sons, like steeds;
My ministers and princes, like rocks;
My vast and great people, like a treasury.

My great jadelike state,
My wives and descendants,
My assembled people,
My beloved country!"

And when he became even more ill, Kilügen Baatur of the Sönid spoke respectfully:

"Your beloved wise Queen Börte Jüsin will surely die.
Your state like a jade jewel will surely be disturbed.
Your two [brothers] Qasar and Belgütei will surely be preoccupied.
Your assembled great people will surely disperse.

Your wise Queen Börte Jüsin, met when you were small, will surely die.
Your high-raised state and government will surely fall low.
Your two sons Ögedei and Tolui will surely be orphaned.
Your subject peoples, so aggressively gathered, will surely come to an end.

Your wise Queen Börte Jüsin, who was rightly chosen for you, will surely die.
Your two younger brothers, Odchigin and Khachigin, will surely be in trouble.
Your beloved great people, assembled in such numbers, will surely disperse.
Your Bo'orchu and Muqali, who form the peak, will surely sorrow.

When they pass by the northern slopes of the Khanggai Mountains,
Your queen and descendants will surely come, wailing and lamenting.
We shall say, 'Where has our Lord and Khan gone?'
My Lord, deign to rise and grant favor!"

The Ruler craned forward and declared:

"Continually and fearlessly render your strength
To my wife and queen, wise Börte Jüsin, my widow who was left behind.
To my two sons Ögedei and Tolui, my orphans left behind,
Act befriending them with true and honest thought.
The words of the child Khubilai have most remarkably emerged. [41v]
In all regards everyone should act in accordance with his words:
'Why worry about making everyone happy
At some time in the future, like after my lifetime?' "

So saying, at the age of sixty-six, in the Ding Pig year [1227], on the twelfth day of the seventh month, in the city of Dörmegei, he departed and rose to his father, Heaven.[107]

Thereupon, when they placed his golden corpse on a two-wheeled cart, the entire great people were going weeping and wailing, and Kilügen Baatur of the Sönid lamented:[108]

"My Lord, have you gone, soaring like a falcon?
My Lord, have you gone, becoming ill from a creaking wagon?
My Lord, have you in truth abandoned your own wife and sons?
My Lord, have you in truth left behind your own assembled subject peoples?
My Lord, did you get lost like a quaking falcon?
My Lord, did you fly in the wind like the gently waving grass?
My Lord, at your age of sixty-six, did you
Depart to demonstrate happiness to your nine-colored peoples?"

Praising him thus, they came to the marshy ground of Muna Mountain, and the wheels of the two-wheeled cart became mired down and did not move. When, after hitching the steeds of the Five-Colored people, they were still unable to move it, the vast great people were in distress. Kilügen Baatur of the Sönid spoke once more:

"My heavenly Holy Lord, Lion of Men,
Born with a destiny from Eternal Blue Heaven!

Abandoning your extensive and great people,
You have gone, attaining your supreme rebirth.

Your queens, whom you met and married,
Your evenly established state,
Your government organized as you desired,
Your people gathered by the myriads, they are here.

Your queen, whom you met and greatly loved,
Your golden tent, palace and dwelling,
Your state established in purity,
Your people, gathered and tributary, they are here.

The land you have ridden upon, the water you washed in, [42r]
Your subject Mongol people, hereditary and increasing,
Your many princes and ministers,
Your home where you were born, Deligün Knoll on the Onon, they are here.

Your protective standard, made from the mane of a chestnut stallion,
Your tambourines, cymbals, trumpets, flutes, piccolos,
Your golden tent palace, where everything is gathered,
Your throne, where you became Khan on Ködege Island in the Kerülen, they are here.

Your wise queen, Börte Jüsin, whom you met before accomplishing anything,
Your great auspicious home camp, Burkhatu Mountain,
Your two close comrades, Bo'orchu and Muqali,
Your state and customs, established in perfection, they are here.

Your wife, Queen Qulan, met through reincarnation,
Your violins, flutes, and others, your music and song,
Your two beautiful queens, Yisü and Yisügen,
Your golden palace home, wherein all is assembled, they are here.

Because the Kharagun Mountains are warm,[109]
Because the foreign Tangut are numerous,
Because Queen Gürbelji is beautiful,
Have you truly abandoned your old Mongols, my Lord?

Although for your warm golden life there is no longer any protection,
Bringing your illumined source [body], which is like a jade jewel,
Should we not display it to your wife Queen Börte Jüsin,
Should we not gratify your whole great people?"

When he said this,

The Lord Khan compassionately gave permission, and
The two-wheeled cart started moving and squeaking.
The amassed great people became joyous;
They brought it to the place called the Khan's Great Land.

Thereupon, his queens and sons at the head,
Everyone weeping and wailing, unable to bring out
His imperial body, they were despairing.
Erecting the eternal stone, here they
Established the Eight White Tents of general veneration.[110]

Thereupon, the Lord's golden corpse,
On the shady side of Altai Mountain,
On the sunny side of Khentei Mountain,
Was interred in the place called Great Öteg. [42v]
Thus his eternal name extending to the end,
The name Fortunate, Holy, Dai Ming Chinggis Khan,
Is famed to the present day.

* * *

CHAPTER FOUR

History of the Yuan Dynasty

Sagang Sechen's cursory history of the Yuan dynasty and the lengthy story of its collapse have one main function: to explain proper rule. As such the narrative, especially the rise of Zhu Yuanzhang and the founding of the Ming dynasty, does double duty: it explains not only why the Mongols lost China but also why they had to seek proper rule under the Manchu Qing. In both cases, of course, the point being made is that the Mongols could no longer maintain peace and order among themselves and therefore had lost the mandate to rule. In particular, in setting the stage for the Mongols' political revival and concurrent Buddhist conversion in the sixteenth century—as well as the subsequent turn to the Buddhist Qing—Sagang Sechen makes it clear that proper rule is based on the "Two Realms," which are the religious and political realms represented by a ruler and a lama, who in a symbiotic relationship oversee the proper functioning of a Buddhist state. Sagang Sechen therefore only highlights the real—or imagined—relations that Mongol rulers had with Tibetan lamas and their Buddhist activities during the Yuan. Moreover, the penultimate mistake of the last Yuan ruler, Toghan Temür Khan, is that he dismisses his lama and sends him back to Tibet. In this telling, not only is Zhu Yuanzhang not criticized for ousting the Mongols, but like the Manchus, he is recognized as a righteous Buddhist ruler who brings back peace and order.

[Chinggis Khan] had four sons: Chagatai, Jochi, Ögedei, and Tolui, and with Princess Sechen Secheyikün, there were five. During the lifetime of the Lord, Chagatai, the eldest,[1] became ruler of the Sarta'ul;[2] the second, named Jochi,[3] became ruler of the Tokmag;[4] the middle one, named Ögedei,[5] guarded the khan's throne; and the youngest, Tolui,[6] being the fire prince guarding the hearth, died during his father's lifetime.

Then Ögedei Khan, born in the Ding Sheep year [1187], ascended the royal throne in the Wu Rat year [1228] when he was forty-two. He had invited the Sakya [Lama] Drakpa Gyeltsen,[7] but there was a delay, and after six years [had elapsed, Ögedei] died at the age of forty-seven in the Gui Snake year [1233].

* * *

His sons were Güyüg and Köden. The elder, Güyüg,[8] was born in the Ji Ox year [1205], and at the age of twenty-nine in the Gui Snake year [1233] ascended the throne, and after six months, died in the same year.

His younger brother, Köden,[9] born in the Bing Tiger year [1206], became khan in the Jia Horse year [1234] when he was twenty-nine. In the Ji Sheep year [1235] he got the dragon king's illness,[10] and when none who tried to aid him succeeded, they said: "In the Eternal Land of the West, they say there is a great remarkable person, perfect in the Five Wisdoms, named Sakya Kungga Gyeltsen. If you invite him, it will be beneficial." Straightaway he dispatched envoys, headed by Doorda Darkhan of the Oyima'ad, and had him brought.[11]

As regards this Sakya Pandita, who was born in the Ren Tiger year [1182], the 3,375th year from that former Wu Rat year, he went to India in the Wu Dragon year [1208] and won a debate with the Six Heretical Teachers. [43r] He having gotten the title of Pandita, and after having returned [to Tibet], his uncle Dakpa Gyeltsen proclaimed a prophecy:[12]

"Henceforth, in a future time, from the eastern direction,
With a hat like a hawk seated on it,
With footwear like the snout of a pig,
With a dwelling like a lattice of wood,
With a curse of three or four words
To the tune of your father's . . . [13]

The lord of the Mongol people, a Khan named Köden, who is a bodhisattva incarnation, will invite you through an envoy named Doorda. At that time, it will be necessary for you to go without fail. Your religion will be disseminated there," he proclaimed.

Then [Sakya Pandita] realized, *That is the prophecy here and now,* and set out in the Jia Dragon year [1244] when he was sixty-three years old. When he was sixty-six, in the Ding Sheep year [1247], he met the khan.[14]

Then, producing the Lion-Voiced Bodhisattva Avalokitesvara, he subjugated the dragon king and gave the khan an initiation and a blessing; and the khan was straightaway saved from that illness, and everyone became joyful. After this, the religion was disseminated into the outermost Mongolian territory for the very first time by the decree of Sakya Pandita. He found the sanctity of nirvana in the Xin Pig year [1251] at the age of seventy, and Köden Khaishi Khan ruled eighteen years, and died in that same Xin Pig year at the age of forty-six. (Thus) the Lama of devotion and the almsmaster, the khan, passed away within a year.

* * *

Then, Lord Tolui's Queen Mother Sorqaqtani Beki[15] had four sons: Möngke, Khubilai, Hülegü, and Ariq Böke. The eldest brother, Möngke,[16] born in the Ding Rabbit year [1207], ascended the throne at the age of forty-six in the Ren Rat year [1252], ruled eight years, and at the age of fifty-four in the Ji Sheep year [1259] passed away. [43v]

* * *

Thereupon his younger brother Khubilai Sechen Khan,[17] born in the Ji Pig year [1215], ascended the throne in the Geng Monkey year [1260] at the age of forty-six, and from the Jia Rat year [1264] when he was fifty to the Xin Sheep year [1271], for eight years he constructed the summer quarters, Shangdu Kaiping City;[18] the winter quarters, the great Daidu City;[19] the White City of Aral on the northern slopes of the Altai; and Erchügi's Lang Ting City—four great cities led by Daidu—and ruled the vast great people and stabilized the Four States.[20] The four cardinal points were made unswerving and the eight compass points made unretractable; he selected the best from all directions and produced tranquility for everything and everyone.

Then the nephew of Sakya Pandita, called Matidhvaja,[21] born in the Yi Sheep year [1235], came in company with his uncle in the Ding Sheep year [1247] when he was thirteen years old.[22] When he was thirty in the

Jia Rat year [1264], the incarnated Queen Chabi the Fair[23] of Holy Khubilai Sechen Khan said, "As for this Matidhvaja, he is [now] our holy Supreme Lama. Let us take from him the initiation of the glorious tutelary deity Hevajra."[24] And when Queen Chabi reported this to the khan, he said, "Though your statement is correct, how am I to sit lower than a small child? You should ask this child if the initiation may be taken with me sitting on the throne and this child sitting below? If so then I shall accept it. If this cannot be, how can I take the initiation?"

When the queen sent the khan's query to the child, Matidhvaja, he said, "In general, to bring about perfection through the initiation, the first step is to enter the gate of the Vajra Vehicle; and second, to perform the detachment of adherence to things. Inasmuch as I am clearly the Vajradhara, [44r] the very meritorious lama who causes bodhi sanctity to be found through these two actions, how can I sit lower than the khan?"

When the two parties could not settle this dispute, Queen Chabi's mind was greatly troubled, and she said: "Now then, what if, when preaching the Dharma or bestowing an initiation, the lama sits on the dais and the khan sits beneath, and then when conducting affairs of state, the lama and the khan sit equally on the dais?" Both agreed and said, "So be it."

Then the khan said, "Now tomorrow, let us two, Monk Matidhvaja [and I], discuss the essence of the tantras of the illustrious Hevajra." The next day while they discussed together this and that, Matidhvaja did not understand a word of the khan's questions. Matidhvaja was therefore troubled and saying, "Now, let us talk again tomorrow!" he left.

This happened because the *Sutra of the Hevajra Tantra*, which had been owned by Sakya Pandita, was now in the hands of the khan, and Matidhvaja had not even seen it. So that night, while Matidhvaja's mind was troubled and he was tossing and turning, there came an old man, in the guise of a Brahman with snow-white hair, and in the topknot of his hair was stuck a human femur trumpet. He said, "Oh my son, don't be troubled! Get a lamp, and wait for me!" He then vanished.

Then after a moment the old man brought a big *pothi* text. "Look at this quickly, and fix it in your mind! Before the light of dawn I shall go and place it back where it was," he said, and again vanished. Then the boy Matidhvaja looked it over three times, and when he had fixed it well in his mind, at the crack of dawn that old man came and said, "If you have finished reading, give me the book. I shall return it." [44v] He furthermore said, "Oh lad, yesterday you were humiliated because you discussed things poorly, you simply pulled things out of thin air. But now, today, when you discuss things with the great khan, by building your argument from the crown of the lama's own head, he will be unable to challenge you. And you must remember to turn this way when he supplicates you, and remember to turn that way when you debate each other," and then vanished.

As for who this was, it was the root Dharma protector of the splendid Sakya father and son, the splendid Shal Mahakala,[25] coming through magical transformation, who had taken the splendid *Hevajra Tantra* from under the khan's pillow. Then the next day, when they debated together, the Great Khan was unable to counter the child, Matidhvaja. Thus the khan greatly venerated and accepted the four initiations of the splendid and thoroughly surpassing Hevajra.[26] The khan also granted him a title: in Tibetan, Gamsum Chöjé Gyalbo Lama Pakpa; in Chinese, Sing Sing Dai Wang Güüshi;[27] and in Mongolian, The Great Lama, Dharma Lord of the Three Lands.

On a golden mandala of a hundred staters[28] he placed a flawless pearl the size of a young camel's dropping given by Surgatu Margata of the Merkid, the father of Queen Chabi.[29] [The khan also] presented him with a silver mandala of a thousand staters on which was Mount Sumeru made from gold along with the four continents, the sun, moon, the seven jewels, and the eight offerings; as well as many other things including gold, silver, lapis lazuli, and various jewels; silk, brocade, and other things; goods and wares, elephants, horses, camels, and so forth; and livestock and horses without number. He also presented the lama with land and the subject people of Silimji City.[30]

Thus [Khubilai] made the sun of religion shine on the dark land of Mongolia. He also brought relics of the Buddha from India, [45r] a Buddha tooth, the begging bowl presented by the Four Maharajas, and a sandalwood Jowo [statue].[31] He followed the rule of the ten meritorious deeds and stabilized the world, and owing to his having pacified and made happy those in the vast world, in this way he became famous in all directions as Cakravartin Sechen Khan, who turns the thousand-spoked golden wheel, and after ruling thirty-six years, at the age of eighty-two in the Geng Monkey year [1296], he went to Heaven.

* * *

Cakravartin Sechen Khan had four sons borne by Queen Chabi the Fair: Dorjé, Manggala, Jinggim, and Nomuqan; and a single princess named Secheg. Then, when Sechen Khan was sixty-six and Pakpa Lama was forty-six, in the Geng Dragon year [1280], he was about to return [to Tibet] when the khan asked, "Who of you, my four sons, will accompany this precious holy lama? The one who does will hold my royal throne forever." The two elder sons said, "We will not go." The third, Jinggim Taiji, in repayment of his father's favor said, "Let me go," and went accompanying Pakpa Lama. But he died in the Eternal Land [of Tibet].[32]

Thereupon [Khubilai Khan said], "I once issued a command [regarding the succession]," and during his own lifetime when he was eighty years old in the Jia Horse year of [1294], he put on the royal throne Öljeitü, the third of Jinggim Taiji's sons: Kamala, Darmabala, and Öljeitü.

This Öljeitü Khan[33] was born in the Yi Ox year [1265] and became khan in the Jia Horse year [1294] when he was thirty, and after his grandfather had become a god, he ruled the realm beginning from the Ding Rooster year [1297]. He appointed the lama called Sakya Manjughosa Ratna[34] to be an offering site, and in accord with former custom, evenly held the Two Realms, thereby establishing welfare and tranquility for the vast great people and the Four Great States. He ruled the khan's state for eleven years, [45v] and died in the Ding Sheep year [1307] at the age of forty-three.

* * *

Then the son of Darmabala, Külüg Khan,[35] born in the Xin Snake year [1281], at the age of twenty-eight in the Wu Monkey year [1308] ascended the throne. By having the monk and translator named Chöjé Özer[36]—the "Light of Dharma"—translate the majority of the Dharma's sutras and dharanis he nurtured everyone through the Two Realms. After ruling the khan's state for four years, in the Xin Pig year [1311] at the age of thirty-one he died.

His younger brother Buyan Khan,[37] born in the Ji Rooster year [1285], ascended the throne at the age of twenty-eight in the Ren Rat year [1312]. He appointed the lama called the Great Sakya Lord Sripada[38] to be an offering site, and as before, established peace for the great jadelike state. After ruling nine years, he died in the Geng Monkey year [1320] at the age of thirty-six.

* * *

His son, Gegen Khan,[39] born in the Gui Rabbit year [1303], ascended the throne in the Xin Rooster year [1321] at the age of nineteen. He appointed the lama Sakya Buddhasri[40] to be an offering site, and spread happiness to all through the religion and state. He slew and killed the Tangut prince named Ching Sang and pacified the Miñag people.[41] He ruled for three years, dying in the Gui Pig year [1323] at the age of twenty-one.

* * *

Then the son of Kamala, Yisün Temür Khan,[42] who was born in the Gui Snake year [1293], ascended the throne in the Jia Rat year [1324] at the age of thirty-two. He had the previously untranslated Dharma books translated by the lama called Sakya Punyabhadra[43] and the Mongol translator and teacher Sherab Senggye. He reigned five years and died in the Wu Dragon year [1328] at the age of thirty-six.

* * *

Külüg Khan's eldest son, Razibag Khan,[44] was born in the Geng Rat year [1300] and ascended the throne in the Ji Snake year [1329] at the age of thirty. After ruling forty days and nights, he died in the same year.

* * *

His younger brother, Khoshila Khan,[45] was born in the Yi Snake year [1305] and ascended the throne in the same Ji Snake year [1329] at the age of twenty-five. After one month [46r] and twenty days he died, also in the same year.

Then the son of Buyantu Khan, Jaya'atu Khan,[46] who was born in the Jia Dragon year [1304], ascended the throne in the same Ji Snake year [1329] at the age of twenty-six. He venerated and appointed as the Crown Ornament of Worship the lama called Sakya Ananda Bhadrakara.[47] He vastly garnered merit offerings of gold, silver, and jewels for the supreme [worship] sites, beginning with the Jowo Sakyamuni [statue in Lhasa], and greatly venerated the religion of the Victorious One. Following the customs of state and religion he ruled for four years, and died in the Ren Monkey year [1332] at the age of twenty-nine.

The son of Khoshila Khan, Rinchenbal Khan, was born in the Bing Tiger year [1326], ascended the throne at the age of seven in the Ren Monkey year [1332], ruled a month and then died.[48]

* * *

The son of Jaya'atu Khan, Toghan Temür Khan[49]—"The Wise"—was born in the Wu Horse year [1318] and ascended the throne in the Gui Rooster year [1333] at the age of sixteen. He worshipped and appointed as the offering site the lama named Sakya Anandamati,[50] and in accord with previous custom, he made the Two Realms operate equitably. As he ruled, rejoicing in state and religion, in the Jia Monkey year [1344] a son was born to an old man of the Juu clan of China.[51] When the boy named Jüge was born, a five-colored rainbow appeared from the house.[52]

At that time Ilakhu Chingsang,[53] the son of Lakhu, a descendant of the descendants of Lord Bo'orchu of the Arlad from long ago,[54] said this to the khan: "When an ordinary man is born, does such an omen appear? He is a person with a foreign countenance.[55] It would be best to kill him while still small." When he said this the khan thought it was a mistake and did not kill him. Therefore Ilakhu Chingsang said again, "Now, not following my words, you may in the end lose your head. After this child grows up, we will see a variety of sufferings."

Afterward, [46v] it turned out that when the child grew up, he was especially clever and wise, and the khan greatly loved him.[56] He then decreed, "Toqta'a and Qarachang, father and son,[57] have been administering the western provinces of my country. [Now] Jüge and Bukha, older and younger brother, the sons of old man Juu, are to administer the eastern provinces of my realm." When he ruled over the eastern provinces, at that time Lord Jüge went and took good counsel with the Chinese Kama Bingjing,[58] and since they joined in confidence, he reported to the khan thus: "Toqta'a Taishi thinks badly of the khan, and appears to be going over to the enemy." In such a manner did Kama Bingjing connivingly report.

At that time the khan had a dream one night: An iron-tusked boar entered a city, and as he went about causing chaos he lost track of where he had entered the city, and thus went running aimlessly. At this time the sun and moon both set simultaneously.[59] The day after dreaming this, he asked the Chinese Wang Shencheng for an interpretation. He said, "It is an omen of the khan losing his state." The khan thought, *What kind of talk is this about a bad omen?*

When he spoke to Ilakhu Chingsang of the Arlad, he replied, "Can it really be a good one?! Have I not said before that from earth covered with dust, smoke will arise here and there?" The khan thought, *What does this little person know?*, and summoned Toqta'a Taishi of the Qonggirad. When [the khan] asked him about [the dream], the taishi said, "As for the iron-tusked boar, it is a sign that people of the Juu clan will make war. As for the sun and moon setting simultaneously, it is a sign that the nobility and commoners will be the same."[60]

When the khan asked, "Now, what should I do to fix it?" [Toqta'a Taishi] replied, "The words Ilakhu Chingsang [47r] previously spoke were correct. Now, there is no other way than to kill that one of the Juu clan." Thinking, *This taishi is a great man, yet because I elevated Lord Jüge, his eyes are filled with jealousy,* the khan did not kill [Jüge]. Lord Jüge then heard about these statements from Kama Bingjing, with whom he had previously had good relations, as well as from many other trusted people. Moreover, Toqta'a Taishi heard about this slander and went to the khan many times saying, "Now, I have told the khan of this many times, but I am not believed. What good can come of this?" And he himself proceeded cautiously.

Meanwhile, Lord Jüge sent a person to conduct surveillance on Toqta'a Taishi. He knew of this, and had previously set up a trick: in front of his door he put a tray of water; in the water he put a few pieces of pine wood; and on top of this he placed sheep shears and hair. When that spy came and saw it, he then returned but said nothing about it. When he did say, "There are such and such things placed at his door," Lord Jüge understood it and said, "The water in the tray, like the ocean, is the great people. The pieces of wood, like boats on the ocean, are the khan, taishis, lords, and jaisangs.[61] The sheep shears and hair, sharper than a cleaver, finer than hair, are the khan's government." Saying this, he thought, *By what means can I kill this evil one? Because if I do not kill him, he will know everything. As long as he is [alive, my plan] will not succeed.* Then he had Kama Bingjing say [to the khan], "It is true that Toqta'a Taishi is thinking evil toward the khan. As proof of this: [47v] when the khan says come and assemble, he will not come. By this you will know."

When other people said this [as well, the khan] sent Kama Bingjing to go and invite the taishi to come. He went part of the way, and then said [to the khan], "When I summoned the taishi, he said it was not possible." The khan said, "If this is true, and he is innocent, why doesn't he come? It must be true that he has evil thoughts!" And he sent Kama Bingjing off saying, "Go, and take an army to kill Toqta'a Taishi!"

Kama Bingjing thus left, and putting his numerous forces at Siruqan city, he [reached the taishi] himself first and said, "There is a decree that must be relayed to the taishi in private." He then said to him secretly, "People are saying to the khan, 'Lord Jüge has evil thoughts toward the khan.' He is therefore asking, 'How is one to know if it is true or false?' and he has decreed, 'Let the taishi come and let us talk together.' " At once the taishi knew [the truth]. But because from before he had been faithful to the khan and he had no power, he went, wondering, *Are these words possibly true?* Kama Bingjing then said, "Let me go first and prepare the relay horses. If we delay, the khan will scold us," and went on ahead, and prepared his forces. Then he overcame the taishi, and upon killing him returned and told the khan of his actions.[62]

The khan said, "Now, let Lord Jüge rule the east and west provinces, all of my people! Let Kama Bingjing rule the internal administration!" Lord Jüge then said, "My Lord, though you have favored me greatly, how can I return to my home and live in peace? If small lords go [as local administrators], they will torment the great people. If I myself go, however, let me squeeze out the country's taxes." [48r] The khan greatly approved, and said, "Let it be so!"

Prince Jüge thus departed, and when he did not return for three years, the khan became furious. He thus cautioned and instructed the gatekeeper, "This Lord Jüge has delayed too long! If he comes, do not allow him to enter the city!"

Then again, one night the khan had this dream: A gray-bearded old man came and said, "You have killed your own guard dog, and now a foreign marauding wolf is coming. What means do you think you [can use against it]?" After rebuking the khan with great anger, the old man instantly vanished. The day after, the khan was afraid of this dream and thought, *Was not my own guard dog Toqta'a Taishi whom I have killed? And the foreign wolf, is that not the waiting Jüge?*

When he told this to his lama, Anandamati, the lama was silent for a moment, then said, "Previously, our supreme lama, the jewel in the crown, he who had reached the limits of knowledge, the Holy Sakya Pandita, explained, in the treatise called the *Treasury of Aphoristic Jewels,* that: 'It may be beneficial if close comrades become enemies, though harmful if bitter enemies become close comrades.'[63] This is the initial meaning of this dream and the harm to come from killing Toqta'a Taishi, [who was] like a guard dog, and having trusted Jüge, who is like a marauding wolf."

When the khan asked, "What should one now do to fix it?" the lama replied: "Long ago, at the time of your holy Khubilai Sechen Khan, our supreme Lord of the Dharma Pakpa Lama was crying for three days. When the khan said, "My lama, why do you cry so much?" [48v] he replied, "Khan, not at the time of you and me, but nine or ten generations beyond us, when a khan named Toghan is born, at that time, the religion and state of ours will be destroyed. I cry because of this." The khan said, "Oh, my lama, since you are so young, how can you know what is so distant?"

"Oh khan, I know this because long ago it rained blood upon this land for seven days and nights." At once the khan searched and had brought forth from the treasury of old books a certain volume [that said]: "Long ago at the time of China's Tang Taisong,[64] it rained blood on this land for seven days and nights. Then China's Tang Jangzang the translator,[65] a disciple of Teacher Suvandu, the younger brother of the Indian 'Without Obstruction,' said: 'Khan, this is not reflective of your time, but it is a sign that more than ten generations after you, when in your lineage one named Tang Inggei Ding[66] is born, your state will be replaced.'"

Looking at this book the khan, proclaiming that he had long been pious, said, "How is anyone able to warn of deeds that have not reached the present, such as this prophecy professes? Is it not enough if one prays to one's supreme lama, worships the three jewels, and devotes oneself to one's tutelary deity? Will that not help?" Then, being possessed by an evil spirit, he grew angry at his own lama and commanded, "Lama, you must now return to your own country!" At this the lama was very happy, and saying, "The command for me to return to my own land, while the khan's golden cord is healthy and his jade great state peaceful, [49r] is not a decree of the khan but grace toward me, the lama!" He immediately left and returned [to Tibet].

Then that Lord Jüge lived three years in the city of Nanjing, and between him and the 880,000 Chinese oaths were firmly exchanged. Then he returned, bringing a letter to the khan that said: "According to the command of the khan, lord of the masses, levying judiciously I have brought the tribute!" When he came, the gatekeeper, on account of the previous command, did not let him in. Then, by bribing the gatekeeper with a great many jewels and goods, he entered and said [to the khan], "Transporting it on 90,000 two-wheeled carts, I have brought jewels, goods, and chattel." Then, having unloaded the wagons, he said, "The first

30,000 wagons have various jewels and goods, the middle 30,000 have assorted weapons, and the final 30,000 have various kinds of food and drink." When they had unloaded the first 30,000 wagons, they were truly full of jewels and goods. The remaining 60,000 wagons, [however, were filled] with soldiers outfitted with armor and weapons of various sorts. And with them were three great cannons covered with wax. "If night should fall before the unloading of these wagons is finished, these lamps are to be lighted," he said, and put them into place.

When that wax had finished burning and the fire reached the lock of the cannon, and it emitted a loud noise, that was to be [the signal] for those soldiers in the wagons to come out. When they had finished unloading the first 30,000 wagons, the cannon shot sounded, and the soldiers came out immediately and began fighting. All being frightened and terrified, no one was able to repel them. The khan entered a crack in the wall that he had seen in a previous dream, [49v][67] and putting the jade jewel seal in his sleeve, he took his queen and children and fled. In the company of Ilakhu Chingsang of the Arlad, Bukha Chingsang of the Naiman,[68] and Doolkhu Baatur, a descendant of Qasar—with these at the head of seven comrades, they fought their way out.

In this way, Wise Khan reigned from the Gui Rooster year [1333] for thirty-six years until the age of fifty-one in the Wu Monkey year [1368]. Deviating [from the Dharma] and accepting a foreign enemy's wiles, he lost his own city Daidu and his jade state. In sum, from the Ren Horse Year [1162] in which brilliant Chinggis Khan was born, two hundred and seven years [had passed]. And from the Ji Rooster year [1189] in which the khan ascended the throne until the Wu Monkey Year [1368], fifteen Mongol rulers held the state.[69]

CHAPTER FIVE

History of the Northern Yuan Dynasty

The collapse of Mongol military and political power and the rise of the Oirats during the first decades of the fifteenth century had many causes. Sagang Sechen, however, claims that the catalyst for this turn of events was a demon possession that generated immoral sexual desires and ultimately fratricidal murder. The historical reality was no doubt more prosaic and was largely the result of Ming military campaigns as well as the court's meddling in the internal affairs of both the Mongols and the Oirats. The upshot of all this was that Mongol rulers were increasingly weak and ineffective and controlled by others, such as Arugtai—first encountered in the *Precious Summary* as the dung-collecting "Basket Boy"—who was the most powerful leader on the steppe during the early decades of the fifteenth century. The Ming court recognized this reality and gave Arugtai the highest-ranking title of taishi in 1411, and then two years later the title Prince of Qaraqorum. Thus the succession of Mongol rulers that Sagang Sechen duly records as the rightful heirs of the Chinggisid mantle were actually largely figureheads with no real power. Oirat leaders such as Mahmud (d. 1416), and his descendants Togan (d. 1438) and Esen (d. 1454) exploited this shifting power dynamic to weaken the Mongols further and thereby take control of Inner Asia.

Thereupon when the khan came out through the Moltasi Gate,[1] in reproaching himself he proceeded to lament and weep as follows:

"My great jewel city, Daidu, replete with various things,
My bustling walled city of Shangdu Kaiping, where I preferred to refresh myself,
My yellow plain of Shangdu, summer residence of the ancient Holy Ones;
I made mistakes and lost my great state, in the jaundiced Yellow Monkey year.

My great Daidu, built of the nine types of jewels,
My Shangdu Kaiping, which tethers ninety-nine white mares,
My happiness in our universally beneficent religion and state,
My great beloved fame and name, which was 'Lord of All.'

If one arises early and looks from on high, it has a lovely mist;
If one looks from in front or behind, it is fine and lovely;
My jeweled Daidu, established by mighty Sechen Khan,
Where one surely may live summer or winter without boredom! [50r]

My great Daidu, the abode where ancestors reposed,
My gathered people, princes, and ministers I have met and associated with,
My regret in not having followed the sagely words of Ilakhu Chingsang,
My stupidity in trusting Lord Jüge, who went and turned on us.

My Toqta'a Taishi whom I wrongly killed;
My misfortune in banishing and expelling my own precious supreme lama,
My beloved name, which is Lord and Khan of the Guard,
My sheer great happiness in having enjoyed all these things.

My Daidu city, in which sanctity has dwelt,
Established in diverse ways by the incarnation Sechen Khan,
Which has been taken through trickery by the Chinese Lord Jüge;
A disgraceful bad name has come to me, Toghan Temür."

So did he eulogize and weep.

Then going in file one after the other they fled, fighting their way through. Of the Forty Tümen Mongols, six tümen got out[2] and thirty-four tümen were cut off and remained behind.[3] At once he assembled from hither and yon the six tümen that had got out and arrived at the banks of the Kerülen River, where they dwelt, building Tiger City.[4] In the Geng Dog year [1370] at the age of fifty-three, [Toghan Temür] passed away.

* * *

His son, Biligtü Khan,[5] was born in the Wu Tiger year [1338], ascended the throne in the Xin Pig year [1371] at the age of thirty-four, ruled eight years, and in the Wu Horse year [1378], at the age of forty-one, passed on.

* * *

His younger brother, Uskhal Khan,[6] born in the Ren Horse year [1342], ascended the throne in the Yi Sheep year [1379] at the age of thirty-eight, ruled ten years, and died in the Wu Dragon year [1388] at the age of forty-seven.

* * *

He had three sons: Engke "The Courageous" Khan, Elbeg "The Merciful" Khan, and Khuurchag Düüreng Temür Khung Taiji.[7] Thereupon Engke "The Courageous" Khan,[8] born in the Ji Pig year [1359], ascended the throne in the Yi Snake year [1389] at the age of thirty-four, ruled four years, and passed on in the Ren Monkey year [1392] at the age of thirty-four. [50v]

* * *

His younger brother, Elbeg Khan,[9] born in the Xin Ox year [1361], ascended the throne in the Gui Rooster year [1393] at the age of thirty-three, and became famous everywhere as Elbeg "The Merciful" Khan. During this time, because his heart suddenly became controlled by a demon, one day he fired a shot at a hare in the snow, and seeing its blood drip onto the snow, said:

"May there be a woman
With a white face like this snow,
With red cheeks like this blood!"

When he said this, Grand Marshall Khuuqai[10] of the Oirat's Border Thousand said, "Khan, the wife of your younger brother Khuurchag

Khung Taiji, the princess Öljeitü Khung the Fair, her complexion and beauty are far more beautiful than that."

"Oh you, my Grand Marshall Khuuqai, you who have conveyed what was just said and evoked what I was thinking, bring her to me! I shall make you a *chingsang*[11] and let you rule the Four Oirat!" Thus, right after [Khuurchag] Düüreng Khung Taiji had gone off on a hunt, Grand Marshall Khuuqai went to Princess Khung the Fair and said: "The command of the khan is as follows: 'Your beauty and loveliness are admired by all. Let me come to your house so I can see you.'"

The princess was very apprehensive and said:

"Is it customary for Heaven and Earth to unite?
Is it legal for supreme khans to look at their younger sisters-in-law?
Have you heard that your younger brother Khuurchag Khung Taiji is dead?
Have you, khan, the elder brother, become no better than a common dog?"

When Khuuqai returned and told him everything, the khan became furious, and meeting his younger brother on the road he killed him, and then he took his sister-in-law in her third month of pregnancy.

His younger brother Khuurchag Khung Taiji had been born in the Gui Rabbit year [1363], and lost his life in the Ji Rabbit year [1399] at the age of thirty-seven. [51r]

* * *

Thereupon, after the khan had gone hawking, Grand Marshall Khuuqai prepared a feast to receive the title of chingsang. Hearing that he was awaiting the khan on the steppe, Princess Khung the Fair dispatched Khuurchag's groom named Yellow Dogsin to say to him, "While you are waiting on the steppe, come to my house and await the khan," thereby inviting him to come. She greatly honored him and paid him respect by proffering buttered goods with twice-distilled brandy served in a silver cup. Princess Khung the Fair then said as follows:

"Making my poor person good,
Making my lowly person great,
Making my name of Princess Khung into Queen Mother Beki,

When I was only the princess of a lowly taiji,
You made me the queen of the supreme khan.
I will not forget your good deeds.
I recognize your great love, khan and lord;
This is my bowl, which I offer you in thanks."

So saying, she gave it to him, and believing her he accepted it, whereby he passed out and fell over. She then lifted Khuuqai up and put him on the bed. Then, tearing loose strands of her hair and scratching herself up here and there, she summoned numerous people from the neighborhood and showed them what he had done.

Thereupon she dispatched Yellow Dogsin, Khuurchag's groom, to fetch the khan, and when he came, she sat weeping with her face turned down. As soon as the khan came in, he said, "Why are you crying?" She told him in full what had happened when she presented the bowl to Khuuqai. "When he got drunk on my liquor he started talking nonsense, and then when he accosted me, I wouldn't," she said. "This is what he did to me!"

Hearing her say that while he was lying there, Khuuqai got up, mounted his horse, and departed in flight. Thereupon the khan said, "This flight by Khuuqai shows that it is true," and they chased and overtook him, and when they were fighting, the khan's little finger was shot off. [51v] Thereupon letting him fall on the ground, [the khan] seized and slew him. Grand Guardian[12] Wangchin of the Sönid had the skin flayed from the base of Khuuqai's spine, and when he gave it to the princess, he said:

"It is said,
'A life in place of a life
Is no satisfaction.' "

Licking the blood from the khan's little finger, she said, "Let me see what men's skin is like," and licked the grease of Khuuqai's skin and said:

"Licking the blood of the evil-minded khan,
Licking the grease of Khuuqai, who spoke sharply;

Although I am a just woman,
I have vindicated the vendetta of my husband,
Even though I now have to die. So if it is no matter to you,
Kill me quickly!"

When the khan said, "Go home," owing to the beauty of Lady Khung the Fair, he was not angry, but said to Batula, son of Khuuqai, "I have wrongly slain your father," and gave him Princess Samur, born of his chief wife, Köbegüntei; made him a chingsang; and had him rule the Four Oirat.[13]

Then Ügechi Khasqa of the Oirat Kerenü'üd said, "This [Elbeg] Khan, having established his state unjustly, has now killed his younger brother Khuurchag and taken his sister-in-law, Lady Khung the Fair, as his wife; he rules the government improperly. My minister Khuuqai was betrayed and killed by the princess. To his own shame, though I the lord am still living, he has let my subject Batula rule the Four [Oirat]."

Hearing that, [Elbeg Khan] was very angry; thus he and his son-in-law Batula talked it over and said, "Let's kill Ügechi Khasqa." But overhearing these two, the Great Queen Köbegüntei dispatched someone to tell this to Ügechi Khasqa; whereupon Ügechi Khasqa immediately rode off and slew Elbeg Khan, took Lady Öljeitü Khung as his wife, and subjugated the majority of the Mongolian people. [52r]

Elbeg Khan became ruler in the Gui Rooster year [1393] and seven years later, at the age of thirty-nine in the Ji Rabbit year [1399], slew Khuurchag, and four months later in the same Ji Rabbit year was slain by Ügechi Khasqa.

* * *

When Lady Öljeitü Khung the Fair married [Elbeg] Khan, she was in her third month, and when she married Ügechi Khasqa, in her seventh month. Thus after three months she gave birth to a son in the Geng Dragon year [1400], and called him Ajai. Ügechi Khasqa treated him as his own son.

Batula Chingsang made Ögedelekü of the Asud tote a wicker basket to gather up dried dung [for use as fuel]. They therefore called him "Basket Boy," and he worked as a servant.[14] After that, for a while, the Mongols were organized in orderly fashion. Elbeg Khan's eldest son, Gün

Temür, born in the Ding Snake year [1377], ascended the throne in the Geng Dragon year [1400] at the age of twenty-four. Three years later he died, in the Ren Horse year [1402] at the age of twenty-six.

* * *

Since he had no descendant, his younger brother Öljei Temür,[15] born in the Ji Sheep year [1379], ascended the throne in the Gui Sheep year [1403] at the age of twenty-five, reigned eight years, and died in the Geng Tiger year [1410] at the age of thirty-two.

* * *

His son, Delbeg Khan, born in the Yi Pig year [1395], ascended the throne in the Xin Rabbit year [1411] at the age of seventeen, reigned five years, and died in the Yi Sheep year [1415] at the age of twenty-one.[16]

CHAPTER SIX

History of the Mongol-Oirat Wars

Sagang Sechen presents the Mongol-Oirat civil war in operatic fashion—complete with rancorous family feuds, conniving relatives, and disputes about inheritance and titles—yet the central theme is the Chinggisid principle: that only the direct descendants of Chinggis Khan can rightfully claim to rule the Mongols. Thus even though the Oirats did ultimately take control of Inner Asia—a fact readily recognized by everyone from the Ming court to Sagang Sechen—from the Mongol perspective they were never legitimate rulers. This sentiment is well captured in the story herein, where the Oirat ruler Togan (d. 1438) goes to the Eight White Tents in order to claim the title of khan and is instead magically killed by Chinggis Khan. Yet, as both the historical record and Sagang Sechen make clear, this divine intervention did not put an end to the rise of the Oirats. Rather, Togan's son Esen (d. 1454) made the Oirats even more powerful, so much so that he captured the Ming emperor at Tumu Fort in 1449, an event that changed world history since it played a role in the Ming's decision to fortify and consolidate the Great Wall and turn inward. But in Sagang Sechen's telling, the Tumu Incident was of little import. What truly mattered was bloodlines: because Esen was not a Chinggisid, his reign was illegitimate, and therefore Oirat power invariably collapsed. And within this wreckage, a lone child of Chinggisid blood—Bayan Möngke—survived on account of a ruse and thereby set the stage for the return of proper Mongol rule.

In the same Yi Sheep year [1415], Ügechi Khasqa had an evil thought, and owing to former enmities, he killed Batula Chingsang, son of Grand Marshall Khuuqai. The Four Oirat immediately convened an assembly, and afterward when three men were returning from this meeting they met on the road "Basket Boy" of the Asud,[1] who was busy collecting dung. When asked by him, "Good sirs, what news from your meeting?" Mergen Nigitei mocked him and laughed, saying:

"They said something like this:
'Affairs were stuck in that basket on your neck:
Because you have suffered so for the great state!'"

They further said:

"They are going to build the city called Qoromqan, [52v]
They are going to slaughter a white-flanked bull;
They are going to elevate Ajai Taiji to khan;
They are going to make 'Basket Boy' a taishi!"[2]

When they had passed by, Arugtai put down his basket and said, "Those are not your words; they are truly the commands of Heaven! What does it mean for me, a commoner? Ajai Taiji is a descendant of Heaven. Father Heaven, do you know?" Then he prayed to Heaven.

Immediately thereupon, Ügechi Khasqa passed away. After this, in that same Yi Sheep year [1415] Ügechi's son named Esekü, born in the Ding Rabbit year [1387], ascended the throne at the age of thirty-nine. He married Princess Samur [the widow] of Batula Chingsang and became famous as Esekü Khan.[3]

Lady Öljeitü Khung the Fair and Ajai Taiji, mother and son, with "Basket Boy" Taishi of the Asud as the third, (all) were servants in the household of Esekü Khan. Eleven years after the Yi Sheep year [1415], Esekü Khan transmigrated in the Yi Snake year [1425] at the age of thirty-nine.

* * *

At once, Princess Samur decided to take revenge for the evil done by Ügechi Khasqa. She thus secretly released Lady Öljeitü Khung the Fair, Ajai Taiji, and Arugtai Taishi, and dispatched them to her paternal Mongol people, saying:

"Esekü Khan has died;
The subject people have lost their chief and head;
After worshipping the Lord and Father [Chinggis Khan] and
beseeching for one's life,
If one campaigns thereupon, it will succeed."

Her son Bagmu said, "Dear mother, although these are relatives, how can you speak thus before strangers!" His mother gave no answer.

At that time, the Khorchin[4] Adai Taiji,[5] a descendant of Lord Odchigin,[6] was ruling the surviving Mongols. When they arrived and related in full the statement of Princess [Samur], Adai Taiji, born in the Bing Dragon year [1388], [53r] married Lady Öljeitu Khung the Fair in the Geng Tiger year [1422] at the age of thirty-five, and ascended the throne in front of the Lord [Chinggis Khan].[7] To Arugtai he gave the title of taishi. And at once the three of them—Adai Khan, Ajai Taiji, and Arugtai Taishi—took control and rode out, attacking the Four Oirat at Jalaman Mountain. Taking Bagmu—the son of Batula Chingsang—Ajai Taiji said, "How would it be if we were to repay the good deeds of Princess [Samur], our mother, and let this boy go?"

Arugtai Taishi replied, "It has been said:

'It won't do to rear the young of a wild animal;
It won't do to bring to manhood the son of an enemy.'
On the day they let us go,
Did that boy not spew malevolent words?"

Adai Khan agreed with Arugtai, and when they brought [Bagmu], Arugtai Taishi said:

"Previously your father, Batula Chingsang, made me carry a
dung basket on my back;
He called me 'Basket Boy' and treated me poorly when I
worked.
Now as the sun turns,
The [fortunes of] states shift,
Thus do I take revenge on the son,
In order to avenge the father's misdeed."

Thereupon he put a kettle on Bagmu's head, named him Togan (kettle), and made him a servant in his house.[8]

The wife of Arugtai Taishi, called Lady Gerel, said, "He is after all a descendant of the princess," and took good care of him. One day while Lady Gerel sat combing Togan's queue, she saw coming one Möngkebei of the Mongoljin. He said, "My lady, instead of sitting there combing his hair, one should snap his spine," and departed.

Later, Princess Samur came in person and asked to take back her son, Togan Taishi. As soon as Togan returned, he said to the leaders of the Four Oirat:

"Now the Mongol people,
Just as we were before,
Have lost their minds.
If we campaign against them at once,
We shall take them without delay."

[53v] His mother, Princess Samur, disagreed and said, "Because this little boy has been made to suffer, he is talking revenge; but why do we have to pursue them with evil and malice?"

They nevertheless rode off and encountered Adai Khan while he was out hunting. Adai Khan had gone off to shoot wild game from horseback and had given his two young Oirat companions, Saimujin and Salamujin, his quiver filled with lances, while he had a quiver filled with four big-tipped arrows.

Yet, recognizing their own Four [Oirat], these two escorts at once switched sides to [the Oirat]. The khan nonetheless felled four men with the four arrows in his quiver. Proceeding to flee, he took refuge in the Lord's palace,[9] but because he was without weapons, they seized and slew him.

Thereupon Togan Taishi, upon the horse called Good Khonggor of Mirasan, circled around the tents of the Lord's palace three times, slashing as he went past, saying: "You may be the White Tent personifying brilliant [Chinggis Khan], but I am Togan, descendant of the female blessedness!"[10] Thereupon the lords and people of both the Forty [Mongols] and the Four [Oirat] spoke among themselves, saying:

"Holy Lord [Chinggis Khan] is not only the lord of the Mongols,
But is the son of Indra, King of the Gods,
And the conqueror of all the Five-Colored People and Four Subjects.
Something disastrous will happen to Togan!"

They told him, "Your behavior is wrong. You should beg the Holy Lord's pardon by making obeisance to him and asking for your own life." Still he would not listen and said, "From whom do I have to ask my own life? Now all the Mongol people are mine. I shall sit on the throne of the khan in accordance with the custom of earlier Mongol khans."

When he made an offering before the Lord and turned around, the golden quiver of the Lord [54r] made a cracking noise, and the people nearby saw an arrow trembling in its middle slot. Just then Togan Taishi fell unconscious, bleeding from the nostrils and mouth. He was undressed and found to have on his back what seemed to be an arrow wound. The quiver was examined and the arrow in the middle was found to be stained with blood. All the people of the Forty [Mongols] and the Four [Oirat] said among themselves, "The Lord did not approve of him!"

[Togan Taishi] summoned his son Esen[11] to come and said:

"The brilliant man has manifested his male power;
The female Sutai was unable to defend me;
While I put my faith in Mother Sutai [his mother of royal blood],
I have been defeated by the Holy Lord.
I have finished clearing away your burden;
There is only Möngkebei of the Monggoljin left."[12]

Saying this, he departed this life.

Adai Khan, born in the Geng Horse year [1390], ascended the throne in the Bing Horse year [1426] at the age of thirty-seven. After thirteen years, in the Wu Horse year [1438] at the age of forty-nine, he was slain by Togan Taishi.

* * *

In this way, Adai Khan and Togan Taishi both passed away one after the other in the same year [1438]. In that same year, Togan's son Esen, born in the Ding Swine year [1419], at the age of thirty-two in the Wu Horse year [1450] ascended the throne in front of the Lord.[13] In accordance with the statement of his father, he slew Möngkebei of the Mongoljin. On that same day, he gathered the two—the Forty [Mongols] and the Four [Oirat]—and they rode out on campaign against the Chinese. Then one night Esen Khan dreamed as follows:

"I myself was being born again,
and everyone was saying, 'Now who will rear him?'
'Who other than Lady Akhadalai,
Wife of Aliman Chingsang, who is
The son of Arugtai Taishi of the Asud.'
That is what I dreamed they were saying." [54v]

When he said, "Interpret this dream!" the Oirat Shiraikhan Bishuun said: "It means that you will seize the Great Ming Emperor of China and will have Aliman Chingsang of the Asud guard him."

Subsequently passing through the Datong area, [Esen] captured the Great Ming Emperor Jingtai[14] and said, "This was the dream omen." And having Aliman Chingsang guard him, he issued an order, "Care for him in the warmth of the place of the Six Thousand Üjiyed."

On the return journey, he proclaimed, "If any person says to my mother before I do, '[Esen] captured the Great Ming emperor,' that person will be killed." When he arrived and embraced his mother, [Esen] said, "Dear Mother! I have now really been born again of you!" When his mother said to her son, "My dear! They say that you have captured the Great Ming emperor," he asked, "Who said that?" She said, "Valiant Sürsün of the Yüngsiyebü happily told me!" Then Esen Khan, not heeding the advice of his mother, slew Valiant Sürsün and had him hung from a bent tree.

Then the Mongol and Oirat nobility said to one another, "When Esen set out on the great campaign, he killed a person, and now when decamping he kills a person. What good is there in this bloodshed?"

Further, the Mongols said,

"Previously he killed Möngkebei.
Now he has killed [Valiant] Sürsün.

If it continues like this, then
He will kill all us Mongols."

Then one after another they all abandoned Esen.

In agreement with these words were the first three sons of Ajai Taiji: Taisung Taiji,[15] born in the Sim Tiger year [1422]; the second, Agbarji Taiji,[16] born in the Gui Rabbit year [1423]; and the youngest, Manduulun Taiji, born in the Bing Horse year [1426]. Thereupon Taisung, at the age of eighteen in the Ji Sheep year [1439], became khan, and he appointed Agbarji to be *jinong*[17] when he was seventeen, [55r] and Manduulun Taiji was fourteen.

When the three brothers rode out they fought the Four Oirat at a place called Black Türin. At that time, saying, "Let us struggle for the circle of the great battle site," they each sent out a good man to fight. The Mongols sent out Baatur Süüsitei, and the Oirats sent out Baatur Guulinchi. Thereupon they asked each other their names and who they were, and they jointly sang forth their names. When they heard each other's names they said, "We two were once here in a time of peace as sworn brothers. Remember how we sat here one day drinking and talking to each other: 'If the Forty [Mongols] and the Four [Oirat] ever split, who else but you and I will come to this fight? If it happens so that we two meet at that time, what will you do to me?'" To which Guulinchi had said, "I am a good shot, and though you bear armor, I will shoot you through!" And Süüsitei had said, "I am a good swordsman, and I will slash you from top to crotch!"

Baatur Süüsitei had put on two layers of armor, and when they met, he came and shouted: "You, man who shoots from afar, take precedence and shoot first!" And when Baatur Guulinchi shot, the arrow went through the two layers of Süüsitei's armor, and going through his body the arrow stuck in the back of his saddle. Thus when he raised up and sat forward, Süüsitei was able to slash and cut Guulinchi from top to bottom.

Thereupon twilight approached, and the [Mongols and Oirat] said to one another, "Let us meet at sunrise." That night they spent the night in alert. The Four Oirat were worried and scared, saying, "Shall we give in now, or what shall we do?" [55v]

Abdula Sechen of the Telenggüs said, "The Mongols are shortsighted; let me go and heap invective on them. If I come back, I expect recognition!

If I die, take care of my children," and departed. He proceeded, saying to himself, *It is known that Taisung Khan is clever, and Agbarji Jinong is dumb; let me try to trick him. But poisonous Kharguchag, the son, will surely figure it out; how can I trick him? Be that as it may, let fate decide!*

Entering the jinong's tent, he said, "Jinong, if you take us together, then we will surrender. But if you and the khan divide us, why should we surrender to you? If it be done by you in this way, it would be better for us all to die on our spear points. Esen Taishi sent me to say [the foregoing]. Furthermore, the khan—your elder brother—is always deprecating you. We have heard it said:

'Though an elder brother sits and eats,
He is giving it to his younger brother.'"

That very evening they sat and spoke among themselves, and the jinong said: "These words of Abdula Sechen are true and correct. My elder brother the khan earlier made me jinong, but when sending me to the Right Tümen, he had everything loaded onto a single blind black male camel and sent me off. Moreover, on the journey he appropriated my groom, White Alagchud. Why should I ally myself with him and call him 'brother'? Let me now instead unite with the Four Oirat and drive him away!"

His son Kharguchag Taiji spoke as follows:

"It is said, 'If one protects his in-laws, he will fail;
If one protects his blood relatives, he will rise higher.'
It is said, 'If one protects his relatives by marriage, he will grow weak;
If one protects his khan, he will be admired.'
Esen Taishi is my father-in-law;
For the sake of your name, my own father, do I speak.
Instead of trusting the word of a stranger,
As soon as the enemy attacks, it would be better to slash him."

[56r] Thereupon the jinong said, "Be you a child or a man, you are ranting nonsense!" And that night he left with Abdula Sechen, as well as Khutubaga of the Solonggod and Möngke of the Khonichuud, and joined up with the Four Oirat.

The next day, when he fought with the Oirat forces, his elder brother Taisung Khan was killing unremittingly, yet when his army was in a desperate fix and beaten, the khan spoke as follows:

"Greatly have you been admired, Baatur Süüsitei!
While I watched, the heavenly orb revolved,
And Agbarji Jinong was deceived by Abdula Sechen.
Greatly despoiled and ruined has been my beloved name."

Taisung Khan then fled on his wild bay horse and headed for the Khentei Mountains by crossing the Kerülen River.

Previously, he had divorced and returned his wife named Altangaljin, who was the daughter of Chabtan of the Khoorlad; and as he fled in this manner, he met [Altangaljin] and her father, who said:

"It is said, 'The person one hates (is the one whom)
One meets on a narrow defile.'
Let me slay him."

But his daughter said:

"The fault of the divorce was mine;
If one harms a Borjigin, misfortune will accrue.
But if we support him in his distress,
Will that not be advantageous sometime in the future?"

Though she so warned her father, he did not agree. Taisung Khan, having ruled from the Ji Sheep year [1439] for fourteen years, departed this life at the hand of Chabtan in his thirty-first year, the Sim Monkey year [1452].

Agbarji Jinong then united with the Four [Oirat], saying, "Yesterday my upstart son Kharguchag said:

'As regards this outsider in distress,
Let me efface the ancient enmity by pursuing and slashing him to death.'
I was apprehensive and made him stop with a warning."

But all the Oirats and Mongols were secretly deriding Agbarji Jinong; laughing together, they said:

"This jinong of ours
Is really no jinong at all!
He is a colossal ass!
So let us bray like you!"

Which is why they say that Agbarji Jinong had become an ass. [56v]

Later, when the Oirat were talking among themselves, they said, "This jinong is like a head of livestock. Kharguchag Taiji is surely one who can take revenge. How can one keep a fox in one's saddlebag? There are many enmities between the Forty [Mongols] and the Four [Oirat]. When one thinks about revenge, how can we let them stay alive? Let us slay both father and son."

Thereupon, Esen Khan, who hated his son-in-law, said: "Although his father [the jinong] is wrong, he pursued his elder brother and joined up with us. The son is a good man, worthy to become a comrade. What will be accomplished by killing them?"

Abdula Sechen replied,

"A father who pursues his elder brother
And slanders his own son is
A person who has no understanding of family and relatives.
How can we let foreign enemies become comrades with us?
We may not treat his son [Kharguchag Taiji] as a man;
Truly it is a dangerous evil.
Is he not on the point of carrying out his obnoxious words?"

Saying this, all approved of it, and they made a plan. Thereupon, Abdula Sechen went and reported as follows to the jinong:

"We two, the Forty [Mongols] and Four [Oirat]
Have become solely your subjects.
Now jinong, our lord, you should be khan!
Bestow (your) jinong title on our Esen Taishi!"

The jinong said, "These words of yours are correct, let it be so!" Then, after they had gone, Kharguchag Taiji said:

"As the sun and moon are in Heaven;
The khan and jinong are on Earth.
There are taishis and chingsangs among the descendants;
Thus how can one give one's title to another?"

Thereupon his father, the jinong, was angry and disapproved, and his son Kharguchag Taiji spoke as follows:

"It is contrary to custom to speak against one's father and khan;
I speak on behalf of the beloved name and jade state [of Chinggis
Khan].
You want to lay down your dark head (i.e., to die); [57r]
You want to exterminate all your Mongols?"

Thereupon the Forty and the Four were assembled and Agbarji ascended the throne, and made Esen Taiji the jinong.

At once the Four Oirat devised a scheme, and constructing two big tents in a row they dug a large hole within the back tent and covered it with felt. Then while they prepared for a stupendously great feast, the evil Abdula Sechen went and said to [Agbarji]:

"Jinong, you are now khan over the Forty and the Four,
And you have bestowed on our favorite the title jinong.
And you having honored us exceedingly well,
Your nephew Esen Jinong is preparing a feast of rejoicing,
And has sent me to invite his uncle the khan."

At once [Agbarji] went, and when he arrived they said, "Let us sing aloud, proffering goblets, and seat you the khan first. Then older and younger brothers with their comrades are to enter two at a time in a single file."

Thus they seated numerous others far off, then summoned the khan with four comrades, and then the taijis with two comrades at a time. And as soon as the first ones entered there was singing, and as everyone sang in a loud voice, they seized them firmly in turn, killed them, and threw them into the hole in the back tent. They assassinated thirty-three plumed ones [i.e., nobility with plumed hats].

Kharguchag Taiji, however, was cautious and had his groom, Inag Gere of the Naiman, go and look in secret. He then returned, saying, "There are no people to be seen, but from the back tent blood is flowing." Kharguchag Taiji said:

> "Let's lie down [i.e., give up];
> Let's lie down and die [i.e., give up and be killed];
> Let's die [i.e., try to escape even if we die],"

and with his groom Inag Gere fled.

Thirty good men of the Oirat came in pursuit, and as they were coming close [Kharguchag and Inag] took refuge at the Onghon ravine. [57v] Then when Silbis Baatur of the Oirat, known as Türin, clad in double armor, came through the pass, Inag Gere shot an arrow through the layered armor, and he fell and rolled down the slope. Then Cheleg Türgen of the Torghud dressed himself in three layers of armor, seized a lance, and came through the pass. Inag Gere said, "Against him I cannot avail; taiji, you shoot him!" When the taiji let him pass and shot him in the heart, the arrow pierced the threefold armor and protruded from the back. Thus when Cheleg Türgen fell, those others fled.

Then [Kharguchag and Inag] said to each other, "Should we go on foot?" And then when night had fallen Inag Gere went and stole the black horse of Esen Khan, named Buura Khabsag, and his bay-blazed mare called Eremeg Sirgagchin. He had the taiji ride the black horse, and Inag Gere rode the bay mare. Then, saying, "The Tokmag princes, descendants of Jochi, are our relatives," they proceeded to Tokmag.[18]

On the way they encountered a rich man named Ag Möngke of the Tokmag, and he and the taiji became friendly, and they stayed with him for a while. [Kharguchag Taiji] then dispatched Inag Gere, saying, "Go and determine whether Esen Taishi is alive, and how things are going with the Forty and Four; moreover, if there is a way—and if no man has married her—try to bring my wife, Secheg."

In the meantime Esen had become khan and was ruling the Forty and the Four.

Later, when the rich man organized a hunt, ten antelopes passed by, and the taiji shot all but one, which made Ag Möngke's younger brother, Yagsi Möngke, extremely jealous. Whereupon he shot and killed [Kharguchag Taiji], saying, "It was an accident."

Thereupon his groom, Inag Gere, came and encountered Ag Möngke's [58r] herdsman on the outskirts of the hunt and asked [about the taiji]. When he said, "Your master was slain in such and such a way," Inag Gere killed him and then went back driving a herd of horses. When he met with Princess Secheg at her place, he explained what had happened and as they wept together he said, "The Tokmag have slain my lord and ill treated me; I rebelled and came here." He then went and met Esen Khan.

Then Princess Secheg said, "Though people may be saying, 'Let your father [Esen] present you to a man!,' until I hear personally of Kharguchag's death, I will not go to another man!" And because she continued to say so, when three months had elapsed from her parting from Kharguchag in her seventh month of pregnancy, she gave birth in that same Ren Monkey year [1452]. Her father, Esen Khan, said, "If this child of Secheg's be a girl, let it live; if it be a boy, kill it!" His daughter, hearing this, drew and tied back the child's testicles and thus displayed him. The people observing said, "It's a girl!"

Thereupon, after they had departed, Princess Secheg placed in a cradle a girl, the daughter of one called Old Lady Odoi of the Chakhar,[19] and left her there. She then went to her great-grandmother, Princess Samur, and when she had related these events, the princess had the boy brought to her and named him Bayan Möngke.[20] She had him suckled and cared for by Grand Mistress Kharagchin, wife of Solongas Sanggaldur.

Then when Esen Khan—[Princess Samur's] grandson—said, "Let's kill this child," the grandmother Princess Samur said, "Do you mean to say that when he grows up and becomes a man, you're afraid he will carry out some sort of revenge? He may be my younger relative, but is he not also your grandson? If my son Togan were alive, he would say as follows, 'Esen, you have sired a grandson; now let him be!'" When she rebuked him in this way, her grandson [Esen] was fearful and left without a sound. He then said:

"I have said, 'I will cut off the descendants of the Borjigin,' [58v]
But my grandmother [who is a Borjigin] does not agree.
Now I will kill him, concealing it from the princess."

Inag Gere heard this and told the princess, whereupon she said, "If there is a trustworthy man [to be found], we should probably send the child to the Mongols." Inag Gere replied, "Grand Guardian Ögedei of the Oirat has told me, 'I have been leading a detachment for thirteen years, and have well given my considerable strength [to the Oirat]. Yet during this time Esen has shown me no favor.' I shall try to find out what he actually means," and departed.

"Baatur Ögedei, if you are seeking honor, Esen is saying to everyone he wants to kill Princess Secheg's three-year-old child. If you make it known to Princess [Samur] that you will bring this child to the Mongols, there is no doubt that this deed will be key to your success, as well as your future generations, not to mention for the Mongols."

Grand Guardian Ögedei approved of these words and went to the princess and said, "Your Esen is trying to kill this child; let me deliver him to the Mongols, your maternal in-laws." The princess was delighted and said, "If these words of yours are true, it is very good." Thus they sent off the child, having him delivered [to the Mongols] by these four: Grand Guardian Ögedei of the Oirat's Gooli Thousand,[21] Bulai Taishi of the Mongol Kharchin,[22] Bayantai Mergen of the Sartu'ul, and Grand Guardian Eselei of the Qonggirad.

In the meantime, Orochu Süüsi of the Urud presented his own daughter Sikhir to [be the wife] of Bayan Möngke. And saying, "Let us deliver him to his remaining relatives," he took the child into his care and kept him there.

At that time, Alag Chingsang of the Right Wing of the Oirat and Temür Chingsang of the Left Wing, these two came and said, "Esen Khan, you have become Khan of the Forty and the Four, now present your taishi title to Alag Chingsang." Esen said, "I do not understand what you mean by this; I have previously given it to my own son." [59r]

The two grew very angry and said, "By the schemes of Abdula Sechen, by the cleverness of Batula Baatur, by the energy of Wise Nigitei, you have taken the Mongol state and put yourself in a fine position. But now, you two, father and son, just try to keep together the state of the Forty and the Four." And at once a force came riding and attacked. As they took and rounded up women, children, servants, and cattle, Esen Khan proceeded to depart in flight. Then, while Esen Khan was fleeing by himself, one called Baghu, son of Valiant Sürsün, slew him and then hung him on a tree upon Kökei mountain.

CHAPTER SEVEN

History of Dayan Khan

The importance of Dayan Khan in Mongol history is hard to overestimate. His revival of Mongol political power in the early sixteenth century, his reorganization of the Mongols into the Six Tümen, and the distribution of the fifty-four *otog*—the recognized territorial units within the Six Tümen—as appanages ruled by his descendants shaped Mongol society for the next four hundred years. Yet, how this all came about is little understood because there are few extant sources explaining these developments. Moreover, as reflected in the history of this period presented in the *Precious Summary*—the murky history of the Mongol rulers prior to Dayan Khan's rise, his troublesome father, and his far-fetched early marriage—there may be certain things that the Mongols wished to forget about Dayan Khan. Indeed, as well evidenced in the violent resistance by the Ordos Mongols, who wanted to preserve their independence in the area within the great bend of the Yellow River, it is clear that Dayan Khan's attempt at Mongol consolidation was not a simple or straightforward process. Even so, by 1510 he had succeeded in suppressing all dissent and forged the Dayan Khanid state, which would survive until the reign of his great-grandson, Ligdan Khan (d. 1634), whose disastrous reign not only alienated his relatives ruling across Mongolia but also set the stage for their eventual submission to the Manchus.

Aliman Chingsang of the Asud gave a wife named Molo to the Great Ming Emperor Jingtai,[1] who had been captured by Esen, renamed White Seüse, and made to be a servant. Thereupon these people suffered a winter storm with much pestilence and plague. One night while White Seüse lay sleeping, a maidservant of Aliman Chingsang, when she rose to milk the cows, saw a reddish-yellow beam emerging from his eyebrows and thereby perceived that he was one to be lauded. She told this to her lady, Akhadalai, and then gradually everyone saw it and marveled together.

"This person is a man of great destiny.
Since after we took him into custody, everything went awry,
And now he has displayed signs different from ordinary men,
Let us deliver him back," they said to one another.[2]

When they returned the Great Ming Emperor Jingtai, he bestowed unsurpassed treasure and presented the title "Great Imperial Favor of Daidu" to the Six Thousand Üjiyed. From the wife of that Jingtai Khan, who was named Molo, there appeared the descendants of Jüü Daasa, and that he is said to be Tabunang Talbai of the Asud is true.

Thereupon, hearing that Esen Khan [59v] was no more, the minor queen of Taisung Khan, Queen Mother Samur, who had produced a son called Markörgis, born in the Bing Tiger year [1446], rode out when he was seven years old. His mother, Queen Mother Samur, girded herself with a sword and went on campaign with an infantry force with horses and oxen. They attacked the Four Oirat on the Könggei and Jabkhan [Rivers], and taking great booty and spoils, they returned home. They then made Markörgis Taiji, at seven years of age, khan. When they gave him the title Ükegtü Khan and while they were organizing the remaining Mongols, at the age of eight, in the Gui Hen year [1453], he was murdered by Doolang Taiji of the Seven Tümed.

Back when they had returned Queen Altaaljin of Taisung Khan, she had left behind her three-year-old Molan Taiji, born in the Ding Snake year [1437]. He was now sixteen years old, and Chabtan had been rearing him, saying, "He is my daughter's son." But in that same year Chabtan was slain, and thus Khabchir of the Khoorlad took [Molan Taiji] into his house.

Suddenly these people suffered a great calamity, and when they asked the soothsayers, because they said, "The misfortune is due to mishandling a Borjigin"; they said to one another, "If this be true, then it must be so," and were afraid. And thus Grand Guardian Dakhatai of the Kemjigüd and Moltai of the Khoorlad delivered [Molan Taiji] to Prince Molakhai of the Ongli'ud.

Thereupon everyone said, "You are the one to establish the state of the great people; thus now be khan!" They then had him mount his yellowish horse and implanted the Golden Vajra, and when they brought him before Lord [Chinggis], at the age of seventeen in the Gui Hen year [1453] they put him on the throne.

Then Khutubaga of the Solongas came before Molan Khan and said, "Prince Molakhai is approaching with his wife Samandi, and with his troops, to take aim at you." [60r]

Molan Khan said, "He once did well by me; why should he now be doing evil?," and did not believe it. When he sent other people to see about this, Prince Molakhai was holding a hunt in his territory and [the messenger,] seeing the dust, turned back. And when he came and said, "It is true; dust was rising up," [Molan Khan] said, "If this be so, let us go meet him," and taking his forces rode out to meet them.

This same Khutubaga then slipped away and said to [Molokhai]: "Molan Khan is approaching on campaign, saying he is going to kill you and take your people." Prince Molakhai did not believe it and said, "I have only helped him, not harmed him, so how can he be riding against me?"

"If you think I am lying, see for yourself by sending out a reconnaissance."

Prince Molakhai said, "It is surely false. Yet let me go up on high and see for myself," and went out and rode onto a height and looked out at the horizon. He put on his armor and poured libations to the heavenly deities and said respectfully:

"Supreme Heaven, Eternal One, you know!
You second, the Holy Lord [Chinggis], know!
I have rendered service to your royal descendant,
And in return he does evil toward me?

Deign to render your command, which will
Graciously distinguish white from black, namely, between

A member of your own imperial family, Molan Khan, and
Prince Molokhai, who has become his subject."

Although they were few, when they fought, Molan Khan was slain. Molan Khan, beginning with the Gui Rooster year [1453], ruled two years, and at the age of eighteen, in the Jia Dog year [1454], died.[3]

* * *

At once Mönggöchei, the queen of Molan Khan, said in her weeping and wailing:

"Oh Khutubaga, who has separated me from the lord khan,
And thus besmirched my lovely and good name!
Oh Khutubaga, who has separated me from the lord of all,
And thus destroyed the established state!
Oh Khutubaga, who has separated me from the lord khan,
And made a rift between father and Molakhai." [60v]

Hearing her lament, Prince Molakhai also mourned for Molan Khan, and cut out Khutubaga's tongue and killed him.

Since [Molan] Khan had died without descendants, his uncle, Manduulun by name, born from an Oirat wife of Ajai Taiji in the Bing Horse year [1426] and thirty-eight years of age in the Gui Sheep year [1463], became khan. When he rode out to take revenge for [Markörgis] Ükegtü Khan, he slew Doolang Taiji, descendant of Khachigin, and subjected the Seven Tümed.

Thereupon, as regards the grandson and younger brother, when the father-in-law Orochu Süüsitei and the four noblemen from before delivered the two—Bayan Möngke Taiji and Princess Sikir—the paternal granduncle, Manduulun Khan, was very happy and at once declaimed, "He is a seed of the Borjigin fruit," and renamed Bayan Möngke as Bolkhu Jinong.[4] Then to take revenge for Molan Khan he rode against Prince Molakhai. Prince Ünebolad—son of Baatur Süüsitei of the Urud—went at the fore with his cinder-colored horse and killed Prince Molakhai at Three Pass Ravine.

Thereupon the relatives of Manduulun Khan and Bolkhu Jinong concluded a peaceful alliance and readied the Six Tümen.[5] Manduulun Khan had two wives. His senior wife was Big Nose Jönggen, daughter of the Oirat Begersen Taiji, and the second wife was Mandukhai Sechen,[6] daughter of the Enggüd Chorogbai Temür Chingsang. Then Khungqola of the Qali'uchin spoke slanderously about Bolkhu Jinong to Manduulun Khan: "Bolkhu Jinong, your younger nephew, is doing evil to the khan. He is saying, 'Let us take Big Nose Jönggen.'"

When told of this the khan did not believe him. When he relayed these words of Khungqola to Bolkhu Jinong, [61r] he said, "What do those evil words mean?" And the khan said, "If this be so, let the one who slanders against two relatives be punished!" and they killed the slanderer Khungqola by cutting him into pieces.

After this Isman Taishi of the Yüngsiyebü said to the khan, "Poor Khungqola's words turned out to be true. In an uninhabited place they have been meeting up." He went to [Bolkhu] Jinong and said, "The khan, your older uncle, considers true the former words of Khungqola, and aims to harm you." And when Bolkhu Jinong did not believe it, Isman Taishi said, "If you don't believe me, there will come a spy," and left.

The khan thought, *I have now heard these words twice, is it true?* and again sent two envoys, who said [to Bolkhu Jinong], "The khan has sent us to say: 'Why do you hate me? A person has said to me, 'It seems that Khungqola's statement is true, [Bolkhu Jinong is sleeping with the khan's wife].'" Bolkhu Jinong thought, *It is true that a spy has been dispatched,* and grew angry and said not a word. Thereupon the envoys returned and said, "The jinong grew angry and said not a word."

The khan, now believing it, became really angry. "Other than my two daughters, Borogchin and Esige, I have no male heirs; and thus at some point all of my people will be [Bolkhu Jinong's subjects]. If he is in such haste now, why should I wait?" And he sent his troops on campaign with Isman Taishi at the fore. Bolkhu Jinong got away and fled, and thus was not captured. [But the khan's forces] took over his people and livestock. Moreover, the Yüngsiyebü Isman Taishi took [Bolkhu Jinong's] wife Queen Sikir. In the Jia Monkey year [1464] Queen Sikir had previously borne a son from Bolkhu Jinong; he was named Batu Möngke[7] and was suckled by Bagai of the Balgachin.

Other than the two daughters, Borogchin and Esige, Manduulun [Khan] was completely without descendants from Big Nose Jönggen. From his queen Mandukhai Sechen came these two, Borogchin and Esige, and thus Princess Borogchin was given to Begersen Taishi of the

Uyigud, and Princess Esige [61v] was given to Son-in-Law Cegüdün Khoosai of the Mongoljin.

Thereupon Manduulun Khan ruled five years from the Gui Sheep year [1463] and died in the Ding Pig year [1467] at the age of forty-two. Then Bayan Möngke Bolkhu Jinong, at the age of twenty-nine, three years elapsing from the Wu Rat year [1468], in the Geng Tiger year [1470] at the age of thirty-one, was slain and killed by these five of the Yüngsiyebü: Keriye, Chagan, Temür, Möngke, and Qara Badai.

When his son Batu Möngke was four, Isman Taishi married [Batu Möngke's] mother, Queen Sikir, and she gave birth to two sons named Babudai and Burkhai. While this was taking place, Bagai of the Balgachin was poorly rearing Batu Möngke; thus Temür Khadag of the Tanglagar forcibly took him away and cared for him. Because he had been separated from his own parents since he was small, [Batu Möngke] had gotten stomach ailments, and Saikhai, the wife of Temür Khadag, rubbed [his stomach] with a silver bowl until the bottom of it was worn thin, and thereby cured him.

Thereupon Prince Ünebalad of the Khorchin said, "I would like to marry Queen Mandukhai Sechen." But Queen Mandukhai Sechen said:

"If the descendants of the Lord [Chinggis Khan] had been completely cut-off,
Then it would be all right [to marry you], since the prince is a descendant of the Lord.
But I have heard it said that the child Batu Möngke, a great-grandson of the Lord,
Is here in the hands of Temür Khadag.

Therefore, I shall not go [to Prince Ünebalad] prior to abandoning all hope [of marrying Batu Möngke]."

Sanggai Örlüg[8] of the Alagchud thoroughly approved and did not give her [to Prince Ünebalad], and thus she waited. Then Queen Mandukhai Sechen asked of Sadai the Khorlad:

"Previously, Prince Ünebalad of the Khorchin brought up the subject [of marriage].
Now this child has shown up.
Of these two, to whom should I go?"

Sadai replied:

"Instead of waiting for this small child,
If you go to Ünebalad, it will be good for us all." [62r]

When she asked the same of Lady Jigan, wife of Sanggai Örlüg, she said:

"If you go to Qasar's descendant [i.e., Prince Ünebalad],
You will pursue a dark path;
Parting from all your own people
You will lose your queenly status.

But if you protect the khan's descendant [Batu Möngke],
Royal Heaven will protect you,
And you will rule your own people,
And your queenly name will be renowned."

Queen Mandukhai Sechen agreed with Lady Jigan and got angry at Sadai, saying:

"You have been telling me,
'The khan's descendant is too small';
'Qasar's descendant is too old';
'My queenly person is like that of a widow';
What are you saying?!" and poured hot tea on Sadai's head.

Straightaway in that same Geng Tiger year [1470] they came leading the seven-year-old Batu Möngke by the hand, and the prince of the household, one named Menggen Iragu, strewed the libations, and Queen Mother Mandukhai said:

"I have performed the daughter-in-law ceremonies in a place where
black and white cannot be distinguished.
When Ünebalad, descendant of Qasar, claimed to be a descendant of
the Khan
Of the Borjigin lineage, saying, 'Let me take her!,'"
I went to the queen mother's palace.[9]

I have performed the daughter-in-law ceremonies at a distance where a dappled horse can be recognized,
And when the uncle, a descendant of Qasar, importuned me,
Saying that the great-grandson [of the late khan] is still a child
I came here at the risk of my fearful life.

Saying, 'Your great, tightly made door is light,
Your great, excellent doorsill is too low, and
The collateral of Prince Ünebalad is great, then
May Eshi, the queen mother, consider me her slave daughter-in-law.'

Holding to my statement that has been proclaimed with
True heart to the Lord and mother,
If I become the wife awaiting and guarding your little descendant Batu Möngke,
If you agree, it becomes my fate according to my wish,
To bear seven boys in the inner flap of my robe and a sole girl in my outer flap.
I shall name the boys the Seven Bolad, and I shall ignite the fire of your [Borjigin] hearth!"

[62v] After she said this and left, Prince Ünebalad weepingly gave his full approval, and withdrawing his spoken statement, gave up.

At that time the honorable elder sister-in-law, Queen Mandukhai Sechen, born in the Wu Horse year [1438], at the age of thirty-three became the wife of Batu Möngke, born in the Jia Monkey year [1464], age seven. In the same Geng Tiger year [1470], in front of Queen Eshi, they said, "Let him rule all the people!" and seating him on the throne they named him Dayan Khan.[10]

Intelligent Queen Mandukhai Sechen put up her hair, which she had previously let hang,[11] and rode off in the lead—conveying in a palanquin Dayan Khan, lord of the people—campaigning against the Four Oirat; upon Tas Bur she attacked and took great spoils and booty.

Then from Queen Mandukhai Sechen were born Törö Bolad[12] and Ulus Bolad,[13] the two twins; later the two twins Princess Töröltü and Barsu Bolad;[14] later, Arsu Bolad[15] by himself, and then Alchu Bolad[16] and Vajra Bolad.[17]

When the Four Oirat attacked, and while they were fleeing the assault, Queen Mandukhai Sechen fell from her horse. The four—Grand Guardian Eselei of the Qonggirad, Jiqui Darkhan[18] of the Kharchin, Bayan Böke of the Balgachin, and Batu Bolad of the Asud—protected her, and had her mount the horse Good Chestnut of the Bayuud's Saikhan and saved her.

Straightaway the two children, the twins [Törö Bolad and Ulus Bolad], were healthily [born], and later on she delivered Arsu Bolad singly, and [the Mongols] said to one another:

"In accord with the routine command of Queen Eshi,
It has come to pass in accord with Mother Mandukhai's sincere wish,"

and set up a feast of great rejoicing.

Then from Queen Sümir—daughter of Junior Preceptor[19] Khutug of the Jalayir—were born Gere Bolad Taiji[20] and Geresenje Taiji;[21] and from Queen Güsei—daughter of Chief Menggelei, son of Alag Chingsang of the Baargun clan of the Oirat Baatud [63r]—were born Ubasanja Ching Taiji[22] and Geretü Taiji.[23] With these two being included, eleven princes branched out [from Dayan Khan].

Thereupon, hearing that Isman Taishi of the Yüngsiyebü was behaving erratically, they dispatched an army headed by Junior Preceptor Togochi of the Khorlas, who killed Isman Taishi. And when they told Queen Sikir to get a horse and ride, she lamented and bemoaned Isman Taishi and would not ride. Junior Preceptor Togochi became really angry and said:

"Was the good jinong, whom you married, bad?
Is your descendant Dayan Khan bad?
Are your people, the Chakhar Tümen, bad?
Was Isman Taishi, on whom we have taken revenge, good?"

Since he was grasping his sword, Queen Sikir was scared and mounted her horse, and then everyone made fun of her. Then Khulatai Uyagan [the daughter] of Isman Taishi married Junior Preceptor Togochi. He brought Queen Sikir and had her meet Dayan Khan.

Meanwhile, from the Right Tümen, three nobles—Bayichugur Darkhan of the Ordos Kharqatan, Jirgugatai Mergen of the Yüngsiyebü Buriat, and Chief Togolan of the Tümed Mau-Minggan—came with thirty allies [to beseech the khan to appoint one of his sons as jinong]:

"Our lord who is destined, sitting on your throne,
Humiliating your enemies of the hither and yon;
Issuing from Queen Mandukhai Sechen, whom you married,
There was born the Seven Bolad in accord with her prayers.

Lighting extremely fragrant incense, and
A shining great lamp in the Eight White Tents of the Holy Lord,
We have come to invite one of your descendants to become jinong,
Who is accordingly empowered to levy tribute on the six great
peoples."[24]

Headed by the khan and queen, everyone agreed to make Ulus Bolad the jinong of the Western Three Tümen, and they dispatched him accompanied by Babagai Örlüg of the Khoorlad.

When he arrived they made him jinong in front of the Lord, [63v] and when he said, "Let me worship the Lord tomorrow," Ibarai Taishi[25] of the Yüngsiyebü and Chief Mandalai[26] of the Ordos took counsel together, saying, "What need do we have of a prince to rule us? Surely we can proceed to rule ourselves? Let us kill that princeling now."[27]

Inciting a man named Sibuuchinu Boljomur, they conspired with him, saying, "Tomorrow when we all assemble to worship the Lord, you, saying 'It is mine!,' start a fight about the princeling's horse; and then when the quarrel has begun, we'll attack!"

The next day they set out and approached, and Boljomur's first words were, "That horse is mine!," and he grabbed the princeling's horse by the bridle. The princeling said, "Let go, let's discuss this later!" But he didn't let go, and the princeling grew angry and slashed his head with the sword at his waist. Whereupon Ibarai and Mandulai got very angry and said:

"No sooner does he come here than he acts like this.
Henceforth he will ruin us.

Let us kill this princeling,
Let us make war on the spot!"

Then Baichugur Darkhan of the Ordos Kharqatan said:

"After him being approved by all and sent here,
How can the common folk function without a lord?
After having said, 'Send us a descendant of the khan,'
If they then do evil to their own sovereign khan,
Will the heavenly Lord [Chinggis Khan] approve?"

Though he said this and warned them, they did not agree, and Ibarai and Mandulai came in full armor at the fore [of a large group], and Kürisün Baatur of the Qonggirad got off his horse Good Gray and said [to the jinong], "The people's mood has changed, leave!"

But since they were somewhat disordered, [Ulus Bolad fled and] sought refuge in the [Eight] White Tents, and as they were fighting, Tümed Bayanmalad of the Ordos shot Ibarai through the breast, and the princeling [Ulus Bolad] also fought [64r] and shot a man through the neck, killing him.

* * *

Then the paternal aunt, elder sister Princess Esige, took care of Barsu Bolad Sain Alag while living in the home of Cegüdün Khoosai of the Monggoljin. When his elder brother [Ulus Bolad] was ruling as jinong, Barsu Bolad said, "Let me pray to the Lord!" To which the Son-in-Law Cegüdün Khoosai said, "These are uncertain days to be showing loyalty. Mount this child upon the horse Good Chestnut, and you, Temür of the Ordos, go at his side," and sent them off.

Yet as things grew worse, Sain Alag with the horse Good Chestnut and Temür, these two fled. Then Princess Esige and Son-in-Law Khoosai spoke angrily:

"We are unable to raise this child;
Let us deliver him to his father!"

In inquiring for a good-hearted man to deliver him, a group of seven men—Temür of the Ordos Köbegüd, Bagsuuli Khorchi of the Üüshin,

Choi Türgen of the Dalad, Toimag of the Urad, Enggür of the Bukhas, Akhatai of the Singqor, and Biligtü of the Mongoljin—said, "Let us deliver him!"

The wife of [Barsu Bolad] Sain Alag, Queen Bodun, accompanied by one woman, brought [their child] Gün Bilig, a three-year-old, and left him with Sinikei Orlüg of the Monggoljin and Lady Ebegei, and then went to his father the khan.

Thereupon their provisions ran out, and while they were going picking and eating wild garlic and onions Temür killed a donkey, and thus with these provisions they were able to make it. [As a result] Dayan Khan bestowed on Temür the title of taishi. As for the seven heroes, they were all made Great Darkhan,[28] and then [Dayan Khan] straightaway went on campaign against the Western Tümen.[29]

Going via the Defile of the Burial Ground, they descended along the edge of the Swift River, where Nüürekei Baatur of the Dalad was driving his numerous oxen. When he went and blew on his horn-trumpet, [64v] immediately the Three Eastern Tümen thought the hooves of the cattle to be the noise of armored forces and said, "An army with banners and trumpets has come!" When they fled in confusion, Dayan Khan's horse named Horned Bay, in the course of leaping a river, fell, and the top of the khan's iron helmet sank into the mud and couldn't be retrieved.

Whereupon Togan of the Besüd cried, "The light bay stallion has got stuck in the mud!" And two of the Ja'ud, Sayin Chegice and Chagan, returned and dismounted, and the two of them got Dayan Khan mounted and then left. When night fell and they had not found the entrance of the pass, they went over the pass via the low parts of the mountain, and since numerous saddles had fallen off and were left behind [when the Three Eastern Tümen fled], they named it "Packsaddle Pass."

Then Nüürekei Baatur sang as follows:

"Although the Eastern Tümen came deliriously in this direction,
The Heavenly Lord examined their good and evil intent;
The Swift River approved [the Lord's wish] and deigned to make them fall;
The Great Golden Lineage sent them in disorder in every direction."

* * *

Then after Dayan Khan had returned and made camp, Ibarai and Mandulai came leading the Three [Western] Tümen on campaign; however, Son-in-Law Khoosai had secretly sent two men from his army to relay a message to Dayan Khan, whereby he could overtake and attack the two clans, Kisigten and Kemjigüd, at Swine Dust, where they had moved after all the confusion.

The two men sent by Khoosai reported as follows to the khan: "While your forces were returning here, our Nüürekei Baatur sang this and that." The khan became furious and declared: "I pray to the Heavenly Lord:

'Thinking evil, [65r] Ibarai and Mandulai have suddenly gone to war;
Prince Ulus Bolad was killed devoid of fault;
Nüürekei Baatur, making mockery, made his boast;
Let my father, the Heavenly Lord, judge as witness!' "

Pleading thus to the Heavenly Lord he strewed the libations, and gathering the Three Eastern Tümen and the Abaga and Khorchin, he rode off. Thereupon, when the Three Western Tümen heard that the khan was on campaign they rode out to meet him at Seventy Peaks,[30] where Dayan Khan proclaimed:

"You of Ordos were a great destined people,
Who have guarded the Lord's Eight White Tents;
And likewise, you Uriyangqan[31] also were a great destined people,
Who protected the Lord's imperial treasury.
With the aid of the Khorchin and Abaga,
And with the twelve clans of the Khalkha, we face the Twelve Tümed;[32]
And with the eight clans of Chakhar, we face the very great Yüngsiyebü!"

and went into battle.

When these five led the battle—Burkhai Baatur Taiji, son of Prince Urtu Guqai of the Khorchin; Baatur Bayakhai of the Uriyangqan; Sayin Chegiche of the Jayud; Son-in-Law Baasun of the Five-Clan Khalkha; and Baatur Öröm of the Kisigten—the Khalka pushed the Tümed, and the Chakhar pushed the Yüngsiyebü to flight.

Then when these seven united together—Baichugur Darkhan of the Ordos Khorqatan; Darma Darkhan of the Khoid; Uda'achi Köndelen of the Khali'uchin; Chief Alchulai of the Tümed Khanglin; Baatur Kürisün of the Qonggirad; Sogtagu Burqanggu of the Yüngsiyebü Buriat; Major Mangguldai of the Kharchin—came entering the fray, they pushed and penetrated through the midst of the Uriyangqan. As they went slashing, Barsu Bolad Sain Alag took and led forty heroes in attack and penetrated into the midst of the Tümed, and from behind the Ordos [troops] [65v] they came slashing in a group of thirty. Whereupon the Ordos standard bearer Mönggekü recognized [Barsu Bolad] Sain Alag, saying

"The black standard of the Lord Khan
Has come to the sovereign descendant!"

And seizing the standard, he attacked.

Whereupon Sain Alag let the standard be taken, but he remained in the same place, and thus the Ordos troops were misled by the silhouette of the standard and the majority of them who were pursuing the Uriyangqan died. Whereupon some of the Western Three surrendered and others fled. Dayan Khan pursued them as far as Blue Lake and taking them prisoner, made the entirety of the Three [Western] Tümen submit. And because Chief Mandulai of the Ordos was killed on the Achina Steppe, they thenceforth called it the Steppe of the Chief.

Ibarai Taishi of the Yüngsiyebü was confused, traveling around by himself, and when he went into the White Turbans' city of Hami,[33] he was killed by someone. Thereupon Dayan Khan fully subdued the Three Western Tümen, and by putting in order the great people as the Six Tümen, from in front of the Lord's Eight White Tents he proclaimed and assumed the title khan.

Thereupon he said: "Let Bodi, son of Törö Bolad, the first of my eleven sons, guard my royal throne. My meritorious Barsu Bolad, because he seized for me the state of the Western Three [Tümen], let him be jinong over the Western Three!" He thereby made [Barsu Bolad] Sain Alag the jinong over the Three Western Tümen.

Further, to the four men who brought Bolkhu Jinong; the four men who assisted Queen Mandukhai; the seven men who served Sain Alag; Temür Khatag of the Tanglagar, who had spirited Dayan Khan away and cared for him; Bayichugur Darkhan of the Kharqatan who had warned him in the slaying of Abakhai; and Kürisün Baatur of the Qonggirad, [66r] who had dismounted and given his own Good Chestnut horse to Abakhai; the princes who had let him take refuge at the Lord's [tent] and had given a sword to Abakhai, the Urtagud Taishi; Bayanmalad Darkhan of the Tümed who shot through the chest of Ibarai; the five men of the Eastern Tümen who had led the attack in the Battle of Seventy Peaks, and others; and to all those who had lent their strength in any way, one after the other, scarlet diplomas, golden seals, and important titles [Dayan Khan] gave. To Son-in-Law Bayasun Darkhan of the Jaruud he gave Princess Töröltü, the sole daughter of Queen Mandukhai Sechen.

Thereupon, when Gegen Chingsang of the Uriyangqan and Tugtai Qara Khulad led the Uriyangqan revolt, Dayan Khan set out against them with the Chakhar and the Khalkha. He also sent a message to his son, Barsu Bolad Jinong, who set out leading the Three Western Tümen and joined [his father's forces] to meet the Uriyangqan for battle upon Jorgalun Jon.[34]

Four men led the forces—from the Eastern Tümen: Bargasun Darkhan of the Khalkha Jaruud and Engkebei Köndelen Khasqa, son of Sain Chegice of the Chakhar Juud; and from the Western Tümen: Bajichugur Darkhan of the Ordos Kharqatan and Chief Alchulai of the Tümed Khanglin—and in meeting the enemy they put the majority of the Uriyangqan to the sword and subjected the rest, thereby integrating them into the other Five Tümen, whereby they made them renounce the name of Tümen.[35]

* * *

Thereby Dayan Khan pacified the people of the Six Tümen and reconciled the great Mongol people, bringing about tranquility and happiness. He ruled as khan for seventy-four years, and at the age of eighty, in the Gui Rabbit year [1543], he became a god.[36]

CHAPTER EIGHT

History of the Six Tümen

In this chapter Sagang Sechen captures the tension around the two significant issues shaping Mongol society in the late sixteenth and early seventeenth centuries: Chinggisid legitimacy and decentralization. In order to highlight the importance of the Chinggisid legacy, it begins with the history of the rulers of the Chakhar Tümen—Dayan Khan's descendants in primogeniture—who were the recognized rulers of all the Mongols. During the reign of Ligdan Khan (d. 1634), however, a Buddhist prophecy comes to fruition and Mongol rule collapses. While this Buddhist story lays the groundwork for the Mongol-Manchu alliances that were soon to develop, it also elides the underlying dynamics of decentralization and civil war that defined Mongol history during this period. In accord with the centrifugal tendencies of the *ulus-törö* model, these new social groupings—such as the Asud, Auqan, Bajar, Khalkha, Kharchin, Khorchin, Naiman, Seven Tümed, and Üüshin, all of which were ruled by various descendants of Dayan Khan—began to assert their independence. These groups not only began to fight each other as the economy collapsed along with the Ming dynasty but also initially allied with the Manchus to secure protection from the depredations of other Mongols. This process animates much of Sagang Sechen's subsequent history. Who were Dayan Khan's descendants that ruled these new communities, and what happened to them during this time of upheaval and fragmentation?

Dayan Khan's sons were Törö Bolad and Ulus Bolad, born in the Ren Tiger year [1482], [the daughter] Princess Töröltü and Barsubolad, [66v] born in the Jia Dragon year [1484]; Arsu Bolad, born in the Ding Sheep year [1487]; Alchu Bolad and Vajra Bolad, born in the Geng Dog year [1490]; and from his Jalayir queen, Gere Bolad and Geresenje Taiji, born in the Ren Tiger year [1482]; Ubasanja Ching Taiji and Geretü Taiji were born from his Oirat Queen Güsei in the Yi Pig year [1491].

Törö Bolad died at the age of forty-two in the Ji Sheep year while his father the khan was still alive, and his son Bodi Taiji,[1] born in the Jia Rat year [1504], ascended the throne in the Jia Dragon year [1544] at the age of forty-one.

Molojai Baatur of the Khorchin said, "To whom are the Three Western [Tümen] any good? Either attack and scatter them, or organize them somehow and apportion them among the Three Eastern [Tümen]."

Bodi Alag Khan agreed, and when they said together, "Let us proceed with a campaign against the Three Western [Tümen]," the Queen Mother Empress[2] Chagajang said: "You are all saying to one another, 'Let us attack and apportion the Three Western Tümen.' Formerly, Prince Urtakhai of the Khorchin, when fighting at the great Battle of Seventy Peaks, said, 'If we let the Western Three stay together, future generations of ours will surely be made to suffer. If we unite the two main peoples, the Chakhar[3] and the Bajar, and link the very great Yüngsiyebü with the twenty thousand Khorchin, and make the Twelve Tümed[4] united with the twelve clans of Khalkha,[5] there will be lasting peace!' Your great-grandfather [Dayan Khan] proclaimed:

'Having sought and found the enemy who killed my blood relatives,
I have seen the punishment of Ibarai and Mandulai.
If I destroy these Six Tümen,
Leftover from the Forty Tümen Mongols of old,
What good will it do me, even if I am khan and lord of all?' [67r]

"By saying so he clearly disapproved [of destroying the Three Western Tümen]. Now, on account of you being born to be more than your great-grandfather, are you going to break this command? Are you too saying, 'Let us destroy the Western Three'? How can one destroy the great dear people—[the Six Tümen]—that your great-grandfather founded, and the jadelike great state that has grown peaceful?

"Furthermore, the middle son of Gün Bilig Mergen Jinong,[6] who is the eldest son of [Barsu Bolad] Sain Alag—namely, Bayangguli Durar Daiching—if he sees an enemy, he cannot restrain himself. They even say he is a great warrior who attacks first unrestrainedly, constantly fighting and making the foe gird up in armor.

"They also say the son of [Barsu Bolad's] middle son Altan,[7] named Sengge Düüreng Temür,[8] can jump over a two-year-old camel in full armor. And another son of Mergen Jinong, the son of Nom Tarni Guua Taiji, called Khutugtai Sechen Taiji,[9] they say he is good at knowing how to deal with what has not yet come, and in running down that which has already passed by.

"Another boy, called Belgei Taibung Taiji, the son of Bayangguli Durar Daiching, when he draws a bow, his two scapula strike together with such force that he has to put a padded box between them. Moreover, they say he can calculate where the joint of a running fox's tail is and shoot it off. It is also said that his younger brother, Bursai Qatan Baatur, can shoot an arrow through three shovel blades.

"If you somehow succeed in destroying them, it will be fine indeed. But if you cannot, will not you yourself, and both two peoples [the East and West Tümens], in turn be diminished?" These were her admonitory words.

Her son, Bodi Alag Khan, agreed with his mother and abandoned the action he had envisaged. Thus, he ruled for four years and made the vast great people tranquil, [67v] and at the age of forty-four in the Ding Sheep year [1547], he passed away.

* * *

His sons were Daraisun Taiji, Kögchüdei Taiji, and Onggon Durar. The elder brother, Daraisun Küdeng Taiji,[10] born in the Jia Dragon year [1520], assumed the title of khan in front of the White Tents at the age of twenty-nine in the Wu Ape year [1548], uniting the Three Western Tümen and bringing them into the peaceful state [of the Six Tümen].

While returning [from Ordos], he encountered Altan, the second son of Barsu Bolad Sain Alag, who said, "Having taken the title of khan, lord of the throne, you have pacified the state. Now, there is a lesser royal title, called Prince Siteü,[11] 'defender of the khan's realm.' Grant this title to me, and I will defend your great state!" The khan agreed and gave to Altan the title Prince Siteü, and then returned.[12]

Calling himself Küdeng Khan, Daraisun was famed to all as one who unified the jadelike great state. While pacifying the universal great people, he was supported by the great wind of destiny, and after ten years of rule, at the age of thirty-eight in the Ding Snake year [1557], he died.

* * *

He had four sons: Tümen Taiji, Jongdu Taiji, Darni Baga Darkhan, and Daiching Taiji. Tümen Taiji,[13] born in the Ji Pig year [1539], became khan at the age of twenty in the Wu Horse year [1558]. In his thirty-eighth year, the Bing Mouse year [1576], meeting with the sword-bearing Karma Lama,[14] he entered the religion.

Having the Six Tümen gathered, he prescribed the Great Law. And with help from the Six Tümen—especially Namudai Khung Taiji of the Chakhar and Üljeng Subuqai of the Khalkha; and from the Western Tümen, Khutugtai Sechen Khung Taiji of the Ordos, Prince Nom Dara Khaulachi of the Asud, and Chürüke Khung Taiji of the Tümed—he upheld the law and became famous in all directions as Jasagtu Khan (i.e., "Khan with the Law"). He established peace and tranquility for the state of the vast great people. [68r] He drew tribute from those of the three languages—Jürchid,[15] Neli'üd,[16] and Daur[17]—and made people and all other sentient beings content with great happiness. He ruled for thirty-five years, and at the age of fifty-four in the Ren Dragon year [1592], he passed away.

His son, Buyan Taiji, was one of eleven brothers. Buyan Taiji, the eldest, born in the Yi Rabbit year [1555], became khan in the Gui Snake year [1593] at the age of thirty-nine, and became famous in all directions as Sechen Khan. He brought peace to the universal great people through religion and the state, and at the age of forty-nine in the Gui Rabbit year [1603], he died.

* * *

He had three sons: Manggus Taiji, Rabkar Taiji, and Bad Chinese Taiji. The eldest, Manggus, died while his father was still alive. His sons were Ligdan Baatur Taiji and Sanggarchi Odkhan Taiji. The elder, Ligdan Baatur Taiji,[18] was born in the Ren Dragon year [1592] and became khan in the Jia Dragon year [1604]. He was called Khutugtu Khan and became famous in all directions.

Having accepted initiations into the profound and secret vehicle from Dharma Lord Maitreya Chöjé Joni and from others, Ligdan defended the religion. At the age of twenty-six in the Ding Snake year [1617], he met with Sakya Dagtsen Sharba Khutugtu and again took initiations into the profound secret vehicle.[19] He erected a grand palace called the Vajra White City and within it established numerous monasteries and shrines, headed by one devoted to Jowo Sakyamuni. All of these were quickly completed in one summer.[20] He then filled them with objects of veneration. While he was evenly establishing the Two Realms in accord with the past, however, the time of the five hundred evils came to pass and many violent deeds were done against the state by everyone who lived in the Six Tümen: the descendants of Dayan Khan, the royal princes, and the commoners. [68v] As a result, he was unable to subject them to his authority through the great peaceful state.

It was like the ancient parable:

If a khan becomes angry, he destroys his state;
If an elephant becomes angry, he destroys his cage.

Because delusion arose in the khan's scintillating mind, the Six Great Tümen were taken over by the Great Qing state. After having been khan for thirty-one years, at the age of forty-three in the Jia Dog year [1634], Ligdan came up against and was destroyed by destiny.

So it was with the descendants of Törö Bolad, the first son of Dayan Khan.

* * *

The second son of Dayan Khan, Ulus Bolad, had no descendants. As a result, Barsu Bolad Sain Alag ruled over the Three Western Tümen, and Arsu Bolad Mergen Mong Taiji ruled over the Seven Tümed; Alchu Bolad ruled over the five clans of the central Khalkha; Gere Bolad ruled over the seven clans of the northern Khalkha; Vajra Bolad ruled over the eight-clan Kisigten of the Chakhar; Geresenje over the Auqan and Naiman of the Chakhar; Ars Bolad over the Kha'uchid of the Chakhar; and Ubasanja over the Asud and the Yüngsiyebü. Geretü Taiji was likewise without descendants.

This Barsu Bolad Sain Alag had seven sons: Gün Bilig Mergen Jinong, Altan Khan, Labug Taiji, Bayaskhal Köndelen Khan,[21] Bayandara Narin Taiji, Bodidara Odkhan Taiji, and Tarakhai Taiji.

The eldest, Gün Bilig Mergen Jinong, born in the Bing Tiger year [1506], ruled over the Ordos Tümen. Altan Khan, born in the Ding Rabbit year [1507], ruled over the Twelve Tümed; Labug Taiji, born in the Ji Rabbit year [1509], ruled over the Üüshin of the Tümed; Bayaskhal, born in the Geng Horse year [1510], ruled over the seven-clan Kharchin of the Yüngsiyebü; Bayandara, born in the Ren Monkey year [1512], ruled over the White Tatars of the Chakhar; and Bodidara, born in the Jia Dog year [1514], [69r] when he was small used to go around singing playfully:

"I hope Aju and Sira kill one another!
I hope I rule over the Asud and Yüngsiyebü!"

Thereupon, when the brothers Aju and Sira did kill each other, the son of Ubasanja Ching Taiji said, "Aju has slain his younger brother, and since Sira does not have any descendants, people said, 'It was a gift of his big mouth,'" and they made Bodidara rule over the Asud and Yüngsiyebü. Tarakhai had died when he was small.

Then the aforementioned Barsu Bolad Sain Alag, the father, became jinong at the age of twenty-nine in the Ren Monkey year [1512], ruled for twenty years, and at the age of forty-eight in the Xin Rabbit year [1531] died. Afterward, his eldest son, Gün Bilig Mergen, at the age of twenty-seven in the Ren Dragon year [1532], became jinong.[22]

He and his younger brother, Altan Khan, took the Three Western Tümen and campaigned against China.[23] When they met the Chinese forces at the narrow passage called Yendege[24] they started fighting, and two individuals—Mergen Jinong's son Buyangguli Durar Daiching and Altan Khan's son Sengge Düüreng Temür—three times attacked the Chinese encampment from this way and that. After fighting the great battle of Yendege they returned and settled down.

* * *

This Gün Bilig Mergen Jinong, from his chief queen named Marvelous—daughter of Ayilan Seger of the Tümed Khanglin—had two sons: Noyandara Jinong and Bayisanggur Lang Taiji. From his second queen, a female relative named Esige—the daughter of Gentleman[25] Esen of the Khalkha

Jalayir—he had one son: Prince Oyidarma Nomoqan. From his Queen Altanchu Sayin—daughter of Son-in-Law Khosai of the Che'üd of the Tümed Mongoljin—he had four sons: Nom Darni Guua Taiji, Buyangguli Durar Daiching, Prince Vajra Üiyeng, [69v] and Padmasambhava Sechen Baatur. From his queen named Amurja—daughter of Ibarai Taishi of the Yüngsiyebü—he had two sons: Prince Namudara Darkhan and Prince Onglaqan Yeldeng. They were called the Nine Princes.

When nineteen years of rule by Gün Bilig Mergen Jinong had elapsed, at the age of forty-five in the Geng Dog year [1550], he passed away.[26]

* * *

His son Noyandara,[27] born in the Ren Horse year [1522], became jinong in the Ren Pig year [1551] at the age of thirty. Then the Nine Princes divided their inheritance: Noyandara Jinong ruled over the Four Khoriya; Bayisanggur, born in the Gui Sheep year [1523], ruled over the Kegüd Sibuuchin of the Right Wing, and the Urad and Tanggud; Oyidarma, born in the Gui Sheep year [1523]. ruled over the Dalad Khanglin Merged and the Ba'anas; Nom Darni, born in the Jia Monkey year [1524], ruled over the Besüd Üüshin of the Right Wing; Buyangguli, born in the Bing Dog year [1526], ruled over the Betegin Khali'uchin of the Right Wing; Vajra Üijeng, born in the Wu Mouse year [1528], ruled over the Khauchid Keriye of the Left Wing; Padmasambhava, born in the Geng Tiger year [1530], ruled over these four, the Cha'ad, Minggad, Khonichin, and Khoyaguchin; Namudara, born in the Xin Rabbit year [1531], ruled over four clans of the Uygurchin of the Right Wing; Onglaqan, born in the Gui Snake year [1533], ruled over the three clans of the Amagaitan of the Right Wing.

* * *

The sons of the first of these, Noyandara Jinong, were Buyan Baatur Khung Taiji, Prince Nomtu Düüreng, Prince Ombo Dalai, and Prince Vibasi Odkhan, and from his Queen Sain was born Duke Manggusa.

The five sons of Bayisanggur were Prince Ayidabis Dayan, Prince Oba Jorigtu, Prince Da'achi Jaisang, and Prince Köndelen.

The six sons of Oyidarma were Marquis Degei Khung Taiji, Prince Khainug Baatur, Akiya Köndelen Daiching, Chürüke Ching Baatur, Tochi Sechen Köngkör, and Küsel Üijeng Jorigtu [70r].

The four sons of Nom Tarni Guua Taiji, from his Queen Tegüs Sechen, were Khutugtai Sechen Khung Taiji, Buyandara Qulachi Baatur,

Saindara Ching Baatur, and from his Queen Delger, Namudai Mergen Taiji.

From Tosun Jula, queen of Buyangguli, were born the two: Prince Belgei Taibung and Bursai Sechen Daiching.

From Vajra's Queen Jula were born the three: Dorjé Darkhan Daiching, Prince Jongtulai Üiyeng, and Prince Marquis Engke.

Since Padmasambhava's Queen Altan Jula had no offspring, they said to one another:

"How can we divide up Padma's people
And thus make unpaired those born as twins [Padma and Vajra]
From their mother, the good queen?
Let us seat Dorjé, son of Vajra, over those four clans."

The three elder brothers were in full accord, and they seated [Dorjé] Darkhan Daiching over the four clans.

Namudara's three sons were Tümei Darkhan Daiching, Prince Minggai Eyechi, and Vibasi Taiji. Onglaqan's three sons were Prince Kichigi Yeldeng, Prince Buyibari, and Khutugtai Taiji.

Thereupon Altan Khan, in the Ren Rat year [1552] at the age of forty-seven, set out against the Four Oirat, and upon Könggei Jabqan slew Mani Minggatu, prince of the Eight Thousand Khoid. His wife, Lady Jigeken; his two sons, Tokhoi and Bökegtütei; and all the people were taken into submission.[28]

When he had thus brought to knee the Four Oirat, who had taken Qonin,[29] after this he campaigned for nineteen years against the Chinese, who had retaken the city, and he destroyed and harassed the lands and people of China. The Chinese people were very scared and dispatched envoys saying:

"To secure the peace we will grant to Altan Khan
The title of *shunyi wang*,[30] and a golden seal."[31]

Altan Khan, at the age of sixty-five in the Xin Sheep year [1571], established a great state[32] with the Lünching emperor of China's Great Ming,[33] [70v] and they opened immeasurably great trade fairs [on the border].[34]

At the age of sixty-seven in the Gui Rooster year [1573], [Altan Khan] campaigned against the Black Tibetans, subjugated the upper and lower divisions of the Yellow Uyghurs,[35] and took into custody the three princes of Lower Adag Kham—Arig Sanggyégab, Dé Lumbum, and Narthang Tseringgab—and their subjects. He also brought back many Tibetans, headed by Asing Lama[36] and Teacher Gumi Soga.

Thereupon Asing Lama preached many times to the khan about the revolving three bad births; the suffering of samsara; the good benefit of being saved and of going to Akanistha [Heaven]; and the difference between grasping and letting go; whereupon in the khan's mind the beginnings of the Dharma was born, and he began to recite the six-syllable dharani.

CHAPTER NINE

History of Khutugtai Sechen Khung Taiji

The fragmentation of the Mongols into smaller social groupings led by descendants of Dayan Khan and their tendency to fight one another was a defining feature of Inner Asian history during the late sixteenth and early seventeenth centuries. This was also why genealogy became such an important facet of Mongolian historical writing at the time: the very legitimacy of these groups depended on them being led by a recognized descendant of Dayan Khan. It was the same when the groups eventually allied themselves with the Manchus: only their genealogy made it possible for the Manchu court to recognize them as legitimate members of the ruling Mongol nobility, with all that entailed. Thus, in one respect, this chapter is another genealogical history. It makes clear that Khutugtai Sechen Khung Taiji and his descendants should be recognized by the Manchu court. At the same time, however, it captures the breakdown and continuous warfare that defined Mongol society in this period. By concluding with a statement of Khutugtai Sechen Khung Taiji warning about the dangers of deviating from traditional Mongol unity, Sagang Sechen sets the stage not only for the next chapter about Altan Khan's revival of Buddhist rule but also for the eventual reunification of the Mongols under the righteous rule of the Buddhist Qing.

It was at this same time that Khutugtai Sechen Khung Taiji, born in the Geng Rat year [1540], at the age of twenty-three in the Ren Dog year [1562] campaigned against the Four Oirat. Upon the Irtysh River he attacked the Torghud,[1] and on killing Qara Buura, [Khutugtai Sechen Khung Taiji] implanted the black standard on his hearth. After incorporating the Silbis and Torghud, he returned.

* * *

Thereupon at the age of twenty-seven in the Bing Tiger year [1566], he campaigned toward Tibet, and when camped at the confluence of the Three Rivers of Silimji[2] he dispatched envoys, first to Great Bursa Lama, Chengse Lama, and Darkhan Lama, then to Gentleman Usungdar, Gentleman Altan, and others, saying: "If you submit to us, we will adopt your religion; if you do not submit, we will attack you!"

The Tibetans were very afraid, and after they had talked among themselves for three days, [Khutugtai Sechen Khung Taiji's] younger brother said:

> "What are we waiting for?
> Let us attack now!"

Then Sechen Khung Taiji, the elder brother, said, "Tomorrow, when the sun rises, three lamas will come. [71r] The one lama who will be sitting in the middle, he is going to have a good conversation with me. Therefore, let us wait for them a little longer."

The next morning the three lamas came, and the middle one was called Darkhan Lama, and while he was talking together with Prince Sechen [Khung Taiji], he asked, "Among your kinsmen is there a wise *nakpa*[3] called Vajra Tümei?"

[Khutugtai Sechen Khung Taiji] replied, "There is no such person among us," promising, "Now, you return and gather your people and submit [to us], and we shall do you no harm."

When they returned, the next morning Nakpa Vajra Tümei was going out to his livestock, and a man riding a tiger, with eyebrows and beard blazing with fire, came pursuing him. When he entered his house, [the man riding the tiger] had disappeared.

When this episode was relayed to everyone, [Nakpa Vajra Tümei's] uncle, Darkhan Lama, said, "That prince [Khutugtai Sechen Khung Taiji] of yesterday was, it seems, no ordinary man. He has indeed revealed his remarkable emanation [in this tiger-riding guise]. Thus, how can one escape? Now it is necessary for us to go and submit."

When they arrived and met each other, the prince himself turned out to be that man who had been riding the tiger. At once, as soon as he met him, as if he had known him previously, [Khutugtai Sechen Khung Taiji] said, "Ah, Nakpa, how did you get away from me? Unless you become a white Garuda, I will capture you forthwith!"

His uncle, Darkhan Lama, said, "Did I not say so?"

Then [Khutugtai Sechen Khung Taiji] took and integrated Tibet of the Three Rivers [into the realm], and he brought three people—Lergen Lama, Asdug Saikhan Bandi, and Asdug Vajra Tümei Nakpa—back to Mongolia. He also presented a wife named Uqanchu Chindan to Vajra Tümei, and gave him the title *güi wang khonjin*[4] and made him the head of ministers. [71v]

Thereupon the two younger brothers, Buyandara Khulachi Baatur, born in the Ren Tiger year [1542], then thirty-one years of age, and Sain Dara Ching Baatur, born in the Yi Snake year [1545], and twenty-eight years of age, campaigned against the Tokmag in the Ren Monkey year [1572]. At the Yellow River they attacked Aqasar Khan,[5] taking and plundering his people and livestock and seizing the queen called Cheügei. Sain Dara Ching Baatur took her for himself.

As they were returning, however, Aqasar Khan caught up with them at Bare Qasulug and attacked with an army of ten thousand. Three men led the counterattack: Sain Dara Ching Baatur, who was then twenty-eight; Bursai Sechen Daiching, who was the eldest son of Khutugtai Sechen Khung Taiji, and born in the Bing Horse year [1546]; and Öljei Ildüchi, born in the Bing Dragon year [1556], then seventeen. The three attacked in unison against the right flank of Aqasar Khan's forces, but when Buyandara Khulachi Baatur was advancing into the middle, someone shot the horse he was riding. Then, as he was mounting another horse, his knee was shot through the kneecap and he fell down. As soldiers moved in and he was about to be ridden down, Sain Dara Ching Baatur dismounted in order to help his elder brother, and thus they perished together.

Seven comrades, headed by Sechen Daiching, Türbei Baatur of the Bukhas, and Togta'a Taishi of the Kharqatan, came out fighting. And since the horse he was riding had been killed, Öljei Ildüchi went into battle on foot in full armor, yet when Kilügen of the Abakhai recognized him, he had Öljei Ildüchi mount the horse he was leading. But since Öljei

Ildüchi leaped onto the horse from the wrong side, it fled and was killed. While he was again going on foot, the page Sain Sainug of the Kharqatan met him, and dismounting from the horse he was riding, gave it to Öljei Ildüchi. [72r] As he set off shouting, "Ride!" Sainug was left standing there and said, "Do I not have a son named Bayar? Take care of him for me! Do not come back for me!" He then entered the fray and was cut down. But on account of this horse, Öljei Ildüchi was able to fight the battle and then return.

* * *

Thereupon the elder brother, Khutugtai Sechen Khung Taiji, at the age of thirty-four in the Gui Rooster year [1573] set out on campaign with seven hundred troops selected from the four encampments of Queen Sain, and the five divisions called the Five Bellies. When they reached Qasulug Marsh they met Aqasar Khan of Tokmag with ten thousand troops. And then when they went into battle at Esil Dabu, Sechen Khung Taiji proclaimed, "Let no one go into this battle before me! I myself need to lead!"

Having donned his golden-red armor made of elephant hide and riding his red horse called Burgucha's Good Mountain Sarbai, he personally led the attack. As he did so, in the eyes of the yonder enemy forces, as he led the charge fire blazed forth from his eyebrows and beard. Moreover, they saw two battalions of soldiers coming from the side on black horses, whose hooves also shot out flames. And immediately as they charged and were about to win, Khutugtai Sechen Khung Taiji fought, creating a clearing, whereupon he recognized Sain Dara Ching Baatur's armor, which he took. He also took alive the three sultans, the sons of Aqasar Khan, and after speaking with them, released them and sent them back to rule. When he had thus well avenged his two younger brothers, he proceeded to return.

* * *

Later, in the Jia Dog year [1574], Buyan Baatur Khung Taiji, with his elder and younger brothers, went on campaign against the Four Oirat. Hearing that they were approaching, Khutugtai Sechen Khung Taiji established his camp at Tiger Lake and then set off toward the Four Oirat. [72v]

When Buyan Baatur Khung Taiji was completely subduing the Eight Thousand Khoid,[6] led by Eselbei Kiya, on the southern slope of Khargai

Mountain, Khutugtai Sechen Khung Taiji was overcoming the Baatud, headed by Khamsu and Düridkü, on the northern slope of Jalaman Mountain.[7]

His son, Öljei Ildüchi, having been pursued for three months and devoid of provisions, was going about eating a kind of stone called *bura tülege*. He subdued the Dörbed, led by Gentleman Bechire of the Chorgas, on the southern slope of Tubkhan Mountain. Then as they returned to pasture in their own place, Khutugtai Sechen Khung Taiji, from the Bulunggir River,[8] dispatched envoys headed by Minister Bekei Sechen[9] and Minister Tibet Khasqa, saying, "Eselbei Kiya's eyes are like the eyes of a condor. He is not a man who behaves appropriately. Let us divide up the Eight Thousand Khoid, and let us break up their power."

Buyan Baatur Khung Taiji disagreed with this statement and had those nobles sit outside. Meanwhile, Eselbei Kiya thought, *Khutugtai Sechen Khung Taiji has always greatly favored me*, and taking charge of the meat in the pot, presented the eight top ribs of a horse to those two nobles. Then after he had them return, Buyan Baatur Khung Taiji got very angry at Eselbei, and he had cut off for him the four top ribs with the nape and the entire trachea of a horse, and said to him:

"You finish this up!
Just like it has been said:
'He has inserted
A finger into the milk,
A lariat into the herd.'

"You have stuck your hands into my pot, taken the meat, and given my resolve to other people!"

As he was making Eselbei Kiya eat the horse meat, the Four Oirat were all talking about it. [73r] When Eselbei Kiya gave up on finishing all the meat he left, saying to himself, "I did not eat the eight ribs of that horse. If only I could eat the eight ribs of my father's horse Sutai Minggatu!" That same night he gathered his forces and went on campaign, and on the Kirchabag River he killed Buyan Baatur Khung Taiji, whereby Eselbei Kiya broke his allegiance and thus fled.

Then Noyandara became jinong in his twenty-third year, and he died in the Jia Dog year [1574] when he was fifty-three.[10]

* * *

The descendants of these nine rulers were born in sequence as follows:

(1) a) The three sons of Buyan Baatur Khung Tayiji were: Boshogtu Jinong, Öljeitü Bingtü Khung Tayiji, and Bandi Mergen Jorigtu.

b) The sons of Nomtu Düüreng were Bandi Düüreng and Manjusri.

c) Prince Ombo Dalai had no descendants.

d) Vibasi Odkhan Baatur with his two sons, Küdedei and Sereng, became the Ongli'ud.

e) The six sons of Duke Manggus were: Bunaban Khung Baatur, Budashiri Ildüchi, Bumba Taiji, Abanai Odqan Jorigtu, Bumbudai Daiching, Buyantai Taiji.

(2) a) The three sons of Prince Ayidabis Dayan were: Prince Achitu Dayan, Prince Echenggi Bingtü, Prince Machig Darkhan.

b) The five sons of Auba Jorigtu were: Prince Marquis Khaatan; Chogtu Taiji; Amu Sengge Taiji, Dorjé Daiching, Tuba Yeldeng.

c) Dagachi Jaisang's son was Banchung Khung Taiji.

d) Köndelen's son was Buyimatu.

(3) a) Marquis Degei's three sons were: China Khung Taiji, Lama Vajra Yeldeng, Marquis Tümendari Sechen.

b) Khainug Baatur had five sons: China Dai Baatur, Güjegechi Khulachi, Prince Tümei Mergen, Prince Vibasi, Prince Küsendei.

c) The sons of Duke Akiya Köndelen were Marquis Oimasun Joisang and Prince Duke Sanjai.

d) The four sons of Tochi Sechen Köngkör were: Önögün Khung Taiji, Esigen Taiji, Sibandara Taiji, Esgel Taiji.

e) The sons of Chürüke Ching Baatur [73v] were two: Khatan Baatur and Ching Baatur.

f) The sons of Küsel Üijeng were Dorjé Üijeng and Sagang Khung Taiji.

(4) a) The seven sons of Khutugtai Sechen Khung Taiji were: Öljei Ildüchi Darkhan Baatur, Duke Sidadai Sechen, Küdedei Bingtü Daiching, Buyantai Sechen Jorigtu, Bumbudai Chogtu Taiji, Bumbasri Sechen Baatur, Dana Sri Khatan Baatur.

b) The son of Buyandara Khulachi Baatur was Manggus Erdeni Khulachi.

c) There were no descendants of Sain Dara Ching Baatur.

d) Namudai Mergen Taiji's son was Türüi Ching Khulachi.

(5) a) The son of Belgei Taibung was Prince Nachin Taibung.

b) The seven sons of Borsai Taibung were: Sadai Guoshi Khung Taiji, Saji Baatur Khung Taiji, Prince Oirat Mergen, Marquis Edei Yeldeng, Chagu Mergen Jorigtu, Sereng Khatan Baatur, Baatud Taiji.

(6) a) The son of Dorjé Darkhan Jaisang was Minggai Ching Daiching.

b) The six sons of Jongtulai Üijeng were: Tashi Üijeng Khung Taiji, Dalai Jaisang, Sherab Chogtu, Duke Onggui, Rasiyan Taiji, Abandai Taiji.

c) The three sons of Marquis Engke were: Marquis Saji, Duke Sidadan, Bumdar Taiji.

(8) a) Tümei Darkhan Daiching's sons were eight: Prince Bumbai Daiching, Bumbasri Taiji, Chibai Taiji, Nekei Taiji, Sakin Taiji, Elenggei Taiji, Bumbu Taiji, Türüi Taiji.

b) Minggai Eyechi's three sons were: Prince Buyantai Eyechi, Engkesri Taiji, Möngkesri Taiji.

(9) a) Kichigi Yeldeng's four sons were: Prince Buyimatu, Prince Jaisang; Jaisanggur Khulachi, Gömbü Taiji.

b) Khutugtai's three sons were: Biba Daiching, Budur Sechen Jorigtu, Boljomur [74r] Taiji.

c) Buyibari's five sons were: Budashiri Khung Taiji, Emegeldei Daiching, Elbei Taiji, Engke Taiji, Engkesiri Taiji.

* * *

After Buyan Baatur Khung Taiji was slain, Khutugtai Sechen Khung Taiji returned in the Yi Pig year [1575] and settled down, proclaiming:

> "When the father dwelt at home, he became a god;
> When the son was on the steppe, he was slain by an enemy,
> "Now that there are no offerings at the Eight White Tents, things are difficult!"

CHAPTER TEN

History of Altan Khan and the Buddhist Conversion

Buddhism is the main organizing principle of the *Precious Summary*, and thus the so-called "second conversion" is a central component of the narrative. It not only confirms that Buddhist rule is required to maintain peace and stability but in this case also makes clear that the Dalai Lama and his Gelukpa lineage—not any other Tibetan school or lama—is the proper choice on account of his extraordinary spiritual power. Of course, the historical reality was quite different in that various Mongol leaders had actually allied with competing Tibetan schools, such as the Kagyü and Sakya, and this was part and parcel of the fragmentation that defined the period. In fact, although Sagang Sechen highlights Altan Khan's conversion and its relation to proper Mongol rule, he also makes it clear that Altan challenged the other component of Mongol rule: the Chinggisid principle and the legitimacy of the Northern Yuan Chakhar rulers. He thereby upended the Dayan Khanid order, which made it possible for other Mongol noblemen ruling their own recognized groups to do the same. In this chapter alone, for example, Sagang Sechen writes about the activities of those leading the Baya'ud, Bügeres, Chakhar, Khalkha, Kharchin, Ma'u Minggan, Mongoljin, Ordos, Tümed, Üüshin, and Yüngsiyebü. The leaders of these groups not only fought with each other but also ultimately came to ally with the Manchus.

Boshogtu, born in the Yi Ox year [1565], became jinong at the age of thirteen in the Bing Rat year [1576].[1] Thereupon in that same year, at the age of thirty-six, Khutugtu Sechen Khung Taiji went to his uncle Altan Khan and said, "You have taken complete revenge on the Chinese who took the ancient city [of Daidu]; you have united with the Chinese into a state;[2] you have taken complete revenge on the Oirat who had seized Qonin;[3] and by making them submit you have seized their state. Thus now, when the khan is getting older, increasing in age, would it not be good—as the wise ones say—to become Buddhist?[4] Indeed, it is said that in the Snowy Land in the west, the all-seeing, powerful, and compassionate Bodhisattva Avalokitesvara is now bodily incarnated. Would it not be wonderful if we established the religion and state according to the Two Realms like holy Khubilai Khan and Khutugtu Pakpa Lama did before?"

When he had respectfully said this, Altan Khan strongly approved and straightaway took counsel with the Western Three Tümen, and in that same Bing Rat year [1576] Altan Khan dispatched envoys—headed by Adusa Darkhan and Engke Darkan, along with Sechen Khung Taiji's teacher, Khongkhudai Dayan[5]—to invite the Holy All-Knowing Sonam Gyatso Khutugtu.[6] [74v]

Just prior to the arrival of these envoys, this holy one was sitting one day and suddenly declared, "Although Altan Khan is getting old, does he have firm resolve?" All the disciples attending him said among themselves, "What kind of royal utterance is this?"

Then those envoys arrived and presented their documents and gifts, and when they respectfully explained the circumstances of their invitation, the holy all-knowing one smiled and proclaimed, "For all of us, on account of previous good deeds, I will now go without delay. But first, you envoys go and tell the khan, as the head almsmaster." Then, having bestowed on them documents and gifts, he had them go first.[7]

As soon as those envoys arrived they said to the Three Tümen: "At the place called Chabchiyal by Kökenuur,[8] a monastery should be built, and in the Ding Ox year [1577] the Western Three [Tümen] should set out and go there."[9]

Then, at the very first encounter-ceremony, with Bargu Daiching of the Yüngsiyebü, Khatan Baatur of the Ordos, and Teacher Mahachin of the Tümed leading eight hundred people, they presented jewels, goods, property, camels, horses, etc. And in order to guide them, when they arrived at the Red River,[10] the Dalai Lama raised his hand in the brandishing gesture at this body of water, and when it flowed backward they all developed a profound faith.

Next, at the second encounter-ceremony, the Dalai Lama met with Ching Baatur of the Ordos and Lord Marshall of the Tümed leading a thousand people. And when they presented their five thousand gifts, from the barren ground a spring gushed forth, whereby everyone found a firm faith. [75r]

That night they camped at the Red River, and the Dalai Lama, mindful of actions to protect the religion, presented an offering to Begtse Mahakala,[11] who hears the command of holy Hayagriva,[12] and issued a command to gather into his own power all the dragons in the land of the Mongols. Then, reaching Gün Ergi,[13] the Dalai Lama gathered into his power the heavenly dragons of Mongolia, as well as the demons, spirits, and beings with the heads of camels, horses, cattle, sheep, cats, hawks, and wolves, and numerous others, and binding them with an oath, he subjugated them to his power.

Then, at the third encounter-ceremony, the Dalai Lama met with Khutugtai Sechen Khung Taiji of the Ordos and Lord Dayan of the Tümed leading three thousand people. When they presented gifts in the thousands including jewels, gold and silver, various clothes and garments, brocaded silks, camels with gold and silver nose plugs, and bejeweled horses with golden saddles and so on, at that time, Sechen Khung Taiji recognized the Dalai Lama as a clear manifestation of the All-Knowing, Four-Armed Bodhisattva Avalokitesvara.[14]

Then on the next day when they were riding, upon the stones of the road stepped on by the roan horse called Norbu Wangzin ridden by the All-Knowing One, the six syllables *om mani padme hum* magically appeared. Everyone seeing this developed great faith.

Thereupon in the Wu Tiger year [1578], having met the holy all-seeing luminous one, every one of the nine births became joyous. And when they beheld the splendor of the holy all-knowing one, especially when the khan and Sechen Khung Taiji closely observed him, it was as if they were scared. Recognizing this, the holy all-knowing one said through the interpreter Vajra Tümei Güi Wang Khonjin: "Why are you two, khan and lord, looking at me like this?" [75v]

First the khan declared, "I have gout in my leg. Previously, when it flared up, people said, 'If you put it inside a horse, it'll get better.' I thus killed a horse and put my leg inside it, but then I suffered from the illness to the limit of my endurance. And then, looking up, I saw a white-colored man in the sky, and he said, 'Khan, why have you done such great evil?' and in an instant vanished. After this, as I proceeded, fearful within, Asing Lama of the Tangut taught me, 'Recite the six syllables!' In accord with the rosary practice of Teacher Gümi, I am to recite it 108 times a day, and now, when I see you, because you were that white-colored man, I am amazed and frightened."

Then Sechen Khung Taiji similarly said, "I was once playing chess at my mother's, and while I was sitting eating a horse udder she gave me, the knife in my hand suddenly flew up and then spiraled down into the ground. Then when looking at my knife I glanced up, and a man with a youthful appearance and a black feltlike coat said, 'Why are you eating horse meat?' After speaking harshly and rebuking me, he suddenly vanished. Since then I have not eaten horse meat, but seeing you, I see that that person was the holy lama. Thus I now understand that the holy lama has been watching us all. But we have not recognized our lama. Therefore, beholding what has gloriously occurred, I was afraid." [76r]

Whereupon the holy all-knowing one smiled, saying, "The words of these two, the khan and lord, are indeed true. We have not only met today, we have seen each other numerous times before.

"Altan Khan, when you were previously known as Khubilai Khan in the true lineage of Chinggis Khan, I was born as Mati Lotsawa Pakpa Lama, the nephew of Sakya Pandita Ananda Lotsawa Sripada. When I initiated Sechen Khan and Queen Chabi into the four initiations, beginning with the fully complete Hevajra, and showed the many types of meditation and powerful mantras, he gave me the title, which in Chinese is *sing sing dai güüshi*,[15] as well as a bejeweled seal with agate, people, lands, and a document in yellow, and made me the lama, offering site adornment of the crown.

"Formerly, at the time of our supreme Buddha, the Lord of Sages, this Sechen Khung Taiji was born as the lord of Magadha, named King Bimbisara, who was an almsmaster to the Buddha. His younger brother, Sechen Daiching, who is quite similar to him, was the lord of Kosala, King Pasenadi. As for this great translator, Vajra Tümei Khonjin, at the time of Teacher Dromton[16] he was called Lobdan Sherab, interpreter of Irgüg. After this, at the time of Pakpa Lama, he became the interpreter named Khara Moritu of Irsang and interpreted for Sechen Khan and Pakpa Lama. And now he is the interpreter for us three; indeed, I have had him as a disciple three times."

Thereupon Altan Khan, who turns the wheel of time and thereby enlightens the dark continent of the borderlands, returned to his territory wearing a white robe and riding a white horse. [76v] Altan Khan and Queen Noyanchu Jönggen,[17] leading tens of thousands of people, set up camp at Chabciyal, and when holding a great feast of joy, as a present upon meeting the offering site [i.e., the Dalai Lama], they gave a bejeweled silver mandala made from 500 staters, with the seven jewels[18] set in ten staters of gold, and a golden bowl of thirty staters adorned with the eight offerings and filled with jewels,[19] as well as fine silks never seen before by the dozens and dozens, five-colored silks by the hundreds, ten white horses with golden saddles adorned with jewels, and so forth; five thousand items of property; five thousand animals; and in this way they presented a great number of gifts. And as they were staying there enjoying this feast of great happiness, Sechen Khung Taiji declared the following, which was translated by Vajra Tümei Güiwang Khonjin.

"Now, on account of former good deeds, the offering site, the lama, and the almsmaster, the khan, dwell like the sun and the moon that have arisen in the blue sky. Now, in this time, on account of the ancient command of the powerful Qormusta Khan, the grandsons of Fortunate Holy Chinggis Khan, who brought into his power the five-colored peoples and four enemies, namely, the bodhisattva incarnation Köden Khan and the wheel-turning Khubilai Sechen Khan; these Dharma lords of the Mongols met with the tantric power-possessing lamas of the Sakyas, Sakya Pandita, who has reached the limits of knowledge, and Pakpa Lama, the Dharma lord and people's refuge. And having met, they made all beings rejoice by means of the Two Realms.

"From the time of Intelligent Sechen Toghan Temür Khan until now, the religion and state have been destroyed, and thus we acted badly, such as when we ate, we made use of flesh and blood in our food.[20] [77r] Now the holy lama, the Sakyamuni of our troubled times, has met Altan Khan, the Qormusta great powerful khan of these lands.

"Beginning on such a fine and auspicious day, when the great stream moving with waves of blood transforms into a transparent sea eddying with milk, and when one follows the white path of the Dharma traversed by earlier holy ones, this will surely benefit us when we rely upon the khan and lama!"

Hearing this—monks and commoners, Chinese, Tibetans, Mongolians, and Uygurs, all those people assembled in the tens of thousands, all those people speaking whatever language who were gathered—when this declaration was heard by all, everyone was amazed. It was like the song of the cuckoo bird in the first month of summer.

Then, led by the holy all-knowing one and Altan Khan, the monks, commoners, princes, and slaves all agreed: "Formerly, among the Mongols, when a person died a number of camels and horses were killed according to their rank, and they were buried together. This was called *khoilaga*. Now, abandoning this tradition, each accordingly is to follow the Dharma. Thus, on the appropriate year and month one is to meditate and follow the eight-part fast.[21]

"If a commoner lays a hand on a monastic, or if one curses or breaks rank, they will be punished. The office of *chöjé* is similar to that of *khung taiji*; *rabjamba* and *kachu* are similar to *taiji*; *gelong* is similar to *son-in-law, khonjin, taishi*, and *jaisang*.[22]

"On the three fast days of the month, one is not to slaughter livestock, nor is one to hunt wild game and birds.

"Monastics who violate the laws of the monastic code—such as by taking a wife—are to be expelled from the samgha according to the laws of the Dharma. They are also to be made to circumambulate the monastery three times in the wrong direction.

"Laymen and laywomen who violate the laws of the Dharma [77v]—such as by taking a life—let them be punished as previously set forth, and be made into slaves.

"If monks and laymen drink wine, let them be expelled."

In order to make things accord with the sutras and old tales from the time of the cakravartin kings of Tibet and the time of the Mongols' Khubilai Sechen Khan, *The Laws of the Ten Meritorious Deeds* was compiled.[23] And the holy all-knowing one was bestowed with the title Vajradhara Dalai Lama; moreover, in accord with the custom of Pakpa Lama, the earlier Dharma lord, the four classes of monastics did not have to pay taxes, provide corvée labor, or participate in group hunts.[24]

In this way the Two Realms were peacefully established.

Thereupon, the Holy All-Knowing Vajradhara Dalai Lama entitled Altan Khan the Cakravartin Sechen Khan Who Makes Revolve the Thousand-Spoked Golden Wheel and Boshogtu Jinong the Cakravartin Sechen Jinong Khasi Qan; to Sechen Khung Taiji he gave the ancient Indian title "Heart of Aggregate";[25] and to Sechen Daiching—saying "Do not translate this title!"—named him Sargyal Sechen Daiching;[26] Marshal Vajra Tümei was named Marshall Günding Güü Wang; Asing Lama became Father Lama;[27] Teacher Gümi was named Marshall Soga; Teacher Ayushi became Ananda Güüshi;[28] and to still other princes, sons-in-law, teachers, and ministers of each *tümen* he bestowed ranks and titles that caused them to behave to the extent of their profound gravity and to accept the Two Realms.

Then the Holy All-Knowing Vajradhara Dalai Lama proclaimed, "Let me erect a statue of Maitreya Buddha on the Nilom Steppe." He then went to the Nilom Steppe.

Then Altan Khan, at Blue City where the nomadic people had gathered,[29] was to fashion from gold, jewels, and silver a statue of Jowo Sakyamuni, [78r] the protector of living beings.[30] Boshogtu Cakravartin Sechen Jinong was to establish a Monastery of the Three Times; Heart of Aggregate Sechen Khung Taiji was to make from jewels, gold, and silver a 108-volume Kanjur, the word of the Buddha;[31] and Sargyal Sechen Daiching was to erect the Monastery of the Three Times. When everyone agreed to follow through on these statements, the Dalai Lama proceeded to the Nilom Steppe.

As the Vajradhara Dalai Lama was going there, along the way many people came to worship him, and because those who heard the teachings and initiations were many, the convoy was delayed. Therefore, the Dalai Lama dispatched a minor reincarnation called Panchen Sonam Dakpa, saying, "When you get there, settle down in the middle of Nilom Steppe, and then bring to mind the holy Hayagriva, whereby you will pacify the local deities of that place. Then, after three seven-day rounds of doing so, the local deities will reveal to you one of my treasures. Then bury that treasure and on top of it build the foundation of a monastery." After saying this he had him go on ahead.

As soon as the minor incarnation arrived, he did as the Supreme Lama had said. He brought to mind the holy Hayagriva, and on the last night of the third round there came a fair and handsome boy, wearing a white robe with a white crystal rosary wrapped on his left wrist and draped in a white monk's robe. And placing his palms together in front of the minor incarnation, he knelt and made obeisance. Then, sitting down, he said: "Formerly, this Supreme Holy Dalai Lama of yours, when he was born as a prince, called 'Slave of the Three Jewels,' he was lord of the Bede people in the southerly direction of India, and he bestowed on me the abstinence vow of a lay disciple. [78v] Then he made me take care of a horse's tack that was perfectly made with jewels and gold, including a golden saddle adorned with various types of jewels. Ever since then I have well taken care of it, and now because you have followed the command of the Supreme Lama, I will give you the tack tomorrow." He then vanished. When Panchen Sonam Dakpa awoke at dawn there was indeed a complete set of tack made of various jewels. Taking it, he said, "The lama's word was true!" He then prayed and properly installed that monastery's treasure. When the foundation was finished the Holy Vajradhara Dalai Lama arrived.

Then it happened that a Tibetan monk had gone to conduct business, and while doing so he had given to the father of the ruler of the Jang people, who was called Sadam,[32] a portrait of this selfsame Vajradhara Dalai Lama; the father accepted it but then threw it on the ground. Straightaway that very night, he dreamed that a man with a felt robe came and stabbed him in the heart with a quartz-handled knife. And the next morning blood poured out of his two nostrils and he died. Now, the son [King Sadam] realized the lama's compassion for himself, and his mind was moved, and the former Buddhist practices were revived. Thereby contriving a pretext on behalf of his father, he said, "Since there is no requirement for me to go and bow my own head, I will offer a replica of my own head."

He thus had a statue of himself made out of a hundred staters of silver, and he offered it along with five hundred staters of gold, a thousand of silver, and various jewels [79r] and silks and clothes in endless quantity. He then dispatched three hundred commoners led by Jaga and Bukha, telling them to say to the Dalai Lama: "I have secretly been praying and worshipping you. If you take pity on me, please make a statue of yourself and send it to me." Saying this, he sent along ten staters of gold. Straightaway the Dalai Lama therefore had some Nepalese make a statue of himself, and bestowing likewise other objects of veneration as well as blessings, he had the envoys return with these things. Then this King Sadam was extremely happy, and by worshipping the golden statue of the Dalai Lama he became eighty-seven years old.

Then, as for the roofing of the monastery being built on the Nilom Steppe, they used the gold presented by that very King Sadam. Then one called Lachan Pelbar, known as "Splendidly Effulgent," made a perfectly joyous image of Maitreya, and Lachan Pelbar himself strewed flowers and consecrated it with the highest wisdom,[33] whereupon everyone saw a rain of flowers come from the sky. As a result, they all had faith.

Then, Sangsung Bonpo Namni cursed the Vajradhara Dalai Lama and brought down thunderbolts upon him. But when they struck the holy lama's robe, the lightning deflected into the water. As a result, the next day Bonpo came and bowed down to the holy lama and said respectfully: "Through curses I have killed ninety-seven men, but when I cursed you three times, holy lama, nothing happened. I am now ninety-seven, and when I die I will go to the three evil rebirths.[34] I repent my earlier deeds and ask you, the living Bodhisattva Avalokitesvara, to purify them in your splendor. Moreover, in my future rebirth I request the sanctity of becoming a buddha. [79v] Now kindly bestow on me the monastic vows. May you guide me on the path when I die in your presence." He then become a monk, and when after seven days he died, the Dalai Lama led him to bodhi sanctity.

* * *

Then, in the Ji Rabbit year [1579],[35] Altan Khan returned to Mongolia with Tongkor Manjusri Khutugtu.[36] He said to Khutugtai Sechen Khung Taiji, "Previously, in the fourth year of the Great Ming's Lungching emperor,[37] the Xin Sheep year [1571], you fervently supported the great state," and he was going to give him the title *lung quu jang jün*,[38] a jade seal, and a yellow imperial script, but in the interval there was a delay, and Khutugtai Sechen Khung Taiji did not get them.

Then in his forty-first year, the Geng Dragon year [1580], Sechen Khung Taiji went and took Irgai City, and from the twenty-one cities between Irgai City and Temeetü City[39] he took an endless amount of treasure.

Thereupon Altan Khan, when he was seventy-six in the Ren Horse year [1582], fell seriously ill, and while he was pulling himself together physically, the princes of the Mongoljin Tümed and other ministers said among themselves: "What is the good of this religion and Dharma? It has not been of any use to the golden life of this khan. Will it be useful later on for something else? These lamas are acting deceitfully. Indeed, we should kill those monks!"

When it was reported what they were saying, Manjusri Khutugtu had all the princes and nobles of the Tümed assembled, and proceeding into the khan's presence, said:

"In general there is no end to deeds originated;
There is no eternity in the body, which is born like the moon reflecting on water;
Like an image in a mirror, in general one is born, dies, and is reborn; [80r]
Because there is no one who has not died, there is none who has overcome death.
In the case of the vajra-body Buddha, who overcame being born and dying,
Because there is thus an overcoming of death and rebirth,
To find the sanctity of a buddha like that
There is nothing other than this true, supreme Dharma.
And prior to whenever this buddhahood is found,
There has been no one at all who did not die.

"In general, all the buddhas of the Three Times, and in particular the protector of living beings in the present, Sakyamuni Buddha, have not taught that one does not die. Now, our supreme lama, the Holy All-Knowing Vajradhara Dalai Lama, were he to come here tomorrow, he would say the same thing. No one is able to overcome the destiny of death, but one can treat against premature death by means of medicines and such things. Now, this khan, because he has reached the end of his life, he will soon not be here. Inasmuch as that is so, the holy all-knowing one has declared that this khan is no ordinary man, but is indeed a bodhisattva!

The jewel of the victorious religion,
A bodhisattva who maintains religion,
A khan who is an almsmaster of the religion.

"And since all three of us have truly met, let the might of the compassionate resolve of the holy all-knowing one and the holy khan's firm faith and devotion prevail!"

Then the precious learned doctor, Yönten Rinchen, gave medicine to the khan through his nose, and when Manjusri Khutugtu said three times: "Oh great khan, for the sake of the religion, deign to arise!," the khan straightaway revived and got up, and everyone was amazed and joyously worshipped.

When everyone talked about what had happened, not concealing anything, [80v] the khan declared: "Princes and nobles of the Twelve Tümed! What is this about you harming the monks and injuring the religion promulgated by me? Have you seen anyone become immortal from among those people who worship spirit dolls and fetishes,[40] as it was before when this land had no monks, nor the Dharma? In general, who previously from among the nobility, or the commoners, became immortal? Who has even become a hundred? At this time I have reached the age of eighty. And Sakyamuni Buddha has taught us the truth that all beings die, since he himself revealed the reality of nirvana [i.e., he passed away]. Did not just yesterday my lama, the holy all-knowing one, say this? Does not each and every one of you know this? Were Khutugtai Sechen Taiji of the Ordos present, he would surely know it!"

As he said so, and after they had overnighted more than ten days, Sechen Khung Taiji, hearing the grave news about the khan, came to greet him together with the queen and children. The khan was very happy and smiled, and explained what had happened without omitting anything. Then they gathered the princes and nobles of the Twelve Tümed, and disseminating the words of Tongkor Manjusri Khutugtu, the khan and Sechen Khung Taiji jointly proclaimed repeatedly the benefit and reward of the religion and Dharma. To promote the words of Manjusri Khutugtu, and so that no harm would come to the religion and the monks, and so that the religion would spread, they jointly swore great vows of brotherhood. Altan Khan lived for another year, which made everyone happy, and in the Gui Sheep year [1583] at the age of seventy-seven, he transmigrated.[41]

* * *

Thereupon his eldest son, Sengge Düüreng Temür, born in the Wu Dog year [1538], at the age of forty-seven ascended the throne in the Jia Monkey year [1584].[42] In that same year he discussed with the Three Western Tümen the need to transfer merit to Altan Khan,[43] [81r] and when they invited him, the Vajradhara Dalai Lama came straightaway.[44]

Along the way, Quu Duutang[45] of Gamsu City in China invited him[46] and prepared a great feast. As they presented the great offerings, in the ashes of the incense, which had been lit in front of the Vajradhara Dalai Lama, the letters forming "Jowo" appeared. And even if one hit the ashes with force, the letters were not destroyed, whereby everyone was amazed. The commoners of Gamsu presented an immeasurable amount of offerings, and listening willingly and well to the initiations and teachings, they found an unshakably firm faith.[47]

* * *

Thereupon the Duutang and Süngbing,[48] and the princes great and small, headed by the Ching Wang of Irgai City, invited the Dalai Lama to come. While he was there they greatly venerated and worshipped the holy all-knowing one, who appeared to them as a deity with a white face and four arms. Two of his hands were held palms together upon his heart, and his other right hand held a lotus blossom, while the other left held a white crystal rosary. He sat with his feet in the vajra posture, and because he was beautifully adorned with signs and marks, as well as adorned in an attractive manner with various jewels and silk scarves, everyone saw him emitting gleaming beams of five colors. As they presented their unimaginable amount of offerings, they listened until satisfied to the deep and profound doctrine with wishful desire and found the power of great devotion and faith.

* * *

Thereupon, in the Yi Rooster year [1585], the Dalai Lama arrived at Great Marsh, the residence of Khutugtai Sechen Khung Taiji, who was then forty-four.[49] Then, on the bank of the Mangrug Spring, he meditated for three months, thereby manifestly completing the rite pertaining to the holy Hayagriva, who gathers the Three Worlds into his power. [81v] Thereupon he bestowed on Khutugtai "Heart of Aggregate" Sechen Khung

Taiji, his queen, Torgan Jula Sechen, and all the almsmasters the limitless, perfected initiation of Hayagriva as well as teaching them with the power of speech.

Thereupon, when the Dalai Lama headed north, many benefactors and princes on the way invited him and presented grand offerings. When he arrived outside Boshogtu Sechen Jinong's place, they indicated to him the Temple of the Three Times, and while they were at Kökebür, the three persons—Boshogtu Sechen Jinong, Sechen Khung Taiji, and Sechen Daiching—received the totally perfected four initiations of the Splendid Hevajra from the Vajradhara Dalai Lama. They also took an oath, saying, "Do not curse one another." Boshogtu Jinong established the Two Realms in accord with yore, and made the sun of religion to shine on the dark continent.

* * *

Then, proceeding and arriving at the Twelve Tümed, the Dalai Lama criticized that they had buried the corpse of Altan Khan according to shamanic practices, saying, "How can you bury in the earth such a beloved and inestimable jewel?" When they exhumed the body and ceremoniously burned it,[50] it distinctly came to be replete with marvelous tokens and incalculably numerous relics.[51] Thus all the people were amazed.

Then further, after his late father had gone to heaven, Bodi Alag Jinong married the third of his three wives, named Queen Molan. From this there was only the single son, called Töbed Taiji. When he died, the queen, heedless of the consequences, said:

"Slaying the children of a hundred persons,
One will make them accompany the deceased;
Slaying the offspring of a hundred female camels,
One will cause them to bellow likewise."

When more than forty [82r] children had been slain, the great people were on the point of an uprising, and the son of Sinikei Örlüg of the Mongoljin, named Jugantulai Kiya Taiji, said:

"In the place of a stranger [i.e., the queen]
Making children suffer, I shall go;

Let her just try to kill me and make me
Accompany her dead son."

Because there was no possibility of slaying him, she gave up, and thus they abandoned the killing. When that queen died, her corpse was buried according to shamanic practices. But on account of her actions, Erlig did not separate her soul from her body,[52] so she could not rise upward and advance to be an unfettered spirit.

The holy Dalai Lama thereby deigned to pacify her spirit. So as to make a fire mandala of the fierce deeds of Yamantaka, performer of frightening things, the splendid vajra one prepared in proper fashion the opening of a triangular gusset. Inside this he placed the queen's robe, which had been folded seven times, and at once great truth was uttered from the lama's mouth. He assembled the lords of death through the four dharanis and four mudra gestures, and when they were made to enter the gusset, a lizard came and crept out of the left sleeve of the robe and stuck out its head. Then, when the holy lama had preached well about the benefit of liberation and the harm of perpetual reincarnation, and the doctrine about the truth of dying in general and so on, that lizard turned around three times as if bowing its head and then died. It was indeed the queen.

Then the Dalai Lama introduced fire through meditative concentration and offered the goods of sacrifice to the mundane and supramundane deities, and when that robe and lizard were burned, there was an unendurably severe and foul odor. Some fainted, some grew hysterical, some awoke and came to themselves, and as they looked, there arose upward a white column of smoke from the mandala, [82v] and on top of it, there was a son of Heaven in the shape of Vajrasattva. When everyone who was there saw how he went they marveled, and they acquired an excessively firm faith. Just as the dawn lights up the dark night, the precious religion greatly expanded, illuminating like the gleaming sun.

* * *

Thereupon, while proceeding to the Kharchin Tümen, princes of the Tümed, Üüshin, Baya'ud, Bügeres, and of the Ma'u Minggan invited the Dalai Lama to visit. And once again when they heard the great and profound Dharma, they offered him an immeasurable amount of offerings.

* * *

At this time, in the Bing Dog year [1586], Khutugtai Sechen Khung Taiji of the Ordos, at the age of forty-seven, passed away. Saikhan Nangso, Vajra Tümei Güi Wang Güüshi, Arachang Üijeng Örlüg, Bekei Sechen Jaya'achi, and others came to present their offerings; moreover, the Vajradhara Dalai Lama was very saddened and proclaimed:

> "When a person goes forth striving for bodhi, what is there to grieve about?
> You lose a part of yourselves;
> Why have you cast on the ground the wondrous object of veneration,
> The beloved pouch of relics and other things?"

Then he offered a prayer for the desired path.

* * *

His son Öljei Ildüchi Darkhan Baatur, at the age of seventeen while his father was still alive, had led the charge at the Battle of Tokmag. Leaping in full armor onto a horse, he rode into the camp of the two princes and destroyed them, whereupon everyone said, "He has confirmed the state." In that very Ding Pig year [1587], he was given the title Baatur Sechen Khung Taiji and made to uphold the law. Then at the age of thirty-four in the Ji Ox year [1589], he died.

* * *

Prior to that year, in the Ding Pig year [1587], [83r] a taiji called Crazy Abatai[53] of the Khalkha came to worship the Dalai Lama. When he offered the Dalai Lama numerous gifts, topped off with a lacquered tent covered with sable skin, his heart's desire was satisfied by the Dharma. Then when the Dalai Lama said to that khan, "Use your hand to take one Buddha statue from among my Buddha statues here," Abatai took a statue of Vajrapani that was in front of him.

Thereupon, when he was about to return, he respectfully asked the Dalai Lama, "In addition to the statue, deign to grant me the title Vajra Khan." The Dalai Lama replied, "That would be very bad for your Mongol state."[54] But Abatai persisted, so the Dalai Lama gave him the title Vajra Khan.

* * *

In that same Ding Pig year [1587], Namudai Khung Taiji of the Chakhar came to worship the Dalai Lama, and he offered gold, silver, goods, camels, horses, livestock, and horse herds numbered in the thousands. When he said, "Our Chakhar Tümen, led by Tümen Khan, longs for the holy lama and is thus sending envoys to invite him for the sake of the religion," the holy all-knowing one said:

"If it comes before next year,
If I am able to go, it will be so.
If it does not come next year,
Then it will not be possible for me to go."

Everyone did not grasp this prediction of his death, and Namudai Khung Taiji said, "What kind of statement is this?" Nevertheless the Dalai Lama gave Namudai Khung Taiji teachings and many initiations.

CHAPTER ELEVEN

History of the Dalai Lamas and Ordos

While glorifying Buddhism, this chapter also reveals the fragmentary nature of Mongol society in the early seventeenth century. The narrative focus is thus not only on the religious activities of the Third, Fourth, and Fifth Dalai Lamas, as well as the Fourth Panchen Lama, but also on the religious activities of the Ordos Mongols. In this way the power of the Dharma and of these particular lamas is amply confirmed. Moreover, by shifting the narrative focus toward his own community of Ordos, Sagang Sechen reveals that it was these smaller communities that really mattered at this time. The idea of the unified Mongols from the time of Chinggis Khan up through the Mongol-Oirat civil war and the Dayan Khanid revival no longer held sway. Sagang Sechen is also able to highlight the contributions of his family and himself in both the promotion of Buddhism and the ruling of Ordos. In so doing he makes clear the tensions that defined Mongol society. The Chinggisid legacy had come to an end, the Ordos Mongols were Buddhist, and thus peace and salvation—as well as political legitimacy—resided elsewhere.

Then, like that, on the first day of the tenth month in the Wu Rat year [1588], while the holy all-knowing one sat on top of a high mountain at the base of a tree, which had flowered and developed fruit and seeds, there came to him a monk in old clothing. They looked at each other, paid respect to each other, then spoke to each other using Indian words, and then parted. [83v] When all the disciples who were present at his side inquired about this, the Dalai Lama said, "That monk is from the Nilom Steppe Monastery. He is called Tarbai Gyeltsen, which in Mongolian is 'The Banner of Victorious Salvation,' and since I am about to depart this life, he came to see me."

Right after he had come, the Dalai Lama became sick. At that time, the Wanli emperor of China's Great Ming sent envoys led by three princes—Süngbing, Buujang, and Sanjang[1]—to invite the Dalai Lama to Beijing.[2] They offered him a golden throne to sit upon, a golden palanquin to be carried in, as well as nine white harnessed horses with golden saddles and three hundred carts filled with treasure, and as welcome gifts, a hundred staters of gold and a thousand staters of silver, and all kinds of various jewels and goods by the hundreds and hundreds, as well as a yellow imperial letter stating: "I have supported the Dharma just like Emperor Taisung of the Tang,[3] the Emperor Yunglo,[4] and Emperor Suvandi,[5] and now according to the custom of the Mongols' Khubilai Sechen Khan, I want to give you the title *sing sing dai wang güüshi*[6] and make you the Lama Adorning the Crown."

When at the same time the envoys of Tümen Khan of the Chakhar—led by Tümei Khung Taiji of the Kesigten and Prince Baga Darkhan of the Kemjigüd—arrived with a thousand men and relay horses, the holy lama said: "The commands of the khan and emperor, lords of the two great people, are right and truthful. It is not solely to benefit the command of these two mighty rulers, the lords of the two great nations, the Chinese and the Mongols, but rather [for] the great merit of supporting the religion, and to benefit all beings, that I have to go without fail. Indeed, before your requests arrived—you great, powerful rulers—did I not last year say to Namudai Khung Taiji:

'If it comes before next year,
If I am able to go, it will be so. [84r]
If it does not come next year,
Then it will not be possible for me to go.'

Those words have now come to pass, and since I have arrived at the end of the deeds to be done, I am going for the benefit of others."

In the presence of these envoys, on the twenty-sixth day of the Hoopoe Moon[7] of the Wu Rat year [1588],[8] the forty-seven-year-old Dalai Lama, who was born in the Ren Tiger year [1542]—the 3,675th since that original Wu Rat year—abandoned his material body marked with all the signs of blessedness, and abiding in the heart of the savior, the Powerful Sainted Perceiver, he ascended to a place called Jiramatai.[9]

Then on the twenty-fifth of the fourth month, when they cremated his splendid body, there emerged letters and innumerable relics including the compassionate eyes of Avalokitesvara, a perfectly completed *kapala*[10] like Cakrasamvara, and Bodhisattva Avalokitesvara, which were put into millions of stupas as Emperor Asoka had done.[11]

* * *

Thereupon, the holy all-knowing one looked at the Mongol people with his eyes of compassion and entered into the womb of Queen Tara, wife of Sümer Daiching,[12] the fourth son of Düüreng Khan. When the entire nine months had passed, at the onset of the tenth month, he was wondrously born in the Ji Ox year [1589].[13] When it was heard that the Holy All-Knowing Vajradara Dalai Lama had reincarnated, and they were going to send envoys to the Eternal Land so they could bring him to Tibet, they said, "Although the wisdom of the Mongols is small, we have our pride, and since our child is small, how can we send him there? We will not send him before he is thirteen." Saying so, they did not send him to Tibet.

Later, Boshogtu Jinong of Ordos, at the age of twenty-eight in the Ren Dragon year [1592], led the Ordos Tümen [84v] on a campaign against China, and for three days and nights at the river called Sinsikü he took vast booty and spoils and then returned.[14] Then when Military Commander Wang from Irgai City came and engaged them in battle, there entered into the fray from the Right Wing Baatur Törö of the Üüshin, Asitu Qara Küji of the Kharqatan, Gilüi Jayachi of the Khali'uchin, and Baatur Türbei of the Bukhas. Moreover, the taiji called Batu, son of Öljei Ildüchi, the eldest son of Khutugtai Sechen Khung Taiji, born in the Geng Dragon year [1580], was then thirteen, and he caught up with and captured a Chinese lancer on account of his chestnut horse called Ökindei. This made everyone happy, including the jinong, who entitled Batu as Darkhan Baatur in accord with the title of his father.

Later, Boshogtu Sechen Jinong, at the age of thirty, in the Jia Horse year [1594] again campaigned against China.[15] As he passed Alag Mountain, Military Commander Maga of Temeetü City came in pursuit, and when they encountered each other, there entered into the fray two from the Left Wing of Minggai Ching Daiching: Son-in-Law Marquis Khutugtai and Togtar Ildüchi Qara Khulad. But when the Chinese caught him and made him lose his red tent, he turned back via Black City[16] and came to Mongolia, arriving at the place called Red Meadow.

That same Batu Darkhan Baatur was then fifteen. He did not ride out on that campaign, but Töbed Khaskha Jaya'achi, at the head of his ministers, took him, and while they rode he protected him in front of his many people. While overnighting prior to uniting under banner and trumpet in battle, they welcomed a man who having gone as a spy told them an attack was imminent. Thus Asitu Qara Küji—son of Tegürge of the same Kharqatan—and Marquis Khainug Dagamai of the Khakilis went first, [85r] and having set things in motion, Batu Darkhan Baatur then entered the fray on his chestnut horse Ökindei and pursued the enemies for half a day from the promontory of Ünügüchi up to the Sukhai River. He took a great amount of plunder and booty, and when he returned and brought forth the armor and horses and such things, everyone was amazed. As a result, they evoked the title of his grandfather, named him Baatur Sechen Khung Taiji, and had him run the administration as his grandfather had previously done.

Afterward, when the incarnation of the all-knowing one was fourteen in the Ren Tiger year [1602], he was brought to Tibet. Upon arriving in the Four Eternal Lands, he took the monastic vows in the presence of the All-Knowing Panchen Jewel,[17] and he comprehended fully the essence of the Dharma's profound and subtle sutras and dharanis that were to be learned. Then, as the previous holy all-knowing one had done, he went to worship the objects of veneration, especially the supreme icon in the temple of Rong, a completely joyous statue of Maitreya called Rong Semchen. Moreover, he had it renovated by fashioning it with copper and jewels and gilting it with gems and gold, so that this great statue measured six feet from its crown to the bottom of its face. Yet then, when this statue suddenly leaned over all by itself, all of the wise men, including the Nepalese, could not straighten it out. Thus when the Holy

All-Knowing Yönten Gyatso worshipped that statue, he sat and looked for a moment, and then said:

"At the roof ridge of the temple, right at the head of this Buddha,
Someone has buried the bones of a master of magic.
This is why it turns away and inclines its body."

Straightaway when they went and looked, there were indeed the bones of a man's corpse. When they took them and threw them into a great river, [85v] and the holy all-knowing one had strewn flowers, that statue became straight as before. When these numerous and various signs were wondrously displayed, he became famous as the All-Knowing Ocean of Knowledge Vajradhara Dalai Lama.

* * *

Like the previous Vajradhara Dalai Lamas, he attained the limits of knowledge and wisdom and established to a full degree the banner of religion of the Fully Realized One. In particular, he made all the directions be illuminated like the Maker of Day [i.e., the sun] through the religion of Tsongkhapa Sumatikirti.[18]

Thereupon the holy wise ones of the Four Eternal Lands spoke with one another regarding how to maintain the religion in Mongolia. Saying, "There is no golden lord in Mongolia," they dispatched a twelve-year-old born in the Ren Dragon year [1592], named Gendün Pelzang Gyatso Sripada, the incarnation of the Most Merciful Samba Gyatso, a disciple of the guru, Holy Padmasambhava. He arrived in the Jia Dragon year [1604] at the age of thirteen and was immediately placed on the golden throne of the Holy All-Knowing Sonam Gyatso Vajradhara Dalai Lama, which was in Mongolia, and he became famous in all directions as the Greatly Merciful Maitreya Khutugtu.

Then, when he was fifteen in the Bing Horse year [1606], Queen Togtai Machig Buyantu Dalai[19]—the wife of Daiching Ejei[20]—invited him to consecrate a Maitreya statue made of jewels.[21] When flowers were strewn from the gates of the mandala of the holy secret collections, everyone beheld a rain of flowers from the sky. When these signs manifestly appeared they were clearly seen by those completely fortunate ones. [86r]

Later, when he was twenty in the Xin Pig year [1611], Prince Dalai Ubasi of the Uru'ud invited him to consecrate his temple, and all jointly marveled at his having left footprints in a rock.

* * *

Prior to this, when Boshogtu Jinong of Ordos was thirty-two in the Bing Monkey year [1596], he campaigned against Tibet's eastern edge and subdued the Yellow Uyghurs led by Gürü Sonam Tsal. How can one even finish relating the deeds of Dharma, and of the world, that he performed afterward?

Such as when Boshogtu Jinong was forty-three in the Ding Sheep year [1607]. First he had made from jewels, gold, and silver a statue of the twelve-year-old Jowo Sakyamuni. Then he established unstintingly various kinds of worship goods, banners, adornments, and so on. In the Gui Ox year [1613] when he was forty-nine, the statue was finished. When he was fifty in the Jia Tiger year [1614], at the full moon of the month of the great magical transformation,[22] he invited the Great Merciful Maitreya Khutugtu, and when he performed the deeds of consecration including strewing flowers, it rained flowers along with many other auspicious signs.

Having organized the occasion of this consecration and its signs, Boshogtu Jinong promoted Vajra Tümei Güiwang Güüshi, Ching Ua Aga Güüshi, and Barasi Üijeng Taiji (son of Jongtulai Üijeng); bestowed on the majesty of Maitreya Khutugtu the title Great Merciful Dharma King; gave Arlig Chöjé the title Dalai Chöjé, Güüwang Güüshi the title of Günding Dai Wang Güüshi,[23] and Aga Güüshi the title of Yogacari Güüshi, and made them become Dharma lords. And to the other monks in order, one after the other, after both major and minor titles were given, there was given a prophecy that all would be reborn in every rebirth with a Dharma king. [86v]

To Boshogtu Sechen Jinong he gave the title Cakravartin Sechen Jinong Khan Who Turns the Golden Wheel; to Queen Taigal Jönggen the title Queen Tara Bodhisattva Nomchi Dalai Sechen Jönggen; to his uncle Duke Manggus the title Dai Khung Taiji; to his younger brother Öljei the title Bingtü Khung Taiji; to Tashi of the Left Wing the title Üijeng Khung Taiji; to Marquis Engke the title Marquis Khung Taiji.

To the great-grandson of Khutugtai Sechen Khung Taiji of the Right Wing, the son of Batu Khung Taiji, namely Sagang Taiji,[24] born in the Jia

Dragon year [1604], at the age of eleven—because the princes of the Six People said among themselves that he was the descendant of the man who initiated the religion and state—was accorded the title of his great-grandfather, Sagang Sechen Khung Taiji. At the age of seventeen he was inducted into the ranks of ministers, and for solidifying the state's rule he was greatly beloved.

To Manggus Khulachi was given the title Jewel Khulachi Khung Taiji; to the eldest son of Sechen Daiching, Sadai Sechen Daiching, the title Güüshi Khung Taiji; to the second son, Sechi, the title Baatur Khung Taiji; to Ubasi, the nephew of Daibung, the title Durar Daiching; in respect of the relative importance of all the other princes and sons-in-law and ministers, they bestowed titles and ranks one after the other. Boshogtu Jinong made the four great states peaceful, and made the vast great people happy.

Later, when he was fifty-seven in the Xin Rooster year [1621], on account of the slaying of sixty envoys who had gone to discuss the state at China's Temeetü city, Boshogtu Jinong Khan was furious. When all the greater and lesser princes and officials of the Ordos Tümen took counsel together, they went with 10,000 troops west toward [87r] Temeetü city via Red Stupa. When they reached Yanggan city, they assembled and besieged it for three days, during which time the princes inside—called the Seven Daoli—dispatched a letter saying: "We have communicated with the *sulang* and *duutang*;[25] hold off beleaguering the city and let us discuss the state."

Boshogtu Jinong Khan agreed and turned back, but at Baogan city there came 20,000 soldiers headed by the two military commanders from the cities of Irgai and Temeetü. When Bogban Khung Taiji, the eldest son of Prince Duke Manggusa of Tegürge—attacked after breaking off by himself on the battlefield—they shot with a gun the horse he was riding, making him fall, but when they grabbed him, he stabbed with a sword the man who was grasping him.

Four officials, namely the two brothers Son-in-Law Lamajab and Son-in-Law Erkei, and Berke Jaisang and Marquis Bolad Khatan, swooped down together on those who had attacked Bogban Khung Taiji, and when they fled he came out still holding his horse's bridle. Straightaway they planned to encircle the battlefield, but since it had grown late, they postponed action, saying, "Let's regroup, spend the night, and attack in the morning!" Yet that night, as they were regrouping, a little prior to dawn, the Chinese furtively fled. Thereupon they took an incalculable amount of loot and booty and returned home.

In the Ren Dog year [1622], the three envoys of Ombo Khung Taiji of the Tümed—Prince Burbai Kiya, Dalatu Chingsang, and Jaya'atu Kiya, the interpreter—held a discussion with the three princes—Manggus Erdeni Khulachi Khung Taiji of the Ordos, Marshall Buyantai Sechen, and [87v] Sagang Sechen Khung Taiji—and agreed to send every year to the Jinong Khan three thousand staters of gold, and every month, two hundred and fifty staters of silver. In compensation for the sixty slain men they also gave six hundred staters of silver. Furthermore, to the princes who ruled the state, and to the sons-in-law and nobles, to each one they gave great treasure, whereby the great state became pacified, regulated, and harmonized.

* * *

Later on, when Boshogtu Jinong was fifty-nine in the Gui Pig year [1623], he had Arig Dalai Chöjé finish writing the Kanjur in gold, and he had Gaba Chagan Khutugtu strew flowers in consecration. Thereupon, although he had promised to bring the Tanjur from the land of Tsongkhapa in the west, when he was sixty in the Jia Rat year [1624], he passed away on account of fate.

* * *

Thereupon his wife, Queen Taigal Tara Bodhisattva Monchi Jönggen, having well performed for one hundred days the earnest merit offerings, at the place where his breath had left him, she did as had previously been done with jewels for the Jowo Erdeni statue: she had a stupa made of a thousand staters of silver and various jewels to house his majestic remains. This object of veneration was put beside the Jowo Sakyamuni statue.

* * *

After discussing it with the greater and lesser princes of the Ordos Tümen, she prepared tea offerings[26] for the many sacred sites in the western Snowy Land, beginning with the Jowo statue in Lhasa. She also presented offerings of jewels and goods, saying, "Let us take the blessings of the many incarnated holy ones, led by the Holy Panchen Jewel and the All-Knowing Dalai Lama." Everyone approved. [88r]

The four sons of that holy one, Boshogtu Jinong, were Sereng Erdeni Khung Taiji, Rinchen Eyechi Daiching, Tuba Taiji, and Choila Taiji. It was the third son, Tuba Taiji, who, to repay the favor of his precious father, said, "Let me go to Tibet to present these offerings." His mother approved, and in the same year she dispatched him forthwith.

Meanwhile, the eldest son, Sereng Erdeni Khung Taiji, born in the Xin Rabbit year [1591], ascended the throne in the Bing Tiger year [1626], when he was thirty-six; six months elapsed and in the same year he died.

* * *

At that time, Tuba Taiji reached the Four Eternal Lands, where he bowed down to the majesty of the Holy Panchen Jewel and the All-Knowing Dalai Lama and distributed the offerings to the many sacred sites beginning with the Jowo Jewel. Then one day, at Ganden monastery[27]—the place of the Second Victorious Holy Sumatikirti, known as Having Perfect Merit—the Holy Panchen Jewel taught the birth story of Victorious Tsongkhapa.

As for this Holy Panchen Jewel,[28] long ago he was Subhuti,[29] a disciple of the Mahayana during the time of the very first Lord of Sages, who taught the *Vajra-Cutting Vajracchedika Sutra*. Then, in the land of Shambhala,[30] which lies to the east, he became famous as the ruler known as The One of Perfect Lineage.[31] He also prophesied that the people of Shambhala would become a repository of the splendid *Kalacakratantra*. Then, in the central land of India, he became a monk called He Who Opens Well in Perfection,[32] and the root disciple of the guru Nagarjuna,[33] whereupon he manifestly revealed the essence of the spoken teachings. [88v]

Thereupon, in the land of Magadha in India, he again became a religious teacher named Abiya Gira, and following his guiding yogini mother, he found the fearless supernatural power of samsara and nirvana, and knowing without hindrance the sutras and tantras, he attained the limits of teaching, disputation, and composition.

Then in the same illustrious land, he became known as the supreme translator and fully revealed the sequence of the path of the splendid secret collection. Then in the land of the splendid Sakyas of Tibet, he became a great pandita called Banner of Joy to All and won a debate with the five hundred heretical teachers. And when he brought to Tibet the teacher of the heretics, called He of Disheveled Hair, he caused his death according to the vows of Padmasambhava of yore. He passed beyond the limits of the five sciences and in general attained all that was to be known.

Then in the same India, he became one called Having the Power of Yogacara and produced the stream of nectar of the old secret dharanis, and by his majesty subjected the beings visible in samsara. Then in the perfect virtuous land of Tibet, he became known as The One of Splendid Good Virtue Who Has Obtained Wisdom, and he attained the yonder shore of the ocean of knowledge beginning with the sutras, dharanis, transcendent paramitas, and wisdom treatises.

Then in the same Snowy Land, he became known as Supreme Elephant, who manifestly understood the essence of the two levels[34] of the three things to be studied.[35] Next, at a monastery in an isolated region of Tibet, he became known as The Victorious Good-Minded Accomplisher of Benefice,[36] and like the powerful khan who thinks extensively and is unhindered in all that is to be understood, he became revered as the pinnacle of the deep profound secret of the complete Vajrayana, [89r] and obtained a Dharma body like an unbreakable vajra.

Thus, when he is now reborn as the one known as the Holy Panchen Sumati Dharma Lotsawa, is there anything his wondrous incarnations and incomparable knowledge do not know? In particular, when Baga Toyin of the Mongol Seven Tümed and Son-in-Law Ögedei Baatur of the Khanglin went on campaign against Tibet in the Ji Sheep year [1619] and were about to meet the ten thousand troops of Jangba Khan[37] at Chagpo Mountain,[38] the Holy Panchen Jewel was sitting in meditation at the monastery, perfect in fortune, sanctity, and majesty and thought: *If we can stop this battle, the merit will be incalculable.* He thus set out on his brown horse named Norbu Wangzin, and arriving swiftly like a wheel of the wind, he dismounted between the two armies, and everyone beheld and greatly marveled together at the path of the horse he had ridden, which clearly imprinted hoofprints in the rock, as if trampled in mud.

As Padmasambhava, who knew the Three Times, had long ago prophesied:

> In a coming time of five hundred troubles,
> On the banks of the Isgisüd River, one named Eng will be born.

At a time when Chagpo Mountain, the place of the powerful one who
  sees clearly,
Is converted solely to a soldiers' camp,

One lama, manifestly an incarnation of Amitabha,
Who contemplated and trained his compassionate bodhi mind,
Will save the lives of ten thousand men,
And thereby perform a vastly great meritorious deed.

Like this I have only written here in summary fashion a mere drop about the sea of virtues of the Holy Panchen Jewel, the buddha of the present time of strife.[39]

* * *

Then, from the majesty of the Holy Panchen Jewel, the door to the deep and profound Vajrayana [89v] was opened with an initiation of the vajra rosary, and he then completely gave them all their desired initiations and hoped-for teachings. Yet, prior to this, in the Bing Dragon year [1616], the Dalai Lama Yönten Gyatso had passed away at the age of twenty-eight.

* * *

Thereupon, in the Ding Snake year [1617], in the land of Sakya Dangbo, the Holy Panchen Jewel became aware in his consciousness that the Dalai Lama bad been reborn as the son of a prince called Diba Guruba.[40] He then said to everyone: "If we bring him to the monastery before he is five years old, it will be a hazard to his life." When he was six years old officials of Drepung monastery[41] were sent to get him, and they brought him a complete monk's robe. When they arrived at the home of that Prince Guruba, everyone was assembled in order to behold and marvel. When they entered that house, the child said, "Ponlob Panchen, why have you taken so long?" Straightaway, Holy Panchen, taking sweets from his sleeve, said, "Oh, my son, have you been bored?" And taking him into his arms, he sat there with him affectionately, and when the child discussed with the Holy Panchen issues of the deep and profound Dharma, everyone was greatly dazzled and amazed.[42]

In this same Ren Dog year [1622] the Holy Panchen Jewel brought him to Drepung, and they dressed him in a complete set of robes and a yellow cap, and shaving his hair, made him into a monk, and when they taught him what was to be learned, he learned it without hindrance. The Holy Panchen thus said: "The fact of his arrival at the limits of knowledge confirms that this is his reincarnation." His monastic name was Lozang Gyatso.

In this way, from the splendor of the All-Knowing Dalai Lama Lozang Gyatso, when he was nine years old in the Yi Ox year [1625], he remembered the monks who had gone to Mongolia, headed by Tuba Taisung Khung Taiji, [90r] and he gave the initiation of the Bestower Mahakala with Six Arms, the purifier of demons.[43] When he did so, and when he taught without any hindrances, everyone was amazed and said: "Truly, he is manifestly the selfsame Bodhisattva Avalokitesvara."

Thereupon, at Drepung monastery—the seat of the holy all-knowing one, known as The Perfectly Splendid Clearly Assembled Place—there was established a stupa for the previous All-Knowing Dalai Lama Yönten Gyatso, and on an auspicious day, flowers were strewn. So as to commemorate this event, from in front of the Protector of Beings, the Holy Panchen Jewel and the All-Knowing Dalai Lama Lozang Gyatso, and Tripa Nangso Aua, sounded forth on the bestowal of the title Taisung Khung Taiji on Tuba Taiji and the titles granted to the other monks and laity present: Sarduk Chöjé got the title Tuulugsan Daiching Chöjé and Arig Rasang Chöjé the title Dalai Chöjé. To Sechen Chöjé, son of Gidung Darkhan Nakpa of the Miñag, the Holy Panchen Jewel declared: "It has been said that you have been my disciple three times; thus I give you the title Güüshi Sechen Chöjé. You are my close son who defends the religion of Sumati; henceforth from here, your deeds will greatly spread."

Regarding Durar Nangso, son of the great interpreter Asdug Vajra Tümei Günding Dai Wang Güüshi, the Panchen Lama said: "In the ancient land of Uddiyana, you were the heart son of Garab Dorjé, and known as the The One Who Laughs with a Lotus Horse Voice.[44] Afterward, in the time of the middle cakravartin khan,[45] in this Snowy Land, [90v] you were born as the interpreter called Jogro Lu Gyeltsen. Now, in this eastern continent of copper, you have been born as Gendün Peljor Wangchuk, and it happens that we meet again. Thus it has come to pass that in three rebirths you have been my disciple." He gave him the title Garab Pandita Lu Gyeltsen, and owing to the existence of the name in the prophecy, he called him that, saying, "In this respect, you are my heart son." To Guru Tabunung he gave the title Güyang Tabunung, to Chidagana

Sanding the title Soga Güüshi, and to Tusatu Sechen Kiya the title Sechen Khonjin. And unto the other monks and laity alike, he made everyone ranked by giving them titles and names.

* * *

Then, when Tuba Taiji was leaving, he said through the interpreter Garab Pandita Lu Gyeltsen: "Previously, the Holy All-Knowing Vajradhara Dalai Lama, who made the sun rise on the dark continent, became our meritorious root supreme holy lama. Later, the All-Knowing Dalai Lama Yönten Gyatso was born into our royal lineage and proved to be very meritorious in support of the religion. And now, if the holy all-knowing one has compassion on us, he will return to the lands that are the country of the Mongols in the East."

Not emitting a single sound, the Dalai Lama cried and wept greatly. Whereupon Tripa Nangso Aua said: "Oh, holy lama, did you have bad thoughts when remembering the two former holy ones? Why are you weeping like this? Did you think, *Why should I go so far from my own native land?* Did you think, *The Mongol people will rob me by force*?" When he said this the Dalai Lama replied, "Not at all." Thereupon, everyone said, "This is a sign, how can it be an ordinary thing?" [91r] Then, as the Mongols were going out, he again summoned them and gave a teaching and did the initiation of the venerable encounter.

Thereupon, in that same Yi Ox year [1625], during the time when Tuba Taiji was returning this way, he said, "Previously Boshogtu Jinong Khan had this promise," and thus he acquired a Tanjur, the repository of the word, written in silver, and arrived safely in the Bing Tiger year [1626].

Then his mother, Queen Jönggen, assembled all the princes of the Ordos Tümen and had them invite Maitreya Dharmaraja, who strewed flowers on the Tanjur, the repository of the word, which was written in silver and gems. At that time, there came many envoys: leading the monks were Dalai Chöjé and Darkhan Chöjé of the Tümed; the envoys of Boshogtu Khan were Uski Yeldeng Tabunung and Kha'agatu Taiji; the envoys of Sereng Khung Taiji were Tanggudai Güyang Tabunung and Dalatu Chingsang; the envoys of of Darjiya Khung Taiji were Son-in-Law Ugchadba Urang Tanggarig and Gentleman Tanggud Güyang; the envoys of the Kharchin Khan[46] were Chöjé Üijeng Chö Gyatso and Tanggudai Güüshi; the envoy of Buyan Aqai was Bumban Öljeitü Kiya.

At that time, the second son of Boshogtu Jinong, Rinchen Eyechi Daiching, born in the Geng Rat year [1600], at the age of twenty-eight in the Ding Rabbit year [1627] ascended the throne. And when Sagang Sechen Khung Taiji proclaimed: "He is a descendant of proper persons of yore," the royal title was proclaimed. Thereupon, saying, "It is the custom for both the khan and ministers," they together listened to the initiation of the Splendid Vajrasattva from the majesty of the Dharmaraja Maitreya Khutugtu. By virtue of this meritorious blessing, they went and formed one group within the domains of Ligdan Khutugtu Khan.

Later, when the great people broke apart, Sagang Sechen Khung Taiji rode out with the army and fought with the nobles of Chakhar who had gone onto the steppe. [91v] In doing so he joined confidently with the three nobles called Julatu Baatur Kiya, Mendükei Darkhan Kiya, and Langso Ildüchi Baatur. By allying with the three hundred commoners they led, at the age of thirty-one in the Jia Dog year [1634], he turned back from the Khua River and returned.

At this time, he said to Rinchen Sechen Jinong, "We allied with the Chakhar and they have turned back. Now, after having taken you as our lord, let us return." Rinchen Jinong was very happy and agreed, thus straightaway they returned.

In this same Jia Dog year [1634], on an auspicious day (the third of the new phase of the fifth month) at a place called Great Marsh—"The Totally Perfect Region" revealed in the prophecy of the all-knowing one—they returned safely to the people of Sagang Sechen Khung Taiji. Rinchen Sechen Jinong went to his own nomadic lands and prayed to his supreme sacred object, the majestic Jowo Sakyamuni. He then settled down at his encampment.

At that time, the Jaisang of the Golden Stupa of the Chakhars, Sereng Bodomal, brought the Lord's White Tents to the younger brother, Tuba Taisung Khung Taiji, and had them pitched at his encampment. In this way the older and younger brother joined together with the great people. And in that same Jia Dog year [1634], when he was thirty-five, from in front of the Lord Father Chinggis Khan, Rinchen ascended to the former khan's throne as the one called Cakravartin Sechen Jinong.

* * *

At that time he assembled the vast, great people headed by the remaining great and lesser princes of the Ordos Tümen. Saying: "Now that we have emerged from the confusion, let us come together and go forward," he gave the title Father Prince to Duke Bodatai. And saying, "Having befriended us from the outset, he delivered us from the enemy [i.e., Ligdan Khan]," he gave to Sagang Sechen Khung Taiji the title Beloved Sechen Khung Taiji [92r] and granted him the right to be the leader in the center during the Grand Hunt. To the many other greater and lesser nobles and ministers who had in general given their might to the cause, he bestowed ranks in accord with prior practice, and they rejoiced peacefully with their hands and feet on the ground.

CHAPTER TWELVE

History of the Ming and Qing Dynasties

In both the epilogue and the colophon to the *Precious Summary* Sagang Sechen states that he wrote it over several months in 1662. In other words, he wrote this history twenty-seven years after the Ordos Mongols—with Sagang Sechen's support—had joined forces with the Manchus. The major thrust of this final chapter is to affirm the validity of the decision, which the narrative does through a twofold framework. First, it highlights again the chaotic and fragmentary situation among the Mongols during the early seventeenth century and thereby makes clear the urgent need for a new and functioning state. And it confirms that the Manchus are the ones destined to build this new political reality because they are both blessed by Heaven and pious Buddhists. In short, they are legitimate rulers—"Holy Ones"—who can build a functioning Buddhist state that offers both peace and salvation.

Nurhaci Baatur Taisui[1] was born into the old Manchu family of Altan Khan.[2] At the very outset he gathered a multitude through his means and strength. He brought into his power the Three Water Jürchid.[3] Next he took the state of Jing Taishi of the Great White Jürchid.[4] After that, in the Wu Horse year [1618] he campaigned against China, and when he captured Loudung,[5] the eastern province of the Great Ming Emperor, a comet came out of the heavens, and it was a major omen.[6] Vajra Tümei Günding Daiwang Güüshi of Ordos said, "Oh, this one called Taisui[7] is a man of great destiny.[8] This star is a brilliant spirit star of a very mighty khan. Hence he is not like ordinary men!" In this way the great powerful Nurhaci Baatur Taisui was famed in all directions.

* * *

His second son, Hong Taiji,[9] was born in the Ren Dragon year [1592], and from the age of twenty-nine in the Geng Tiger year,[10] he led the army. When he went campaigning outside the Manchu homeland toward China's violent Commander Duu, he fought valiantly and then returned. After this, those called the Three Taishis attacked through the city and seized very great booty and spoils. And when the land and people were destroyed, a prince called Sog Jaisang of the Five-Banner Khalkha[11] asked, "Why are you destroying the city that feeds my treasury?"

Whereupon Hong Taiji seized Prince Jaisang. [92v] Then his queen, sons, and people proclaimed, "While you are taking revenge on the enemy who seized the old city, why are you harming your own people?"

Hong Taiji replied, "If this is the case, so that I do no harm to the Mongols, you should think of the state, and for the peace of your princes, you need to admit your mistake and pay a fine, and then we can discuss it." He then took two taishis and 10,000 head of cattle, and released Prince Jaisang.[12]

After that, as more and more decrees and documents came out profusely, his strength and power became great. And while the Mongols on the borders were becoming scared, Hong Taiji went on campaign against Ligdan Khutugtu Khan and the Three Western Tümen.[13] Peacefully drawing in the princes of Khorchin, he made them bend the knee. He became famous to all as Sechen Khan.[14]

Thereupon, after Ligdan Khutugtu had been overcome by fate, his wife, Queen Mother Sutai—daughter of Delger Taishi, the son of Jing Taishi of the Jürchid—together with her son Erke Khonggur Khan, by Heavenly decree abandoned their own Chakhar and were received by four princes of royal rank in the fifth month of the Yi Pig year [1635] at Toli in Ordos's Otog Banner.[15] Taking the second wife of Ligdan, Empress Queen Mother, to his own royal body, Hong Taiji gave to Erke Khonggur his own daughter, Princess Erke Gürüne, who was born from the chief queen of his own people. Hong Taiji considerately treated as his own the two brothers Erke Khonggor and his younger brother, Abanai, who was born of Empress Queen Mother in the same month Ligdan Khutugtu

Khan died.[16] In this way, by taking the state of the Mongol khan at the age of forty-four in the Yi Pig year [1635], he became famed as the widely merciful one, the supremely virtuous, peaceful holy Sechen Khan.[17] [93r]

After this, when he was forty-six in the Ding Ox year [1637], he campaigned against China and besieged the city of Jingju for one year.[18] When he destroyed the forces of thirteen military commanders headed by Khung Sulang Baatur Süngbing,[19] he subdued the city of Jingju and then settled down healthy and well.[20]

Then the protectors of beings, the Holy Panchen Jewel and the All-Knowing Dalai Lama—who had bestowed the title Victorious Khutugtu on Güüshi Chöjé of the Miñag as prophesied before—dispatched him to the Qormusta of the East, the supreme wise holy Sechen Khan, with a document proclaiming: "When one considers the many other beings who are reborn in samsara of the three worlds, finding the precious body of one who has the opportunity for salvation is rarer than stars rising in the daytime. And within this, the appearance of a khan who gathers everything into his might is as difficult as finding a wish-fulfilling cintamani jewel. Therefore, having become the very mighty khan—who nurtures the great people with religion and the state—and thus an adversary of the present time of strife is indeed an achievement that merits being called a khan. Thus, to protect the religion of the Victorious One you must become an almsmaster of our precious religion."

When they dispatched this letter, with a seal and gifts, the khan himself received Victorious Khutugtu and made obeisance. And when he was invited to enter into the city of Mukden—"Which Gathers All Together"—Hong Taiji elevated Victorious Khutugtu to be the Achitu Lama, and with compassion in mind he received an initiation.[21] [93v]

Having heard the profound Dharma and finding the beginnings of religion, and since Victorious Khutugtu was going to return to Tibet in the Gui Sheep year [1643], Hong Taiji presented to his supreme lama an incomparable, unending amount of offerings. In the absence of the two holy lamas, he bestowed jewels, gold, silver, and various goods beyond measure, saying, "I am about to take Daidu, the city of the Great Ming Emperor; thus before completing my own worldly deeds, let me invite the two holy lamas, make obeisance to their majesty, and thereby promote the spread of the Buddha's religion." Having said these profound words and more, he dispatched the Victorious Khutugtu to Tibet.

* * *

Thereupon he set out on a campaign, saying, "Let me now take Daidu City!" While he was campaigning toward China, at the age of fifty-two in the Gui Sheep year [1643], by the power of fate he rose up to his Heavenly Father.

* * *

Thereafter in accordance with the deceased khan's order, the wangs, princes, and ministers went on campaign, and when they were laying siege to the city known as the Nine-Gated One,[22] the head of the Chinese bandits, named Chuvang Wang,[23] killed the Great Ming Chongjing emperor[24] and captured Daidu City. Thereupon the lord of Qaratai City,[25] Commander Wu,[26] surrendered to the khan's princes, who immediately unified the Manchus and Chinese and drove out Emperor Chuvang. In the Jia Monkey year [1644] [the Manchus] took the state of the Chinese emperor.

Thus, from that former Toghan Temür "the Intelligent" Khan of the Mongols, in the Wu Monkey year [1368], the Chinese Prince Jüge took Daidu City, and in his twenty-fifth year, the Wu Monkey year, he ascended the royal throne and became famed as the Great Ming Juu Khunggu emperor.[27] [94r]

* * *

Then the Intelligent Toghan Temür Khan and his third wife, Queen Gereltü, the daughter of Togta'a Taishi of the Qonggirad—who was then seven months pregnant—were separated. Having been abandoned, she was taken by the Khunggu emperor, and after three months, in that same Wu Monkey year [1368], a boy was born, whereupon Juu Khunggu proclaimed:

> "Formerly, my Heavenlike Lord showed me great favor.
> Now, be this his child or be he mine, let me nicely return the good graces;
> Let me make him a descendant of mine. Let not one of you not do likewise!"

and made him his descendant.[28]

With his second Chinese queen he had two sons, including the one named Juu Dagaya.[29] Then the father, Emperor Juu Khunggu, held the state of the people for thirty-one years, and at the age of fifty-five in the Wu Tiger year [1398], he died. Whereupon the greater and lesser Chinese ministers said, "Although the son of the Mongol queen is the elder brother, he is of a different man. After he grows up, there is no way to know if he will take revenge on the Chinese people. Although the son of the Chinese queen is the younger brother, because he is a descendant of ours, let us elevate him as emperor."

Juu Dagaya, born in the Ging Dog year [1370], at the age of twenty-nine in the Wu Tiger year [1398] was seated on the throne. But he departed this life in the same Wu Tiger year, after only four months and eighteen days elapsed.

* * *

Since he did not have any sons, the son of the Mongol queen, named Lord Yunglo,[30] at the age of thirty-two in the Ji Rabbit year [1399] ascended the throne. He invited one after the other the reincarnation of the Karmapa, Rolpé Dorjé;[31] the great lama of the Sakya, Tegchen Chöjé;[32] and the great caretaker of Sera monastery, Semchen Chöjé,[33] and when both the religion and the state were evenly established the vast great people were peaceful for the twenty-two years that he held the royal throne. [94v] In his fiftieth year, in the Ging Rat year [1420], he died.[34]

His son, Emperor Suvandi,[35] born in the Bing Tiger year [1386], ascended the throne at the age of thirty-six in the Xin Ox year [1421], and he made his own father's Semchen Chöjé the religious leader.[36] By the Two Realms of religion and state the vast great people were made happy, and after holding the throne for ten years, at the age of forty-five in the Ging Dog year [1430] he died. His son, Emperor Khungki,[37] born in the Ren Horse year [1402], ascended the throne at the age of thirty in the Xin Pig year [1431], and after three years, at the age of thirty-two in the Gui Ox year [1433], he died.

* * *

His son, Emperor Jingtai,[38] born in the Wu Dog year [1418], ascended the throne at the age of seventeen in the Ga Tiger year [1434]; after five years, in the Wu Horse year [1438]—when he was twenty-one—the Oirat Esen Taishi captured him. Immediately his younger brother, Emperor Jingtung,[39] born in the Ging Rat year [1420], ascended the throne in the Ji Sheep year [1439], when he was twenty. Five years later, in the Gui Pig year [1443], the Oirat returned the Jingtai emperor. The younger brother,

Emperor Jingtung, said, "You are the legitimate one, you should sit on the royal throne." Although he said that, his elder brother, Emperor Jingtai, said, "You rule! I have already been disfavored by Heaven; you should continue to rule." So it was that the younger brother remained as ruler. After three more years, for a total of eight, at the age of twenty-seven in the Bing Tiger year [1446], he died.

* * *

Then Emperor Jingtai, at the age of thirty in the Ding Hare year [1447], again peacefully ascended the throne and became famous as Emperor Teshün,[40] meaning "Bestowed by Heaven." After seventeen years, at the age of forty-six in the Gui Sheep year [1463], he died.

* * *

His son, Emperor Chingkhua,[41] born in the Jia Tiger year [1434], became ruler at the age of thirty-one in the Jia Monkey year [1464], and after twenty-three years, at the age of fifty-four in the Bing Horse year [1486], he died. His younger brother, Emperor Khungji,[42] born in the Gui Snake year [1449], became emperor at the age of thirty-nine in the Ding Sheep year [1487], and after eighteen years, at the age of fifty-six in the Jia Rat year [1504], he died.

* * *

His son, Emperor Jingden,[43] born in the Bing Dog year [1466], became ruler at the age of forty in the Yi Ox year [1505], [95r] and after sixteen years, at the age of fifty-five in the Ging Dragon year [1520], he died.

* * *

His son, Emperor Ji'ajing,[44] born in the Wu Horse year [1498], became ruler at the age of twenty-four in the Xin Snake year [1521], and after forty-five years, at the age of sixty-eight in the Yi Ox year [1565], he died.

* * *

His son, Emperor Lungching,[45] born in the Sim Horse year [1522], ascended the throne at the age of forty-five in the Bing Tiger year [1567], and after seven years elapsed, at the age of fifty-one in the Ren Monkey year [1572], he died.

* * *

His son, Emperor Wanli,[46] born in the Xin Pig year [1551], ascended the throne at the age of twenty-three in the Gui Rooster year [1573] and held the imperial state for forty-eight years. During the time he was ruler, as in the time of Yunglo and Suvandi, the vast great people became excessively happy. Then at the age of seventy in the Ging Monkey year [1620], he died.

His son, Emperor Taichang,[47] born in the Xin Snake year [1581], ascended the throne at the age of forty-one in the Xin Rooster year [1621], and after eleven months, at the same age of forty-one in the Xin Rooster year [1621], he died.

* * *

His son, Emperor Tenchi,[48] born in the Jia Dragon year [1604], ascended the throne at the age of nineteen in the Ren Dog year [1622], and after seven years, at the age of twenty-five in the Wu Dragon year [1628], he died.

His nephew, Emperor Chongjing,[49] born in the Ji Pig year [1599], ascended the throne at the age of thirty-one in the Ji Snake year [1629], and after sixteen years, in the Jia Monkey year [1644], the Ruling Peacefully Emperor of the Manchus took the imperial state.[50]

This Ruling Peacefully Emperor was born in the Wu Tiger year [1638], and at the age of seven in the Jia Monkey year [1644] sat upon the golden throne of China's Great Ming emperor and became famed in all directions as the Ruling Peacefully Emperor by taking into his power the Eighty Tümen of Chinese in the south, the Twenty-Six Tümen of Tibetans of Adag Kham in the west, [95v] the Four Tümen of Oirat in the east, the Thirty Tümen of White Koreans, the four central provinces of the Manchus, and the Six Tümen of Mongols. He bestowed among all the people such titles as *wang*, *beile*, *beise*, and *gong*, and more on the royal princes and officials, and showed favor unto each, high and low; justly ruling the vast great people, he maintained the jade great state in peace and tranquility.[51]

* * *

Thereupon, at the age of fourteen, in the Xin Rabbit year [1651], he proclaimed, "Previously, when my good father took Daidu City, he said, 'After having completed these worldly deeds, let me invite the two holy lamas to promote the Dharma.'" Thus [the Shunzhi emperor] sent for them, but when the two holy lamas were invited, the Holy Panchen Jewel said, "I am too old to travel," and declined to go. But the All-Knowing Dalai Lama Lozang Gyatso arose and came.

At the age of fifteen, in the Ren Dragon year [1652], outside the city of Daidu, [the Shunzhi emperor] had the Yellow Temple prepared and within it established in wondrous fashion a temple of the Buddhas of the Three Times.[52] In addition, he erected in a beautiful style a house for living, and a house for resting for the lama jewel and his retinue, as well as a treasury; thereby he greatly supported the powerful religion of the Victorious One.

He venerated the holy all-knowing one—the son of the Victorious One—making him an ornament of the crown. In absentia he took the Holy Panchen Jewel, the protector of living beings, as his lama. By very greatly supporting the religion of the Buddha, he fully established and pacified greatly the state of the holy ones. And by his not rocking the four directions and not upsetting the eight borders, the vast great people were pacified, [96r] which was the grace of this lord khan,[53] who had caused the gleaming sun of the Dharma to rise in the east. In this way, by satisfying the desires of men and beings of the outer regions and bringing peace to all sentient beings, he made everyone happy. In this way he held the imperial state for eighteen years, and at the age of twenty-four, in the Ren Ox year [1661], he proceeded to the land of the gods.

His son, Emperor Peace and Tranquility, born in the Jia Horse year [1654], ascended the throne at the age of nine in the Ren Tiger year [1662] and became famed in all directions as the "peace and tranquility emperor."[54] In the same year, when performing mourning rites for his late father he handed down a decree that allowed people in all directions to follow their own mourning customs, thereby making it legal for all to do their customary religious and worldly rites that benefited those who had passed on.

Thereupon, in order to receive a blessing from the two holy lamas, he dispatched and presented an incalculable amount of offerings to them, which included gold, silver, brocade, silk brocade, fur coats,[55] silk, velvet, and silken prayer scarfs.

Then the lord of the Tibetan people sent to Vajra Khan of the Oirat a yellow imperial decree and a seal with a weighty title, as well as presents.[56] Thereby Vajra Khan repaired the white road traversed by his fine father of yore, removing obstacles so that the majesty of the two holy lamas could go back and forth. Moreover, so that they could learn music, the essence of the paramitas, the treatises of knowledge, the sutras and dharanis, selected commentaries, and suitable melodies, he sent sixteen Oirat men to reside in the schools of the supreme land of Tibet.

At that time, in the Ren Tiger year [1662], the protector of beings, the Holy Panchen Jewel, who was born in the Xin Sheep year [1571] [96v]—which was 3,632 years from that same Wu Rat year—was ninety-two. Abandoning his bodily aggregates, he transmigrated by means of nirvana and arrived at the time of aiding beings in the land of Shambhala. Yet, although he evidently did go to that land, he also looked with eyes of compassion on beings in general—including the perfectly fated disciples of the present time, the meritorious almsmasters—and therefore said, "I will come straightaway and aid beings through my reincarnation, causing them to hear the happiness of the commandment of prophecy."[57]

When the emissary and document came to the supreme khan, there was great rejoicing.

* * *

Thus, by the grace of this lord khan, all the vast people had their desires fulfilled and rejoiced with their hands and feet resting on the ground.

CHAPTER THIRTEEN

Epilogue

About that former worldly material universe and
The various living beings relying on it,
Regarding the living beings from India's ruler Elevated by the Many,
Down to now, to the present time of strife,

About the birth of holy ones and powerful khans pacifying the earth,
The birth of meritorious bodhisattvas leading living beings,
And about all having been made joyful by the religion of the Buddha
    and the state of the holy ones,
Being unable to relate this fully, I am summarizing it at some length.

Great-grandson of the most Supreme Khutugtai Sechen Khung Taiji,
I, named Sagang Sechen Taiji, of very small intellect,
Relying thus on what I have seen and kept in mind of things necessary
    to know,
Speaking thus have I completed this book called *The Precious
    Summary of the Origin of Khans.*

Accordingly, by having examined a sutra called *The Meaningful and
    Important Necessity,*[1] [97r]
A treatise called *The Flower Bouquet Marvelous to Behold,*[2]

As well as *The Red Book, Causing one to Understand Nature, Circumstance, and Origin,*[3]

Likewise, *The Story of the Origin of the Khans,* composed by Sharba Khutugtu,[4]

The Chinese sastra called *The Flower Garden Illuminating the Mind of Savants,*[5]

The White History of the Dharma brought into being by the Supreme Sublime Cakravartin [Khubilai] Khan,[6] and

The Great Yellow History of the Origin of the Former Mongolian Khans,[7]

In this manner, by having seen and compared these seven works did I complete it.

From the year of my birth, called the Nine Red Wrathful Ones, this is the fifty-ninth

From the year just having waxed in the firmament [1662], called the Eight White Initiators,

Beginning in the second month, Uttaraphalguni, the eleventh day, that wood planet day of the victorious star (March 30),

I concluded it in Purvasadha month, at the entering of the first decade of the new moon, the Nali planet, and the Pausya star day (July 15).

* * *

Having tolerantly taken notice of the mistakes and erroneous faults in this,

Ye scholars, wise men and savants, examine, investigate, and correct it, without deriding it.

And as for the very small amount that is correct and is to be understood by aid of the heavenly wish-fulfilling jewel,

Let there be opened the lotus of intellect of those who have particular need to study it!

* * *

CHAPTER FOURTEEN

Colophon

I say these very words in verse.
Following what I have heard from the mouths of outstanding sages
And read in the truthful sutras and commentaries,
I offer them as illustration, an embellishment to the ears of the wise.

Following thus the teachings of ancient sages,
First I will deal with the joy that comes with liberation;
Then with the doleful suffering of the distressing cycle of rebirth;
The rise and fall of the material world;

The noble virtues of the original eminent people;
The good and evil deeds of such persons who are mediocre; [97v]
The evil faults of common people, clinging to the material world;
Together with the merits of the great people; of these seven,

The very first is the beneficial pleasure of liberation.
Thus, in the land of Akanistha that is not below anything,
There dwell limitless buddhas, headed by
The Supreme Vajradhara, the sixth over the Five Buddhas.

Those who have found the bliss of enlightenment in that realm
Are born from an immaculate lotus and

Have no suffering, only the joy of obtaining
The perfect and immortal vajra body.

If someone, in order to achieve this sanctity of pure enlightenment,
Trusts in the steadfast Three Jewels
And initiates undistracted bodhicitta mind,
It is needless to say, that person will become a purified buddha.

As for these three sublime and rare jewels,
They are blended into one in the person of one's benevolent lama.
Although one seek a refuge other than that one,
It is very difficult to find. Therefore,

The brilliant mind of one's benevolent lama
Embodies the many buddhas.
His spoken words are exclusively sublime teachings;
Moreover, his material body represents the holy samgha.

Therefore, until you find the bliss of true enlightenment,
You should rely completely on this meritorious teacher.
Until you fully understand the way of existence,
You should listen steadfastly to many teachings.

Of the various things to be said on the value of liberation:
How can I explain them completely?
Yet, according to my ability, what I am able to explain,
I have written here, as an adornment to the ears of those who need to know.

As for the second, it is the doleful sufferings of the rebirth cycle. [98r]
If one speaks of the beings in the dreary realm of hell,
They suffer, being cooked until they are boiled to jelly and peel apart;
Or die by bursting from cold on all sides, then recovering again.

When they finally die and are then reborn as hungry ghosts,
They will suffer hunger, unable to find food and drink.

Even if they find a little, they will be unable to satisfy their hunger.
Another suffering is when strong ones steal the food and do not let
them eat.

If one, in turn, is born as an animal,
There is the suffering of dying by various means
Because such animals possess hides and meat to be eaten,
Or the suffering of being laden and harnessed and afflicted with pack
sores.

Being born and dying in the cycle of rebirth, if one now finds a human
rebirth,
One revolves in samsara by the power of the corruption of birth:
Birth, death, illness, old age, and the like,
From these four great seas one cannot be delivered.

Then, if one transmigrates and is born among the demigods
Owing to the thought of desiring the pleasure of gods,
Thus letting blaze the fire of thedefilement of hatred and
By fighting and struggling with one another, there is eternal
suffering.

If one then transmigrates upward, being reborn as a god,
One will indulge in pleasures without comprehension,
Give birth to aversion to the guiding Dharma, and
Suffer on account of downfall, decline, and such things.

As for these evil sufferings of the rebirth cycle,
Who indeed can relate them perfectly and completely?
Even if it is so, I have related the six kinds of suffering,
Summing up each in one strophe only.

The third is the rise and fall of the material world, with
The suffering and mental anguish of elevated supreme ones,
The despair and bodily suffering of lowly small ones, and [98v]
The offensive harassment by vulgar evil people.

Very rich people may exhaust their property and become impoverished, and
When they beg from others, they are not given anything, though those see their need.
Great supreme ones may fall from their rank, and
Become slaves of ordinary men.

And again, even those who enjoy great happiness
May fall and see many various sufferings.
Stalwart youths, endowed with heroic strength,
May suffer being captured and forced to comply with the enemy's will.

Those whose mind is confused by treacherous devils
May become separated from their own liberating supreme teacher,
And fleeing from all their dear beloved ones
May be made to enter the trap of the murderous demons.

Now, accepting as true the words of evil people,
They become separated from their parents and kinfolk,
Even particularly suspecting their comrades whom they believed;
And being separated from these, they join the enemy.

Although one may become very wealthy, one cannot acquire everything.
As for the indigent and beggars, they too may be unable to find [what they need].
Even if living as a commoner, one may be taken by the enemy.
Obviously, happiness and suffering alternate.

Who indeed is able to relate to the end
The rise and fall of this material world?
If one says even a little, will not our thoughts be awakened?
With such a thought I summed up and relayed this in alliterating verses.

As for the fourth, if one speaks of the virtues of leading people:
They are the ten virtues, which comprise the four elements;

Like the pinnacle of the tent of the fully perfected holy ones,
They are suitable for the supreme lama who is to be relied upon.

It has been the rule of the holy ones, those with surpassing merits, [99r]
Who are like the jewel, the diamond, to not have mercy
On their own lives in striving for the bliss of buddhahood;
Nor on their bodies, indeed, for the benefit of others.

If one profoundly understands one's firmly intended deeds,
Keeping them like an inscription laid out and cut into stone,
And does not shy from being crushed by anybody,
That is the principle of the nobles, whom one should venerate.

If one is a fearless hero, he is the weapon of the army;
If an infallible shot, the marvel of the hunt;
If a trustworthy sage, an eternal ornament;
If a guileless wise man, a universal treasury.

The sublime sages and the wise, the gems, the gold,
The truly valiant men, and select geldings
Are the ornaments in their own land when they are at home
And objects of veneration when they go to other places.

However much extraordinary sages and savants weaken [with age],
Nonetheless, their knowledge and intellect increase all the more;
Like the marvelously precious jewel of gold, which
Increases its own color by burning in the fire.

Even famous nobles may be ruined at some time,
But from that they will have another instructive lesson.
However much one may cover the *sumana* flower,
Its fine fragrance will be felt everywhere.

Even if one oppresses select wise nobles,
Their royal virtue emerges once more.
Even if one take and turn upside down a lighted lamp,
Its burning fire goes blazing upward.

Even if two intelligent people argue with each other,
Some useful good words will be heard.
As when one makes steel and flint strike each other, [99v]
Behold the glowing fire blazing and burning.

Even when excellent sages and wise people live apart,
The words they say do indeed match as one.
As the shadow of a bird traveling through the heavens is,
When one regards it, just like the one sitting on the ground.

Those who abandon from the outset wicked sin and
Initiate meritorious thought from the heart are
Like the lotus flower that has grown
From the midst of a murky swamp.

Those who do not grow boastful, although having become
 very important, and
Who do not lose their senses, although being truly
 discouraged, are
Truly like fine gold, which when covered with dirt
Does not lose its color.

How is it possible to relate the excellent virtues
Of those abovementioned sublime foremost people?
I have thus discussed them a little
And written a few words after conversing a little with others.

As to the fifth, the mixed deeds of mediocre people:
Virtue pursued without a revered teacher is harmful.
Although salt improves the taste of food,
If one eat it plain, its bitter nature is astringent.

Those of little knowledge who have not studied profoundly
Recount their own virtues as soon as one meets them.
The mighty tiger angrily roars with pride;
The cat approaches a mouse stealthily in silence.

Even if they are truly knowledgable sages,
If they should become rough and tough,
They are like the beautiful peacock that has bright colors
Even though it eats poisonous food continuously.

Those who externally display an upright and honest
character [100r]
While internally being deceitful
Are, verily, like the interior of a silk scarf
That has amassed sharp and tough thorns.

One who, while perfecting unhindered his intellect and
wisdom,
Has fallen into the power of hindering laziness,
Is like a fine swift-running gelding
That has been tethered by hindering hobbles.

While studying the virtues only a little, most people
Speak excessively of other things out of pride.
Just as an arrow shot into the sky falls down,
Where else will it go than hitting the shooter's head?

Thus, since the difference in the merit and evil
Of the mixed deeds of mediocre people is so great,
How is one to relate all about such a varied group?
Consequently, I have written as such according to my ability.

As to the sixth, the faults of ill-mannered people:
The pupil who reveres his own teacher, but
Speaks evil about him when he is away,
What else is this pupil than a twin-tongued serpent?

An evil man who discloses to others
The confidential words of the heart
Is like a rough and wild powerful falcon
Who attacks his own shadow.

Those who are very greatly favored by princes and the elite
But who repay them with evil deeds
Are like a man sitting in the top of a tree on the edge of a cliff,
Who is, verily, cutting off the trunk.

Dissolute people, who repay with evil openly, and
Those who receive benefits but are not grateful
Are like what happens if one raises the cub of a savage wild wolf,
[100v]
Which thinks to attack its owner.

Those who, having become good friends immediately upon meeting,
Disrupt on the spot their own harmony straightaway;
What difference is there from travelers who encounter each other on their way
And then disperse, turning their backs, parting from each other?

One who does not know his own faults until he has grown old
But who relates nonetheless the faults of other men
Is like a despised ugly raven
Who has called the beautiful vulture blacker than himself.

The evil faults of these dissolute people,
Although unspeakable and unutterable by all means;
Since it is not befitting to speak very much of them,
I have spoken thus only summarizing here and there.

As to the seventh, the meritorious conduct of great men:
If they rely on the Three Jewels and the lama unfailingly,
He is like an arrow shot from below into the sky.
Why seek it here when it goes to places other than here?

One cannot reach the end of knowing the mighty Buddha's Dharma;
There is no coming to the end of religious actions taken by men;
The doctrine of samsara reveals that the end of one's life is transitory;
There is no separation of virtue at the end of the jeweled and beneficent Dharma.

Surely, this virtue, inseparable in the two fates [of reincarnation],
Is to be studied assiduously today, since one may die tomorrow;
If one delay greatly at present, saying it is not necessary until the next life;
Then one need consider what the eminent Nagarjuna has preached.

If one adorn well with perfect and desirable virtues
The body of a man who is provided with complete freedom,
It will be like dispersing the fruit that was obtained
From the leaves of the kalpavrksa tree evenly for all.

The words that have been said by knowledgable sages and savants, [101r]
Who well understand the consequences of past deeds,
Are like the beams of the rising moon; their light increases in the first decade
And later becomes brighter and brighter.

The admonishing words taught by our gracious parents,
Although heard first as stern, are later useful;
The king of pure medicines, named myrobalan,
Although bitter to the taste, is later delicious.

Although one long associates with nobles of lineage,
Its soothing benefit, that works both overtly and hidden,
Illuminates the four continents indiscriminately
By the beams of the shining sun, which illuminates clearly.

Improving and getting worse are not one and the same;
If one becomes disturbed, let one's own virtue not be forgotten;
Although the moon fades when the sun approaches,
Behold the full moon again in the first half of the month!

Even if one's life is going well, there should not be excessive pride;
And if things get worse, one should not get especially discouraged.

Although the gleaming sun disappears behind Mount Sumeru at night,
It gleams again so much the more the next day.

For those who strive to learn many virtues,
What need is there for excessive cruel pride?
Those who boast while having no virtue
Are like dead tiger skins stuffed with grass.

Now even if one sees many other living beings,
It is much more important to seek and obtain
The jewel-like human body endowed with freedom
Than to become a powerful heavenly cakravartin khan.

While it is very difficult to obtain such a thing,
It is likewise very easy to lose it,
Like the immediate, swift coming [101v]
Of a thunderclap descending from heaven.

Reflecting on this principle , if one thus investigates and comprehends them,
Striving valiantly, one will be delighted with pleasure,
But be aware, the beautiful and colorful rainbow
May go away, vanishing into the same emptiness.

The corporeal body adorned with materiality, and
The jewel-like body adorned with understanding and wisdom,
Both follow the law of reincarnation and will pass away,
Which is like the law of day turning to night.

If one lets the meritorious human body, which is endowed with freedom,
Decay by lowly evil conduct,
It is like having wrongly traded black charcoal for
An elaborate and exquisite fine golden jewel.

Wise and sagacious men, who are adorned with virtues,
Should consider the precious human body that is complete in various ways,

Like as if they found in the jewel-endowed great ocean
The actual *cintamani*, the wish-fulfilling jewel.

If, in general, you consider this fully functioning human body,
It is the basic support, necessary for at least the two fates,
And is like a great ship that is able to carry
Those of the nine kinds of birth across the ocean of samsara. Then

That which, in various ways, is a marvel for all is the words of the Dharma.
Its resounding fame is a source of joy in this world.
To help now the living beings is the adornment of nirvana, and
Thus, the merit that goes to the next world is a source of joy.

The prophetic name, given as soon as one is born,
The renowned name, having transmitted one's fame when mature, and
The eternal name, to be remembered by posterity alone,
If all these are manifestly complete, that is the merit of human existence.

As for the reasons for my having arranged, uttered, and written down [102r]
All these and other words,
It was not because I suddenly sat down and felt myself to be wise
And spoke spontaneously with excessive pride,

But relying on what some few juniors and children, desirous of learning, said:
"Write something for our instruction in rhyming quatrains
About the good, the bad, and the mixed behaviors to be studied,
And being ready to learn, we will keep it in our minds!"

So I, named and called Erke Sechen Sagang Taiji,
Who was born of the grandson of the very first son
Of Sechen Khung Taiji, the aggregate jewel heart,
Wrote these words I came up with in relation to my abilities.

Faithfully, kneeling and praying by means of the third gate (i.e., the mind),
To Vajradhara, the guru with complete threefold grace,
I joined thirty times ten and four times four verses[1]
Into seven times ten plus three times three verses.[2]

In the fifty-ninth year from the one of my birth, called the Wrathful One [1604],
In the Asvini month of the year called Founder of Merit [1662], when this poem was started,
On the 22nd, at the time of the great festival of the descent from Tusita heaven,
On the wood planet day of the Pausya star,[3] I have finished it.

For the mistakes and erroneous faults in it,
I respectfully beg pardon from the learned savants.
By the meritorious sun, the little amount that has been gotten right,
Let the lotus flower of the mind of those who need it be opened.

May the meritorious fundamental supreme lama
Open the gate of the immortal vajra body, [102v]
Let him cause flawless tranquility greatly to blaze, and
Cause the predominant immortal vajra body to be found.

May the unhindered meritorious fundamental supreme lama
Open the gate of the unhindered vajra speech,
May he allow us to obtain that unimpaired vajra speech,
Unrestricted, full of all the sixty branches.

May the jewel-like meritorious fundamental supreme lama
Open the gate of the faultless vajra mind,
And may he let us obtain the indestructible vajra mind
That combines emptiness and quietude without attachments to this world.

Notes

INTRODUCTION

1. The scholarship reevaluating the history of the Mongol empire has expanded greatly over the last two decades. See, for example, Thomas T. Allsen, *Culture and Conquest in Mongol Eurasia* (Cambridge: Cambridge University Press, 2001); Thomas T. Allsen, *Commodity and Exchange in the Mongol Empire: A Cultural History of Islamic Textiles* (Cambridge: Cambridge University Press, 1997); Michal Biran, *Chinggis Khan* (Oxford: Oneworld Publications, 2007); Marie Favereau, *The Horde: How the Mongols Changed the World* (Cambridge: Belknap Press, 2021); Peter Jackson, *The Mongols and the Islamic World: From Conquest to Conversion* (New Haven, CT: Yale University Press, 2017); Timothy May, *The Mongol Empire* (Edinburgh: Edinburgh University Press, 2018); Timothy May, *The Mongol Conquests in World History* (London: Reaktion Books, 2012); Roxann Prazniak, *Sudden Appearances: The Mongol Turn in Commerce, Belief, and Art* (Honolulu: University of Hawai'i Press, 2019); Morris Rossabi, *The Mongols and Global History* (New York: Norton, 2010).
2. On the impact of Mongolian nationalist and communist historiography in shaping the modern understanding of Mongol history see Johan Elverskog, "The Story of Zhu and the Mongols of the 17th century," *Ming Studies* 50 (2004): 39–76.
3. On the lasting power of the Northern Yuan and Zhu Yuanzhang's attempts to deal with it see David M. Robinson, *In the Shadow of the Mongol Empire: Ming China and Eurasia* (New York: Cambridge University Press, 2020).

4. Jasper Becker, *City of Heavenly Tranquility: Beijing in the History of China* (New York: Oxford University Press. 2008), 18.
5. On the Ming-Mongol horse trade see Henry Serruys, *Sino-Mongol Relations During the Ming III. Trade Relations: The Horse Fairs (1400–1600)* (Bruxelles: Institut Belge des Hautes Études Chinoises, 1975).
6. Elliot Sperling, "The Szechwan-Tibet Frontier in the Fifteenth Century," *Ming Studies* 26 (1988): 37–55. On the earlier Sino-Tibetan tea trade see Paul J. Smith, *Taxing Heaven's Storehouse: Horses, Bureaucrats, and the Destruction of the Sichuan Tea Trade, 1074–1224* (Cambridge, MA: Council on East Asian Studies, 1991).
7. Morris Rossabi, "Ming Foreign Policy: The Case of Hami," in *China and Her Neighbours: Borders, Visions of the Other, Foreign Policy 10th to 19th Century*, ed. Sabine Dabringhaus and Roderich Ptak (Wiesbaden: Harrassowitz, 1997), 79–97.
8. The Oirat seizure of the emperor had profound consequences for the Ming (F. W. Mote, "The T'u-mu Incident of 1449," in *Chinese Ways in Warfare*, ed. Frank Kierman Jr. and John K. Fairbank [Cambridge: Harvard University Press, 1974], 243–272); one scholar has claimed that it changed forever the Ming intellectual world (Chu Hung-lam, "Intellectual Trends in the Fifteenth Century," *Ming Studies* 27 [1989]: 9), and another has suggested that it played a fundamental role in the subsequent Ming turn inward (Timothy Brook, "Commerce: The Ming in the World," in *Ming: 50 Years that Changed China*, ed. Craig Clunas et al. [Seattle: University of Washington Press, 2014], 274).
9. On the issue of environmental problems on the Mongolian plateau and their impact see Okada Hidehiro, "Outer Mongolia in the Sixteenth and Seventeenth Centuries," *Journal of Asian and African Studies* 5 (1972): 69–85; and James Geiss, "The Chia-ching reign, 1522–1566," in *The Cambridge History of China, vol 8,1*, ed. F. W. Mote (New York: Cambridge University Press, 1988), 440–510.
10. Louis Hambis, "Note sur l'installation des Mongols dans la Boucle du Fleuve Jaune," in *Mongolian Studies*, ed. Louis Ligeti (Amsterdam: B. R. Grüner, 1970), 167–179.
11. The six groups were divided into two wings: the Western Tümen comprised the Ordos, Tümed, and Yüngshiyebü (with the Asud and Kharchin); and the Eastern Tümen the Chakhar, Khalkha, and Khorchin (it had also included the Uriyangkhan; however, they were dismantled as a Tümen after their 1538 revolt). After Dayan Khan reunited the Six Tümen in 1510, he divided them among his sons. He made his son Barsubolod the *jinong*, or "viceroy" of the Three Western Tümen, who not only ruled over them but also administered the cult of Chinggis Khan in Ordos, where Mongol rulers were ritually recognized.

12. Christopher P. Atwood, "Banner, Otog, Thousand: Appanage Communities as the Basic Unit of Traditional Mongolian Society," *Mongolian Studies* 34 (2012): 20.
13. The same idea is also reflected in Nurhaci's letter sent to the Khalkhas in 1620, wherein Chinggis Khan is described as taking the Jin state (Man. *doro*). "Thinking the worst, [the Jin] attacked, but Heaven favored Temüjin, and so the Mongol Chinggis Khan took the state from the Jin Khan," quoted in Mark C. Elliott, "Manchu Historical Consciousness in the Early Qing," in *Temporalities of the Ming-Qing Transition*, ed. Lynn Struve (Honolulu: University of Hawai'i Press, 2004), 31.
14. On the theory of "Great States" in Inner and East Asian history see Timothy Brook, "Great States," *The Journal of Asian Studies* 75, no. 4 (2016): 957–972.
15. In this regard it is also relevant that the "Kitad Ulus"—the Chinese nation—did not include the former Song territories, which in the Mongols' imperial categorization were the "Southern" Nanggiyad Ulus.
16. The seventeenth-century Mongol histories are often identified together as the Mongol chronicles. In addition to Sagang Sechen's *Precious Summary*, they include Lubsangdanjin's *Golden Summary* (*Altan Tobči*) from the 1650s, the undated and anonymous *Golden Summary* (*Altan Tobči*), the anonymous *Yellow History* (*Šira Tuyuji*), and Byamba Erke Daiching's late seventeenth-century *Asaragchi's History* (*Asarayči neretü-yin teüke*). While these sources follow the same theory of world history in a similar structural format and contain many of the same episodes, poems, and stories drawn from the *Secret History*, oral lore, and Buddhist historiography, there are also differences based on regional orientations. For an introduction to and overview of these works see Walther Heissig, *Die Familien- und Kirchengeschichts-schreibung der Mongolen. Teil I: 16.-18. Jahrhundert* (Wiesbaden: Otto Harrassowitz, 1959) and Shagdaryn Bira, *Mongolian Historical Writing from 1200 to 1700*, trans. John R. Krueger (Bellingham: Center for East Asian Studies, Western Washington University, 2002). There is also an extant Mongolian history from 1607, the *Jewel Translucent Sutra* (*Erdeni tunumal sudur*), which focuses on Altan Khan and his descendants.
17. For a detailed study of the "Two Realms" (M. *qoyar yosu*, T. *yon mchod*) theory of rule see David S. Ruegg, *Ordre spiritual et ordre temporal dans la pensée bouddhique de l'Inde et du Tibet* (Paris: Collège de France, 1995).
18. Trade between the Mongols and the Ming court was essential for the functioning of their economic, military, and political systems; however, with the chaos of the early seventeenth century these trade networks collapsed. A telling example of this disruption is the horse trade: in the early fifteenth century the Ming army received 1,700,000 horses from the Mongols, but during the rise of the

Qing they could barely maintain 100,000 regular mounts for its cavalry. Frederic Wakeman, Jr., *The Great Enterprise: The Manchu Reconstruction of Imperial Order in Seventeenth-Century China* (Berkeley: University of California Press, 1985), 202–203. This deficit clearly affected not only how the Ming could respond to Qing encroachments but also the socioeconomic environment among the Mongols and their decisions regarding their relations with the Manchus.

19. Li Baowen, *Arban doloduγar jaγun-u emün-e qaγas-tu qolbuγdaγu Mongγol üsüg-ün bicig debter. Shiqi shiji menggu wen wenshu dang'an (1600–1650)* (Tongliao: Obör Mongγol-un baγacud keüked-ün keblel-ün qoriy-a, 1997), 143. On the ferocity of this war and its implications see Nicola Di Cosmo, "Military Aspects of the Manchu Wars against the Caqars," in *Warfare in Inner Asian History (500–1800)*, ed. Nicola Di Cosmo (Leiden: Brill, 2002), 337–367.
20. Sabine Dabringhaus, "Chinese Emperors and Tibetan Monks: Religion as an Instrument of Rule," in *China and Her Neighbours: Borders, Visions of the Other, Foreign Policy 10th to 19th Century China*, ed. Sabine Dabringhaus and Roderich Ptak (Wiesbaden: Harrassowitz, 1997), 122.
21. Samuel Grupper, "Manchu Patronage and Tibetan Buddhism During the First Half of the Ch'ing Dynasty," *The Journal of the Tibet Society* 4 (1984): 53.
22. On Sagang Sechen's life see Antoine Mostaert, *Erdeni-yin Tobči: Mongolian Chronicle by Saγang Sečen* (Cambridge, MA: Harvard University Press. 1956), 1–29.
23. After a rebellion against Manchu rule in 1649 the Ordos was divided into six banners. This may have been when Sagang Sechen moved north. Regardless, northern Üüshin banner is where his grave is located and where the rituals commemorating Sagang Sechen that developed later were performed. Antoine Mostaert, "Sur le culte de Saγang Sečen et de son bisaieul Qutuγtai Sečen chez les Ordos," *Harvard Journal of Asiatic Studies* 20 (1957): 534–566.
24. Chiodo notes that the recently discovered manuscript from Kentei Aimag "provides further evidence that Sagang Sechen's masterwork was held in high esteem by the Mongols of different areas." Elisabetta Chiodo, *Saγang Sečen. Erdeni-yin Tobči: A Manuscript from Kentei Ayimaγ* (Wiesbaden: Harrassowitz Verlag, 1996), 4.
25. On the numerous extant manuscript copies of the *Precious Summary* held in the archives of China, Mongolia, and Russia see Saγang Sečen, *Erdeni-yin Tobči. ('Precious Summary') A Mongolian Chronicle of 1662. vol. I*, ed. M. GØ, I. de Rachewiltz, J. R. Krueger, and B. Ulaan (Canberra: The Australian National University, 1990), v–vii. On the interrelationship of these manuscripts see Morikawa Tetsuo, "Manuscripts of *Erdeni-yin Tobči* and Their Connections," *Journal of Asian and African Studies* 50 (1995): 1–41; and Morikawa Tetsuo, "The

Manuscripts and Manuscript Families of the *Erdeni-yin tobči*," *Memoirs of the Research Department of the Toyo Bunko* 59 (2001): 49–86.

26. This translation into German was prepared by Isaak Jacob Schmidt (1779–1847), a Moravian missionary among the Kalmyks in southern Russia. Hartmut Walravens, *Isaak Jacob Schmidt (1779–1847)—Leben und Werk des Pioneers der mongolischen und tibetischen Studien: Eine Dokumentation* (Wiesbaden: Harrassowitz Verlag, 2005). It has recently been republished in a modern German version: Sagang Sechen, *Geschichte der Mongolen und ihres Fürstenhauses, Herausgegeben und mit einem Nachwort von Walther Heissig* (Zürich: Manesse Verlag, 1985).
27. On the soteriological significance of the Manchu rulers see Matthew W. King, *Ocean of Milk, Ocean of Blood: A Mongolian Monk in the Ruins of the Qing Empire* (New York: Columbia University Press, 2019).
28. On the many Buddhist works that Sagang Sechen drew upon see György Kara, "On Some Sources of Sagang Sechen's Teachings (1662)," *Acta Orientalia Academiae Scieniarum Hungaricae* 73, no. 4 (2020): 603–615; György Kara, "Sagang Sechen's Teachings Reconsidered," *Acta Orientalia Academiae Scientiarum Hungaricae* 74, 2 (2021): 267–324.
29. On Sagang Sechen's use of Chinese and Tibetan sources see Heissig, *Die Familien*, 48–50, 103.
30. Although Lubsangdanjin's *Golden Summary* includes almost two-thirds of the *Secret History*, Sagang Sechen only includes the earliest part that covers the legendary prehistory of the Mongols and the early life of Chinggis Khan (up to *Secret History* § 93). Igor de Rachewiltz, *The Secret History of the Mongols: A Mongolian Epic Chronicle of the Thirteenth Century* (Leiden: Brill, 2004), 1–29.
31. The most important of these sources was the *Golden Summary of Chinggis Khan* (*Činggis Qaγan-u Altan Tobči*), a compilation of seventeen distinct stories about Chinggis Khan that had developed in the fourteenth and fifteenth centuries. Sagang Sechen incorporates fifteen of them in his telling of the history of Chinggis Khan. It is also likely that he used both versions of the *Golden Summary* in writing the *Precious Summary*.
32. On the elaborate poetic forms used by Sagang Sechen see John R. Krueger, *Poetical Passages in the Erdeni-yin Tobči. A Mongolian Chronicle of the Year 1662 by Saγang Sečen* (The Hague: Mouton, 1961).
33. Although this scholarly history is beyond the scope of this study see, for example, Johan Elverskog, "Things & the Qing: Mongol Culture in the Visual Narrative," *Inner Asia* 6 (2004): 137–178; Johan Elverskog, "Sagang Sechen on the Qing Conquest," in *The Black Master: Essays on Central Eurasia in Honor of Professor György Kara on his 70th Birthday*, ed. Stéphane Grivelet, Ruth Meserve, Àgnes Birtalan, and Giovanni Stary (Wiesbaden: Harrassowitz Verlag, 2005),

43–56. One memorable episode is the *Uiguren-Streit* between Julius Klaproth (1783–1835) and I. J. Schmidt. This debate pitted the German philologist—who argued that there was a link between the ancient Uighurs of the steppe and those of Xinjiang—against the Moravian missionary, who, based on the *Precious Summary*, argued that the ancient Uighurs were actually Tibetan; more specifically, that they were related to the Tanguts. David Brophy, *Uyghur Nation: Reform and Revolution on the Russia-China Frontier* (Cambridge, MA: Harvard University Press, 2016), 44–47.

34. This translation is based on the "enhanced" version of the Urga manuscript published by Igor de Rachewiltz and John R. Krueger in 1990 (Saγang Sečen, *Erdeni-yin Tobči*).

35. To organize the material into coherent historical sections I have divided the text into chapters that do not exist in the original; however, I have preserved the punctuation marks (the three asterixes) that are used in the manuscript to mark off discrete episodes in the narrative.

36. To enhance the reading experience I have also tried to simplify as much as possible the complicated Mongolian, Tibetan, and Chinese terms found throughout the text. To this end I use the transcription of Mongolian from Christopher P. Atwood's *Encyclopedia of Mongolia and the Mongol Empire* (New York: Facts on File, 2004). I have transliterated all the Tibetan terms into the current scholarly standard: THDL. For Chinese terms, I have transliterated Sagang Sechen's phonological transliterations and then provided the characters and *pinyin* in the notes.

1. HISTORY OF THE UNIVERSE, THE BUDDHA, AND INDIA

1. The Three Jewels are the "three principal objects of veneration: the Buddha, the Dharma, and the samgha. One of the most common practices that define a Buddhist is 'taking refuge' in the three jewels. This formula, which accompanies many lay and monastic rituals, involves a formal declaration that the practitioner 'goes to' each of the above three jewels for refuge (śaraṇa) or protection." Robert E. Buswell, Jr., and Donald S. Lopez, Jr., *The Princeton Dictionary of Buddhism* (Princeton, NJ: Princeton University Press, 2014), 704.

2. The Three Bodies of the Buddha is "one of the central doctrines of Mahayana buddhology. The three bodies refer specifically to the three distinct bodies or aspects of a buddha: Dharmakāya, the 'dharma body' or 'truth body'; Saṃbhogakāya, the 'enjoyment body' or 'reward body'; and Nirmāṇakāya, 'emanation body' or 'transformation body' (Buswell and Lopez, *Dictionary*, 923).

3. The Three Times refers to the past, present, and future.

4. Vajradhara is "an important buddha of the tantric systems, where he appears in some texts as an ādhibuddha (primordial buddha). He is closely related to Vajrapāṇī; indeed, Vajrapāṇī and Vajradhara may have originally been two names for the same deity (the Chinese translations of the two deities' names are the same). . . . Vajradhara is sometimes referred to as the sixth buddha, representing the quintessence of the five buddhas (pañcatathāgata) and the five Buddha families. In Tibetan Buddhism, he is one of two buddhas considered as both a primordial Buddha (ādibuddha) and as a dharmakāya. . . . Vajradhara is the primordial buddha of the three new, or gsar ma, sects, Sa skya, Bka' rgyud, and Dge lugs" (Buswell and Lopez, *Dictionary*, 954).
5. There are Three Realms of existence in samsara "in which beings take rebirth: the sensuous, or desire, realm (kāmadhātu); the subtle-materiality, or form, realm (rūpadhātu); and the immaterial, or formless, realm (ārāpyadhātu)" (Buswell and Lopez, *Dictionary*, 920).
6. The Three Perfect Ones are the Bodhisattvas Avalokitesvara, Manjusri, and Vajrapani (Buswell and Lopez, *Dictionary*, 1094).
7. It is unclear who the "three benevolent lamas" are in this case; however, it is likely that two of them are the Dalai Lama and Panchen Lama, both of whom play important roles in the history of Mongolian Buddhism.
8. This passage encapsulates the Buddhist religiopolitical vision that frames the *Precious Summary*: for there to be both the possibility of liberation and just rule, there need to be both "bodhisattvas"—or lamas—who can teach the Dharma and righteous rulers, "Holy Ones"—like the Tibetan emperors, Mongol khans, or Manchu emperors—who both support the Dharma and rule according to its principles.
9. The myth of Mahasammata is a Buddhist version of the Hindu story of the lawgiver Manu and is found in a wide array of Buddhist literature. Ronald M. Davidson, *Indian Esoteric Buddhism: A Social History of the Tantric Movement* (New York: Columbia University Press, 2002), 132.
10. The Buddhist cosmological creation story presented here comes from Vasubandhu's fourth-century *Abhidharmakośabhāṣya*, which became a foundational part of the Inner Asian Buddhist tradition through its incorporation in Pakpa Lama's thirteenth-century primer on Buddhism written for Khubilai Khan's son, *What Is to Be Known* (*Shes bya rab gsal*). Constance Hoog, *Prince Jin-gim's Textbook of Tibetan Buddhism* (Leiden: E. J. Brill. 1983), 7, 83.
11. Mount Sumeru is the central axis in Buddhist cosmology. It is said to be eight leagues high, and its four faces are flat and each composed of a "different precious stone: gold in the north, silver in the east, lapis lazuli in the south, and crystal in the west. The substance determines the color of the sky over each of the continents. The sky is blue in the southern continent of Jambudvipa because

the southern face of Mount Sumeru is made of lapis. The slopes of Sumeru are the abode of the demigods (asura), and its upper reaches are the heavens of the four heavenly kings. At the summit of the mountain is the heaven of the thirty-three, ruled by the king of the gods, Sakra. Above Mount Sumeru are located the remaining heavens of the sensuous realm" (Buswell and Lopez, *Dictionary,* 869).

12. Mount Sumeru is surrounded by four island continents, one in each of the cardinal directions, all of which are flanked by two island subcontinents. "The northern continent is square, the eastern semi-circular, the southern triangular, and the western round. Although humans inhabit all four continents, the 'known world' is the southern continent, named Jambudvīpa" (Buswell and Lopez, *Dictionary,* 869).
13. Buddha Samantabhadra is the primordial Buddha according to the Nyingma tradition of Tibetan Buddhism. "He is depicted naked, blue, and in sexual union with his consort Samantabhadri. He is the embodiment of the original purity of all phenomena of saṃsāra and nirvāṇa. Called the 'primordial basis' (*ye gzhi*), he is regarded as the eternal union of awareness (*rig pa*) and emptiness (*śūnyatā*), of emptiness and appearance, and of the nature of the mind and compassion. As such he is the wellspring of the Atiyoga teachings" (Buswell and Lopez, *Dictionary,* 745).
14. Each cakravartin, or "wheel-turning king," is supposed to possess an actual wheel, floating in space, that represents his sovereign power. Robert E. Buswell, Jr., *Encyclopedia of Buddhism* (New York: Macmillan Reference, 2004), 424–425.
15. In Buddhist cosmology, Jambudvipa is the southern continent where humans reside (see note 12).
16. According to the earliest Buddhist texts there are seven Buddhas that have appeared through history: Vipasyin, Sikhin, Visvabhu, Krakucchanda, Kanakamuni, Kasyapa, and Sakyamuni.
17. In the Tibetan tradition the story of all the Buddha's lives is structured around twelve acts: 1. dwelling in Tusita heaven; 2. descent from Tusita heaven; 3. entering his mother's womb; 4. birth; 5. enjoyment of proficiency in worldly skills and sensuality; 6. disenchantment with a life of pleasure; 7. leaving the palace; 8. practice of asceticism; 9. defeat of Mara; 10. attainment of complete awakening; 11. teaching the Dharma; 12. "full going out," *parinirvana*. Rupert Gethin, *The Foundations of Buddhism* (New York: Oxford University Press, 1998), 17–27.
18. Atisa (982–1054), the son of a minor northeast Indian ruler, entered the monkhood after some years of marriage and was given the name Dipankara Srijnana. He studied at the four great monastic universities of the Pala dynasty, then traveled south, probably to Sumatra, where he studied Mind-Only philosophy.

Atisa then returned to India and was appointed abbot of Vikramasila monastery, where he promoted monastic renewal. Thereafter, Yeshe Ö, the king of Ngari, invited Atisa to Tibet. He arrived in 1042 and in collaboration with Tibetans translated the *Perfection of Wisdom* literature, fundamental texts of the Madhyamaka, and composed the *Lamp for the Path* (*Byang chub sgron me*). His most important disciple was Dromtonpa Gyelwa Jungne (1005–1064), who founded Reting, the first Kadampa monastery (Buswell, *Encyclopedia*, 35–36).

19. As is evident from this section, the dating of the Buddha has long been debated by Buddhist scholars. More recently, modern scholars have identified two chronologies for the life of the Buddha, long and short. For the scholarly debates, see Heinz Bechert, ed., *The Dating of the Historical Buddha*, 3 vols. (Göttingen: Vandenhoeck & Ruprecht, 1991–1992).
20. The actual date of the Jia Monkey year is unclear; however, what it—and the preceding Yi Ox year—reveal is Sagang Sechen's distinctive form of calendar reckoning. Thus, unlike all the other Mongolian histories from the seventeenth century that use the Tibetan system of calendar reckoning, Sagang Sechen uses neither the Tibetan system nor the widely used color-animal form, but rather the old Uygur form that combines the ten Chinese heavenly stems with the traditional twelve-animal cycle. On the history and development of this earlier Sino-Uygur-Mongol system of calendar reckoning see Brian Baumann, *Divine Knowledge: Buddhist Mathematics According to the Anonymous Manual of Mongolian Astrology and Divination* (Leiden: Brill, 2008), 61–63.
21. The *Wheel of Time* (*Kalacakratantra*) is the most important Buddhist tantric teaching in the Gelukpa tradition.
22. Sakya Pandita Kungga Gyeltsen (1182–1251) was the leader of Sakya monastery who in 1244 was invited by the Mongol Prince Köden to Liangzhou 涼州. He arrived there late in 1246, though he did not meet Köden till early 1247 because the latter was in Mongolia. After this meeting Sakya Pandita sent a manifesto to all the political and ecclesiastical leaders of Tibet urging their acceptance of Mongol sovereignty with the Sakya as their feudatory representatives. However, this agreement became only theoretical because Güyük Khan died in 1248, leaving Mongol politics in disarray. In 1251 when Möngke became khan the Tibet policy altered drastically, in that the Sakya were neglected and Tibet was instead divided into appanages and then subsequently invaded. Not until Khubilai Khan and Pakpa Lama was there a return to the Mongol-Sakya relationship envisioned by Köden and Sakya Pandita. He died at his monastery in Liangzhou in 1251; his remains are still kept there in a stupa. David Jackson, *The Entrance Gate for the Wise (Section III). Sa-skya Pandita on Indian and Tibetan Traditions of Pramana and Philosophical Debate. 2 vols.* (Wien: Arbeitskreis für Tibetische und Buddhistische Studien Universität Wien, 1989), 15–29; Luciano Petech,

Central Tibet and the Mongols: The Yüan-Sa-skya Period of Tibetan History (Rome: Istituto Italiano per il Medio Estremo Oriente. 1990), 5–16.

23. The *Golden Beam Sutra* (*Suvarnaprabhāsottama Sūtra*) is a central text of the Mahayana tradition, which became an especially important work among the Mongols. Ts. Damdinsüren, "Two Mongolian Colophons of the *Suvarnaprabhāsottama-Sutra*," *Acta Orientalia Academiae Scientiarum Hungaricae* 33, 1 (1979): 39–58.
24. Sagang Sechen's two-verse poetic rendering is based on a prose passage in chapter 2 of the *Golden Beam Sutra*: "The Buddha does not enter complete Nirvāna (and) the Law does not disappear. For the ripening of beings does he teach complete Nirvāna. The Lord Buddha is inconceivable. The Tathāgata has an eternal body. He shows various manifestations by reason of the welfare of beings." R. E. Emmerick, *The Sūtra of Golden Light: Being a Translation of the Suvarnabhsāsottamasūtra* (London: Luzac & Company, 1970), 8.
25. Dampa Togkar (T. *Dam pa tog dkar*, Holy White Peak) is the Buddha's name during his pre-existence in Tusita heaven.
26. Airavata, the god Indra's steed, is a white elephant with five trunks and ten tusks.
27. Lumbini is the name of the Buddha's birthplace, which is now "Rummindei in the Terai region of modern Nepal. The Buddha's mother Maya was traveling from her home in Kapilavastu to her parents' home to give birth when she went into labor at Lumbini. According to traditional accounts, she gave birth while standing between two śāla trees. It is said that the Buddha stepped out of her right side and was born" (Buswell and Lopez, *Dictionary*, 483).
28. Kapilavastu was "the capital city of the Sakya tribe and the hometown of the buddha Gautama. The city was located north of the larger region of Kosala, in the foothills of modern-day Nepal" (Buswell and Lopez, *Dictionary*, 418).
29. In their astrological manuals the Mongols collated five different calendar systems in order to identify the months—1. Indian; 2. "Chinese peasant"; 3. "Chinese scholarly"; 4. Tibetan; 5. Mongolian—and in this case Sagang Sechen uses the Mongolian term (Mo. *šušay*), which corresponds to the Sanskrit month of Vishaka. In India, this is the last month of spring, for "Chinese peasants" the middle month of summer, for "Chinese scholars" the first month of summer; in Tibet it is the Snake month, and in Mongolia it is the fourth month (Baumann, *Divine Knowledge*, 70–74).
30. This two-week period and its Great Miracles (T. *cho 'phrul chen mo*) refers to the time when the Buddha defeated the heretical teachers at Sravasti, which included the performance of miracles. This event is celebrated in Lhasa during New Year's Monlam Chenmo (Great Prayer) festival, which was established by Tsongkhapa in 1409 (Buswell and Lopez, *Dictionary*, 831).

31. The Jetavana Park was located to the south of Sravasti and was donated to the Buddha by the banker Anathapindada, who also built several buildings to house the community during the rain retreats, including the Buddha's own residence, the "perfumed chamber" (Buswell and Lopez, *Dictionary,* 383).
32. The wheel of the Three Doctrines comprises the Dharma wheel of the Four Noble Truths, the Dharma wheel of the absence of defining characteristics, and the Dharma wheel of the thorough delineations (Buswell and Lopez, *Dictionary,* 1068).
33. Udayana was the king of Vatsa and a follower of the Buddha (Buswell and Lopez, *Dictionary,* 962).
34. Maha Maudgalyayana was "one of the two chief disciples of the Buddha, often depicted together with his friend Śāriputra flanking the Buddha. Mahāmaudgalyāyana was considered supreme among the Buddha's disciples in supranormal powers . . . [He] is additionally famous in East Asian Buddhism for his role in the *Yulanben Jing.* The text describes his efforts to save his mother from the tortures of her rebirth as a ghost (*preta*). Mahāmaudgalyāyana (Ch. Mulian) is able to use his supranormal powers to visit his mother in the realm of ghosts, but the food that he offers her immediately bursts into flames. The Buddha explains that it is impossible for the living to make offerings directly to the dead; instead, one should make offerings to the samgha in a bowl, and the power of their meditative practices will be able to save one's ancestors and loved ones from rebirths in the unfortunate realms" (Buswell and Lopez, *Dictionary,* 498–499).
35. The legend of the Sandalwood Buddha and its migration from India to Central Asia and finally to China arose in the fifth century as part of the process of Dharma localization. The famous Sandalwood Buddha in Beijing, which is what this story is about, was an important part of Chinese religiopolitical ideology from the eleventh century on. As a result of its significance during the Yuan dynasty, and especially for the Manchu Qing dynasty, the statue was also an important component of Mongol religious life. Isabelle Charleux, "From North India to Buryatia: The 'Sandalwood Buddha' from the Mongols' Perspective," in *Studies on Sino-Tibetan Buddhist Art: Proceedings of the Fourth International Conference on Tibetan Archaeology and Art,* ed. Xie Jisheng, Luo Wenhua, and Shi Yangang (Shanghai: Shanghai Classics Publishing, 2014), 539–558.
36. Black Chinese (Mong. *Qara Kitad*) is a calque of the Tibetan name for China *rgya-nag* and refers to the Han of north China. During the Yuan dynasty the Mongols divided the Han Chinese into the *Kitad* in the north (those who had been under the Jurchen's Jin dynasty), and the *Nanggiyad* in the south (i.e., the Han of the Song dynasty).

37. "Heart of Aggregate" is the Mongolian translation of the Sanskrit Bimbisāra (essence of the absolute), who was the ruler of Magadha and an avid supporter of the Buddha.
38. Magadha was "the largest of the sixteen states (Mahājanapada) that flourished in northern India between the sixth and third centuries BCE. As described in Pali sources, its capital was Rājagrha and, during the lifetime of the Buddha was ruled by king Bimbisāra and his usurper son Ajātaśatru, both of whom became patrons of Buddhism" (Buswell and Lopez, *Dictionary,* 491).
39. Kosala was one of the important kingdoms at the time of the Buddha, located in the foothills of modern-day Nepal. It was eventually conquered by King Ajatasatru of Magadha (Buswell and Lopez, *Dictionary,* 471).
40. Kausambi was the capital of Vatsa, located on the Yamuna river to the south of modern-day Prayagraj in Uttar Pradesh.
41. "Almsmaster" is a literal translation of the Mongolian (*öglige-yin ejen*), which refers to a secular ruler who supports the Buddhist community (the offering site, M. *takil-un oron*) as part of the religiopolitical system that defines the narrative of the *Precious Summary.*
42. It is unclear what "Vimala-jang Vina Köndi" refers to since the First Council to confirm and preserve the Buddha's teachings supposedly took place in Rajagrha in the year of the Buddha's death.
43. Ananda was the Buddha's main disciple, who according to tradition recited all the Buddha's teachings later compiled in the *Sutrapitaka*.
44. The Important One is Upali, who according to tradition recited the monastic rules known as the *Vinayapitaka*.
45. Kasyapa was one of the Buddha's main disciples, who according to tradition was appointed president of the first council and selected the 500 monks that participated in the event.
46. The Four Truths, also known as the Four Noble Truths, are an encapsulation of the Buddha's insight into the nature of the world: suffering (*dukkha*), origination (*samudaya*), cessation (*narodha*), and path (*marga*).
47. Although all Buddhist traditions assert that this First Council, which codified the Buddha's teachings, "was a historical event, its historicity is questioned by virtually all Buddhist scholars" (Buswell, *Encyclopedia*, 187).
48. Asoka (ca. 300–232 BCE, r. 268–232 BCE) was the third ruler of the Indian Mauryan empire (ca. 321–185 BCE), who through his edicts and subsequent Buddhist historiography became the model of Buddhist rule all over Asia. John S. Strong, *The Legend of King Aśoka* (Princeton, NJ: Princeton University Press, 1983).
49. This presentation inaccurately collapses the Second and Third Councils into one. The Second Council, which occurred about a hundred years after

the Buddha's death, was convened at Vaisali in order to address illicit monastic behavior, such as accepting gold and silver. "It has been postulated that Buddhist sectarianism began shortly after the Vaisali council, with the Mahasamgika school and Sthviras emerging as individual sects following a non-canonical council held shortly after the Vaisali event. Another council was held in Pataliputra around 250 BCE during the reign of Asoka. Asoka convened the council under Moggaliputta Tissa with the intention of establishing the orthodoxy of the dharma. A thousand monks were assembled, and, under Tissa's guidance, various viewpoints were considered and either sanctioned or rejected, with the proponents of rejected views being expelled from the city" (Buswell, *Encyclopedia*, 188).

50. Body, speech, and mind—the so-called "three gates"—are the three types of karmic activity (Buswell and Lopez, *Dictionary*, 1067).
51. Kaniska (c. 127–151 CE) was the "third king of the Kushan kingdom in the northwest of India and legendary patron of Buddhism. . . . The story of his conversion to Buddhism is widely found in the literature, but it seems to belong to the realm of legend, not history. . . . Thanks to Kaniṣka's putative support, the Kushan kingdom has traditionally been assumed to have been an important conduit for the introduction of Buddhist materials into China via the Silk Road of Central Asia. Recent evidence of the decline in western Central Asian trade during the Kushan period, however, may suggest instead that the Kushans were more of an obstacle than a help to this dissemination. Hence, it may not have been the Kushans who facilitated the transmission of Buddhism but their Indo-Scythian predecessors in the region, the Saka tribe" (Buswell and Lopez, *Dictionary*, 416).
52. "Around 100 CE another council was held under the Kushan king Kaniṣka, probably in Gandhara. A great scholar named Vasumitra presided, assisted by the learned Aśvaghosa. In addition to compiling a new Vinaya, they prepared a commentary called the *Mahāvibhāṣā* (*Great Exegesis*) on the Abhidharma text *Jñānaprasthāna* (*Foundation of Knowledge*), which became the standard reference work for all Sarvāstivāda abhidharma issues" (Buswell, *Encyclopedia*, 188).
53. "Chandra kings" refers to the Arakan-based Chandra dynasty of the tenth and eleventh centuries, which was a neighbor of the powerful Pala dynasty and also a flourishing center of Tantric Buddhism.
54. All the kings of the Pala dynasty (ca. 750–1150), who ruled what is today's Bengal and Bihar, bore names ending with the suffix *pala* ("protector" in Sanskrit) and were supporters of the Dharma. Jhunu Bagchi, *The History and Culture of the Palas of Bengal and Bihar (cir. 750 A.D.–cir. 1200 A.D.)* (New Delhi: Abhinav Publications, 1993).

55. The Sena dynasty (ca. 1070–1230) also ruled the area that is today's Bengal; however, contrary to what is claimed in the *Precious Summary*, it was not a Buddhist dynasty but a Hindu one.

2. HISTORY OF TIBET

1. Matthew T. Kapstein, *The Tibetans* (London: Wiley-Blackwell, 2006), 75.
2. The origin of the Tibetan royal lineage was an issue of great debate in Tibetan historiography, and Sagang Sechen follows the conventional narrative whereby the lineage begins with the third son. Per Sørensen, *Tibetan Buddhist Historiography: The Mirror Illuminating the Royal Genealogies. An Annotated Translation of the XIVth Century Tibetan Chronicle: rGyal-rabs gsal-ba'i me-long* (Wiesbaden: Harrassowitz Verlag, 1994), 137–138.
3. Vatsa was "one of the three powerful kingdoms of the Gangā (Ganges) river valley at the time of the Buddha, together with Magadha and Kośala. Vatsa was located south of the Gangā River, in what is today the Indian state of Uttar Pradesh, and had its capital at Kauśāmbī." Robert E. Buswell, Jr., and Donald S. Lopez, Jr., *The Princeton Dictionary of Buddhism* (Princeton, NJ: Princeton University Press, 2014), 962.
4. Every "Great Man," either a buddha or a cakravartin, acquires thirty-two specific bodily distinctions, as well as eighty signs of beauty. John Powers, *A Bull of a Man: Images of Masculinity, Sex and the Body in Indian Buddhism* (Cambridge, MA: Harvard University Press, 2009).
5. This Moses-like story comes from Butön Rinchen Drub's fourteenth-century history of Buddhism. Eugene Obermiller, *The History of Buddhism* (Heidelberg: Otto Harrassowitz, 1931–32), 181–182.
6. Vaisali was the capital of the Licchavis, which was part of the Vrji republic at the time of the Buddha. It was located approximately 25 miles to the northwest of modern-day Patna in the state of Bihar (Buswell and Lopez, *Dictionary*, 950).
7. Mount Shampo is a mountain located in the Yarlung valley in central Tibet. It is considered to be the place where the first king of Tibet, Nyatri Tsenpo, descended from the sky to the earth.
8. Tibet's first monarch's name was originally Nyaktri, Notch Throne, which "seems to be related to the numerologically significant position of his father as the 'joint' between three older and three younger brothers. The term, however, was obscure to later generations, and in the well-known literary versions of the legend it was reinterpreted as 'Nyatri,' 'Shoulder(-borne) Throne.' The account was accordingly amplified to state that, after the people had acclaimed him as king, they hoisted him up in a palanquin" (Kapstein, *The Tibetans*, 36).

9. "Kongpo, in eastern Tibet, where the Tsangpo river begins its great turn south to descend precipitously into Assam, to emerge from the gorges as the Brahmaputra, has long had a peculiar reputation in the Tibetan world as a place of black magic, but also of great spiritual power. It would become the base from which the dynasty of the Tsenpo would eventually reassert itself, following the revenge taken upon the regicide Lo-ngam" (Kapstein, *The Tibetans*, 40).
10. According to tradition, Yumbu Lhakang was built for Tibet's first king, Nyatri Tsenpo, on a hill on the eastern bank of the Yarlung River about 100 miles southeast of Lhasa. In fact, it was built during the turn of the eighth century and became the summer palace of Songtsen Gampo (604–650). When he moved his government to Lhasa the Yumbu Lhakang became a temple.
11. The *Mudras of Pangkong* is the *Pang kong phyag rgya pa*, which, as Sam van Schaik has pointed out, is the name of the text found in early Tibetan histories. In more recent histories, however, the name has been changed to the canonical *Spang-skong phyag brgya-pa'i mdo* (*The Hundred Salutations Repairing Branches*). To explain this, van Schaik notes that the "most convincing early title of our text (*Pam kong brgya rtsa brgyad)* suggests a text either translated from Chinese, or composed in a Sino-Tibetan culture like that of Dunhuang. If we can draw a moral from this little philological enquiry, it may be that the presence of a Chinese text along with more well-known Indian ones in Lhatotori's casket is emblematic of the mixed sources from which early Tibetan Buddhism was made. While Chinese Buddhist sources never truly featured as importantly as Indian ones, they were there, and China was certainly not spurned as a source of authentic dharma before the 11th century (notwithstanding a certain debate at Samyé), as it often would be later" (https://earlytibet.com/2007/10/30/dharma-from-the-sky-ii-indian-or-chinese-dharma/). See also Sam van Schaik, "Dharma from the Sky: The Pangkong Prayer," *Central Asiatic Journal* 61, 1 (2018): 61–70.
12. The original six syllables are the famous mantra: *Om Mani Padme Hum*.
13. The *Zamatog Sutra* (*Mdo-sde za-ma-tog bkod-pa*) is the Tibetan translation of the *Kāraṇḍavyūha Sūtra*, which extols the virtues and power of the Bodhisattva Avalokitesvara and especially the mantra *Om Mani Padme Hum*.
14. *Vimana* is the Sanskrit word for mansion, or palace, which Sagang Sechen here includes along with the Mongolian word for palace (*qarsi*).
15. In Buddhist sources, Bon is the name given to the indigenous religion of Tibet that was ultimately defeated by the Dharma. For the followers of Bon, it is a tradition that preserves an earlier form of the Dharma transmitted from northwest India in the early centuries of the common era, which eventually became formalized as a distinct tradition in the eleventh century. Samten G. Karmay

and Jeff Watt, *Bon: The Magic Word. The Indigenous Religion of Tibet* (New York: Rubin Museum of Art, 2007).

16. The *Collected Precepts of Mani* (*Ma ṇi bka' bum*) is a collection of various mythical, ritual, and doctrinal texts attributed to the seventh-century Tibetan king Songtsen Gampo that focuses mainly on Avalokitesvara, especially the idea that Songtsen Gampo is an emanation of this bodhisattva. Matthew T. Kapstein, "Remarks on the Maṇi Bka'-'bum and the Cult of Āvalokiteśvara in Tibet," in *Tibetan Buddhism: Reason and Revelation*, ed. Steven Goodman and Ronald Davidson (Albany: State University of New York Press, 1992), 79–93.
17. Amitabha, meaning "Limitless Light," is one of the most widely worshipped buddhas in the Mahayana tradition. In particular, people pray to Amitabha so that they can be reborn in his western pure land of Sukhavati (Buswell and Lopez, *Dictionary*, 34).
18. Songsten Gampo was born with Amitabha on his forehead because this confirms that he was an incarnation of Avalokitesvara; "according to legend, Avalokiteśvara was produced from a beam of light that radiated from the forehead of Amitābha while that Buddha was deep in meditation. For this reason, Buddhist iconography often depicts Amitabha as embedded in Avalokiteśvara's crown" (Buswell and Lopez, *Dictionary*, 82).
19. Although the *Old Tibetan Chronicle* from Dunhuang, written about 800, does record the development of a Tibetan script during the reign of Songtsen Gampo, the legend of Thonmi Sambhota—and much else about his reign—are largely the creation of later Buddhist narratives from the twelfth century. Brandon Dotson, *The Old Tibetan Annals: An Annotated Translation of Tibet's First History, with an Annotated Cartographical Documentation by Guntram Hazod* (Vienna: Verlag der Österreichischen Akademie der Wissenschaften, 2009).
20. The "all-perceiving one with eleven faces" is the Eleven-Headed Avalokitesvara, one of the most common iconographic forms of the bodhisattva of compassion. "While theories abound about why he has eleven heads, it is likely that the ten small bodhisattva heads topped by a buddha head represent the ten stages of the bodhisattva path, along with the final attainment of Buddhahood" (Buswell and Lopez, *Dictionary*, 280).
21. Akanistha "is the eighth and highest level of the realm of subtle materiality (rūpadhātu), which is accessible only through experiencing the fourth meditative absorption (dhyāna)" (Buswell and Lopez, *Dictionary*, 25).
22. Airavata is a white elephant with five trunks and ten tusks who the carries the deity Indra.
23. The following stories about the Nepalese and Chinese princesses are drawn from traditional Tibetan historiography as found in the fourteenth-century *The*

Mirror Illuminating the Royal Genealogies (Sørensen, *Tibetan Buddhist Historiography*, 199–249).

24. The *Treasury of Jewels* is Sakya Pandita's collection of wisdom verses, the *Subhasitaratnanidhi*. James Bosson, *A Treasury of Aphoristic Jewels: The Subhasitaratnanidhi of Sa Skya Pandita in Tibetan and Mongolian* (Bloomington: Indiana University Publications, 1969).
25. Tang Taisong is Taizong 太宗 (598–649, r. 626–649), the second emperor of the Tang dynasty.
26. Princess Munchang is the Tibetan name for Princess Wencheng (Wencheng Gongzhu 文成公主), the Tang princess who was sent to Tibet to marry the crown prince Gungsong Gungtsen. When he died in 646, however, she became her father-in-law's queen, which is how she is remembered in Tibetan history. On the historiography of Princess Wencheng, especially in terms of Sino-Tibetan relations, see Robert Barnett, *Lhasa: Streets with Memories* (New York: Columbia University Press, 2006), and Clare E. Harris, *The Museum on the Roof of the World: Art, Politics, and the Representation of Tibet* (Chicago: University of Chicago Press, 2012), 191–203.
27. Uran Tanggarig, literally "crafty oath," is the Mongolian name for Gar Tongtsen, the wise prime minister who served Songtsen Gampo and who succeeded in winning the hand of Princess Wenchang. Okada Hidehiro, "The Third Dalai Lama and Altan Khan of the Tümed," in *Tibetan Studies. Proceedings of the 5th Seminar of the International Association of Tibetan Studies*, ed. Ihara Shoren and Yamaguchi Zuiho (Narita: Naritasan Shinshoji, 1992), 647.
28. The identification of the Nepalese princess Bhrkuti as an incarnation of White Tara—and Princess Wencheng as an incarnation of Green Tara—only developed in the Tibetan historical tradition during the fourteenth century. Regardless, Tara is a female bodhisattva who saves her devotees from all dangers when they recite her mantra: *om tare tuttare ture svaha*. She is said to have appeared from a tear that Avalokitesvara shed when he saw the world's suffering; it fell into a valley, forming a lake, out of which grew a lotus from which Tara appeared. Her worship began in Tibet in the eleventh century after Atisa claimed that Tara had not only helped him during times of trouble but also told him to spread the Dharma in Tibet (Buswell and Lopez, *Dictionary*, 895–896).
29. The "ten virtues" refer to the ten precepts that monastic novices—and members of the laity—should follow: 1. not to kill living beings; 2. not to steal; 3. not to engage in sexual activity; 4. not to lie (about spiritual attainments); 5. not to use intoxicants; 6. not to eat at improper times; 7. not to use perfumes, garlands, or cosmetics; 8. not to sing, dance, play music, or attend entertainments; 9. not to sleep on high and luxurious beds; 10. not to handle gold and silver/money (Buswell and Lopez, *Dictionary*, 1085).

30. Süngbing is Zongping 總兵, a military regional commander. Charles O. Hucker, *A Dictionary of Official Titles in Imperial China* (Stanford, CA: Stanford University Press, 1985), 533.

31. A *dharani* is a "verbal formula believed to 'retain' or 'encapsulate' the meaning of lengthier texts and prolix doctrines, thus functioning as a mnemonic device. It is said that those who memorize these formulae (which may or may not have semantic meaning) gain the power to retain the fuller teachings that the dhāraṇī retain" (Buswell and Lopez, *Dictionary,* 241).

32. In the practice of Buddhist tantra, a tutelary deity (T. *yi dam*) is the enlightened deity that is the focus of one's meditation practice. "Traditionally, the yi dam is selected by throwing a flower onto a mandala, with the deity upon whom the flower lands becoming the 'chosen deity.' However, when one receives a tantric initiation, the central deity of that tantra typically becomes the yi dam, with daily practices of offering and meditation often required. Through the propitiation of the deity and recitation of mantra, it is said that the deity will bestow accomplishments (siddhi)" (Buswell and Lopez, *Dictionary,* 1027).

33. During the second half of the seventh century the real power in Tibet was held not by the kings but rather by the Gar clan, "which dominated the key civil and military posts of the empire. . . . The power and influence of the Gar increased further with the death of the monarch Manglön Mangtsen in 676, the year of the birth of his son and heir Düsong (676–704)" (Kapstein, *The Tibetans,* 62; Hugh Richardson, "The Mgar Family in Seventh-Century Tibet," in *High Peaks, Pure Earth: Collected Writings on Tibetan History and Culture,* ed. Michael Aris, 114–123 [London: Serindia, 1988]).

34. Düsong was the ruler who finally broke the power of the Gar clan and also revived the expansion of the Tibetan empire. Most notably, he led the campaigns against the Nanzhao kingdom in Yunnan, where he supposedly built a Buddhist temple and ultimately died (Kapstein, *The Tibetans,* 62).

35. Gyimshing Gongju (T. *gyim shing kong jo*) is the Tibetan transliteration of Princess Jincheng (Jincheng Gongzhu 金城公主, 698–739), a minor Tang princess who was sent to Tibet to marry Düsong, the father of Tridé Tsukten. "Later Tibetan legend reverses the tale and maintains that the princess was to wed Tri Detsyuktsen's son Lhawön, who died before the arrival of his betrothed . . . [Regardless,] during the three decades of her residence in Tibet, until her death in 739, she appears to have played a major role in promoting Chinese learning, as well as the Buddhist religion, to which she was deeply devoted" (Kapstein, *The Tibetans,* 63–64).

36. Tang Chuchung was the Zhongzong 中宗 emperor (656–710, r. 705–710), the fourth emperor of the Tang dynasty.

37. Khenpo Bodhisattva is the Mongolian translation of Santaraksita's Tibetan title, Mkhan po byang chub sems dpa'. Santaraksita was the famous abbot of the Indian monastery Vikramasila, who ordained the first Tibetan monks and recommended inviting both Padmasambhava and Kamalasila to Tibet.
38. Mang[yül] Güngtang (T. *mang yul gung thang*) is the name of a Tibetan kingdom established under Sakya overlordship in southwest Tibet around 1265, which was ultimately destroyed by the king of Tsang in 1620. It was situated on the main route between Tibet and Nepal, which passed through the Kyirong valley and led to Katmandu. "According to the *dBa' bzhed* (folios 5–10) and other sources, this was the route taken by Padmasambhava and Santaraksita in the eighth century on their way from India to Tibet." Hildegard Diemberger, *When a Woman Becomes a Religious Dynasty: The Samding Dorje Phagmo of Tibet* (New York: Columbia University Press, 2007), 34–35.
39. Haspo Mountain (T. has po ri) is a hill that rises 560 feet above Samyé monastery in the Yarlung valley, where Trisong Detsen's palace is said to have been located and where Padmasambhava appeared in his guise as Dorjé Trolo, one of his Eight Manifestations. It is also recognized as one of Tibet's four holy mountains.
40. Padmasambhava was the famous yogi and tantric master from Uddiyana invited to Tibet by the emperor Trisong Detsen in the late eighth century. His mythical status as one of the central figures in the Buddhist conversion of Tibet has resulted in an enormous amount of hagiographical literature. He is most famous for his fight against the indigenous demons and his conversion of local deities into protectors of Buddhism, and his hiding of treasure texts (*gter-ma*). Daniel A. Hirshberg, *Remembering the Lotus-Born: Padmasambhava in the History of Tibet's Golden Age* (Cambridge, MA: Wisdom, 2016).
41. In Buddhist cosmology, Uddiyana is one of the two peripheral continents of Jambudvipa, and is now identified with either the Swat Valley in Pakistan or the area around Kabul (Sørensen, *Tibetan Buddhist Historiography*, 47).
42. This refers to Dorjé Dudjum, who was sent to invite Padmasambhava. Zahiruddin Ahmad, *The Song of the Queen of Spring or A History of Tibet: Nag-dBan Blo-bZan rGya-mTSHo Fifth Dalai Lama of Tibet* (New Delhi: Aditya Prakashan, 2008), 42.
43. Dragons, or nagas, are "beings said to inhabit bodies of water and the roots of great trees, often guarding treasures hidden there. They are depicted iconographically with human heads and torsos but with the tail and hood of a cobra. They inhabit an underwater kingdom filled with magnificent palaces, and they possess a range of magical powers. . . . Digging the earth is said to displease the nagas, who must therefore be propitiated prior to the construction of a building" (Buswell and Lopez, *Dictionary*, 561).

44. On the vast array of Tibetan autochthonous deities that were Buddhicized in the course of Tibet's conversion see Christopher Bell, "Worldly Protector Deities in Tibet," in *The Brill Encyclopedia of Buddhism*, ed. Jonathan A. Silk et al. (Leiden: Brill, 2019), 1254–1266.
45. The Twelve Powerful Mothers were the female protector deities of Tibet, which according to tradition Padmasambhava subdued during his promotion of the Dharma. On this story see Janet Gyatso, "Down with the Demoness: Reflections on a Feminine Ground in Tibet," in *Feminine Ground: Essays on Women and Tibet*, ed. Janice Dean Willis (Ithaca, NY: Snow Lion, 1987), 33–51.
46. The Three Baskets of the canon (S. *Tripitika*) are the basket of discourses (*sutrapitika*), the basket of discipline (*vinayapitaka*), and the basket of scholastic exegesis (*abhidharmapitika*) (Buswell and Lopez, *Dictionary*, 1066).
47. Abhidharma is the corpus of the Buddhist canon that entails the scholarly interpretation of the Buddha's teachings.
48. Samyé monastery was built during the reign of Trisong Detsen and was not only Tibet's first monastery but also a central component in the project of making Buddhism the state religion. It was built to represent a three-dimensional mandala, presumably of the Buddha Vairocana, who had become intertwined with the Tibetan imperial cult (Buswell, *Encyclopedia*, 68–69).
49. The Four Immeasurables are loving-kindness, compassion, empathetic joy, and equanimity, and the Four Activities are pacification, enrichment, control, and wrath (Buswell and Lopez, *Dictionary*, 1096, 1095).
50. The four major continents are Videha (east), Jambudvipa (south), Godaniya (west), and Uttarakuru (north) (Buswell and Lopez, *Dictionary*, 1096).
51. *Yaksas* are "a class of nature spirit, commonly serving as local guardians of the earth and trees and the treasures hidden there. They possess supernatural powers—including the ability to fly, to change their appearance, and to disappear—which they can employ for good or for evil. They often appear in Buddhist texts, sometimes serving as benevolent protectors and messengers for the Buddha and his disciples" (Buswell and Lopez, *Dictionary*, 1018).
52. In the Buddhist pantheon Yama is the lord of death and king of hell (Buswell and Lopez, *Dictionary*, 1018).
53. Mahakala is a wrathful manifestation of the Bodhisattva Avalokitesvara, who protects the Dharma. "He has many aspects, including two-, four-, and six-armed forms, and appears in several colors, the most famous being black and white. He wears a crown of five skulls, symbolizing the transmutation of the five afflictions (kleśa) into the five wisdoms (pañcajñāna) of a buddha. One of his most popular forms in Tibet is as Pañjaranātha or 'Protector of the Pavilion.' In this form, which derives from the *Vajrapañjaratantra*, he is the protector of the *Hevajratantra* cycle" (Buswell and Lopez, *Dictionary*, 496).

54. The Indian monastery of Otantapuri in Magadha is regarded as the model for Samyé. R. A. Stein, *Tibetan Civilization* (Stanford, CA: Stanford University Press, 1972), 66.
55. Dharmakirti (c. 600–670 CE) was one of the most important and influential figures in Indian Buddhist philosophy, whose thought eventually became pivotal in Tibetan scholarship (Buswell and Lopez, *Dictionary,* 246–247).
56. After the consecration of Samye monastery twelve monks of the Sarvastivadins were invited from India to form the initial monastic community, whereupon seven Tibetans were then ordained (Buswell, *Encyclopedia*, 190).
57. Vajrapani, "Holder of the Vajra," was the Buddha's enforcer in early Buddhism. "It is said that whoever refuses three times to respond to a reasonable question from the Buddha would have his head split into pieces on the spot; carrying out this punishment was Vajrapāṇi's duty." In later Mahayana and tantric Buddhist texts Vajrapani becomes a major figure, but he retains his role as an enforcer by suppressing "all of the worldly divinities of the universe and brings them to the summit of Mount Sumeru, where they seek refuge in the three jewels" (Buswell and Lopez, *Dictionary,* 955).
58. "According to Buddhist mythology, Mañjuśrī, the bodhisattva of wisdom, took the form of the terrifying bull-headed deity in order to destroy the Lord of Death (Yama), who was ravaging the country; hence the epithet Yamantaka (Destroyer of Death). . . . In Tibetan Buddhism, he was one of the three primary Yi Dam of the Dge lugs pa sect (together with Guhyasamaja and Cakrasamvara)" (Buswell and Lopez, *Dictionary,* 1020).
59. Hayagriva, "Horse-Necked One," is "an early Buddhist deity who developed from a yaksa attendant of Avalokiteśvara into a tantric wrathful deity important in the second diffusion of Buddhism in Tibet" (Buswell and Lopez, *Dictionary,* 347).
60. Vajrakilaya, "Vajra dagger," is the "deification of the kīla (see phur pa), the ritual dagger used in tantric ceremonies. In the rituals involving the use of the kīla, the tantric dagger is typically used to subdue a ritual site, to subjugate the local demon by pinning him or her to the ground; the mandala is thus planted and established on top of the offending demon. . . . As a deity, Vajrakīlaya originally held the same duties as the ritual dagger; to protect the borders of the ritual space and pin down and destroy enemies, human or otherwise" (Buswell and Lopez, *Dictionary,* 954).
61. Vairocana the Interpreter was one of the first seven Tibetans to be ordained as a monk by Santaraksita at Samyé, whereupon he was sent to India to study the Dharma. Upon his return he taught Trisong Detsen, and "he is renowned as one of the three major figures (along with Padmasambhava and Vimalamitra) in the dissemination of the rdzogs chen teachings in Tibet and translated many

texts from Sanskrit into Tibetan; the manuscripts of some of his translations have been discovered at Dunhuang" (Buswell and Lopez, *Dictionary*, 950).

62. Vimalamitra was supposedly invited to Tibet when he was 200 years old and is revered in Tibetan history as one of the main figures who transmitted the Dzokchen teachings, and for translating a number of texts from Sanskrit to Tibetan (Buswell and Lopez, *Dictionary*, 971).

63. Manjusri, meaning "Gentle Glory," also known as Manjughosa, "Gentle Voice," is the bodhisattva of wisdom "and sometimes is said to be the embodiment of all wisdom of all the buddhas. Mañjuśrī, Avalokiteśvara, and Vajrapāṇi are together known as the 'protectors of the three families' (*trikulanātha*), representing wisdom, compassion, and power, respectively. Among his many epithets, the most common is Kumārabhūta, 'Ever Youthful'" (Buswell and Lopez, *Dictionary*, 526–527).

64. Muné Tsenpo was supposedly a devout Buddhist layman who established several important religious festivals that are still observed in Lhasa today. He also supposedly tried three times to distribute equally the wealth between rich and poor subjects, but failed, and finally he was poisoned to death by his mother, who favored the old religion over Buddhism.

65. He was exiled because he murdered the son of a nobleman.

66. Mutik Tsenpo, who ruled as Tri Désongsten, reigned from 804 to 815.

67. Tri Désongsten's support of Buddhism is well documented, most famously in the so-called "Karchung Inscription," which records his building of a grand monastery at Ramasang near Lhasa that is mentioned in this passage. Hugh Richardson, "The sKar-Cung Inscription," *The Journal of the Royal Asiatic Society of Great Britain and Ireland* 1 (1973): 12–20.

68. Dharmapala (ca. 780–820) was the second ruler of the Pala dynasty, who not only greatly expanded the Pala domains but also was a great patron of Buddhism.

69. Tang Yichung refers to the Yizong 懿宗 emperor (833–873, r. 859–873), the seventeenth emperor of the Tang dynasty, who was a devout Buddhist.

70. It is unclear to whom Tang Chuchung refers. Regardless, this supposed killing of a Tang emperor during the reign of Relpachen did not happen. This most likely refers to the last of this period's Sino-Tibetan treaties, which was signed in 822 during the reign of Relpachen and set the border between Tibet and China on terms dictated by the Tibetans. Sam van Schaik, *Tibet: A History* (New Haven, CT: Yale University Press, 2011), 42–44.

71. This list of translators goes back to "the preamble to the *Two-Fascicle Lexicon*, a bilingual glossary of Buddhist terminology prepared by order of the throne: 'In the horse year (814) the Emperor Tri Desongtsen dwelt in Önchangdo palace in Kyi. The old armies of east and west had been rotated and the brigands

quelled. The messengers of the Karluk offered homage. The Great Ministers Zhang Trizur Ramshag, Mangjé Lhalö and others brought much tribute from the territories, and offered most of the camels, horses and cattle to his majesty. As a follow-up to the awards that he granted to the each according to rank from *zhanglön* down, he gave his command that the Bactrian preceptors Acharya Jinamitra, Surendrabodhi, Shilendrabodhi, Danashila and Bodhimitra, and the Tibetan preceptors Ratnarakshita and Dharmatashila, and those who had become master translators, including Jñanasena, Jayarakshita, Mañjushrivarma and Ratnendrashila, should write a catalogue of the Tibetan translations and coinages derived from the Sanskrit of the Great and Lesser Vehicles, saying, 'Make it fit to be learned by all, so that they never depart from those textual traditions'" (Kapstein, *The Tibetans*, 76–77).

72. Relpachen (r. 815–838) avidly supported Buddhism, "most notably by instituting a tax to support monastics, and by fostering the creation of the first standard Sanskrit-Tibetan dictionary—the *Mahavyutpatti*—which greatly advanced the translation of Buddhist texts into Tibetan. Moreover, during his reign the Tibetan empire reached its greatest extent, conquering regions of China, India, Nepal, Khotan, Turkestan and Gansu. After Tibetan armies attacked Yanzhou in modern Shandong province, the Chinese sued for peace. A peace treaty in 821 set the boundaries between the two countries, marking a period of peaceful relations along the border" (Buswell and Lopez, *Dictionary*, 695).

73. Later Tibetan historians identified Songtsen Gampo, Trisong Detsen, and Relpachen as the three great Buddhist rulers, and also recognized each respectively as an incarnation of Avalokitesvara, Manjusri, and Vajrapani. David L. Snellgrove, *Indo-Tibetan Buddhism* (Boston: Shambhala, 1987), 383.

74. Langdarma, "Darma the Ox," is famously blamed for destroying the Dharma in Tibetan history; however, as with many of the stories told about this period, this was actually a later development. Scholars today question whether Langdarma's persecution of Buddhism ever even happened. "Several scholars have now argued that little more than a reduction of patronage may have been at stake, and there is some evidence suggesting Lang Darma himself was initially a Buddhist king, who enjoyed the good wishes of the clergy. It seems possible that the persecution, despite its great importance in later thought, was in essence a withdrawal of funding, no doubt due to a poor current-accounts balance rather than to anti-Buddhist sentiment, that came to be very much exaggerated in its retelling" (Kapstein, *The Tibetans*, 81).

75. The four provinces of Tibet: Amdo, Kham, Tsang, and U.

76. Chief of the Sun is Kyide Nyima Gon, who fled from central Tibet to Ngari following the assassination of his father, Pal Khortsen (893–923), and thereupon took over this western kingdom. In turn, his three sons—Majestic Chief (Rikpa

Gon), Fortunate Chief (Tashi Gon), and Ranked Chief (Destuk Gon)—each inherited part of the kingdom. Majestic Chief took over Ladakh, Fortunate Chief took over Purang, and Ranked Chief took over Guge. Roberto Vitali, *The Kingdoms of Gu.ge Pu.hrang: According to the mkhan.chen Ngag.dbang grags.pa* (Chicago: Serindia, 1997).

77. Although many Tibetan sources identify ten monks as being ordained by Gongpa Rabsal, the names often differ (Sørensen, *Tibetan Buddhist Historiography*, 446).

78. Dantig is a mountain valley—and a religious retreat site—on the bank of the Yellow River to the southeast of Xining in Qinghai 清海. Sam van Schaik and Imre Galambos, *Manucripts and Travellers: The Sino-Tibetan Documents of a Tenth Century Buddhist Pilgrim* (Berlin: de Gruyter, 2012), 40–43.

79. As Davidson has noted, "the events as they occurred were far more complex than this flat formulaic rendition. Our early sources mention . . . [that] twenty of the thirty teaching temples (*chos grwa*) constructed or supported by Relpachen were located in the eastern Tibetan areas of Kham or Amdo." Ronald M. Davidson, *Tibetan Renaissance: Tantric Buddhism in the Rebirth of Tibetan Culture* (New York: Columbia University Press, 2005), 88.

80. Lha Lama Jnanarasmi is Lha Lama Yeshe Ö (947–1019/1024), who first became a monk and then reclaimed the Guge throne. He is famous for both reviving the Dharma and establishing a new legal code. Jacob P. Dalton, *The Taming of the Demons: Violence and Liberation in Tibetan Buddhism* (New Haven, CT: Yale University Press, 2011), 110–125.

81. According to tradition, Rinchen Zangpo (958–1055) traveled to India as a teenager, studying first in Kashmir and then at Vikramasila monastery, then returned to Tibet, where his accomplishments were recognized by the Guge ruler Yeshe Ö, who "was then engaged in reforming Buddhism in Tibet, sweeping away what he considered the Tibetan corruptions of the religion that had arisen since the collapse of the Yarlung Dynasty in the mid ninth century." To this end, Rinchen Zangpo was supposedly sent again to India, whereupon he came to be credited with promoting not only Prajñāpāramitā literature but also several tantric traditions, as well as composing commentaries on topics such as Prajñāpāramitā, *sādhāna*, and *abhiṣeka*. "Rinchen Zangpo is equally famous for his contribution to the creation of temples; he is said to have constructed one hundred and eight temples . . . [Nevertheless] most of the attributions to Rinchen Zangpo must be taken with some suspicion, as they are the invention of later tradition" (https://treasuryoflives.org/biographies/view/Rinchen-Zangpo/10199, accessed October 23, 2020).

82. Toling monastery was founded by Rinchen Zangpo in 996 under the patronage of Lha Lama Yeshe Ö. Roberto Vitali, *Records of Tho.ling: A Literary and Visual*

Reconstruction of the "Mother" Monastery in Gu.ge (Delhi: Marg Publishing, 1999).

83. According to tradition, of these twenty-one, all but two—Rinchen Zangpo and Drakjor Sherab—died on the journey on account of the foreign climate, disease, and other factors.
84. Songnye is Lha Lama Yeshe Ö's given name, Song Nge.
85. Tsunpa Beam of the Sakyas is Lha Lama Jangchub Ö, the nephew and successor of Lha Lama Yeshe Ö as ruler of Purang.
86. Naktso Lotsawa Tsultrim Gyelwé (1011–1064) was sent to India by Lha Lama Jangchub Ö in order to invite Atisa to Tibet, which he successfully did. He studied under Atisa for nineteen years and is credited with "around one hundred translations in the Kangyur, including texts in the Prajnaparamita and tantra sections, and in the Tengyur, including works by Atisa" (https://treasuryoflives.org/biographies/view/Naktso-Lotsawa-Tsultrim-Gyelwa/5801, accessed October 23, 2020).

3. HISTORY OF CHINGGIS KHAN

1. It has been hypothesized that "Bede" is a Mongolian transcription of the Chinese *Beida* 北韃 (Shagdaryn Bira, *Mongolian Historical Writing from 1200 to 1700*, trans. John R. Krueger [Bellingham: Center for East Asian Studies, Western Washington University, 2002], 200), a contraction of Bei Dada 北韃靼, "Northern Tatars," a name for northern nomads that dates from at least the ninth century (Mark C. Elliott, "The Limits of Tartary: Manchuria in Imperial and National Geographies," *The Journal of Asian Studies* 59, 3 [2000]: 625). Whether this is correct or not is unclear; it does follow the Buddhist historiographical model of a people—like the Tibetans or Mongols—only being fully formed after they are discovered and ruled by a descendant of the primordial Mahasammata, "Elevated by the Many."
2. Burkhan Khaldun, the sacred mountain associated with Chinggis Khan and his ancestors, refers to today's Khentei Khan mountain in the Great Khentei range in northeastern Mongolia.
3. This narrative framework, whereby a people are only fully formed when ruled by a legitimate ruler, mythologizes the strict social stratification in Mongol society between the nobility and the commoner class. On Mongol social hierarchies and political power see David Sneath, *The Headless State: Aristocratic Orders, Kinship Society, and Misrepresentations of Nomadic Inner Asia* (New York: Columbia University Press, 2008).
4. The following genealogy corresponds to the *Secret History* (and is charted in Igor de Rachewiltz, *The Secret History of the Mongols: A Mongolian Epic*

Chronicle of the Thirteenth Century [Leiden: Brill, 2004], 1349). It is also found in all the seventeenth-century chronicles and later Mongol histories. During the Yuan dynasty, however, there were six competing genealogies, which shows "that genealogy remained a major site of intellectual disputation and production throughout the Mongol empire period." Christopher P. Atwood, "Six Pre-Chinggisid Geneaologies in the Mongol Empire," *Archivum Eurasiae Medii Aevi* 19 (2012): 42.

5. The Oirat, who originally inhabited the area of present-day Khöwsgöl province, are first mentioned in 1202 as members of a coalition force campaigning against both Ong Khan and Chinggis Khan. In 1208 they submitted to Chinggis Khan and maintained matrimonial affiliations with all four Chinggisid lines, particularly the Toluids. In Yuan dynasty sources there is no record of the Oirat, presumably on account of their support of Arig Böke during his war of succession with Khubilai Khan; however, they are mentioned by Marco Polo (Henry Yule, *The Book of Ser Marco Polo the Venetian concerning the Kingdoms and Marvels of the East, Translated and Edited, with Notes, by Colonel Sir Henry Yule, R.E., C.B., K.C.S.I., Corr. Inst. France, Third Edition, Revised Throughout in the Light of Recent Discoveries by Henri Cordier (of Paris)* [New York: Charles Scribner, 1929], 300). In 1388 Arig Böke's descendant Prince Yesüder, with the support of the Four Oirat, killed the last Mongol ruler of the Northern Yuan and created a new tribal confederation. At this time the Four Oirat were not the same as the thirteenth-century group; the term was an overarching designation for four peoples inhabiting the northwest, the original Oirat, Naiman, Kereit, and Bargud. Later, the Oirat were composed of eight different groups: the Khoid, Baatud, Bargu, Buraad, Dörböd, Züün Gar, Khoshud, and Torghud. Beginning in the fifteenth century, this new confederation continued to struggle for ascendency against the Mongols in the south and west. Oirat success was greatest under the rule of Togan (d. 1439/40) and his son Esen (d. 1455). After Dayan Khan had reunified the fractious eastern Mongols, however, the Oirat were greatly weakened. Under repeated attacks by various Mongols in the late sixteenth century they were pushed out of their territory on the central Mongolian plateau. During the seventeenth and eighteenth centuries, the Oirat again became a regional power in western Inner Asia, particularly under Galdan Boshogtu Khan; however, in 1755 they were defeated by the Manchus and incorporated into the Qing imperium. Okada Hidehiro, "Origins of the Dörben Oyirad," *Ural-Altaische Jahrbücher* Neue Folge 7 (1987): 181–211; Miyawaki Junko, "The Birth of Oyirad Khanship," *Central Asiatic Journal* 41 (1997): 38–75.
6. The *Secret History* is far more detailed about this union: "At Ariq Usun, in the land of the Qori Tumat, that girl named Alan Qo'a was born to Barqujin Qo'a, wife of Qorilartai Mergen. As in their land the Qori Tumat had imposed bans

on one another's sable, squirrel and wild-game hunting grounds, and mutual relations were bad as a result, Qorilartai Mergen separated from the Qori Tumat and took the clan name Qorilar. Saying that the land of Burqan Qaldun was good, and that it was suitable for game hunting, he was now moving into the territory of the Uriangqai Burqan Bosqaqsan and Sinci Bayan, lords of Bayan Qaldun. This is how Dobun Mergen asked there and then for Alan Qo'a." de Rachewiltz, *Secret History*, 2–3.

7. Traditionally, Mongol parents gave their children protective names that would deceive evil spirits from harming the child. Judit Vinkovics, "Name-Giving Among the Mongols: An Ethnographico-Bibliographical Survey," *Acta Orientalia Academiae Scientiarum Hungaricae* 39, 1 (1985): 29.
8. Although the term "Tatar" has been used for a wide array of people from the eighth century until today, in Mongol sources it refers to a specific group who inhabited what is now northeast Inner Mongolia and were at odds with both the Mongols and the Kereit Khanate. Their feud with the Mongols escalated when they supported Chinggis Khan's rival Jamuqa, who was enthroned in 1201. When they were defeated in 1202 Chinggis decreed that "all Tatars taller than a linch pole would be slaughtered and the small children enslaved. When the Tatars learned of this decision, they organized for a desparate last stand but were destroyed, and the sentence carried out. The Tatars disappeared as a corporate tribal body." Christopher P. Atwood, *Encyclopedia of Mongolia and the Mongol Empire* (New York: Facts on File, 2004), 529.
9. Odchigin is based on the epithet *odčigin* (< Turkic *od*, "fire," and *tegin*, "prince"), given to Chinggis Khan's youngest brother, Temüge, and designates his role as the "guardian of the hearth." By tradition the youngest inherited the native territory and domestic patrimony; thus Temüge inherited the Mongol ancestral lands in the northeastern corner of Mongolia. Isenbike Togan, "Otchigin's Place in the Transformation from Family to Dynasty," in *Interpreting the Turkic Runiform Sources and the Position of the Altai Corpus*, ed. Marcel Erdal (Berlin: Klaus Schwarz Verlag, 2020), 403–421.
10. The Qonggirad were one of the main groups of eastern Mongolia and the main group with whom the Mongols practiced exogamous marriage relations. This relationship, wherein the Qonggirad supplied imperial brides for the ruling Mongols, continued up through the fourteenth century (de Rachewiltz, *Secret History*, 326).
11. The Seven Qongqotan descended from Chaujin Örtegei and were continually at odds with Chinggis Khan during the rise to power. This tension peaked when the shaman Teb Tenggeri and his Qongqotan challenged his authority, with devastating consequences for both Teb Tenggeri and the Qongqotan (de Rachewiltz, *Secret History*, 286, 878).

12. The Tayichi'ud were an early leading group among the Mongols, consisting of a ruling lineage descended from Charakha Lingkhum and their subject peoples the Suldus, Besüd, Targhud, and Je'üred. After the death of Yisügei Baatur, a leader of the rival Kiyad clan, the Tayichi'ud seized power, thereby earning the lifelong enmity of his son, Chinggis Khan. After his defeat of Jamuqa of the Jajiraid, whom the Tayichi'ud supported as khan, Chinggis Khan enslaved them. Atwood, *Encyclopedia*, 530.
13. Bo'orchu (1165?–1227?) was Chinggis Khan's first friend and ally (de Rachewiltz, *Secret History*, § 90–93). On account of his continued loyalty he became the first member of the elite "Four Steeds," and was also placed in charge of the right wing of the Mongol army. Paul Pelliot and Louis Hambis, *Histoire des campagnes de Gengis Khan. Cheng-wou ts'in-tcheng lou*, vol. I (Leiden: E. J. Brill, 1951), 342–360.
14. Temüjin was elected supreme tribal leader and entitled Chinggis Khan in 1206, the sixth year of the Taihe 泰和 period of the Jin 金 emperor Zhangzong 章宗 (r. 1190–1209). Yet, according to the *Secret History* he was enthroned at an earlier date and given the less grandiose title *qan*; when this occurred is unknown. Based on Sagang Sechen and the other seventeenth-century chronicles, some scholars have suggested 1189. But, as de Rachewiltz has pointed out, the locality where this took place is different in the *Secret History* and the chronicles, and thus "we are dealing with different traditions" (de Rachewiltz, *Secret History*, 458).
15. *Qasbao* is a combination of the Mongolian *qas*, "jade," and Chinese *bao* 寶, "precious, jewel."
16. The "Jade Seal" refers to the imperial seal of government that was "discovered" in 1294 and declared to be the imperial seal of Qinshi Huangdi 秦始皇帝, the *chuanguo xi* 傳國璽 "seal transmitting the State," that had been used by all successive dynasties until it was lost by the Jurchens, who had taken it when they finally defeated the Song. Although Chinese scholars declared it a fraud, it became an important aspect of propaganda for Mongol legitimacy to rule China, and its importance only grew with time. In the Mongol chronicles of the seventeenth century the seal appears first to Chinggis Khan, coming out of a rock, or he was born with it in his hand, or it was given to him by the dragon kings. The import of this potent symbol of legitimate rule was again revived by the Manchus, a fact with different interpretations in the historical tradition. Michael Weiers, "Die historische Dimension des Jade-siegels zur Zeit des mandschuherrschers Hongtaiji," *Zentralasiatische Studien* 24 (1994): 119–145.
17. These two banners, both made with horse hair hanging from a circular disk atop a pole, were symbols respectively of peace (white) and war (black).
18. A Tümen refers to a group of 10,000, so in this case there are supposed to be 40,000 Mongols, which becomes the basis of their standard moniker: the Forty.

The Oirat become known as "the Four," after the initial four groups they comprised.

19. This story, which is also in the other seventeenth-century chronicles, is first found in the sixteenth-century collection of Chinggis Khan tales, the *Golden Summary of Chinggis Khan*. Leland Liu Rogers, *The Golden Summary of Cinggis Qayan: Cinggis Qayan-u Altan Tobci* (Wiesbaden: Harrassowitz Verlag, 2009).

20. The people of the Five Colors are part of the Mongolian geographical/sacred division of the known world and its peoples. Though this classificatory scheme is not in the *Secret History*, the division is found in all later sources. As noted by several scholars, however, there is a marked difference in the sources over time as to which are the five colored peoples and the concomitant four subject peoples (*dörben qari*). It is likely that the fundamental construction of this geography is as follows:

	North Tibet / Black	
West Turkestan / Yellow	Center Mongolia / Blue	East Korea / White
	South China / Red	

In later sources under different influences, most notably Buddhist, these divisions are reformulated in multifarious ways. Klaus Sagaster, *Die Weisse Geschicte. Eine mongolische Quelle zur Lehre von den Beiden Ordnungen Religion und Staat in Tibet und der Mongolei* (Wiesbaden: Harrassowitz, 1976), 304–317.

21. The Enggüd (< Önggüt) were a Turkic people that had been resettled in the Ordos region by the Tang 唐 court in the ninth century. Gradually their territory expanded over much of the area that is now central Inner Mongolia; they also converted to Nestorian Christianity. In 1204 their leader Alaqag submitted to Chinggis Khan, an alliance that was sealed by the marriage of Alaqag's younger son to Chinggis's daughter Alaqai Beki. The marriage alliance between these two courts continued during the reigns of the subsequent Mongol rulers. de Rachewiltz, *Secret History*, 656.

22. Like the preceding story about the arrogance of Qasar and Belgütei, this story about Chenggui is not in the *Secret History* but is first found in the *Golden Summary of Chinggis Khan*. Therein, the story ends differently: "For this Qasar was awarded a woman called Bombolun. After that the skillful Cinggüi sent a crystal stupa to the incarnate wise emperor, for which Činggis Khan gave his daughter Al Altan." Rogers, *Golden Summary*, 84.

23. "The Buriats are the northernmost branch of the Mongolian peoples. Inhabiting southern Siberia on both sides of Lake Baikal, they were brought under Russian control in the 17th century." Atwood, *Encyclopedia*, 60.
24. Wangzun is probably a corrupted version of the clan name—Wanyan—of the Jurchen rulers of the Jin dynasty. Atwood, *Encyclopedia*, 275–278.
25. Like the two preceding stories, this is first found in the *Golden Summary of Chinggis Khan*. It is also in the other seventeenth-century chronicles. Rogers, *Golden Summary*, 85–86.
26. This story, "The Marriage of Qulan," and the following one, "The Trial of Argasun Khorchi," are first recorded in the *Golden Summary of Chinggis Khan*. Rogers, *Golden Summary*, 87–95.
27. "The Yüan [Mongol] demands for artisans and women to do embroidery work dates to 1232, but the Koryo response to such demands, especially in the presentation of women to the Yüan throne, did not begin until 1275. In that year, ten maidens were presented to the throne and this practice continued until 1353. . . . These girls probably gave rise to the legend of the beautiful Qulan, Korean bride of Cinggis, who rode with him in battle. . . . Like most legends of this type it combines truth with half-truth and fiction. Cinggis had a wife named Qulan 忽蘭 (cf. *YS* 106.1b) who was renowned for her beauty. There is, however, little doubt that she was of the Merkit, namely the daughter of Dayir-Üsün, the ruler of the Uhaz-Merkit. The identification of Qulan with Korea undoubtedly stems in large part from the intermarriage between Yüan and Koryo royal families and from the Koryo tribute girls. As far as is known, Cinggis himself never set foot in Korea, never gave any of his daughters to a Korean ruler, nor were any of his Empresses Korean." William E. Henthorn, *Korea: The Mongol Invasions* (Leiden: E. J. Brill, 1963), 214.
28. Although this legend is found in all the seventeenth-century chronicles, it is a distortion based on events that took place after Chinggis Khan's death. In particular, during the 1230s the Mongols continually invaded Korea; finally in 1239 negotiations began about Koryo's submission. The Mongols demanded that the Koryo king present himself at the Mongol court; however, using various excuses such as the death of the Queen Dowager, mourning period, illness, etc., the king continued to evade this demand. The Mongols also requested a royal "hostage," and for several years Chon, the Duke of Sinan, was passed off as the king's younger brother and shuttled back and forth between the Mongol and Koryo courts. Yet the Mongol demands persisted and the Koreans sent Wang Sun (1224–1283) to the Mongol court in 1241, saying he was the crown prince. He was not, a fact not discovered by the Mongols until fourteen years later. Regardless, during this time he married one of Möngke's daughters and eventually became the supreme commander of the Korean community in the Shenyang 瀋陽 area. He also joined

Mongol campaigns against Koryo, and in 1270 he led a contingent of troops there to suppress the rebellion of the Patrols. Henthorn, *Korea*, 104–105, 118.

29. The Nine Comrades, or Nine Paladins (*yisün örlüg*), of later Mongol histories and epics, derive from the main companions of Chinggis Khan found in the *Secret History*. In particular, the "Four Hounds" (Jebe, Khubilai, Jelme, and Sübe'tei) and the "Four Steeds" (Bo'orchu, Muqali, Boroqul, and Chila'un) were his hand-picked chief lieutenants. Over time Siki Khutug was added to these initial eight, thus forming the Nine Comrades celebrated in Mongolian literature and rituals. See Elisabetta Chiodo, "History and Legend: The Nine Paladins of Činggis (*Yisün Örlüg*) According to the Great Prayer (*Yeke öčig*)," *Ural-Altaische Jahrbücher* 13 (1994): 219–223.

30. Muqali was presented to Chinggis Khan as a personal or hereditary slave after his father, Gü'ün Qan, declared allegiance. However, over time he showed his merit and became a member of Chinggis Khan's elite group of "Four Steeds." After taking part in campaigns against the Kereit (1203) and Naiman (1204), in 1206 Muqali was appointed commander of the left wing of the Mongol army. He subsequently played a leading role in the campaigns against the Jin 金 dynasty (1211–1215). In 1217 Chinggis Khan gave him the titles Prince of the State (M. *güi ong*, < Ch. *guowang* 國王) and Grand Preceptor, and made him commander-in-chief of operations in North China. In this position he continued the campaigns against the Jin until his death near the Yellow River in 1223. Igor de Rachewiltz, *In the Service of the Khan: Eminent Personalities of the Early Mongol-Yüan Period* (Wiesbaden: Otto Harrassowitz, 1993), 3–8.

31. The Jalayir was a group that once rivaled the Mongols, and whose members became powerful aristocrats in the Mongol empire and its successor states. "In the 16th century the name Jalayir (as Jalair or Jalaid) was one of the fourteen clans of the Khalkha in northern Mongolia. It is found at present as a clan name among the Khalkha of Mongolia as well as a Banner and clan name in eastern and southeastern Inner Mongolia." Atwood, *Encyclopedia*, 257–258.

32. This story, "The Plot of Wrestler Böke," is first found in the *Golden Summary of Chinggis Khan*. Rogers, *Golden Summary*, 79–81.

33. The origin of this story is unclear, since it does not correspond to the stories of Qabul Khan and Ambagai Khan in the *Secret History* (de Rachewiltz, *Secret History*, § 47, 52–53, 57–58) or any other known source. Moreover, because this episode actually occurred before the rise of Chinggis Khan, it is unclear why it is included at this particular juncture in the narrative of the *Precious Summary*.

34. According to Mongol history, "Qabul Khan, his cousin [Ambagai] Khan, and Qabul Khan's son Qutula Khan ruled the Mongols in succession until about 1164, when Qutula died in battle with the Tatars, a group allied with the Jin. Earlier, the Tatars had captured first [Ambagai] Khan and then Qabul Khan's

eldest son, Ökin Barqaq, and handed them over to be nailed to a wooden mule by the Jin rulers. Under these blows the early Mongol Khanate disintegrated. The Chinese envoy Zhao Gong described the Jin rulers as mounting yearly expeditions against the Mongols, which they called 'thinning the ranks.' From 1160 to 1190 the victories of the Jin and their tribal allies filled the North China markets with Mongol slaves. Even so, the Mongol rulers regularly paid tribute to the Jin dynasty, really a form of state-subsidized trade. Chinggis Khan discontinued this tribute only in 1210." Atwood, *Encyclopedia*, 389–390.

35. On the introduction of the Mongols to newer forms of alcohol as the empire expanded and its deleterious consequences see Thomas T. Allsen, "Ögedei and Alcohol," *Mongolian Studies* 29 (2007): 3–12.
36. This story, "The Bejeweled Jade Cup," is first found in the *Golden Summary of Chinggis Khan*. It is also in all the other seventeenth-century chronicles. Rogers, *Golden Summary*, 99–101.
37. Qormusta derives from the Persian Ormuzd—a variant of Ahura Mazda, the creator and highest deity in Zoroastrianism—which, in the context of Buddhist Central Asia, came to be the standard translation of the Sanskrit Indra, the ancient supreme Vedic god, later a powerful deity in both Hinduism and Buddhism.
38. "Heaven" (M. *tengri*) is the supreme deity of the Mongolian pantheon, which is engaged in regulating the powers and events of the world. The role of Heaven and Mother Earth in recognizing the authority of Chinggis Khan's reign is found throughout the *Secret History*; in later Mongol sources the role of Mother Earth is omitted, and his legitimacy derives from the blessing of Heaven and his relationship with Tibetan Buddhism.
39. Qan Gaochung is Gaozu 高祖 (247–195 BCE, r. 202–195 BCE), the founder of the Han 漢 dynasty (202 BCE–220 CE).
40. Ang Lang is Wang Mang 王莽 (45 BCE–23 CE, r. 9–23 CE), a Han dynasty official who seized the throne and founded the Xin 新 dynasty, which ended when he died and the Han dynasty was restored.
41. Kliü Güngbü is Liu Guangwu 劉光武 (5 BCE–57 CE, r. 25–29 CE), the restorer and thus the founder of the Later or Eastern Han dynasty (25–220 CE).
42. Qan Mingdi is Mingdi 明帝 (15–75 CE, r. 58–75 CE). the fourth son of emperor Guangwu, and the second ruler of the Eastern Han dynasty.
43. The legend of Emperor Mingdi's dream about the Buddha, which supposedly inspired him to send envoys to Central Asia to bring back the Dharma, developed sometime in the third century and has no basis in historical fact. Erik Zürcher, *The Buddhist Conquest of China: The Spread and Adaptation of Buddhism in Early Medieval China* (Leiden: Brill, 1959), 22.
44. Qan Qindi is Xiandi 獻帝 (181–234, r. 189–220 CE), the fourteenth and last emperor of the Eastern Han dynasty.

45. This is a convoluted history of the Jin 晉 dynasty (266–420 CE), which followed the Three Kingdoms period and was founded by Sima Yan 司馬炎.
46. Sui Yangdai is Yangdi 煬帝 (569–618, r. 604–618), the second emperor of the Sui 隋 dynasty (581–618).
47. Tang Gaochung is Gaozu 高祖 (566–635, r. 618–625), the founder of the Tang 唐 dynasty (618–907).
48. Tayangbu is Taiyuan 太原 in today's Shanxi 山西.
49. Tang Taisong is Taizong 太宗 (598–649, r. 626–649), the second emperor of the Tang.
50. Tang Jangzang is a variant of the more common Tang san chang, the Mongolian name for the famous Tang dynasty pilgrim and translator Xuanzang 玄奘. The name, however, is not based on the original historical sources about Xuanzang but derives from the sixteenth-century novel *Journey to the West*, wherein the Xuanzang-like main character is called Tang Sanzang 唐三藏, meaning Tang Tripitaka. The influence of this novel on Mongol historiography is also evident in the fact that Xuanzang is identified as the emperor's son, which he was not.
51. The "Two Realms" are generally recognized as the two spheres of religion and state (M. *qoyar yosu*, T, *lugs-nyis/lugs-zung*), with Buddhist teachers manifesting religious doctrine and providing ideological legitimacy for the khan, who controls the political affairs of state.
52. Munchang is the Tibetan name for Princess Wencheng (Wencheng Gongzhu 文成公主), the Tang princess who was sent to Tibet (see page #, note #).
53. Tang Ciguuchung is Gaozong 高宗 (628–683, r. 649–684), the third emperor of the Tang.
54. Tang Zochung is Tang Zhongzong 唐中宗 (656–710, r. 684–684), the fourth emperor of the Tang.
55. Yichung is Ruizong 睿宗 (656–710, r. 662–716), the fifth emperor of the Tang.
56. Qanchung is Xuanzong 玄宗 (685–762, r. 712–756), the sixth emperor of the Tang.
57. Tang Zungchung is Suzong 玄宗 (711–762, r. 756–762), the seventh emperor of the Tang.
58. This episode, which is also recounted in the preceding chapter on Tibet, is not correct. Nevertheless, it may refer to Trisong Detsen's invasion of China in 763, during which his forces not only conquered Chang'an 長安 but also installed a puppet emperor while Emperor Daizong 代宗 was in Luoyang 洛陽.
59. Tang Dangchung is Daizong 代宗 (727–779, r. 762–779), the eighth emperor of the Tang.
60. Tang Dingchung is Dezong 德宗 (742–805, r. 779–805), the ninth emperor of the Tang.
61. Tang Sünchung is Shunzong 順宗 (761–806, r. 805–805), the tenth emperor of the Tang.

62. Tang Qunchung is Xianzong 憲宗 (778–820, r. 805–820), the eleventh emperor of the Tang.
63. Tang Muchung is Muzong 穆宗 (795–824, r. 820–824), the twelfth emperor of the Tang.
64. Tang Juchung is Jingzong 敬宗 (809–827, r. 824–827), the thirteenth emperor of the Tang.
65. Tang Sunchung is Wenzong 文宗 (809–840, r. 827–840), the fourteenth emperor of the Tang.
66. Tang Kyuchung is Wuzong 武宗 (814–846, r. 840–846), the fifteenth emperor of the Tang.
67. Tang Krichung is Xuanzong 宣宗 (810–859, r. 846–859), the sixteenth emperor of the Tang.
68. Tang Yichung is Yizong 懿宗 (833–873, r. 859–873), the seventeenth emperor of the Tang.
69. Tang Jinchung is Xizong 僖宗 (862–888, r. 873–888), the eighteenth emperor of the Tang.
70. Tang Inggeyiding is Zhaozong 昭宗 (867–904, r. 888–904), the nineteenth emperor of the Tang.
71. Prince Layang (Liang 梁) of south China refers to Zhu Quanzhong 朱全忠 (852–912, r. 907–912), who killed the last Tang emperor and founded the Later Liang 後梁 dynasty (907–923).
72. This appears to be a confused history of the Later Zhou 後周 dynasty (951–960).
73. Joo Taizu Wang refers to Abaoji (872–926, r. 916–926), the founder of the Khitan's Liao 遼 dynasty (916–1125), posthumously known as Emperor Taizu 太祖.
74. In early Qing historiography the Mongolic-speaking Khitans and their Liao dynasty (916–1125), as well as the Jurchens' Jin 金 dynasty (1115–1234), were understood as being part of the Manchu's imperial heritage.
75. Altan Khan, which means "Gold Khan," refers to Wanyan Chenglin 完顏承麟 (d. 1234) the last emperor of the Jin (金 gold) dynasty.
76. Chinggis Khan actually launched his first campaign against the Jurchen's Jin 金 dynasty (1115–1234) in the spring of 1211. This initial foray was more for reconnaissance, and only the following year was a large-scale invasion undertaken. Through the winter of 1214 the Mongols blockaded the Jin capital. In the spring of 1214 the Jin court sued for peace and offered a Jurchen princess to Chinggis Khan, and the Mongols withdrew from the capital. The Xuanzong 宣宗 emperor (1163–1224, r. 1213–1224), however, was wary and moved the capital south to Kaifeng 開封, an action Chinggis Khan saw as a preparation for war, and the following year he launched another campaign. On May 31, 1215, the Jin capital surrendered to the Mongols; it was not until 1234 that the Jin was completely defeated by Ögedei Khan's forces. Herbert Franke and Denis Twitchett, *The Cambridge*

History of China: Alien Regimes and Border States, 97–1368 (New York: Cambridge University Press, 1994), 250–265.

77. Dai Ming (< Ch. 大命, "great mandate") is a Chinese title confirming that Chinggis Khan had the mandate of Heaven.

78. The title Sidurgu Khan ("Honest Khan") was bestowed on the Tangut ruler Iluqu Burqan by Chinggis Khan after the Tangut had been defeated (de Rachewiltz, *Secret History*, 199). "The name is ironic, since it was given to the Tangut emperor for being dishonest and going back on his word." Rogers, *Golden Summary*, 96.

79. The Tangut were a Tibeto-Burman group of people who had moved into northwest China in the tenth century and shortly thereafter founded the Xixia 西夏 dynasty (1038–1227).

80. This story, "The Treachery of Sidurgu Khan," is first found in the *Golden Summary of Chinggis Khan*. Rogers, *Golden Summary*, 82–83.

81. As noted by Rogers, this name is most likely a distortion of Jamuqa, Chinggis Khan's sworn brother, since it is correctly written as such in Lubsangdanjin's *Golden Summary*, which—unlike the other seventeenth-century chronicles—extensively used the *Secret History* as a source. Rogers, *Golden Summary*, 97.

82. Sarta'ul refers very broadly to the entire Eastern Turkestan region, and in general to any Central and Western Asian Muslim. de Rachewiltz, *Secret History*, 562–563.

83. Tokmag is not found in any records from the empire period; it only developed as an important medieval Central Asian trading center in the post-Yuan period. It was located on the Chu River west of Lake Isyk Köl in contemporary Kazakhstan. Lubsangdanjin, *Altan Tobci*, ed. Coyiji (Kökeqota: Öbör Monggol-un arad-un keblel-ün qoriy-a, 1983), 513.

84. Ong Khan was the ruler of the Kereit, who were mostly Nestorian Christians, and controlled the territory of central Mongolia (de Rachewiltz, *Secret History*, 394). Although he and Chinggis Khan's father had been sworn friends, the power of Ong Khan and his Kereits threatened the rise of Chinggis, and thus they were eventually "ethnically cleansed." The *Secret History* tells us, "When the Mongols subjugated the Kereyit people, they distributed them among each other so that nobody went short. They distributed the Tümen Tübe'en and they all took of them until they had plenty. They despoiled the Olon Dongqayit in less than a day. As for the brave Jirgin who used to strip the blood-stained clothing and possessions from the enemy, they divided and apportioned them, but could not give some to everybody. Having in this way annihilated the Kereyit people, Cinggis Qa'an spent that winter at Abji'a Ködeger. Ong Qan and Senggüm escaped with their bare lives and went away, unwilling to submit to Cinggis Qa'an. Ong Qan, who was suffering from thirst, was going to drink at Nekün

Usun of Didik Saqal when he came across the Naiman patrolman Qori Sübeci. Qori Sübeci seized Ong Qan and although the latter declared, 'I am Ong Qan,' Qori Sübeci did not recognise him and, disbelieving him, slew him on the spot." de Rachewiltz, *Secret History*, 109.

85. Tayan Khan was the ruler of the powerful Naiman, who inhabited the area east and west of the Altai mountain range in western Mongolia, whom Chinggis Khan defeated in 1204 according to the *Secret History* (§ 196).
86. Prince Buurul of Üüshin (a group not found in the *Secret History*) is Boroqul of the Jürkin in the *Secret History*. As a boy he was taken from the Jürkin camp and raised by Chinggis Khan's mother, whereupon he became one of the khan's loyal commanders, eventually promoted to lord (M. *noyan*), commander of a thousand. de Rachewiltz, *Secret History*, 508.
87. As noted by de Rachewiltz, it is unlikely that the submission of the Qonggirad and Ikires-related Khorolas group found in the *Secret History* (§ 141) corresponds to this later story about the Khorlad, as others have suggested. de Rachewiltz, *Secret History*, 517–518.
88. Darkhan is an old title in the Turco-Mongol tradition, given to those with both special rights and exemption from various requirements, such as paying taxes. In the Mongol tradition "the range of possible rights and exemptions include: the right to nomadize freely over wide territory, the right to hold women captured in war without forwarding them to the khan, immunity to prosecution for up to nine transgressions, the right to serve as quiver bearers for the khan, and the right to drink *ötög*, a special ceremonial liquor (probably a milk liquor) offered at great assemblies. All these rights were hereditary, being granted 'unto the seed of the seed.' Rewards of subjects and goods inevitably accompanied them, too. While many in the Mongol elite received these exemptions, the actual title *darqan* was mostly reserved for those outside the ruling inner circle." Atwood, *Encyclopedia*, 133.
89. Although Temüjin was enthroned as khan in 1206, contrary to later Mongolian and Tibetan histories, he never campaigned against Tibet. On the early relations between the Mongols and Tibet see Christopher P. Atwood, "The First Mongol Contacts with the Tibetans," in *Trails of the Tibetan Tradition: Papers for Elliot Sperling*, ed. Roberto Vitali (Dharamsala: Amnye Machen Institute, 2014), 21–46.
90. Sakya Chag Lotsawa Ananda Garbi is Kungga Nyingpo (1092–1158), the son of Konchog Gyalpo (1034–1102) of the Khon family, who founded Sakya monastery in 1073. In turn, Kungga Nyingpo formulated the tantric teachings of the Virupa lineage into a distinctive school that was to become the Sakya. More to the point, however, the fact that he died in 1158 belies the notion that he met Chinggis Khan in 1206.

91. Although later Mongol and Tibetan sources claim that Chinggis Khan was the first to initiate relations with Tibetan Buddhists, this has long been recognized as a later historical fabrication. However, he and the Mongols did come into contact with Tibetans and Tibetan Buddhism during this early period, especially through their relations with the Tanguts. Elliot Sperling, "Rtsa-mi Lo-tsa-ba Sangs-rgyas grags-pa and the Tangut Background to Early Mongol-Tibetan Relations," in *Tibetan Studies: Proceedings of the 6th Seminar of the International Association of Tibetan Studies*, ed. Per Kvaerne (Oslo: The Institute for Comparative Research in Human Culture, 1994), 801–824.
92. The three provinces are Ü-Tsang, Kham, and Amdo.
93. The three provinces of Ngari, or western Tibet, are Guge, Maryul, and Purang.
94. After his campaigns in Central Asia, Chinggis Khan had planned "to follow the Indus River north through a route roughly tracking the Pakistan-China highway of today," but he was dissuaded from doing so by his advisor Yelü Chucai. This later story about meeting a rhinoceros was "derived from Song Zichen's encomium of the official Yelü Chucai." Christopher P. Atwood, "*The History of the Yuan*, chapter 1," *Mongolian Studies* 34 (2017–2018): 78.
95. Centurions, chiliarchs, and myriarchs were commanders of units of 100, 1000, and 10,000 men, respectively.
96. "Bujin" is the title "Lady" (*Furen* 夫人) given to high-ranking women, and "Taibujin" is the title "Commandery Grand Mistress" (*Taifuren* 太夫人), an "honorific designation granted to mothers and grandmothers of various high-ranking officials." Charles O. Hucker, *A Dictionary of Official Titles in Imperial China* (Stanford, CA: Stanford University Press, 1985), #1793.
97. This is a famous Mongolian saying that means "completely sated and relaxed," alluding to the act of lying on one's back with outstretched arms and legs. It is first found in a speech of Ögedei Khan in the *Secret History*.
98. Muna Mountain lies to the west of Baotou 包头 in Inner Mongolia.
99. On the historiography of this prophecy and the narrative of Chinggis Khan's death, especially how it relates to the post-Yuan Mongols claiming the territory of what is now Inner Mongolia as their "homeland," see Johan Elverskog, "The Legend of Muna Mountain," *Inner Asia* 8, 1 (2006): 99–122.
100. This story, "The Incarceration of Qasar," is first found in the *Golden Summary of Chinggis Khan*. It is also in all the other seventeenth-century chronicles. Rogers, *Golden Summary*, 104–106.
101. Dörmegei is the Mongolian name for Lingzhou 靈州, which is present-day Lingwuxian 靈武縣 in Ningxia 寧夏.
102. This story, "The Conquest of the Tangut," is first found in the *Golden Summary of Chinggis Khan*. It is also in all the other seventeenth-century chronicles. Rogers, *Golden Summary*, 107–111.

103. Miñag (< T. mi nyag) is the Tangut name for themselves.

104. "Queen Mother" or "Queen's River" is the Mongol name for the Yellow River 黃河.

105. Irgai is Zhencheng 鎮城 in Ningxia 寧夏, modern-day Yinchuan 銀川. The Mongol name is borrowed from the Tangut Erigaya, noted by Marco Polo as Egrigaya. Henry Serruys, *Sino-Mongol Relations during the Ming II. The Tribute System and Diplomatic Missions (1400–1600)* (Bruxelles: Institut Belge des Hautes Études Chinoises, 1967), 24 n. 8.

106. Although Sagang Sechen drew upon the story of Chinggis Khan's death as found in the *Golden Summary of Chinggis Khan*—especially in terms of Kilügen Baatur's speech—he presents it in a truncated fashion. Rogers, *Golden Summary*, 112–116.

107. In contradistinction to the many legendary accounts of Chinggis Khan's death, scholars have recently argued that he died of bubonic plague during the Xixia campaign (You Wenpeng et al., "Genghis Khan's death (AD 1227): An Unsolvable Riddle or Simply a Pandemic Disease?" *International Journal of Infectious Diseases* 104 (2021): 347–348. On the ongoing debate about the origins of the medieval Black Death—whether it started in the twelfth or thirteenth century, and originated in Qinghai-Gansu or the Tianshan mountains—see John Brook and Monica Green, "Thinking Big About the Plague," *Inference* 4, 2 (2018), https://inference-review.com/letter/thinking-big-about-the-plague.

108. "The Lament for Chinggis Khan," is first found in the *Golden Summary of Chinggis Khan*. Rogers, *Golden Summary*,117–120.

109. The Kharagun Mountains are the Daqing 大青 Mountains north of Hohhot in Inner Mongolia.

110. The Eight White Tents as the main site of the Chinggis Khan cult developed in the late fifteenth–early sixteenth centuries when the Mongols first moved into the Ordos region in the wake of the 1449 Tumu Incident. While the cult drew on precedents from the empire period, it also developed new rituals and traditions related to the upheavals of the Mongol-Oirat wars. The Eight White Tents became the site where all Mongol rulers came to be enthroned "in front of the Lord." Johan Elverskog, *Our Great Qing: The Mongols, Buddhism, and the State in Late Imperial China* (Honolulu: University of Hawai'i Press, 2006), 40–62.

4. HISTORY OF THE YUAN DYNASTY

1. Chagatai (d. 1241/2) was Chinggis Khan's second son. His first campaign was with Chinggis against the Jurchen Jin 金 dynasty in 1211–1216. Afterward, during the Western Campaign (1219–1224), Chagatai and Ögedei were ordered to seize the city of Utrar, and then with Jochi the city of Urganch. When the

Khorezm Shah fled, Chagatai was responsible for his capture and therefore spent the winter of 1221–1222 pursuing the shah in northwest India. During Chinggis's final campaign against the Tanguts, Chagatai as the eldest surviving son remained in Mongolia with the court and various forces. Upon Chinggis's death Chagatai headed the Khuriltai that elected Ögedei as khan. Even though he was not selected to be khan by Chinggis, Chagatai maintained a modicum of authority as the eldest surviving son and the main keeper of the *jasag*, or Mongol law. After Ögedei's enthronement Chagatai returned to his bequeathed territory in Central Asia and stayed at his summer and winter residences in the Ili Valley and Kulja. In Muslim sources Chagatai is frequently portrayed as anti-Islam in that he ruled harshly against Muslims who broke the *jasag*, which contained laws contrary to the *shari'a*, yet in fact he appointed and employed many Muslim ministers and officials. The sources differ on his time of death, either just before Ögedei (late 1241) or five months later (early 1242). *The Encyclopaedia of Islam* (Leiden: E. J. Brill, 1960), vol. II, 2–3.

2. Sarta'ul refers very broadly to the entire Eastern Turkestan region, and in general to any Central or Western Asian Muslim.
3. Although claimed as a son by Chinggis Khan, Jochi (which means "guest," d. 1225?) was born after Börte had been captured by a Merkid leader, and this stigma plagued his life. Nevertheless, he was apparently initially groomed as the heir apparent and did take command of the Merkid conquest in 1204. After the unification of Mongolia, Chinggis Khan sent Jochi north to conquer Siberia in 1207. Later he also campaigned against North China (1211–1213) and the Kipchaks (1218–1219), and took part in the Western Campaigns (1220–1221). However, Chinggis eventually decided upon Ögedei as his heir, and Jochi was given Khorezm and the west as his appanage. After he died prematurely his realm (*ulus*) passed to his son Batu, the founder of the Golden Horde, or Ulus of Jochi. Christopher P. Atwood, *Encyclopedia of Mongolia and the Mongol Empire* (New York: Facts on File, 2004), 278–279.
4. As noted above, Tokmag was not an important city in the Yuan period, and thus Jochi was actually bequeathed Khorezm and the unconquered areas to its west. After those areas were conquered, Jochi's descendants established themselves as the rulers of the Golden Horde in what is now southern Russia.
5. Ögedei Khan (1186–1241, r. 1229–1241, Taizong 太宗) was the third son of Chinggis Khan and his designated heir. During his reign in 1234 the Mongols finally defeated the Jurchen Jin dynasty in north China. In the following year the western campaigns were initiated, leading to the establishment of the Golden Horde. Ögedei also initiated the empirewide postal system and built the Mongol capital at Qaraqorum in the Orkhon valley, where he also began the construction of a Buddhist stupa. Waltraut Abramowski, "Die chinesischen Annalen von Ögedei

und Güyük: Übersetzung des 2. Kapitels des Yüan-shih," *Zentralasiatische Studien* 10 (1975): 117–167; Christina Franken, *Die "Grosse Halle" von Karakorum: Zur archäologischen Untersuchung des ersten buddhistischen Tempels der alten mongolischen Haupstadt* (Wiesbaden: Reichert Verlag, 2015).

6. Although Tolui was apparently Chinggis Khan's favorite son and recognized as the best warrior by his father, he was never appointed heir apparent. He began his distinguished military career with the 1213 campaign against the Jin 金, during which he purportedly scaled a city's walls during an attack. In 1221 Chinggis Khan sent him on his first independent campaign to Khorasan, Iran; after there were revolts, Tolui ordered the total massacre of Merv and Nishapur. Later he joined his father on the final campaign against the Tanguts; after Chinggis's death, Tolui supported the empire till the election of Ögedei in 1229. His appanage was the ancestral homeland of northwest Mongolia, from where he helped coordinate Ögedei's final defeat of the Jin. Atwood, *Encyclopedia*, 542.
7. Drakpa Gyeltsen (1147–1216) was the third throne holder of Sakya monastery for forty-three years. He was also the uncle of Sakya Pandita, who was one of his main disciples. https://treasuryoflives.org/biographies/view/Drakpa-Gyeltsen/2915 (accessed October 27, 2020).
8. Güyüg Khan (r. 1246–1248) was enthroned five years after the death of Ögedei, after the stiff resistance of other Mongol princes, especially Batu, had finally been quelled by his mother, Töregene, who had ruled as regent in the interim. Once elevated as khan he bestowed lavish gifts on his supporters, a practice he continued with debilitating financial implications, but without appeasing his opponents. During his rule the administration veered toward decentralization and political fragmentation. His weak and ineffectual reign came to an end when he died during a punitive campaign against his rival Batu in the west. Herbert Franke and Denis Twitchett, *The Cambridge History of China: Alien Regimes and Border States, 97–1368* (New York: Cambridge University Press, 1994), 382–390.
9. Köden (fl. 1235–1247), the second son of Ögedei, began his career by conquering Gansu 甘肅 in 1235. From there he marched south into Sichuan 四川, attacking Chengdu 成都 in November 1236. He returned to his appanage at Liangzhou 涼州 in 1239, and the following year sent an army led by Dorda Darkhan to subjugate Tibet. Being told of Sakya Pandita, Köden sent an envoy to invite him in 1244, though Köden himself returned to Mongolia to attend the Khuriltai convened upon the death of Ögedei. After his brother Güyüg was made khan, Köden returned to Liangzhou and finally met Sakya Pandita in 1247. Although Köden received Buddhist teachings and tantric initiations, Sakya Pandita advised Tibetan hierarchs to submit to the Mongols. Köden died shortly thereafter. Atwood, *Encyclopedia*, 321.

10. While the dragon king refers to Muchalinda, the ruler of the nagas, it is unclear what this illness may have been.
11. In 1240 Köden did not send envoys to Tibet, but rather a military force led by Dorda Darkhan, who left a wake of devastation as they marched south to the Phanyul valley. They also damaged the Kadampa monasteries of Reting and Gyel Lhakhang, where five hundred men were slaughtered. The Taglung monastery was spared due to heavy fog, as was Drigung, which, according to tradition, the abbot defended by calling forth a shower of stones. Witnessing this miraculous display, Dorda wanted to bring the abbot back to the Mongol court to teach the Dharma; however, he refused and recommended he contact Sakya Pandita. Thus in 1244 Köden sent envoys to invite Sakya Pandita with a letter warning of invasion in case of noncompliance. Dieter Schuh, *Erlasse und Sendschreiben mongolischer Herrscher für tibetische Geistliche* (St. Augustin: VGH-Wissenschaftsverlag, 1977), 31–41.
12. This prophecy is first found in Tsalpa Kungga Dorjé's (1309–1364) *Red Annals.* 'Tshal-pa Kun-dga' rdo-rje, *Deb-ther dmar-po* (Beijing: Mi-rigs dpe-skrun khang, 1981), 47.
13. According to Nicholas Poppe, this is an old Mongolian curse, here cited by only sufficient words to identify it. The full form is, "I urinate on your father's head and will rape your mother." I thank John R. Krueger for explaining this passage.
14. Sakya Pandita actually set out in 1245 and arrived at Liangzhou 涼州 in 1246, only to find Köden had returned to the Khuriltai that elected Güyüg as khan. They finally met the following year when Köden returned, and their future relations were established: "Sa-skya Pandita entered into a new role as an agent of Mongol policy in his home country. He sent a circular letter to the ecclesiastical and lay notables of Tibet, advising them to submit and to allow the Mongols to exact taxes and to levy troops. To cement the agreement, the boy Phyag-na-rdo-rje was promised in marriage a daughter of Köden's. Moreover, Güyüg sent substantial presents to the Tibetan monasteries: 4 *bre-chen* of gold (1 *bre-chen* = 20 *bre*; 1 *bre* = ca. 2 pints), 20 *bre-chen* of silver, and 200 precious stones." Luciano Petech, "Tibetan Relations with Sung China and with the Mongols," in *China Among Equals: The Middle Kingdom and Its Neighbors, 10th–14th Centuries*, ed. Morris Rossabi (Berkeley: University of California Press, 1983), 182.
15. Sorqaqtani Beki, Princess Sorqaqtani (d. 1252), was the niece of Ong Khan, the ruler of the Kereit; when they were conquered by Chinggis Khan, he gave her in marriage to his son Tolui. When he died prematurely in 1232, Ögedei Khan gave her control of Tolui's appanage, whereupon she became a major figure in Mongol history. Most notably, upon the death of Güyüg Khan she played a key role in moving control of the throne from the descendants of Ögedei to those of Tolui. Moreover, although she was a Nestorian Christian she advocated

ecumenicalism, so much so that she financed the construction of a madrasa in Bukhara. She taught this pluralistic vision to her sons, which in turn shaped subsequent Mongol religious policies. Atwood, *Encyclopedia*, 511–512.

16. Möngke Khan (r. 1251–1259) had the support of the Jochid and Toluid lineages, but only on the day of his enthronement was an Ögedeid and Chaghataid assassination plot against him thwarted. Thus wary of the continuing fractious nature of the empire, Möngke launched a massive purge of his real and imagined enemies, then consolidated his control over the administrative apparatus. He instituted new policies of internal reform, especially of the tax system, and also prepared for military expansion. In 1252 he launched three campaigns: Hülegü against Iran, Prince Yekü against Korea, and Khubilai against the Dali 大理 kingdom of Yunnan 雲南. From this southern vantage point in 1258, Möngke and his forces attacked the Southern Song 南宋 (1127–1279). In the following year the Song was surrounded by Mongol forces from the north, south, and west; however, on August 12, 1259, Möngke died. This not only saved the Southern Song from military defeat but also precipitated the civil war that finally shattered the unity of the Mongol Empire. Franke and Twitchett, *The Cambridge History*, 390–413.

17. Sechen, "Wise," is the Mongol title for Khubilai Khan (1215–1294, r. 1260–1294, Shizu 世祖). In 1251 his elder brother Möngke was elected khan, wresting power from the designated successors of Ögedei's lineage. Khubilai was given northern China as an appanage and the duty of defeating the Dali 大理 kingdom in Yunnan 雲南. After this success he began consolidating his power in north China and building Shangdu 上都, and acted as mediator in the fierce Buddhist-Daoist debates of the 1250s. In 1258 Möngke and Khubilai began the conquest of the Southern Song 南宋 (1127–1279), though a year later Möngke died. Although Khubilai was elected khan, a bitter succession struggle ensued with his younger brother Ariq Böke, until Ariq Böke suddenly died in 1266. Afterward Khubilai focused on conquering the Song, fighting on both land and sea, yet did not succeed until the last Song emperor died in 1279. In 1272 Khubilai proclaimed the founding of the Yuan 元 dynasty (1272–1368), subjugated Korea, and launched a disastrous invasion of Japan in 1274. Yet as his power increased in the East, his right to rule was being threatened from Central Asia by steppe-oriented Mongols under Qaidu, also defeated in 1279. After he had consolidated his control, Khubilai turned to reforming the government, particularly in the economic and legal spheres. Yet his rule was beset with financial problems, stemming from tax policies, the building of the Grand Canal extension to the capital, and failed campaigns in South Asia. Nevertheless, there were improvements in other areas, including science, trade, and the arts. Morris

Rossabi, *Khubilai Khan: His Life and Times* (Berkeley: University of California Press, 1988).

18. In 1256 Khubilai built Kaiping 開平 in what is now Inner Mongolia, and during the war with Ariq Böke it became his main military headquarters. In 1263 it was renamed Shangdu 上都 (Upper Capital) and was subsequently used by the Yuan rulers during the summer months. During the Ming dynasty Shangdu was used as a frontier garrison until it was abandoned in 1430. Atwood, *Encyclopedia*, 497; Hok-lam Chan, "Exorcising the Dragon: A Legend about the Building of the Mongolian Upper Capital (Shangdu)," *Central Asiatic Journal* 55, 1 (2011): 1–32.
19. Daidu 大都, "Great Capital," was the name Khubilai Khan gave to the former Jin 金 dynasty capital on March 4, 1272. It is now the site of modern Beijing 北京.
20. The Four States refers to the four khanates (or *ulus*) that composed the Mongol Empire—the Yuan dynasty in China, the Chagataid dynasty in Central Asia, the Il-Khans in Iran and Iraq, and the Golden Horde in southern Russia—all of which were technically under the control of the Great Khan.
21. Matidhvaja is Pakpa Lama (1235–1280), "Holy Lama," the honorific title of Lodro Gyeltsen. He was born at Lukhung in western Tibet and pursued his religious studies at Sakya monastery under the tutelage of his uncle Sakya Pandita (1182–1251), and accompanied him when summoned by Köden. Four years later, upon Sakya Pandita's death, Pakpa inherited his office; in 1253 Khubilai summoned him to his court and in 1254 bestowed on him all the monasteries of Tsang. In 1258 Pakpa initiated Khubilai into Buddhism and played a decisive role in the third and final Buddhist-Daoist debate held at court. After Khubilai's enthronement and victorious succession feud with Ariq Böke, Pakpa Lama became the main Tibetan Buddhist teacher at court, since his erstwhile competitor Karma Paksi (1206–1283) of the Black Hat (Zhva-nag) sect of the Karmapas had been purged on account of his alleged affiliations with Ariq Böke. Thus in 1264 Khubilai appointed Pakpa as the National Preceptor (*guoshi* 國師) and supreme head of the entire Tibetan clergy, whereupon he returned to Sakya. Shortly afterward, there was widespread rebellion spearheaded by the Drigungpa, who opposed Sakya dominance enforced by their Mongol protectors. The revolt was quelled by Mongol forces, and Pakpa was evacuated to Gansu 甘肅 and then continued to the capital. During this time he was commissioned to devise a national script, capable of writing all languages within the empire, which was submitted and adopted by the court in 1269. Within a year he was granted the title Imperial Preceptor (*dishi* 帝師). For the next several years he traveled, and in 1274 he renounced his title and returned to Tibet, arriving at Sakya in 1276. The following year he convened a general council that affirmed the eccelestical

authority of the Sakya in Tibet. He then retired to Sakya and wrote his most important work, the *Shes bya rab gsal*, an introductory guidebook to Buddhism for the heir apparent Jinggim. János Szerb, "Glosses on the Oeuvre of Bla-ma 'Phags-pa: II. Some notes on the events of the years 1251–1254," *Acta Orientalia Hungarica* 34 (1980): 263–285; János Szerb, "Glosses on the Oeuvre of Bla-ma 'Phags-pa: III. The 'Patron-Patronized' Relationship," in *Soundings in Tibetan Civilization*, ed. Barbara Nimri Aziz and Matthew Kapstein (New Delhi: Manohar, 1985), 165–173.

22. Khubilai Khan actually requested Köden to send him Pakpa Lama and Chagna Dorjé as he was preparing for his 1253 campaign against Yunnan 雲南. The two brothers joined Khubilai's camp during his return northward from the successful campaign in the south. While Pakpa taught the Dharma, Khubilai issued a decree exempting the Sakya monks from taxation and military and corvée service. A similar decree exempting lamas of central Tibet was given to the Nyingma lama Zur Sakya Ö. Luciano Petech, *Central Tibet and the Mongols. The Yüan-Sa-skya Period of Tibetan History* (Rome: Istituto Italiano per il Medio Estremo Oriente, 1990), 14–15.
23. Queen Chabi (d. 1281) was a Qonggirad and Khubilai Khan's second wife, but she soon eclipsed both his first wife and his other five wives. She was famous for her frugality, and for giving her sons both Buddhist initiations and Confucian educations. In fact, she supported Confucian officials and once even "criticized Liu Bingzhong for not opposing a plan of Qubilai's *keshig* nobility to make the suburbs of the capital a grazing ground." Atwood, *Encyclopedia*, 82.
24. Hevajra is a tantric deity that developed in India and by the eighth century was the main deity in the *Hevajratantra*. "Hevajra is most commonly depicted as dark blue in color and naked. One of his most common forms is Kapāladhārin ('Skull Bearing') Hevajra, with four legs, eight faces with three eyes each, and sixteen hands, each of which holds a skull cup. Each face has three bloodshot eyes, four fangs, and a protruding tongue. The skulls in his right hands hold various animals and the skulls in his left hand hold various deities. He is often depicted in sexual union with his consort Nairātmyā ('Selflessness'), who holds a curved knife and skull cup, the couple surrounded by a retinue of eight yoginis." Robert E. Buswell, Jr., and Donald S. Lopez, Jr., *The Princeton Dictionary of Buddhism* (Princeton, NJ: Princeton University Press, 2014), 348.
25. Mahakala, "The Great Black One," is a wrathful emanation of the Bodhisattva Avalokitesvara and had become a powerful state protector in the Tangut empire. Legend has it that Mahakala enabled the Tanguts to initially defeat Chinggis Khan. Once the Mongols did defeat the Tanguts they adopted Mahakala as the protector of their own state. Karl Debreczeny, "Faith and Empire: An Overview,"

in *Faith and Empire: The Art of Politics in Tibetan Buddhism*, ed. K. Debreczeny (New York: Rubin Museum of Art, 2019), 31–33.

26. According to the biography of Pakpa Lama this initiation took place at Khubilai Khan's court in 1258, and it is mentioned in the colophon of a short eulogy written by Pakpa Lama dedicated to the goddesses of the Hevajra mandala (Szerb, "Glosses on the Oeuvre of Bla-ma 'Phags-pa: III. The 'Patron-Patronized' Relationship," 166). It is often identified as the beginning of Buddhism among the Mongols; however, we know from Situ Panchen's *History of the Kagyu Sect* that Karma Paksi (1204 or 1206–1283/4) the second Black Hat Karmapa had initiated Möngke Khan into the Cakrasamvara mandala already in 1256. Si-tu Pan-chen Chos-kyi-'byung-gnas and Be-lo Tshe-dbang kun-khyab, *Sgrub brgyud karma kam tshang brgyud pa rin po che'i rnam par thar pa rab 'byam nor bu zla ba chu shel gyi phreng ba vol. 1* (New Delhi: 1972), 109.

27. According to the *Yuan Shi*, Khubilai Khan gave Pakpa Lama the title national preceptor (*guoshi* 國師) on January 9, 1261, and the title imperial preceptor (*dishi* 帝師) in late 1269 or early 1270 (*Yuan Shi* 元史) (Beijing: Zhonghua Shuju Chubanshe, 1995), 202:1b. In later Tibetan histories the role of Pakpa Lama was greatly amplified, and thus he supposedly initiated Khubilai Khan three times and each time was granted something new. The first time he received the thirteen districts (*khri' skor*) of central Tibet; the second time, the three regions (M. *cölge*, T. *chol kha*) of Tibet; and finally, numerous relics and various subjects (Igor de Rachewiltz, *In the Service of the Khan: Eminent Personalities of the Early Mongol-Yüan Period [1200–1300]* [Wiesbaden: Harrassowitz, 1993], 651). This retelling has shaped the idea that Pakpa Lama was made to rule Tibet, which is incorrect; he had absolutely no political control. The title given here is based on the Chinese: national preceptor, great prince of the three provinces (*sansheng daiwang guoshi* 三省太王國師).

28. A stater was a Greek coin that over time played a fundamental role in international trade, especially in the Black Sea area. As a result, it was adjusted to a standard of 16.05 grams, and this weight subsequently became standard in the trade networks of Inner Asia. A.D.H. Bivar, "Coins," in *The Oxford Encyclopedia of Archaeology in the Near East*, ed. Eric M. Meyers (New York: Oxford University Press, 1997), 41–52.

29. On the importance of pearls in Mongol imperial ideology, especially in the rituals of gift giving, see Thomas T. Allsen, *The Steppe and the Sea: Pearls in the Mongol Empire* (Philadelphia: University of Pennsylvania Press, 2019).

30. As noted by Petech, the common misconception that the Sakya abbots were temporal rulers of Tibet "must be abandoned." Nevertheless, it is true that the Mongols divided the whole Tibetan-speaking area into three units, the *cölge*

(Tib. *chol-kha*), comprising Mdo-smad (modern Amdo and northern Kham), Mdo-khams or Dmo-stod (modern Kham), and Dbus-gtsang (modern central and western Tibet). Petech, *Central Tibet*, 36–39.

31. According to Marco Polo, in 1284 Khubilai Khan sent three envoys to Sri Lanka to obtain not only these Buddha relics but also the world's largest ruby, which was in the Sri Lankan king's possession. "The king declined the offer. It was not so easy to resist the request for the tooth, however. The king managed that request by sending two other teeth of the Buddha, though not the one Khubilai coveted, along with a begging bowl and a tuft of the Buddha's hair. Khubilai was realistic enough to know that the gifts that reached him might not be the real things. To discourage anyone else from having this thought, he staged a huge reception outside the walls of Beijing to greet their arrival. Who then dared to suggest that these were not the genuine articles?" Timothy Brook, *Great State: China and the World* (New York: Harper, 2020), 101. See also Henry Yule, *The Book of Ser Marco Polo the Venetian concerning the Kingdoms and Marvels of the East, Translated and Edited, with Notes, by Colonel Sir Henry Yule, R.E., C.B., K.C.S.I., Corr. Inst. France, Third Edition, Revised Throughout in the Light of Recent Discoveries by Henri Cordier (of Paris)* (New York: Charles Scribner, 1929), 319–330.

32. Khubilai Khan's second son was born in 1243, nominated heir apparent in 1273, and died in 1286. The name Jinggim (< Tib. Jing-gim < Ch. Zhenjin 真金) was given to him by the Chan 禪 monk Haiyun 海雲, who was replaced as head of the Buddhist community by the Tibetan priest Namo in 1252. In 1275 Jinggim accompanied Pakpa Lama back to Tibet, and upon his request the lama wrote his most famous exposition of the Dharma, the *Shes bya rab gsal* (*What Is to Be Known*) of 1278.

33. Although in contention with his older brother Kamala, Öljeitü (r. 1294–1307, Chengzong 成宗) was made khan in April 1294 with the backing of his mother and the Mongol military and administrative elite. Once elevated he tried to continue the policies of his father, Khubilai; however, his reign was plagued with fiscal mismanagement and endemic corruption. Nevertheless, Öljeitü Khan oversaw the transformation of the empire's expansionist policies to general peace and stability, once the long-running war with the Ögedeid and Chagataid lineages was concluded. Franke and Twitchett, *The Cambridge History*, 490–505.

34. Manjughosa Ratna (T. 'Jam dbyang rin chen rgyal mtshan, d. 1305), according to the *Red Annals*, was "by Qubilai Sechen's command, [made] Bla chos of Sa skya's Bshi thog for sixteen years. Later, he was invited to the Imperial Court by the Emperor Ol ja du (成宗) and became Imperial Preceptor (Ti çrhi). He passed away at the Imperial Court at the age of 49. He was perfect in

understanding the Scriptures and practicing them. The Holy Sa skya became large [and influential] at this time." Inaba Shoju, "The Lineage of the Sa skya pa: A Chapter of the Red Annals," *Memoirs of the Research Department of the Toyo Bunko* 22 (1963): 111.

35. Külüg is the Mongolian temple name of Khaisan (< Ch. Hai-shan 海山, r. 1307–1311, Wuzong 武宗), the eldest son of Darmabala, Jinggim's second son. He was born in 1281, and at the age of eighteen in 1299 he led the campaign against Qaidu in the Mongolian steppe in order to consolidate Yuan rule. As a result of his success and subsequent power, when Oljeitü died in February 1307, Khaisan was selected to succeed him. During his reign he stressed the importance of controlling the steppe for the Yuan and therefore launched several steppe-oriented policies, including the building of a new capital, Zhongdu 中都, north of present-day Zhangjiakou 張家口. Although it was never completed and the policies not fully implemented, they had lasting resonance in the discussions of theories of rule throughout the Yuan. John W. Dardess, *Conquerors and Confucians: Aspects of Political Change in Late Yüan China* (New York: Columbia University Press, 1973).

36. The full biography of Chöjé Özer (fl. 1307–1321) is still unknown: we know neither his dates nor whether he was Mongol, Tibetan, or Uygur, though it is clear he was fluent in all three languages. He was a disciple of Pakpa Lama and was then in the service of Öljeitü (1294–1307) and Khaisan (1307–1311) and translated Buddhist works (Paul Pelliot, "Les systèmes d'ecriture en usage chez les anciens Mongols," *Asia Major* 2 [1925]: 286). There are five works attributed to him, the *Jirüken-ü tolta*; a Mongolian translation of the *Pañcaraksa* from Uyghur; a versified hymn to Mahakala; a translation of the *Bodhicaryavatara* with an autocommentary; and an original Tibetan compilation that is an abridgment of the *Lalitavistara*. A Yuan period translation of the *Mañjusrinamasamgiti* was also done within Chöjé Özer's circle of translators.

37. Buyan[tu] is the temple name of Ayushiridara (r. 1311–1320, Renzong 仁宗), who had been designated heir apparent by Khaisan already in 1307; thus his enthronement was the first peaceful and smooth transition in Yuan history. Even so, the Confucian-trained Buyantu systematically set out to reverse the steppe-oriented policies of his elder brother Khaisan. Buyantu not only purged the ministries of Khaisan's officials, replacing them with Chinese scholar-officials, but also revived the Neo-Confucian-oriented civil service exams in 1313. In 1316 he also ordered the codification of Yuan laws, a project completed in 1324 with the 2,400 legal documents of the *Da Yuan tongzhi* 大元通制. Although Buyantu tried to "Confucianize" the Yuan, he was not able to solve the state's continuing fiscal problems or resolve the violent factional disputes within the imperial elite. Franke and Twitchett, *The Cambridge History*, 513–527.

38. The identity of Lord Sripada is unclear; it presumably refers to Pel Zangpo (T. Kun dga' legs pa'i 'byung nas rgyal mtshan dpal bzang po, 1262–1330), who was the Imperial Preceptor 帝師 from 1328 to 1330. Leonard van der Kuijp, "From *Chongzhen lishu* 崇禎曆書 to *Tengri-yin udq-a* and *Rgya rtsis chen mo*," in *Tibetan Printing: Comparison, Continuities and Change*, ed. H. Diemberger, F. Ehrhard, and P. Kornicki (Leiden: Brill, 2016), 61.

39. When Shidebala, temple name Gegen (r. 1321–1323, Yingzong 英宗), took the throne at the age of eighteen, true power was wielded by Temüder, the Grand Councillor of the Right and a favorite of the Empress Dowager Targi, who set about reversing the "Confucianist" policies of Buyantu Khan. To counteract Temüder and the dissension he ushered in, Gegen Khan appointed the Confucian statesman Baiju—a descendant of Muqali—as Grand Councillor of the Left. Shortly thereafter an alleged coup plot enabled Baiju and other Chinese scholar-officials to promote the reforms launched by Buyantu Khan. Yet, Gegen Khan was also a devout Buddhist who, in honor of Pakpa Lama, ordered a larger temple than its Confucian counterpart to be built in every province. He also executed or exiled four officials who protested his profligacy in temple building. Nevertheless, in September 1323 a group of disenfranchised Mongol princes and others aligned with the Temüder faction carried out a coup d'état that killed both Gegen Khan and Baiju. Franke and Twitchett, *The Cambridge History*, 527–534.

40. Although the dates do not correspond, Buddhasri (T. Sang gyas dpal) presumably refers to the Imperial Preceptor 帝師 Sanggye Pel (1267–1314, r. 1305–1314).

41. Miñag (< Tib. mi-nyag) is what the Tanguts called themselves. It is now used to refer specifically to their distinctive language, the only historically documented language of the Qiangic family found along the eastern edge of the Tibetan plateau. "The Qiangic family is part of the larger Sino-Tibetan (or Tibeto-Burman) language family. But whether the Qiangic family is more closely related to Burmese, Tibetan, or Chinese or is its own separate branch is currently disputed. The family is named after the Qiang, the only people in the language family currently recognized as a separate ethnic group in China today." Christopher P. Atwood, *The Rise of the Mongols: Five Chinese Sources* (Indianapolis: Hackett, 2021), 8 n. 7.

42. Yisün Temür (r. 1323–1328, Taiding 泰定) was presumably a member of the group that killed Gegen Khan, though after being enthroned he launched a countercampaign against the members of Temüder's faction tied to the coup. He still largely rejected his predecessor's "Confucianist" policies and adopted a policy of reconciliation among all the competing groups. This enabled Muslims to gain unprecedented importance during his reign. Franke and Twitchett, *The Cambridge History*, 535–541.

43. The identity of Punyabhadra, or Sonam Zangpo in Tibetan, is unclear; it presumably refers to Rinchen Dak, who was an interim imperial preceptor in 1329–1330. Leonard van der Kuijp, *The Kalacakra and the Patronage of Tibetan Buddhism by the Mongol Imperial Family* (Bloomington: Department of Central Eurasian Studies, Indiana University, 2004), 43–46.
44. Razibag Khan (1320–1328, r. 1328, Tianshun 天順) was put on the throne by a powerful clique of ministers led by El Temür after his father, Yisün Temür, passed away. By so doing, El Temür and his Muslim allies "touched off the bloodiest and most destructive succession struggle of Yüan history, a struggle that resulted in the imperial line's shifting back to the Khaisan house for the rest of the dynasty. . . . All in all, the war of restoration and its repercussions made the entire reign of Tugh Temür a war-torn era." Franke and Twitchett, *The Cambridge History*, 541, 545.
45. Khoshila (r. 1329, Mingzong 明宗) was Khaisan's eldest son, exiled to Yunnan 雲南 in order to ensure the succession of Gegen Khan in 1321. In protest, Khoshila staged a failed revolt and ended up a political refugee among the Chagatai Khans of Central Asia. After the murder of Yisün Temür and the call for a restoration of Khaisan's lineage, Khoshila was summoned to take the throne. On February 27, 1329, he enthroned himself as khan and appointed his younger half-brother, Tug Temür, as heir apparent. Tug Temür and his powerful supporter El Temür did not want Khoshila as khan, and four days after the two brothers met on August 26, Khoshila mysteriously died. Tug Temür was enthroned on September 8, 1329. Franke and Twitchett, *The Cambridge History*, 541–547.
46. Tug Temür, temple name Jaya'atu (r. 1329–32, Wenzong 文宗), who had been exiled to Hainan 海南 in 1321 and reinstated as a prince in 1324, was put on the throne by the powerful Kipchak Turk El Temür, who as a loyal general of Khaisan had supported the restoration of his lineage. Once Khoshila had died and Tug Temür was enthroned, El Temür and his comrade Bayan effectively took control of the government and set about purging it of all remnants and influences of the previous khans descended from Kamala. This included not only desecrating their imperial temples but also removing from power Chinese scholar-officials and Muslims connected with these earlier reigns. To garner support and counter their image of illegitimacy the new court lavished rewards on the nobility and officialdom, yet apparently to no avail. Both groups continued to challenge the state, as did various other groups of the general populace who were suffering from a host of natural calamities. These events coupled with fiscal disarray foreshadowed the loss of control and widespread rebellion that would eventually lead to the Yuan's demise. Nevertheless, Tug Temür actively promoted Chinese learning by founding the Academy of the Pavilion of the Star of Literature. Franke and Twitchett, *The Cambridge History*, 541–547.

47. Ananda Bhadrakara presumably refers to Kungga Gyeltsen (1310–1358), imperial preceptor from 1331 to 1358. Petech, *Central Tibet*, 144.
48. On his deathbed Tug Temür supposedly feared retribution for the role he had played in the death of his brother Khoshila, and thus wanted Khoshila's eldest son, Toghan Temür, to succeed him rather than his own son, El Tegüs. The powerful El Temür feared the implications of this and promoted El Tegüs, but he was overruled by Empress Dowager Budashiri, who suggested the compromise candidate, Khoshila's second son, the six-year-old Rinchenbal (r. 1332, Ningzong 寧宗). He was enthroned on October 13, 1332, and died fifty-three days later.
49. Toghan Temür Khan (1320–1370, r. 1333–1368, Shundi 順帝) was exiled to an island off Korea's northwest coast when he was ten, and later to Guangxi 廣西, as a perceived threat in the succession feuds at the court. Nevertheless, after a struggle with his supporters and the son of Tug Temür, El Tegüs, who was supported by the powerful El Temür, he became emperor in 1333. Since he was only thirteen, power continued to be held by feuding Mongol lords, whose most contentious issue was whether to adopt a pro- or anti-Chinese stance. Eventually the pro-Chinese faction gained the upper hand, leading to a reestablishment of the classical examinations and the rise of Confucian literati in the government. The factional fighting continued and the power of the emperor was weakened with the rise of Mongol warlords and Chinese rebels. There were also massive environmental and social problems, including famines resulting from the flooding of the Yellow River and outbreaks of disease that killed enormous numbers of the population in the 1350s, all of which influenced a breakdown in the exchange of commodities. In reaction, the government began printing money and driving up inflation, another factor that escalated the problems, which in turn fueled the rebels in the south. Finally, all these rebels were united under Zhu Yuanzhang 朱元璋, who expelled Toghan Temür and the Mongols from Beijing on September 10, 1368. Toghan Temür fled and continued ruling the so-called "Northern Yuan." He died two years later of dysentery at Yingchang 應昌. L. Carrington Goodrich and Chaoyang Fang, *Dictionary of Ming Biography 1368–1644* (New York: Columbia University Press, 1976), 1290–1293.
50. The Sanskrit name of a Sakya monk, Anandamati (T. Kun-dga blos-gros); his presence at the Yuan court is recorded in several Mongol sources. This name is not corroborated in any of the relevant Chinese or Tibetan sources. It may refer to Kungga Lodro Gyeltsen, who was imperial preceptor in 1314–1327. Dharma, *Altan kürdün mingγan kegesütü*, ed. Coyiji (Kökeqota: Öbör Mongγol-un arad-un keblel-ün qoriy-a, 1987), 178.
51. This refers to Zhu Yuanzhang 朱元璋 (1328–1398), the founder of the Ming 明 dynasty (1368–1644), who was not actually born in 1344. On the Hongwu 洪武 emperor and the Ming conquest in Mongol historiography, especially in terms

of how it relates to the context of the later Qing conquest, see Johan Elverskog, "The Story of Zhu and the Mongols of the Seventeenth Century," in *Long Live the Emperor: Uses of the Ming Founder Across Six Centuries of East Asian History*, ed. Sarah Schneewind (Minneapolis: Society for Ming Studies. 2007), 211–243.

52. This same miracle is also recorded in Zhu Yuanzhang's autobiography, as well as the *Ming Shi.* Charles Bawden, *The Mongol Chronicle Altan Tobči* (Wiesbaden: Otto Harrassowitz, 1955), 150 n. 2.

53. It is unclear to which historical figure, if any, Ilakhu Chingsang refers. Okada Hidehiro, "An Analysis of the Lament of Togon Temür," *Zentralasiatische Studien* 1 (1967): 65–66.

54. Bo'orchu (1165?–1227?) was Chinggis Khan's first friend and ally.

55. Whether this remark has anything to do with the oft-noted "unique" appearance of Zhu Yuanzhang, such as his large lower jaw and pock-marked face, is unclear.

56. There is no historical evidence to support the existence of this relationship. Nevertheless, materials preserved in Korea suggest that Zhu Yuanzhang may have at some point served as a soldier in the Yuan army. Goodrich and Fang, *Dictionary of Ming Biography*, 381.

57. Toqta'a (1314–1356) was a well-known grand councillor (*chengxiang* 丞相) of the Yuan dynasty, and Qarachang (the Mongol name of Yunnan 雲南) was his son. Franke and Twitchett, *The Cambridge History*, 572–580.

58. Okada identifies Kama Bingjing as Hama Pingzhang 哈馬平章 (d. 1356), a Turkic Qangli Confucian statesman who was one of the chief administrators (*pingzhang zhengshi* 平章政事) of the Central Secretariat (*Zhongshu sheng* 中書省) from 1354 to 1355. Okada, "Lament of Togon Temür," 69.

59. It is possible that "the sun and moon setting simultaneously" may refer to the Ming 明 dynasty, the character of which is made up of the sun and moon: 日+月=明, meaning "bright." I thank David Robinson for this suggestion.

60. Mongol society was defined by its social stratification, and as this passage reveals, if these hierarchies were not maintained by the ruler and his state, it was a sign of failure and impending collapse.

61. These are descending ranks of officials in the Mongol government beginning with the khan, then the taishi (< Ch. *taishi* 太師), "grand preceptor"; lord is the Mongolian title of nobility, *noyan*; and *jaisang* (< Ch. *zaixiang* 宰相) "was a colloquial name for all kinds of prime ministers in the Chinese bureaucratic government, such as *cheng-xiang* 丞相 or *ping-zhang* 平章." Ho Kai-lung, "The Office and Noble Titles of the Mongols from the 14th to 16th Century, and the Study of the 'White History' *Čayan Teüke*," *Central Asiatic Journal* 59, 1–2 (2016): 164.

62. After Toqta'a (1314–1356), as grand councillor (1340–1344 and 1349–1345), was unable to quell the Red Turban revolt or halt the continuing piracy on the southern coast, and generated hyperinflation by printing money, he was exiled by imperial decree to Yunnan 雲南 in 1344. The following year his rival at court, Hama (i.e., Kama Bingjing), sent agents to poison him. Atwood, *Encyclopedia*, 543–544.

63. This is a poetic version of stanza 113 in Sakya Pandita's *Subhāsitaratnanidhi*, which in the original reads: "Even the one who does harm to the excellent may become a companion, (but) the one who does harm to the base suffers harm. The wind, to be sure, ignites the forest fire, and that wind extinguishes a little lamp." James Bosson, *A Treasury of Aphoristic Jewels: The Subhasitaratnanidhi of Sa Skya Pandita in Tibetan and Mongolian* (Bloomington: Indiana University Publications, 1969), 225.

64. Tang Taisong is the Taizong 太宗 emperor (r. 626–649), who consolidated the authority of the Tang dynasty. In Buddhist sources he is also lauded for his relationship with the famous pilgrim and translator Xuanzang 玄奘 (600–664).

65. Tang Jangzang is the Tang dynasty pilgrim and translator Xuanzang 玄奘 (see p. #, n. #).

66. It is unclear which Tang dynasty emperor this Mongolian transliteration refers to, since it does not correspond remotely to any of the final rulers: Yizong 懿宗 (r. 859–873), Xizong 僖宗 (r. 873–888), and Zhaozong 昭宗 (r. 888–904).

67. According to the *Yuan Shi* 元史, Toghan Temür fled the city by opening the Jiande Gate 健德門 at midnight and escaping northward. Okada, "Lament of Togon Temür," 63.

68. Bukha Temür Chingsang was the fourth son of the Zhennan Prince 鎮南王 Toghan. In 1329 he was given the title Prince Xuanrang 宣讓王 and moved to Zhenlu Zhou 鎮廬州, which is now Hefei 合肥 in Anhui 安徽. Later he moved north and settled in the capital. In 1367 he was given the title Prince Zhun 凖王. The *Yuan Shi* 元史 records that in 1368 he was appointed as grand councillor 丞相, and that he remained in the capital when the emperor fled north and was subsequently killed by Ming troops. Zhurongga 珠榮嘎, 阿鞑坦汗傳 (Hohhot: Nei Menggu Renmin Chubanshe, 1990), 10 n. 2.

69. In earlier Mongol sources there were only "Fourteen Great Khans" since the reign of Köden was not included: 1. Chinggis (d. 1227); 2. Ögedei (r. 1229–1241); 3. Güyüg (r. 1246–1248); 4. Möngke (r. 1251–1259); 5. Khubilai (r. 1260–1294); 6. Temür (r. 1294–1307); 7. Khaisan (r. 1307–1311); 8. Ayurbarwada (r. 1311–1320); 9. Shidebala (r. 1320–1323); 10. Yesün Temür (r. 1323–1328); 11. Khoshila (r. 1329); 12. Tug Temür (r. 1329–1332); 13. Rinchenbal (r. 1332); 14. Toghan Temür (r. 1333–1368). The reason was that after the death of Güyüg and the elevation of Möngke, the Mongol throne had passed from the lineage of Ögedei to that of

Tolui (where it was to remain). Thus not only were Köden's descendants not allowed to inherit the appanage of Liangzhou, but also they were not allowed to have relations with Tibet. As one can therefore expect, Köden's history—especially his role in establishing Tibeto-Mongol relations—tended to be minimized in Yuan-era histories. With the so-called "second conversion" of the Mongols, however, Köden's role and his relations with Tibet were again highlighted, resulting in Sagang Sechen's identification of "fifteen Mongol rulers."

5. HISTORY OF THE NORTHERN YUAN DYNASTY

1. The Moltasi Gate is the Mongol name for Gubeikou 古北口, the "Old Northern Pass" in the Great Wall, which is ninety miles north of Beijing. Hidehiro Okada, "An Analysis of the Lament of Togon Temür," *Zentralasiatische Studien* 1 (1967): 66.
2. By claiming that only six of the supposed Forty Tümen of Mongols escaped to the north, Sagang Sechen is foreshadowing the Mongol revival of the late fifteenth century, when Dayan Khan reorganized the disparate Mongols into the Six Tümen, which were the sociomilitary and territorial units of the Ordos, Tümed, Yüngsiyebü, Chakhar, Khalkha, and Uriyangkhan.
3. On the Mongols who remained behind and their subsequent alliances with the Ming dynasty see David M. Robinson, *Ming China and Its Allies: Imperial Rule in Eurasia* (New York: Cambridge University Press, 2019).
4. Tiger City is Yingchang 應昌 on Dalai Nuur Lake, near today's Xilinhot in Inner Mongolia.
5. Biligtü Khan is the posthumous reign title of Ayushidara (1340–1378, r. 1370–1378), who succeeded his father, Toghan Temür, apparently without any succession struggles. Yet almost immediately after his enthronement the Ming launched a devastating invasion that almost led to the collapse of the Northern Yuan. Ayushidara survived, and with the help of the Chinggisid legacy, as well as jade seals and tablets of investiture stretching back to the Song dynasty, he was able to maintain legitimate claims as the Great Khan of the Yuan. He even "proclaimed a Chinese reign name, Xuanguang, to mark his rule's beginning. Scholars since the Qing dynasty have explained Xuanguang as an allusion to a well-known passage in a work by the famous poet, Du Fu (712–70) of the Tang period. 'The Zhou and Han achieved restorations; Xuan and Guang were indeed brilliantly wise.' Xuan refers to the Prince of Xuan (r. 827–782 BCE) of the Zhou dynasty and Guang to Emperor Guangwu (r. 145–146) of the Han dynasty. Both were men who accomplished dynastic restorations after internal and external threats had forced the capital's relocation and threatened to topple the regime. Thus Ayushidara's reign name announces his determination to restore the Great

Yuan. Such a lofty mission also places Ayushidara in the ranks of the great rulers of the past. Finally, such a message in such a form suggests that its primary audience was men with a Sinophone classical education, whether they were of Chinese, Korean, Jurchen, Kitan, Mongol or Turkic background and whether they were subjects of the Yuan, Ming, or Koryo dynasties." David M. Robinson, *In the Shadow of the Mongol Empire: Ming China and Eurasia* (New York: Cambridge University Press, 2020), 69. Ayushidara did subsequently secure support from rulers stretching from Korea to Central Asia to Yunnan, and thereby did revive the fortunes of the Great Yuan.

6. Uskhal Khan is the posthumous reign title of Togus Temür (1342–1388, r. 1378–1388), who unlike his older brother ushered in the collapse of the Great Yuan as a result of numerous military losses during Ming invasions of the steppe. Most notably, he and his army were roundly defeated by Ming forces at Lake Buir in 1388, after which, during their retreat back to central Mongolia, Togus Temür was killed by Yisüder (whose identity remains obscure). "The Yüan imperial family then entered upon a period of short reigns by weak rulers who were mainly puppets in the hands of rival leaders." L. Carrington Goodrich and Chaoyang Fang, *Dictionary of Ming Biography 1368–1644* (New York: Columbia University Press, 1976), 1294. See also Robinson, *In the Shadow*, 79–84.
7. The title Khung Taiji derives from the Chinese "heir apparent" (*huang taizi* 皇太子); however, in the post-Yuan period it lost this meaning and became instead a term like *taiji*, which signified a nobleman of the Chinggisid lineage. In the wake of Dayan Khan's restoration of the Mongols the title was used specifically to denote his own descendants.
8. Little is known about Engke Khan or the succession struggles among the Mongols during the late fourteenth and early fifteenth centuries. Much of this has to do with the lack of Mongolian sources, but also with the lack of Chinese sources. Indeed, why the Ming, which had assiduously followed developments among the Northern Yuan during the Hongwu 洪武 period (r. 1368–1398), suddenly gave up interest is something of a mystery. The succession struggles and the subsequent devastating invasions of the steppe by the Yongle 永樂 emperor (r. 1402–1424) no doubt played a role in weakening the Northern Yuan and thereby minimizing Ming interest in Mongol affairs. In fact, "a 1408 communication from the Ming court offers the following summary of the years after Toghus-Temür's death. 'The Yuan's allotted span of rule has already ended. After the Obedient Emperor (Toghan-Temür), [rulership] passed to Ayushidara [and has now] come to Gün Temür. In total six men have replaced each other in succession within the span of a blink of the eye or the drawing of a breath. Further, not a single person came to a good end.'" Robinson, *In the Shadow*, 85.

9. Even less is known about Elbeg Khan, not even whether he was of Khubilai Khan's lineage or that of his brother and archrival Ariq Böke. Nevertheless, as the following story makes clear, all the seventeenth-century chronicles maintain that after Elbeg Khan's reign (1393–1399?) the power of the Mongols waned in the face of Oirat power. Yet in Ming records, the rise of the Oirat truly began only in 1412 when the Oirat ruler Mahmud (d. 1416) deposed the Mongol ruler Punyashri (r. 1408–1411) and placed his son, Delbeg (r. 1412–1414), on the throne. Moreover, it was really during the reigns of Mahmud's descendants, Togan (d. 1438) and Esen (r. 1438–1454), that the Oirat took control of Inner Asia. Nevertheless, as seen in the *Precious Summary*, this folkloric family feud and the death of Elbeg Khan were the pivotal episode that shaped the subsequent Mongol-Oirat wars of the fifteenth century. Christopher P. Atwood, *Encyclopedia of Mongolia and the Mongol Empire* (New York: Facts on File, 2004), 420.
10. The title grand marshall (M. *dayiu*) derives from the Chinese title "grand instructor" (*taiwei* 太尉), "which was a temporary post mainly in charge of Chinese Confucian ceremonies for the Heir-Apparent and Queen. . . . It later became a permanent honorary title for important figures" (Ho Kai-lung, "The Office and Noble Titles of the Mongols from the 14th to 16th Century, and the Study of the 'White History' *Čayan Teüke*," *Central Asiatic Journal* 59, 1–2 [2016]: 149–150). Among the post-Yuan Mongols it was the third highest rank, just below chingsang.
11. Chingsang (< Ch. *chengxiang* 丞相, grand councillor) was—after taishi (< Ch. *taishi* 太師, grand preceptor)—the second highest rank among the post-Yuan Mongols.
12. The title grand guardian (M. *taibu*) derives from the Yuan dynasty rank *taibao* 太保.
13. Although the historicity of these events is uncertain, the narrative does reveal the nature of the tensions defining life on the steppe at this time. Not only was there the struggle between the Oirat and the Mongols regarding the Chinggisid principle, but also among the Oirat themselves there were tensions regarding who should rightfully be ruling. As we know from Chinese sources, the Ming court stoked these divisions in order to sow discord among both the Mongols and Oirats. In 1411, for example, the Ming not only recognized two different taishi among the Oirats but also gave three other contending Oirat rulers the title prince (*wang* 王), including Mahmud, who would in turn become the most powerful Oirat ruler.
14. "Basket Boy" is an overtranslation of Arugtai, meaning "with a basket," referring to the basket worn on one's back while collecting dung. In other words, the nickname Arugtai is making fun of him for being a low-status servant. Yet, Arugtai (d. 1434) was actually to become the Mongol khan's chief minister and

one of the, if not the most powerful individuals on the steppe in the early decades of the fifteenth century. The Ming court recognized this and gave Arugtai the title taishi in 1411, and in 1413 the title prince of Hening 和寧王 (prince of Qaraqorum). Several years later, however, on account of Arugtai's power and machinations on the steppe—including invasions of China—the Yongle emperor launched two campaigns in 1421 and 1423–24 to bring Arugtai to heel. Neither one was successful, and Arugtai continued to be a key power broker on the steppe. However, as control of the Oirat was subsequently taken by the descendants of Mahmud, they challenged not only the power of the Mongol khans but also that of Arugtai. He was killed by the Oirat in 1434. Goodrich and Fang, *Dictionary of Ming Biography*, 12–15.

15. Although the *Precious Summary* presents the conventional narrative that Gün Temür's brother, Öljei Temür (1379–1410), took the Mongol throne at age twenty-five and died eight years later, this is not exactly correct. After the death of Gün Temür in 1402(?), the throne was taken by Güilichi (Ch. Guilizhi 鬼力赤, r. 1403–1408?), who, rather than enhancing relations and trade with China, actually further alienated the Ming court by poisoning Engke Temür, the prince of Hami 哈密, whom the court had enfeoffed. With tensions escalating, Arugtai therefore killed Güilichi and put Punyashri, a descendant of the imperial Yuan lineage resident in Beshbaliq, on the throne. With a new ruler in place the Ming tried again to establish relations; however, Punyashri and Arugtai killed the Chinese envoys. In response the Chinese bestowed titles and privileges on the Mongols' main rival, the Oirat Mahmud, who, to repay the favor, launched an assault on the Mongols. The Oirat thereby killed Punyashri and put his compliant son Delbeg on the throne. Goodrich and Fang, *Dictionary of Ming Biography*, 1035–1036.
16. Delbeg (1395–1414, Ch. Daliba 答里巴, r. 1412–1414) was put on the throne by the Oirat ruler Mahmud in 1412, and three years later was succeeded by Oiratai (r. 1415–1425?).

6. HISTORY OF THE MONGOL-OIRAT WARS

1. "Basket Boy" of the Asud refers to Arugtai, one of the most powerful individuals on the steppe in the early decades of the fifteenth century (see page 253, note 14).
2. As explained in the introduction, one of the main driving factors of post-Mongol Eurasian history was the Chinggisid principle, which proclaimed that only direct heirs of Chinggis Khan could rule. This issue—along with issues of power and financial resources—played an important role in the Mongol-Oirat wars, since the Oirat were not Chinggisids and thus could not claim the Mongol

throne. Even though they eventually came to be the dominant power in Inner Asia, they ruled through various weak and ineffectual Mongol rulers or married into the Chinggisid lineage and thereby had their children declared Chinggisids. The Oirats were ultimately defeated; however, the Chinggisid reality that shaped their interactions throughout the fifteenth century is well captured in this poem and the titles used. Ajai—a proper Chinggisid—holds the title taiji (< Ch. *taizi* 太子, heir apparent), which was reserved for Chinggisids. Powerful non-Chinggisids—such as Arugtai—could hold the title taishi (< Ch. *taishi* 太師, grand preceptor), which in the fifteenth century "indicated a powerful functionary in Mongol society, apparently hardly less influential than the qaγan himself, and often with enough power to overshadow and even to remove him." Henry Serruys, "The Office of Tayisi in Mongolia in the Fifteenth Century," *Harvard Journal of Asiatic Studies* 37, 2 (1977): 356.

3. Little is known about Esekü Khan (r. 1415?–1425?), also known as Oiratai Khan; his reign was constrained by the Oirats as well as by Arugtai (d. 1434).
4. The Khorchin descend from the Mongols of the Üjiyed~Fuyu 福餘 Guard formed by the Ming after their surrender in 1389, and were ruled by descendants of Qasar. Having fled south after Esen's campaigns, they eventually allied themselves with the Manchus in 1612, for which they were handsomely rewarded. Along with the Gorlos, Dörbed, and Jalaid Banners, the Khorchin became part of the Jirim League. The Khorchins were further divided into two wings (north and south), each with three Banners. Christopher P. Atwood, *Encyclopedia of Mongolia and the Mongol Empire* (New York: Facts on File, 2004), 308.
5. Adai (r. 1426–1438) was the successor of Esekü Khan, and his reign also was largely in the hands of Arugtai. Yet, on account of Togan's consolidation of the Oirat at this time, the power of the Mongols was weakening precipitously. In 1433 Arugtai was pushed out east of the Khinggan Mountains, where he subjugated the Ming-allied Three Guards. Yet, one year later Arugtai and Adai Khan were defeated by Ming forces and fled west, where both were subsequently killed by the Oirat. Atwood, *Encyclopedia*, 408.
6. Odchigin was the younger brother of Chinggis Khan.
7. In the post-Yuan period the coronation of a new khan was always done "in front of the Lord Chinggis Khan": the ritual was performed at the Eight White Tents, which housed the relics of Chinggis Khan. On the cult of Chinggis Khan and Mongol rituals of political legitimacy see Johan Elverskog, *Our Great Qing: The Mongols, Buddhism and the State in Late Imperial China* (Honolulu: University of Hawai'i Press, 2006), 65–95.
8. Bagmuu, or Togan (kettle) is Togan Taishi (d. 1438), son of the Oirat ruler Mahmud (d. 1416), who continued the consolidation of Oirat power that began with the murder of the Mongol~Chinggisid ruler Punyashiri and the

enthronement of his son Delbeg under Oirat control in 1412. In turn, Togan consolidated his own power by first killing two rival Oirat chieftains, thereby uniting the Oirat, which the Ming recognized by giving him his father's title, Prince Shunning (*Shunning Wang* 順寧王, Obedient and Righteous Prince). Thereupon he began campaigning against the Mongols in order to weaken the power of Arugtai. And although Togan killed Arugtai, as a non-Chinggisid, he could not take the Mongol throne. To maintain control he married his daughter to the Mongol ruler Taisung Khan. L. Carrington Goodrich and Chaoyang Fang, *Dictionary of Ming Biography 1368–1644* (New York: Columbia University Press, 1976), 12–15, 1035–1037.

9. The "Lord's palace" refers to the Eight White Tents that housed the relics of Chinggis Khan.
10. This passage again encapsulates the Chinggisid principle defining the Mongol-Oirat conflict, since here, Togan Taishi, an Oirat, is claiming to be legitimate because he has "female blessedness" (M. *sutai*), or Chinggisid blood through his mother, Princess Samur, who was the daughter of Elbeg Khan. It is on account of this bloodline that Togan challenges Adai Khan, who is a direct descendant of the male "brilliant" line of Chinggis Khan. Of course, as the story reveals, according to the Chinggisid principle, Togan's claim is not enough to gain the Mongol throne.
11. Esen (d. 1455) began his career with three successful campaigns against Eastern Moghulistan in the 1420s, which extended Oirat power as far west as Beshbaliq. After his father's death in 1440 he gave himself the titles taishi 太師 and prince of Huai 淮王 and began launching campaigns against the Ming 明. This included Hami 哈密, but he also went into Gansu 甘肅 and eventually conquered the three Uriyangkhad guards in the northeast. Once Esen controlled virtually the entire swath of Inner Asia from Xinjiang 新疆 to Korea, the Ming became apprehensive, especially about the appropriate protocols concerning trade and tribute relations. Most often the Ming court felt Esen sent too many envoys and demanded too much in return. These continuing disputes eventually came to a head, and Esen launched an attack against the Ming in 1449. The emperor met Esen in the field and was captured at Tumu Fort 土木堡 outside Beijing 北京. The court, however, thwarted any ransom demands by placing the emperor's brother on the throne and continued their support of rival Mongol groups, even offering a reward for the assassination of Esen. After repeated negotiations, the emperor was returned and Esen continued his trade and tribute relations with the Ming. He also turned his focus from the Ming to the Mongols, in particular the young ruler Taisung Khan. In 1450 they jointly attacked the Jurchens in the northeast, but one year later Esen turned on his former ally, and Taisung was eventually killed while retreating from Oirat attacks. In 1452 Esen, unlike

his father, thus proclaimed himself khan, which the Ming emperor grudgingly approved. Yet it was precisely the usurpation of the Chinggisid throne that finally consolidated Mongol resistance, which led to not only the death of Esen but also the eventual eclipse of Oirat power. Goodrich and Fang, *Dictionary of Ming Biography*, 416–420.

12. Whether or not Togan Taishi actually gave this speech to his son is unknown; however, Esen Taishi was well aware of the Chinggisid principle and the dangers of claiming the Mongol throne as a non-Chinggisid. He wanted his daughter to marry Taisung Khan and then have their child—Esen's grandchild—become the Mongol khan. However, Taisung Khan refused to marry his daughter, whereupon conflict erupted and Esen killed Taisung in 1452. Then, contrary to the Chinggisid principle, Esen proclaimed himself khan, "the Heavenly blessed Great Khan of the Great Yuan" (*Dayuan tiansheng da kehan* 大元天聖大可汗). This rallied the Mongols to finally challenge Oirat power; however, Esen's fall actually had more to do with internal Oirat feuds. The Oirat nobleman Alag wanted to be appointed taishi (or second in command), but Esen gave the position to his second son. Alag rebelled, and in the ensuing battle Esen was killed in 1454. Serruys, "Office of Tayisi," 364–366.
13. At this time the coronation of the khan was done "in front of the Lord [i.e., Chinggis Khan]" at the Eight White Tents.
14. This a confusion between the Jingtai 景泰 emperor (1428–1457, r. 1449–1457), who was not captured at Tumu 土木 but was put on the throne when the Zhengtong 正統 (1427–1464, r. 1435–1449 and 1457–1464) emperor was captured at Tumu. For a historical reevaluation of the Tumu Incident and its larger Eurasian implications, see David M. Robinson, *Ming China and Its Allies: Imperial Rule in Eurasia* (New York: Cambridge University Press, 2019), 131–195.
15. Taisung (< Ch. Taizong 太宗, r. 1433–1452) is the reign title of Toqta'a-Bukha, the son of Adai Khan, who was put on the throne by the Oirat in order to weaken the power of not only his father but also the powerful chief minister Arugtai. From 1439 the Oirat ruler Esen and his Mongol-appointed ruler, Taisung, began sending joint tribute missions to the Ming court. Over time, these missions expanded from a hundred to several thousand men, and the Ming court grew increasingly annoyed at both the expense of these trade relations and the effrontery of Esen Khan. In response the court tried to drive a wedge between Esen and Taisung by treating the latter with great respect and lavishing gifts on his envoys. Although Taisung contemplated aligning the Mongols with the Ming against the Oirat, he could not actually break free from Oirat control. Thus when Esen was further slighted by the Ming court in 1448, Taisung joined in the retaliatory 1449 campaigns by leading the Mongol forces into Liaodong 遼東. The following year Esen and Taisung together attacked the Jurchens.

Yet tensions between the two remained, no doubt fueled by the Ming court, who in response to the Tumu Incident—and to counteract the growing power of the Oirats—wanted to make an alliance with the Mongol khan. The lavish rewards were apparently not the deciding factor in Taisung's decision to go against Esen, but rather the question of Mongol succession. In 1452, with the support of the Three Uriyangkhad Guards, Taisung attacked Esen in the area of Turfan. But when Taisung's brother Agbarji Jinong defected to the Oirat, Taisung and his forces were defeated, and while retreating he was eventually killed, presumably by the Uriyangkhad. Goodrich and Fang, *Dictionary of Ming Biography*, 418–419.

16. Agbarji was Taisung's younger brother who was appointed as jinong, or viceroy, of the western wing of the Mongols; however, he defected to the Oirat during the failed Mongol campaign against the Oirat in 1452. Esen Khan had promised to put Agbarji on the Mongol throne if he fought against his brother; however, after the Oirat eventually defeated Taisung, Esen had Agbarji murdered and himself installed as the Mongol khan. Esen also appointed his son as jinong. Atwood, *Encyclopedia*, 171.
17. Although the title jinong (< Ch. *jinwang* 晉王, prince of Jin) goes back to the Empire period, it was only revived in the fifteenth century to denote the khan's viceroy, or second in command, who ruled the western flank of the Mongols. During the reign of Dayan Khan and after, the jinong was the recognized ruler of the Three Western Tümen.
18. At this time, the descendant of Jochi who ruled this area of Central Asia was Abu'l Khayr Khan (1412–1468), the founder of the Uzbek Khanate.
19. The Chakhar first appear in the late fifteenth century as one of the Six Tümen. In particular, after the reign of Dayan Khan (1480?–1517?), the Chakhar became the personal appanage of the Mongol ruler. It has been suggested that the name Chakhar derives from the Sogdian *čākar* "the ruler's guard corps" and was brought to the Dayan Khanid court by Queen Mandukhai, the famous and powerful empress of Dayan Khan during his minority and the daughter of the Önggüd, a mixed Turco-Sogdian people of central Inner Mongolia (Christopher P. Atwood, "Six Pre-Chinggisid Geneaologies in the Mongol Empire," *Archivum Eurasiae Medii Aevi* 19 (2012): 46). Regardless, after this name was adopted the Chakhar became the Dayan Khanid ruler's fief, and under Daraisun Küdeng Khan (1548–1557) moved east over the Great Khinggan range into the Shara Mören valley. "In 1627 the princes of the Chakhar's Sönid, Üjümüchin, Naiman, and the Aohan *otogs* (camp districts) revolted against the centralization of Ligdan Khan (1604–34). After being attacked by the rising Manchus in 1632, Ligdan Khan took the remaining Chakhars and fled west to Ordos and then Kökenuur (Qinghai). After his death his sons surrendered to the Manchus'

new Qing dynasty (1636–1912) and the remaining Chakhars were resettled as autonomous banners in south-central Inner Mongolia." Atwood, *Encyclopedia*, 88.

20. Bayan Möngke was the father of Dayan Khan. According to Sagang Sechen, Bayan Möngke was the son of Kharguchag (a nephew of Manduul Khan) and Princess Secheg (Esen Taiji's daughter). After Molan Khan was killed in 1466, the Mongol throne was vacant for a decade, until in 1475 Beg Arslan, the most powerful Mongol ruler living in Turfan, tried to enthrone Bayan Möngke. When he refused, Manduul of the Chakhar was made khan and reigned from 1475 to 1479. During this time Bayan Möngke was made ruler of the Ordos. After Manduul Khan's death, Bayan Möngke was made khan in 1480; he was killed by Yüngsiyebü Mongols in 1487. Mongol sources proclaim he was assassinated by Ibarai; however, the *Ming Shi* 明史 identifies the murderer as Beg Arslan. This confusion may have arisen out of the fact that Ibarai eventually took over Beg Arslan's post as taishi in the West. Henry Serruys, *Genealogical Tables of the Descendants of Dayan-Qan* ('S-Gravenhage: Mouton, 1958), 12–15; Okada Hidehiro, "Life of Dayan Khan," *Acta Asiatica* 11 (1966): 46–55.

21. There are three interpretations concerning who the Gooli Thousand are. The first identifies it as another name for the Khoid Oirat, who are also called the Yeke Minggatu and the Naiman Minggatu (Altan'orgil Badai and Erdeni, *Oyirad teüken surbulji bicig* [Qayilar: Öbör Mongγol-un soyul-un keblel-ün qoriy-a, 1985], 77–78 n. 29). The second, based on the *Precious Summary*, argues that at this time the Oirats were divided into two wings, the Jaga Minggan, "Border Thousand," and the Gooli Thousand, "Central Thousand" (Yoshida Jun'ichi 吉田順一, et al., *Altan Qagan-u Tuγuji* [Tokyo: Kazama-shobo, 1998], 286–287). The third is that Gooli Minggan, "the thousand Gooli," refers to a "thousand" whose ancestors were Koreans (Gooli < Ch. Gaoli 高麗) brought to Mongolia, who became part of the Khoid confederation (Christopher P. Atwood, personal communication).

22. After several Mongol groups submitted to the Ming, in 1389 the court organized them into the Three Guards on the eastern slopes of the Khinggan Mountains, comprising the Uriyangkhan~Duoyan 朵顏, Üjiyed~Fuyu 福餘, and Ongnigud~Taining 泰寧. These three groups, commonly though mistakenly called the Uriyangkhad, were said to be the descendants of Chinggis Khan's companion Jelme of the Uriyangkhan. After the Oirat ruler Esen's crushing assault, most of them fled south toward the Ming border, to what became the territory of the Josotu League. During the Mongol-Oirat war the Kharchin, descendants of the Mongol empire's Kipchak guards, who had until then been part of the Yüngshiyebü Tümen in Ordos, moved east and joined with the Uriyangkhan Mongols. When these mixed groups submitted to the Manchus in

1626, they were reorganized into the Three Kharchin Banners in the Josotu League, each ruled by a nobleman of the old Uriyangkhan lineage. Atwood, *Encyclopedia*, 303–304, 535.

7. HISTORY OF DAYAN KHAN

1. As noted above, Emperor Jingtai 景泰 (1428–1457, r. 1449–1457) is a mistake for the Zhengtong 正統 emperor (1427–1464, r. 1435–1449).
2. On the historiography of the Mongol recognition of the Ming emperor as a rightful ruler in the Chinggisid mold and its relation to the Mongol legacy in East Asian history, see Johan Elverskog, "The Tumu Incident and the Chinggisid Legacy in Inner Asia," *The Silk Road Journal* 15 (2017): 142–152.
3. It is unclear from the available sources what actually happened during this period. It is commonly held that after Molan Khan's death in 1466 the Mongol throne was empty for a decade, and then Manduulun of the Chakhars became khan and reigned from 1475 to 1479. Upon his death, Bayan Möngke (Dayan Khan's father), who was ruling as *jinong* over the Ordos, was made khan, and upon his death, his young son became khan. Henry Serruys, *Genealogical Tables of the Descendants of Dayan-Qan* ('S-Gravenhage: Mouton, 1958), 12–15.
4. Bayan Möngke Bolkhu Jinong was the son of Kharguchag (a nephew of Manduulun Khan) and Secheg Beiji (Esen Khan's daughter), and the father of Dayan Khan; however, apart from these facts his history is shrouded in mystery. Some sources record that Bayan Möngke ruled as khan for a period of time, while others maintain that he did not. According to Lubsangdanjin's *Golden Summary* and Chinese sources, Bayan Möngke took the Mongol throne after Manduulun Khan's death in 1479, and ruled for four years (Hidehiro Okada, "The Ordos Jinong in *Erdeni-yin Tobči*," *Journal of Asian and African Studies* 27 [1984]: 160). The *Precious Summary*, on the other hand, claims that Manduulun Khan died in 1467 and Bayan Möngke was killed in 1470 by five Yüngshiyebü Mongols. The *Jewel Translucent Sutra* claims that Dayan Khan was an orphan at age one, after his father died in 1475. This variation in the historical narrative is clearly problematic, and it hints at the difficulties in attempting to solve the mystery of Bayan Möngke's life as well as describe the transition period from Molon Khan until Dayan Khan. On these problems and the Dayan Khan-descended aristocrats' subsequent desire to forget these chronological and historical problems see Johan Elverskog, *The Jewel Translucent Sutra: Altan Khan and the Mongols in the Sixteenth Century* (Leiden: Brill, 2003), 48–53.
5. The Six Tümen were the sociomilitary units into which Dayan Khan organized the Mongols. The six groups were divided into two wings: the Western Tümen

comprised the Ordos, Tümed, and Yüngsiyebü (with the Asud and Kharchin), and the Eastern Tümen the Chakhar, Khalkha, and Uriyangkhan. Although all of these were traditionally identified groups among the Mongols, Dayan Khan institutionalized their structure and their territorial homeland (which was further systematized in the bureaucratic enterprise of the Qing dynasty); see Nicola Di Cosmo, "Qing Colonial Administration in Inner Asia," *The International History Review* 20 (1998): 287–309. Yet even so, all of these groups traced their lineages to the Empire period. The Ordos group originated in 1292 when Khubilai Khan enfeoffed his grandson Kamala as Prince of the Four Great Ordos of Chinggis Khan on the Kerülen River. The Tümed descended from the Turkic Önggüd kingdom in the Yinshan 陰山 Mountains, and the Yüngsiyebü derived from Köden's fief in Gansu 甘肅. Of the eastern groups, the Chakhar originated from Khubilai Khan's personal fief in Shaanxi 陝西, the Khalkha went back to the five elite corps commanded by Muqali of the Jalayir, and the Uriyangkhan were the original people assigned to guard Chinggis Khan's tomb in the Kentei (Henry Serruys, "A Mongol Settlement in North China at the End of the 16th Century." *Central Asiatic Journal* 4 [1959]: 47–50).

6. Queen Mandukhai was the younger wife of Manduulun and after he died she acted as regent. When Ünebalad Ong of the Khorchin asked her to marry in order to bolster his claim to legitimacy, she refused (which is the event herein described). The following year, to maintain Mongol rule she married Batu Möngke and supported his ascension as khan (Jürungγa, *Erdeni tunumal neretü sudur orosiba* [Beijing: Ündüsüten-ü keblel-ün qoriy-a, 1984], 17 n. 2).

7. Batu Möngke Dayan Sechen Khan was the most important Mongol ruler of this period; however, there is no certainty about his years of birth, rule, or death. Nevertheless, he was the ruler who finally consolidated the fractious post-Yuan Mongols into a confederation of Six Tümens. After the death of his father, Dayan Khan married Queen Mandukhai, the wife of the Chakhar ruler Manduulun, to ensure the power of the Chakhar rulers as the rightful heirs of Chinggisid Mongol rule. With this mandate of rule Dayan Khan campaigned against his enemies and was able to forge a new alliance that continued until the reign of Ligdan Khan and the ultimate submission of the Mongols to the Manchus in the 1630s. Although Chakhar rule and the Six Tümen of Dayan Khan were destroyed, the lasting importance of his rule is reflected in the fact that when the Manchus established their 135 banners among the Mongols, 106 were ruled by descendants of Dayan Khan (Hidehiro Okada, "Life of Dayan Khan." *Acta Asiatica* 11 [1966]: 46–47).

8. Örlüg was a title given to the husband of the foster mother of a royal prince. "The so-called foster-parent taking care of a royal prince was quite similar to having a political hostage for the maintenance of a close alliance. Clearly, the

nonroyal leader was trusted by the Qagan and then was invited to look after a prince. Therefore, the title Örlög was with great honour. Very few posts carried the right as this did to hold a banquet just like a royal family member" (Ho Kai-lung, "The Office and Noble Titles of the Mongols from the 14th to 16th Century, and the Study of the 'White History' *Čayan Teüke*," *Central Asiatic Journal* 59, 1–2 [2016]: 174).

9. The queen mother's palace is the shrine of Queen Eshi, a deification of Sorqoqtani Beki, the wife of Tolui (Chinggis Khan's youngest son) and the mother of Khubilai Khan (Okada Hidehiro, "The Chakhar Shrine of Eshi Khatun," in *Aspects of Altaic Civilization III*, ed. Denis Sinor [Bloomington: Research Institute for Inner Asian Studies, 1990], 176). It is probable that her worship began with Khubilai Khan and was maintained by the successive princes of Anxi 安西王 in their fief in Shanxi 山西. However, the first direct mention is in the *Yuan Shi* (ch. 38), wherein Toghan Temür Khan in 1335 grants permission for the offering of sacrifices to Empress Dowager Beki in a Christian church in Gansu. After the fall of the Yuan and the subsequent rise of Dayan Khan, the Queen Eshi shrine became affiliated with the Chakhars. It appears to have functioned as a female counterpart to the Chinggis Khan shrine maintained by the Western Tümen at the Eight White Tents in Ordos. This created a balance of power whereby the politically dominant Eastern Tümen controlled the weaker sacred object while the politically weaker Western Tümen controlled the more powerful Chinggis Khan cult (Christopher P. Atwood, *Encyclopedia of Mongolia and the Mongol Empire* [New York: Facts on File, 2004], 512).

10. Although Dayan is written as Da Yuan 大元 in Chinese sources, and has thus been taken to imply a restoration of the Yuan dynasty, "Dayan" does not refer to the "Great Yuan" but is instead the Mongolian word *dayan*, meaning "whole, entire" (Antoine Mostaert, "Introduction," *Bolor Erike: Mongolian Chronicle, vol. I* [Cambridge, MA: Harvard University Press, 1959], 12–15 n. 43.

11. Mongol women, as a sign of marriage, wore their hair in elaborate headdresses.

12. Törö Bolad was born a twin with Ulus Bolad in 1482. He died in 1523, and therefore when Dayan Khan died between 1524 and 1543, Törö Bolad's eldest son Bodi Taiji became khan after an interim rule by his uncle Barsu Bolad Sain Alag. Serruys, *Genealogical Tables*, 16, 22.

13. Ulus Bolad was born a twin with Törö Bolad in 1482. Dayan Khan appointed him jinong of the Three Eastern Tümens; however, he was assassinated by Ibarai Taishi and left no descendants. Serruys, *Genealogical Tables*, 16.

14. Barsu Bolad was born as a twin with Princess Töröltü in 1484. After his elder brother was murdered he was appointed in 1512 as jinong of the Three Western Tümen. When Dayan Khan died, however, the *Golden Summary* notes that since Törö Bolad's son—Bodi Alag—was too young, Barsu Bolad made himself

khan. However, when Bodi Alag was old enough (and with the support of the Three Eastern Tümen) he went before the White Tents of Chinggis Khan and protested against Barsu Bolad's alleged usurpation. Subsequently, Barsu Bolad stepped down and Bodi Alag was enthroned as khan. Afterward, Barsu Bolad died; the sources differ as to when. The *Precious Summary* maintains 1531, the *Wanli Wugong Lu* proclaims 1521 and the *Jewel Translucent Sutra* says it was 1519. Serruys, *Genealogical Tables*, 16, 22.

15. Arsu Bolad had the Khaachud of the Chakhar as his appanage. The Khaachud consisted of at least five different groups, including the Asud, Sarkhad, Ha-pu-shen 哈不瞫 (possibly < M. Qabsin), Uygurchin, and Dalan Minggan. Serruys, *Genealogical Tables*, 16, 15.
16. Alchu Bolad was the twin of Vajra Bolad. He was given as an appanage one part of the Khalkha Tümen; the other was given to Geresenji. When a rift developed between Daraisun, the khan of the Eastern Tümen, and Altan Khan, presumably over Altan Khan's growing power, Daraisun and Alchu Bolad moved east of the Khinggan Mountains. Alchu Bolad and his appanage remained in this area, and it was later divided among the five sons of Khurkhachi, son of Alchu Bolad, and became known as the Five-Banner Khalkha or the Inner Khalkha. They are now substantially the Jarud and Baarin of Jehol. Serruys, *Genealogical Tables*, 16, 152; Junko Miyawaki, "The Birth of Oyirad Khanship," *Central Asiatic Journal* 41 (1997): 55.
17. Vajra Bolad was born as the twin of Alchu Bolad in 1490. His appanage was the Kesigten of the Chakhars. Serruys, *Genealogical Tables*, 16.
18. Jiqui darkhan is not a name but a title: the second-highest rank for a free nobleman.
19. The title junior preceptor (M. *sigüsi*) derives from the Chinese *shaoshi* 少師, and it "was quite popular and many non-royal tribe leaders got this title after the 15th century" (Ho, "The Office and Noble Titles," 150).
20. Gere Bolad was born in 1482. His appanage was the Aukhan and Naiman of the Chakhar. Serruys, *Genealogical Tables*, 16.
21. Geresenji Taiji (1513–1548) had as his appanage one part of the Khalkha (Serruys, *Genealogical Tables*, 16). The anonymous *Yellow History* and *Asaragchi's History* say he was born in 1513 as the son of Queen Jimisken. They also explain how Geresenji subsequently became the ruler of the Khalkha: Uda Bolad of the Chinos used to send dried meat to Dayan Khan, and once when leaving he asked for one of the khan's sons to rule his people. The khan gave him Gere Bolad; however, Uda Bolad returned him, then kidnapped Geresenji. Dayan Khan was told of this, yet told his ministers to do nothing, and eventually Geresenji became the ruler of the Khalkha. Other sources claim Geresenji married into the Khalkha, taking two wives, one from the Üjiyed, the other from the

Uriyangqan. He had seven sons, and as a result the thirteen clans (*otog*) of the Khalkhas north of the Gobi became known as the Seven-Banner Khalkha, as opposed to the Five-Banner Khalkha who stayed in the area of Jehol. Geresenji died in 1548 at Borong on the Kerülen. The direct descendants of Geresenji's eldest son bore the title Jasagtu Khan and were the leaders of the Khalkha Right Wing. The descendants of Geresenji's third son bore the title Tüshiyetü Khan and were the leaders of the Khalkha Left Wing. Elverskog, *The Jewel Translucent Sutra*, 73.

22. Ubasanja Ching Taiji had the Asud and Yüngsiyebü as his appanage. Serruys, *Genealogical Tables*, 154.
23. Geretü Taiji was born in 1491. He had no descendants. Serruys, *Genealogical Tables*, 16.
24. The "six great peoples" refers to the Six Tümen.
25. Ibarai < Ibrahim (Ch. Yi-bu-la 亦不剌, died 1533) was an important figure in Inner Asian politics in the early sixteenth century, though his ancestry is unclear (one source claims he was a grandson of the Oirat khan, Esen). In 1495 he petitioned the Ming to settle near the Chinese border and pay tribute, which was granted, though after a few years he returned to the area north of Shaanxi 陝西 and started raiding China. In 1509 he was defeated by a Chinese force, and this may have been involved in his subsequent feud with Dayan Khan, who was simultaneously trying to consolidate his power by incorporating the Ordos into his own realm as the Western Tümen. Since Ibarai was the most powerful leader in the area, he was clearly a hindrance to Dayan Khan's plans. Thus, when Dayan Khan appointed Ulus Bolod as jinong over the Western Tümen, Ibarai saw his power threatened and killed him, then fled to the southwest, where in 1511 he attacked Lanzhou 蘭州 and the next year other areas in Gansu. Over the years he continued to consolidate his power in the northwest, in particular controlling the important trade routes. In 1513 he again requested to initiate tribute relations with the Ming and receive a four-clawed dragon robe but was rejected. He then continued raiding Tibet, border trading areas, and Hami 哈密, becoming the dominant power in the area. Finally, in 1533, Gün Bilig Mergen Jinong feigned an attack on Yansui 延綏, then marched west and defeated Ibarai's forces. L. Carrington Goodrich and Chaoyang Fang, *Dictionary of Ming Biography 1368–1644* (New York: Columbia University Press, 1976), 683–685.
26. Chief Mandulai (Ch. A-er-tu-si 阿爾禿) was the leader of the Ordos Tümen and an ally of Ibarai Taishi, who after the assassination of Ulus Bolod fled with Ibarai to the southwest. In the campaigns of Dayan Khan and Barsubolod, Mandulai was killed. Goodrich and Fang, *Dictionary of Ming Biography*, 683.
27. Both the *Precious Summary* and the *Golden Summary* contain this story of Ulus Bolad's assassination; however, although the chain of events is similar, the

details differ. In the *Precious Summary*, as Ulus Bolad is on his way to the Chinggis Khan shrine he is confronted by a man who questions his ownership of his horse. The dispute escalates and the prince decapitates the man, whereupon Ibarai and Mandulai incite the onlookers to attack and kill the prince. But in the *Golden Summary* the dispute begins with a horse theft, and Ulus Bolad is sent by Dayan Khan to the Ordos to help resolve it. However, when he arrives his retainers are beaten, and in anger he kills the man responsible. After witnessing this, Ibarai and another leader launch a campaign against Ulus Bolad and kill him. Okada Hidehiro, "Dayan Khan in the Battle of Dalan Terigün," in *Gedanke und Wirkung. Festschrift zum 90. Geburtstag von Nikolaus Poppe*, ed. Walther Heissig and Klaus Sagaster (Wiesbaden: Harrassowitz Verlag. 1989), 262–270.

28. Although *darkhan* is an old and well-known title in the Turco-Mongol tradition, the specific title "Great Darkhan" (M. *dayi darqan*) developed in the post-Yuan period to denote the highest rank of free nobleman. The ranks below it were: Baatur Darkhan, the lowest; one rank up, Üijeng Darkhan; then Guowang Darkhan, and the highest, Jiqui Darkhan. Ho, "The Office and Noble Titles," 168, 174.
29. The preceding stories of conflict set the stage for this campaign, which was Dayan Khan's greatest achievement because it finally unified the fractious Mongols into the Six Tümen.
30. Dalan Terigün, Seventy Chiefs, is the Mongolian name of the mountain range just north of Hohhot (in Chinese, the Yinshan Mountains), where Dayan Khan's army confronted the forces of the Three Western Tümen and defeated them. Afterward he pursued the fleeing remnants south, all the way to Kökenuur, where he eventually killed Mandulai. Returning to the Ordos, having reunited the Mongols of Inner Mongolia under his rule and organizing them into the Six Tümen, he received the title of khan in front of the Chinggis Khan shrine. Okada, "Dayan Khan," 265.
31. The Uriyangqan, reportedly a blond-haired people, were an old group who had long inhabited the Onon Valley and dominated the Mongolian steppe until their defeat in 1538. After Chinggis Khan died, Rashid al-Din records that the emirs of the Uriyangqan were to guard the royal Borjigid tombs in the Khentei Mountains, which is here confirmed by the following line: "who protected the lord's imperial treasury." As a result of this connection the Uriyangqan continued to be a powerful group until their ultimate defeat in the early sixteenth century, which is described below.
32. It is unclear what groups composed the Twelve Tümed, which was to become the appanage of Altan Khan. Jürungγa notes that in one Chinese source they consisted of the Seven Tümed, Uyigurchin, Üüsin, Bayaud, Urugud, and

Khonggirad. Morikawa, on the other hand, has argued that the Twelve Tümed comprised two wings, Right and Left, each with six groups. The Left Wing, inherited by the descendants of Altan Khan and headed by the Uyigurchin, consisted of the Üüshin, Baya'ud, Urud, Muu Minggan, Qonggirad, and Seven Tümed. The Right Wing, headed by the Mongoljin, was controlled by Daiching Ejei and his descendants, and it consisted of the Chegüd, Dalad, and others (Jun'ichi Yoshida, ed. *Altan Qayan-u Tuyuǰi* [Tokyo: Kazama-shobo, 1998], 325).

33. The "White Turbans" (< Ch. Chantou 纏頭) refers to the Muslim inhabitants of Inner Asia. Antoine Mostaert, *Dictionanaire ordos* (New York: Johnson Reprint Corporation, 1968), 451a.

34. The location of Jorgalun Jon is uncertain; it is either a mountain in Tüsiyetü Khan's Banner, now in the southwest of Töw Aimag, or another located close to the source of the Kerülen River. Yoshida, *Altan Qayan-u Tuyuǰi*, 253.

35. As noted above, the Uriyangqan, who guarded the royal Borjigid tombs in the Khentei Mountains, had been a powerful group of Mongols throughout the fifteenth century. This continued into the sixteenth century since Dayan Khan's mother was also a member of the Uriyangqan, and thus he felt an affinity toward them and did not engage them in battle. However, after he died, his successors engaged in the six successive battles herein described that finally destroyed the power of the Uriyangqan. As a result of the vacuum created by their defeat, a part of the Khalkhas—the Seven-Banner Khalkha—were able to move from the east into the traditional Uriyangqan territory and assume control in what was to become Outer Mongolia. The remaining Uriyangqan were pushed west toward the area of what is now Tuva. Okada Hidehiro, "The Fall of the Uriyangqan Mongols," *Mongolian Studies* 10 (1986–87): 49–57.

36. The dates of Dayan Khan are extensively debated; however, it is unlikely that he died in 1543 as claimed in the *Precious Summary*. He probably passed away in 1524. Nevertheless, the dates of his birth and enthronement—whether in 1470, 1480, or 1487—are still unclear. Moreover, the chronological confusion in the transition period from Manduluun Khan's death around 1470–1480 to the eventual rise of Dayan Khan in the 1490s is not as simple as later histories would have us believe. This was a period of intense conflict, as evidenced in the Western Tümens' assassination of Dayan Khan's son, Ulus Bolod. Clearly, neither Bayan Möngke nor Dayan Khan had resolved these tensions between the two wings of the Mongol community. Contrary to later historiography, when Dayan Khan's ascension as the Mongol khan is taken for granted as the natural order of things, at the time, Bayan Möngke becoming khan and then being succeeded by his son must have appeared to be a gross aberration of Chinggisid principles, or at least a usurpation by one powerful clique. Of course, it was

precisely this fact that Dayan Khan and later Mongol historians and Dayan Khan-descended aristocrats wished to forget. As a result, the history from Manduluun Khan's death to Dayan Khan's dominance is either obscured or wrapped in hagiographic legend. Elverskog, *Jewel Translucent*, 51–52.

8. HISTORY OF THE SIX TÜMEN

1. Although some sources claim that Törö Bolad had no children, it is maintained in the chronicle tradition that Bodi Taiji—or Bodi Alag Khan—was his son. But Dayan Khan died much earlier than 1543, and his uncle, Barsu Bolad Sain Alag, with the support of the Three Western Tümen, seized the throne in this interregnum period. Shortly thereafter, under pressure from the Three Eastern Tümen, Barsu Bolad was forced to step down and Bodi Alag ascended the throne. After his death in 1547 he was succeeded by his son Daraisun. Johan Elverskog, *The Jewel Translucent Sutra: Altan Khan and the Mongols in the Sixteenth Century* (Leiden: Brill, 2003), 50, 81, 88.
2. The title "Queen Mother Empress" (M. *tayiqu nangnang*) derives from the Chinese *taihou* 太后 and *niangniang* 娘娘.
3. The Chakhars first appeared in the second half of the fifteenth century, and during the reign of Dayan Khan they became the personal appanage of the Chinggisid khans. At the time it comprised Eight Otogs (camp districts); however, during the reign of Ligdan Khan (1604–1634) four of these groups, the Sünid, Üjümüchin, Naiman, and Aokhan, revolted. Ligdan Khan with the remaining groups subsequently fled to Kökenuur, and after his father's death, Erke Khonggor submitted to the Qing. The court in turn resettled these groups in south-central Inner Mongolia as autonomous banners; however, after the 1675 rebellion of Ligdan Khan's grandson and the prince of the Naiman Banner, Burni, the Chakhar's Chinggisid nobility was stripped of its privileges. The Chakhar Banners were integrated directly into the Eight-Banner system and put under the Manchu official in Zhangjiakou 張家口. Christopher P. Atwood, *Encyclopedia of Mongolia and the Mongol Empire* (New York: Facts on File, 2004), 88.
4. The Twelve Tümed were to become the appanage of Altan Khan, but it is not clear what groups it comprised. Jürungγa notes that in one Chinese source the Twelve Tümed consisted of the Seven Tümed, Uyigurchin, Ügüsin, Baya'ud, Uru'ud, and Qonggirad. Morikawa, on the other hand, has argued that the Twelve Tümed comprised two wings, Right and Left, each with six groups. The Left Wing was inherited by the descendants of Altan Khan and was headed by the Uyigurchin, consisting of the Üüsin, Baya'ud, Urud, Muu Minggan, Qonggirad, and Seven Tümed. The Right Wing was headed by the Mongoljin and

controlled by Daiching Ejei and his descendants; it consisted of the Chegüd, Dalad, and others. Jun'ichi Yoshida, *Altan Qagan-u Tuyuji* (Tokyo: Kazama-shobo, 1998), 325.

5. The twelve clans of Khalkha refer to the Five-Banner Khalkha in Inner Mongolia and the Seven-Banner Khalkha in Outer Mongolia.
6. According to the *Precious Summary* and the *Jewel Translucent Sutra*, Gün Bilig Mergen Jinong (1506–1542), also known as Kümel and Kümel Khara Jinong, was born in 1506. Chinese sources do not provide a date of birth; however, he is first mentioned in Chinese records in 1532 as part of a military raid into Ming territory. From then until his death he is repeatedly mentioned in regard to Mongol incursions into China. The *Precious Summary* notes that he died in 1551, at the age of forty-four. The *Jewel Translucent Sutra* and the majority of Chinese sources claim that he died in 1542 after raiding over the border into China.
7. Altan Khan (1507–1582) was the lord of the Twelve Tümed in Ordos, who during his life was to become the most powerful ruler among the Mongols.
8. Sengge Düüreng (1522–1586) was the eldest son of Altan Khan, by his first wife. He lived in the area of Xinghe 興和, north of Kalgan, and had a market at Xinping 新平, yet also frequented the market at Shoukoupu 守口堡. The possible reason for his "illegal" use of two markets, which is found in all the Chinese sources, is that he was perpetually destitute, no doubt in part fueled by his bitter feud with his father. This revolved around two issues:Altan Khan had disinherited his first wife, Sengge Düüreng's mother, in favor of his third wife, Queen Jönggen; and Sengge Düüreng felt that Altan was hoarding more than his fair share of the revenue from the border markets. This conflict reached such a level that Sengge's wife went to Wang Chonggu 王崇古, the governor in Datong 大同, to plead with him to increase Sengge's revenue and help "'her husband dispel this hatred for his father'" (Henry Serruys, "Two Remarkable Women in Mongolia: The Third Lady Erketü Qatun and Dayicing-Beyiji," *Asia Major* New Series 19, 2 [1974/75]: 202–203). The *Wanli Wugong Lu* also notes that he took so many wives he could not support them and thus sent them away begging. He even used some as warriors in raids over the border. Yet despite this bitter rivalry, as part of the 1571 peace accords Sengge received the rank of vice commissioner-in-chief (*dudu tongzhi* 都督同知), and upon his father's death he became ruler of the Tümed Mongols. However, the Chinese did not grant him the title Shunyi Wang 順義王 until he married the pro-Chinese Queen Jönggen, who was his archrival, in late 1582. After he received this rank Sengge Düüreng moved from the east and settled in Altan Khan's territory; he died four years later. Henry Serruys, *Genealogical Tables of the Descendants of Dayan-Qan* ('S-Gravenhage: Mouton, 1958), 83–87; Henry Serruys, "A Mongol Settlement

in North China at the End of the 16th Century," *Central Asiatic Journal* 4 (1959): 240.

9. Khutugtai Sechen Khung Taiji (1540–1586) was the eldest son of Guua Taiji, a grandson of Gün Bilig Mergen Jinong. He was involved in many campaigns with Altan Khan, particularly against the Oirat (in 1562, 1572, 1574), and also against northern Tibet in 1566. During this campaign into Tibet, the *Precious Summary*, written by his great-grandson Sagang Sechen, reports that Khung Taiji was converted to Buddhism; however, the veracity of this claim is dubious since it seems his interest began earlier. Nevertheless, it is clear Khung Taiji was a Buddhist and as an advisor to his uncle Altan Khan, was involved in Tibeto-Mongol relations. Khung Taiji was also engaged in Sino-Mongol relations, thus during the 1570 peace negotiations, Noyandara Jinong sent him to the court of Altan Khan in order to ensure markets and tribute relations for the Ordos Mongols. On account of Wang Chonggu's 王崇古 argument in support of Ordos markets, the court conceded, and in recognition of Khung Taiji's work and vigilance in maintaining the peace he was made a manager of the market (*zhuzhang* 主張). In 1571 he was given the rank assistant military commander (*zhihui qianshi* 指揮僉事), and in 1579 the honorary rank general of dragon and tiger (*longhu jiangjun* 龍虎將軍). He is also credited as the redactor of the famous *White History*, a manual outlining the Tibeto-Mongol theory of rule through the two spheres of religion and state and the cult of Chinggis Khan. L. Carrington Goodrich and Chaoyang Fang, *Dictionary of Ming Biography 1368–1644* (New York: Columbia University Press, 1976), 1128–1131.
10. Daraisun Küdeng Khan (r. 1548–1557) was the recognized heir in primogeniture to the title "Great Khan of the Great Yuan" and controlled the Chakhar. Yet during his reign, he had to recognize his cousins Altan of the Tümed, and Bayaskhal of the Kharchin as "khans," and in consolidating his own power, Altan Khan banished Daraisun to the east of the Khingan mountains. Atwood, *Encyclopedia*, 410.
11. It is unclear what the title *siteü* actually was; however, it may be *situ* 司徒, which from the Han to the Liao dynasties was "intermittently the title of one of the eminent central government officials called the Three Dukes (*san kung*); until 1122 in Sung and Liao used almost interchangeably with *ta ssu-t'u*, *ch'eng-hsiang*, etc., minister over the masses . . . [and during the Yuan dynasty]: though not considered one of the Three Dukes, sometimes used for similar quasi-honorific appointments."Charles O. Hucker, *A Dictionary of Official Titles in Imperial China* (Stanford, CA: Stanford University Press, 1985), 458.
12. This passage belies the decentralization of authority during the reign of Daraisun Khan. Granting Altan this title not only confirmed his status but also

perpetuated the fiction that the Chakhar Khan was still the ruler of the Mongols. The fact is that Altan Khan was then the most powerful ruler on the steppe.

13. Tümen Jasagtu Khan (r. 1557–1592) is always lauded in Mongolian sources for meeting with Karma Lama and introducing Buddhism to the Chakhars, as well as for establishing a legal code. Okada Hidehiro, "Origin of the Caqar Mongols," *Mongolian Studies* 14 (1991): 166.

14. The identity of Karma Lama remains unclear; however, a recently published Tibetan history of the Jonangpa sect (Ngawang Lodro Drakpa, *Jo nang chos 'byung zla ba'i sgron me*) notes: "The Mongol king Abai and King Ching Baatur, etc. respectfully proffered service and the Karma Lama from the Karma Temple, etc. monks, students, and patrons, were very many." Of course, whether this Karma Lama of the Jonangpa order is the one noted herein—and in the *Jewel Translucent Sutra*—is uncertain. Elverskog, *Jewel Translucent*, 168.

15. Although it is not clear what exactly is meant by "Jürchid," it presumably refers to speakers of what would become Manchu in northeast China.

16. Although it is not clear what exactly is meant by "Neli'üd," it may refer to the Evenki, speakers of a Tungusic language who were originally reindeer herders.

17. "The name Daur goes back to the medieval Kitans, speakers of a very distinct language of the Mongolic family who called their 10th- to 12th-century empire the 'Daur Gurun,' or Daur Empire. The Daur language today retains a few Kitan features, such as the peculiar word *kasoo* for 'iron' (versus Mongolian *temür*, a borrowing from Turkic), yet the Daur language is mostly a development of Middle Mongolian, the language of the Mongol empire. Moreover, the Daur clan name Boskochaina may be the same as the Qonggirad tribe's Bosqur lineage, from whom came Chinggis Khan's wife Börte Üjin. The Daurs thus appear to be a population of provincial Kitans who were heavily 'Mongolized' during Mongolian rule of Manchuria. The Daurs emerged into history in 1616, when the nascent Manchu Empire found 'Solon' tribesmen distributed along the northern bank of the Amur river. . . . The Solons were divided into *khalas* (clans), a Manchu-Tungusic word, and composed of predominantly agricultural Daurs in symbiosis with bands of hunting and farming Ewenkis." Atwood, *Encyclopedia*, 135.

18. Ligdan Khan (b. 1588, r. 1604–1634) began his career by aligning with the southern Five-Banner Khalkha and raiding China, which subsequently gave him an annual subsidy of 40,000 taels of silver to prevent further raids. By 1614 the Khalkhas and other Mongol groups had become marriage partners with the Manchus, and Ligdan eventually broke off relations with their leader Nurhaci in 1620. Tensions escalated when Manchu forces came to the aid of the Khorchin as Ligdan was besieging them. Nevertheless, Ligdan maintained control of some

Mongol groups, and after allying himself with the northern Seven-Banner Khalkha leader, Tsogtu Taiji, he also began promoting the Dharma. He invited the Sakya Sharba Khutugtu and had the entire Kanjur translated. Regardless, by 1627 other Mongols were in open revolt, and in 1632 Hong Taiji and his Khorchin allies assaulted Ligdan Khan and his Chakhar Mongols. They fled to Ordos, where their presence only exacerbated the tenuous situation, and eventually to Kökenuur with Boshogtu Jinong's wife and the relics of Chinggis Khan. In 1634 Ligdan died of smallpox, and his wives and sons surrendered to Hong Taiji's forces. Atwood, *Encyclopedia*, 334–335.

19. As a counter to the other Mongol leaders, who had allied themselves with the Dalai Lama and his Gelukpa order, Ligdan Khan wanted to revive the Mongol-Sakya relations of the Yuan period. He thus invited the Sakya monk Sharba Khutugtu (fl. 1617–1629), who installed in Ligdan Khan's capital an image of Mahakala that Khubilai Khan had supposedly presented to Pakpa Lama. Atwood, *Encyclopedia*, 335.
20. Ligdan Khan's White City was built near modern Lindong. Georg Huth, *Die Inschriften von Tsaghan Baisin. Tibetisch-Mongolischer Text* (Leipzig: F. A. Brockhaus, 1894).
21. Bayaskhal Köndelen Khan was born in 1510, and after his father died, he took control of the Seven Kharchin of the Yüngsiyebü. The *Wanli Wugong Lu* notes that he had over 30,000 well-trained troops under his command, who continually harassed the Chinese in Ming territory. As a result, during the 1571 negotiations between Altan Khan and the Ming, Bayaskhal Taiji was greatly opposed to his older brother's overtures of peace. However, after the Yüngsiyebü's animals were struck by lightning, he saw it as a sign from heaven and followed Altan's lead. As part of the 1571 peace accords, the Ming court gave Bayaskhal Taiji the high-ranking title of vice commissioner-in-chief (*dudu tongzhi* 都督同知). One year later he became ill, probably from gout, and died. When the Ming government heard of his death they sent emissaries to his family; however, his two wives, who believed the Chinese had caused the illness through evil magic, sent them away. Serruys, *Genealogical Tables*, 119–121.
22. The jinong was the "viceroy" appointed by the khan to rule over the Western Three Tümen (see page 258, note 17).
23. Although there is no date provided for this invasion, based on the individuals involved—and its inclusion in the *Precious Summary*—it presumably involves Altan Khan's assault on Beijing in 1550, during which he demanded that tribute relations between the Ming court and the Tümed be established. Elverskog, *Jewel Translucent*, 97–102.
24. Although it is not possible to definitely identify Yendege, Chinese sources record that the 1550 invasion began in Dashawo 大沙窩, the "Great Sands," north of

Dushikou 獨石口, where Altan Khan's brother resided and where their meeting prior to the invasion took place. In his 1630 work, the *Huangming Shifa lu* 皇明世法錄, Chen Renxi 陳仁錫 points out the danger Mongols in this area posed to China if they decided to march south. Drawing upon his knowledge of the area or from the historical evidence of this 1550 attack, he claimed that the Mongols could easily move south, pass through Yongning 永寧 and Sihaiye 四海冶, and then attack Huanghua 黃花, which is almost due north of Beijing, just south of the Great Wall at the Juyong Pass 居庸關. It may therefore be possible that the Mongols passed through the Dashawo, and that the ravine here noted is the Juyong Pass, where the Chinese made a failed attempt to stop the Mongol advance. Henry Serruys, "A Note on Two Place Names in Mongolia," in *Documenta Barbarorum. Festschrift für Walther Heissig zum 70. Geburtstag*, ed. Annemarie von Gabain and Wolfgang Veenker (Wiesbaden: Otto Harrassowitz, 1983), 370–381.

25. The title gentleman (< Ch. *sheren* 舍人) was used to denote the son of a *tabunang* (a son-in-law married to a daughter of a Chinggisid nobleman) who was himself not married to a Chinggisid. "If a son of a *Tabunang* did not marry a royal princess, then he could not be *Tabunang*. In this case, he needed to have another specific title to show his relationship with the royal family. Therefore, a new title *Sigejin* was introduced. In the Khalkha (Qalqa) law codes in 1620 A.D., *Tabunang* and *Sigejin* were listed together in their privileges to show that they were different from the commoners." Kai-lung Ho, "The Office and Noble Titles of the Mongols from the 14th to 16th Century, and the study of the "White History" *Čayan Teüke*." *Central Asiatic Journal* 59, 1–2 (2016): 163.
26. Although the *Precious Summary* claims that he died in 1550, at the age of forty-four, the *Jewel Translucent Sutra* and the majority of Chinese sources confirm that he died in 1542 after raiding over the border in China.
27. Noyandara Jinong (1522–1572) was the eldest son of Mergen Jinong, and after his father died he became jinong in 1544 (Sagang Sechen incorrectly gives the year 1551). His appanage was the Four Khoriya, and he resided in the western part of Ordos. The *Wanli Wugong Lu* notes that he died of illness on the third day of the third month of 1572. Serruys, *Genealogical Tables*, 43–44.
28. On Altan Khan's numerous campaigns against the Oirat see Elverskog, *Jewel Translucent*, 108–117.
29. Qonin is Hening 和寧, which was the new administrative name of Qaraqorum adopted by the Yuan government early in the fourteenth century. It was subsequently adopted by the Ming court and used as part of their strategies in dealing with the Mongols, such as after the failed Yongle campaigns when they gave Arugtai the title Prince of Hening 和寧王 in 1413 (David M. Robinson, *Ming China and Its Allies: Imperial Rule in Eurasia* [New York: Cambridge University

Press, 2019], 56). In this case, however, it confirms the power of the Oirat, who controlled the old imperial capital.

30. The title *shunyi wang* 順義王 ("obedient and righteous prince") was given to Altan Khan on April 21, 1571; however, the official ceremony of investiture did not take place until June 13, 1571. Henry Serruys, "Four Documents Relating to the Sino-Mongol Peace of 1570–1571," *Monumenta Serica* 19 (1960): 23.
31. This is incorrect. At the ceremony of 1571, Altan Khan did not receive a seal, so it has to be assumed that during this time he continued using his own seal in Mongolian script. Later in June 1572, Wang Chonggu 王崇古 sent a memorial to the court requesting four items for the Mongols, including a seal for Altan Khan. The court issued him a gilt silver seal on July 3, 1572. This greatly upset Tümen Khan, who was technically Altan Khan's superior as the Great Khan of the Eastern Tümen yet received no recognition from the Ming court. The *Wanli Wugong Lu* notes that in 1577 his envoys declared, "the Altan-qan is Tümen-qagan's subject, but now that he has received a princely title and a golden seal as big as a peck (*tou* 斗) is it not as if he was the husband, and Tümen-qagan has been reduced to the status of wife?" (quoted in Henry Serruys, *Sino-Mongol Relations during the Ming II. The Tribute System and Diplomatic Missions [1400–1600]* [Bruxelles: Institut Belge des Hautes Études Chinoises, 1967], 104). In April 1577, as Altan Khan was planning his trip to Kökenuur to meet the Dalai Lama, to facilitate his travel through Ming territory he requested a new seal, a "golden seal of a *dudu* 都督" (commissioner-in-chief). The court apparently rejected his request. Serruys, *The Tribute System*, 77–78 nn. 41, 103, 445.
32. As outlined in the introduction, Mongol political ideology at this time was defined by the theory of *ulus* and *törö*, which is well captured in this passage. And, as explained in the introduction, this *törö* could collapse, and did, and the two ulus were able to subsequently go their own ways.
33. Serruys has published a full translation of the Chinese version of this agreement ("Four Documents," 23–47). In the initial agreement of 1571, the Mongols swore an oath that they would no longer attack China, and then a thirteen-point agreement was established on the issues of refugees and deserters and in particular judicial matters concerning the punishment of Chinese and Mongols who committed criminal acts in the other's territory. In 1577 when Altan Khan was on his way to Kökenuur to meet the Dalai Lama, the agreement was renewed, with an additional five regulations heightening Mongol patrols to prevent Chinese from entering Mongol territory, granting permission for Chinese to gather wood in Mongol territory, and imposing fines on Mongols who stole from Chinese. When Sengge Düüreng became *shunyi wang* 順義王 in 1587 the Mongols and Chinese negotiated anew, and again in 1603 when Namudai Sechen Khan came to the border requesting tribute relations. At this time four more

laws were added: forbidding Mongols to surrender to the Chinese, request gifts for deceased relatives, accompany leaders on tribute missions, or be cruel to horses and mules. In 1613 when Boshogtu was enfeoffed as *shunyi sang* the regulations were again ratified, with the addition of fourteen laws pertaining to criminal acts and appropriate punishments.

34. The Ministry of the Army allowed two markets to be opened for the Ordos Mongols at Hong Shan 紅山 and Qingshuiying 清水營 in Ningxia 寧夏. The Court of the Imperial Stud forwarded 20,000 taels of silver from the Horse Fund to purchase horses. There was also another 20,000 taels of silver from other sources to pay for the entertainment and daily rations of the Mongols who came to the market. (Serruys, *The Tribute System*, 384 n. 44). There is no record of what was bought in 1571, though in 1572 at Hong Shan the government purchased over 1,500 horses and private traders bought a total of 1,800 horses and mules. At Qingshui Ying the court bought over 1,500 horses and cattle, while private merchants bought 600 horses (Serruys, *The Tribute System*, 169–170, 213). The market for the Tümed was located at Deshengpu 得勝堡, where the government purchased 1,370 horses for 10,545 taels of silver. Private buyers bought a total of 6,000 head of horses, mules, donkeys, cattle and sheep (Serruys, *Trade Relations*, 170, 203). Besides the transactions done at the market, Altan Khan was allowed to present tribute of 500 horses. In 1571 he presented 509 horses, the extra nine as a special gift to the emperor. The court gave two lined garments in varicolored satin, one bolt of coarse silk and five taels of silver for the 30 best horses; for the remaining 479 the Court of the Imperial Stud paid 5,000 taels of silver and distributed them among garrisons of Shanxi 山西, Datong 大同 and Xuanfu 宣府 (Serruys, "Four Documents," 47–66; Serruys, *The Tribute System*, 187–190). The Kharchin and Yüngshiyebü had their market at Zhangjia Kou 張家口, where the government bought 1993 horses for 15,277 taels of silver and private merchants bought 9,000 horses, mules, cattle, and sheep.

35. The Yellow Uyghurs are descendants of the Gansu 甘肅 Uyghurs. In the face of Tangut attacks they moved into the territory of the Tsong Kha confederation in what is now northern Qinghai. Bianca Horlemann, "The Relations of the Eleventh-Century Tsong Kha Tribal Confederation to Its Neighbour States on the Silk Road," in *Contributions to the Early History of Tibet*, ed. M. T. Kapstein and B. Dotson (Leiden: Brill, 2007), 83–106. In the *Yuan Shi* 元史 it is recorded that in 1226 Chinggis Khan's general Sübütei attacked them, and throughout the Yuan and Ming, Chinese sources always record them as living in border areas, particularly in the Tsaidam Basin. The *Ta'rikh-i Rashidi* of Mirza Haidar, compiled in 1547, also notes that they were living on the southern perimeter of the Tarim Basin and that they were Buddhists. Saguchi Toru,

"Historical Development of the Sarïgh Uyghurs," *Memoirs of the Research Department of the Toyo Bunko* 44 (1986): 1–26.

36. Little is known about Asing Lama, except that he was the principal Buddhist monk who initiated Altan Khan's involvement with Tibet. Herein it is claimed that he was captured during Altan Khan's campaigns in Tibet in 1573, and then taught the khan the theory of reincarnation and the six-syllable mantra. In the *Jewel Translucent Sutra,* however, and as in corroborated by Tibetan sources, he simply came to Altan Khan's court and gave teachings (Zahiruddin Ahmad, *Sino-Tibetan Relations in the Seventeenth Century* [Roma: Istituto Italiano per il Medio ed Estremo Oriente, 1970], 87). A recently discovered local history from Küriye Banner, which claims Asing Lama as the first local lama, provides a more detailed history of his life. Asing Lama was born in Amdo in the Samlau (< Tibetan?) lineage and was originally named Sherab. He studied in central Tibet, then went to Wutai Shan 五台山 in Shanxi 山西, then crossed the Great Wall and lived at Chagan Khada, north of present-day Hohhot, whereupon he met Altan Khan, the history of which is described in the *Jewel Translucent Sutra*. Altan Khan decreed, "You are the cause of my root of merit. Thus I'll call you Echige Lama [Father Lama]." Later, at the beginning of the seventeenth century, he began proselytizing in the Baarin and Kharchin areas. Eventually he came into contact with the Manchus, and when Hong Taiji moved the capital to Mukden, he invited Asing Lama to live there. He lived on Bagun Mountain, west of Mukden, and became famous as Manjusri Khutugtu. Later he returned to Inner Mongolia and established what came to be Manjusri monastery. He died on the twenty-fifth day of the eighth month of 1636, age eighty. Čigči, "Asing Lama-yin udum üile-yi tobči tanilčaγulqu ni," *Öbör Mongγol-un neyigem-ün sinjilekü uqagan* 3 (1983): 177–181.

9. HISTORY OF KHUTUGTAI SECHEN KHUNG TAIJI

1. The Torghud trace their origin to the Kereit ruler Ong Khan (d. 1203), and first appear as a group among the Oirat in the mid-sixteenth century. In 1630 the majority of the Torghud migrated west to the Volga, forming the base of the Kalmyks. Other Torghud princes joined Güüshi Khan and moved into the area of Kökenuur. In 1698 a Torghud Kalmyk prince with 500 subjects went to Tibet on pilgrimage, and when they could not return the Qing resettled them in Alashan; they are the Ejene Torghuds. The following year 15,000 Torghud households returned from Russia, and the Zünghar ruler Tsewang Rabtan Khung Taiji attached them to the Khoid. Sixteen years after the Qing conquest of the Zünghars, most of the Volga Torghud returned, and the Qing resettled them

in Xinjiang as the "Old Torghuds." Similarly in 1771, some of the Zünghar Torghud were resettled in western Mongolia (today's Khowd province) as the "New Torghud." Christopher P. Atwood, *Encyclopedia of Mongolia and the Mongol Empire* (New York: Facts on File, 2004), 544–545.

2. The "confluence of the Three Rivers of Silimji" is known in Chinese and Tibetan as the "Source of Three Rivers" (Ch. *Sanjiangyuan* 三江源, T. *rma 'bri rdza gsum gyi mgo khungs*), an area of the Tibetan plateau in Qinghai province that contains the headwaters of the three great rivers of Asia: the Yellow, Yangtze, and Mekong.
3. A *nakpa* (T. *snags-pa*) is an ordained nonmonastic practitioner of tantra.
4. The title *güi wang khonjin* is composed of two Chinese titles: *güi wang* (< Ch. *guowang* 國王), "prince of the state," and *khonjin* (< Ch. *guanren* 官人), "Lord," a new title that developed in the post-Dayan Khan period to denote a high-ranking official who was not of royal blood (Kai-lung Ho, "The Office and Noble Titles of the Mongols from the 14th to 16th Century, and the Study of the 'White History' *Čayan Teüke*," *Central Asiatic Journal* 59, 1–2 (2016): 1). Unlike in the fifteenth century, when non-Chinggisids could hold titles such as *taishi*, *chingsang*, and *jaisang*, after Dayan Khan's restoration only his descendants could hold any such ranks. Thus in the sixteenth century *khonjin* was adopted for when non-Dayan Khanids were to be entitled, such as this Tibetan, Vajra Tümei.
5. Aqasar Khan presumably refers to the Moghul ruler 'Abd al-Karim Khan (r. 1566–1594), the grandson of Sultan Said Khan (r. 1514–1533) and the son of 'Abd al-Rashid Khan (r. 1534–1566). Jun'ichi Yoshida, *Altan Qagan-u Tuyuji* (Tokyo: Kazama-shobo, 1998), 371–372.
6. Originally the Four Oirat was an overarching term connoting four groups of people inhabiting northwest Mongolia: the Oirat, Naiman, Kereit, and Bargud. By the sixteenth century, however, the Oirat were composed of eight different groups: the Khoid, Baatud, Bargu, Buraad, Dörböd, Zünghar, Khoshud, and Torghud.
7. Jalaman Mountain is located northeast of Hami 哈密 and borders the southern side of the recognized homeland of the Four Oirat. Jürungγ-a, *Erdeni tunumal neretü sudur orosiba* (Beijing: Ündüsüten-ü keblel-ün qoriy-a, 1984), 63 n. 1.
8. The Bulunggir River is the Shule River 疏勒河, which flows north from the Qilian Mountains 祁連山 on the Tibetan plateau and then west through Gansu province toward Dunhuang 敦煌. Historically it flowed seasonally into Lop Nur, an intermittent salt lake in the Taklamakan Desert. Jürungγ-a, *Erdeni tunumal*, 60 n. 1.
9. The title "minister" (M. *jayayači*) actually meant "fortune-teller" in both the imperial and Qing periods; however, in the wake of Dayan Khan's reformulation of Mongol ranks and titles it came to be a "high-ranking post in charge of

important foreign affairs and the tribe's internal military affairs." Ho, "The Office and Noble Titles," 175.

10. Noyandara (1522–1572) was the eldest son of Gün Bilig Mergen Jinong. After his father died he became *jinong*, "viceroy," in 1544. His appanage was the Four Khoriya, and he resided in the western part of Ordos. The *Wanli Wugong Lu* notes that he died of an illness on the third day of the third month of 1572. Henry Serruys, *Genealogical Tables of the Descendants of Dayan-Qan* ('S-Gravenhage: Mouton, 1958), 43–44.

10. HISTORY OF ALTAN KHAN AND THE BUDDHIST CONVERSION

1. Boshogtu (1565–1624) was the son of Buyan Baatur Taiji, the son of Noyandara Jinong. In 1577 at the age of thirteen he became jinong because his father had been killed in a campaign against the Oirat. Boshogtu Jinong is well known for his Buddhist activities, which included building a Kalacakra temple in 1585 and commissioning a Sakyamuni statue in 1607 and later another monastery in Ordos. He is also identified as the sponsor of several important Buddhist texts, the *Dasasahasrika Sutra*, the *Gegen Toli* (Tib. *Rgyal-rabs gsal-ba'i me-long*) translated by Sakya Dondub, and the *Mani ka-'bum* translated by Shireetü Güüsi. He also had the *Altan bicig*, the ritual text for the cult of Chinggis Khan, written down in gold letters. His son Rinchen Jinong (d. 1656), as leader of the Ordos, submitted to the Manchus in 1635. Henry Serruys, *Genealogical Tables of the Descendants of Dayan-Qan* ('S-Gravenhage: Mouton, 1958), 59–61; Walther Heissig, "Zur Entstehungsgeschichte der Mongolischen Kandjur-Redaktion der Ligdan Khan-Zeit (1628–1629)," in *Studia Altaica. Festschrift für Nikolaus Poppe zm 60. Geburtstag am 8. August 1957* (Wiesbaden: Otto Harrassowitz, 1957), 110; Walther Heissig, "Eine kleine mongolische Klosterbibliothek aus Tsakhar," *Jahrbuch des Bernischen Historischen Museums in Bern* 41 (1961–1962): 576 n. 68.
2. This refers to the 1571 peace accord between the Ming dynasty and Altan Khan, which according to Mongol political ideology was understood in terms of two *ulus* (China and the Tümed) forming an alliance in a state (*törö*).
3. Qonin (Ch. Hening 和寧) was the Ming-era name of the old Mongol capital Qaraqorum.
4. Although Mongol sources, particularly the *Precious Summary*, maintain that after the Yuan dynasty the Mongols completely forgot or ignored Buddhism until Altan Khan, this is is incorrect. Before aligning with the Gelukpa tradition Altan Khan had maintained relations with several other Tibetan Buddhist schools, as well as the Chinese White Lotus. He continually asked the

Ming court to provide him with Buddhist texts and other religious items (including statues, rosaries, and paint for thangkas). In 1573 the Ming acquiesced and sent statues and twelve Tibetan sutras, accompanied by lamas who were resident in Beijing to recite them. The following year they gave these monks gifts and titles for their activities and sent two more monks to Altan's court. This Ming policy of supporting Buddhism, which continued long after Altan Khan's death, was premised on the idea that Buddhism would pacify the Mongols.

5. The *Jewel Translucent Sutra* records not only a different list of envoys (Taglung Nangso, Üijeng Jaisang, Dayan Kiya, and Bombu Sanding) but also that they were actually sent in 1575. Johan Elverskog, *The Jewel Translucent Sutra: Altan Khan and the Mongols in the Sixteenth Century* (Leiden: Brill, 2003), 139–140.
6. Sonam Gyatso (1543–1588) was recognized at age two as an incarnation of Gedün Gyatso and thus brought to Drepung monastery and installed as abbot. In the 1560s he began his political career by seeking support for the Gelukpa order, which was threatened by the growing power of the Rinpung rulers of Tsang, supporters of the rival Karmapas. When their forces began to threaten Lhasa, Sonam Gyatso began looking for outside help, turning in particular to the Tümed ruler Altan Khan. When they met on June 19, 1578, near Kökenuur, the khan gave him the title Dalai Lama, which was retroactively bestowed on his two predecessors. After this meeting, the Dalai Lama sent a letter and gifts to the Chinese court, then proceeded to southeastern Tibet. In response to his letter the Wanli 萬曆 emperor sent a letter granting the Dalai Lama a title and gifts. During his time in eastern Tibet the Dalai Lama established close relations with local rulers, and after the death of Altan Khan in 1582 he was invited to Mongolia by the khan's descendants. Upon arriving he made allegiances with the Tümed, Khalkha, and Kharchin. In 1588 he was also invited to Beijing, but he died in Mongol territory that same year. L. Carrington Goodrich and Chaoyang Fang, *Dictionary of Ming Biography 1368–1644* (New York: Columbia University Press, 1976), 22–23.
7. Contrary to how it is presented here, the main Tibetan source describing these events, the Fifth Dalai Lama's biography of the Third Dalai Lama, notes that Tibetans were wary of establishing relations with the Mongols: "Although it was time for opening the door on his work in that direction, he did not make up his mind for a while, and went to Gong-dkar. Among the patrons and monks there arose many opinions both for and against his going. He adopted the advice of those represented by Ngag-dbang grag-pa, the Lha-gzig-mi ruler (of the Rlangs clan), that it might be proper to fulfill the wishes of the king of the frontier, and made his decision before arriving back at 'Bras-spungs." Okada Hidehiro, "The

Mongolian Literary Tradition in Early Manchu Culture," in *Proceedings of the 35th Permanent International Altaistic Conference*, ed. Chieh-hsien Ch'en (Taipei: National Taiwan University and Center for Chinese Studies Materials, 1992), 645.

8. Where exactly Chabchiyal (steep ravine, gully, clearing in forest) was is not certain. Jürungya notes it was in the area of Gonghe 共和 (Jürungya, *Erdeni tunumal neretü sudur orosiba* [Beijing: Ündüsüten-ü keblel-ün qoriy-a, 1984], 100 n. 1). The *Ming shi lu* 明史錄 identifies its location as Cha-cha cheng 叉叉城 (itself a transcription of the Mongol Chabchiyal), to the southeast of Kökenuur. Henry Serruys, "Four Documents Relating to the Sino-Mongol Peace of 1570–1571," *Monumenta Serica* 19 (1960): 36 n. 74.
9. The temple that was built is known in Mongol sources as Chabchiyal monastery; however, the exact history of its construction is unclear. The *Ming Shi* 明史 notes that already in 1573 Bingtü, Altan Khan's fourth son, requested permission from the Ming to build a temple at Kökenuur. According to the *Ming shi lu* 明史錄, it was Khutugtai Sechen Khung Taiji who in 1575 asked for permission (Serruys, "Four Documents," 36 n. 74). Either way, it was eventually completed in 1577 on the southeastern shores of Qinghai lake. The *Shi lu* also notes that in 1576 Altan Khan and Bingtü requested help from the Chinese to build the temple, a fact also recorded in the Fifth Dalai Lama's *History of the Third Dalai Lama*, which is copied in Nata's 1817 *Altan Erike*: "The ground having been consecrated, at the place where the lama and almsmaster had met, a monastery was built. Many Black Chinese craftsmen were made to build it. Inside the monastery there were statues of the Buddhas of the three times, Tsongkhapa, and also holy statues. In the four directions there was a temple to Yamantaka and Avalokitesvara, each of which had sixteen pillars. In between these two were a Bodhisattva and Yaksa temple. In the four corners of the pavilion there was the Palace of the Shining Saviour and the Great Bliss Palace. It was built in a Chinese fashion with a Chinese manner. It was called the 'Monastery of the Turner of Great Vehicle's Dharmacakra.'" Nata, *Altan Erike*, ed. Coyiji (Kökeqota: Öbör Mongγol-un arad-un keblel-ün qoriy-a, 1989), 123–124. In 1577 the Ming government recognized the temple and gave it the title Look up to China Monastery (Yanghua Si 仰華寺). After it was completed many Mongols went to this monastery; however, to do so they had to pass through Ming-controlled Gansu 甘肅. Chinese officials suggested that it should be burned down in order to prevent Mongol raids, and the *Ming Shi* records that Ming troops destroyed it in 1591 (Nata, *Altan Erike*, 210).
10. Red River is the Mongol name for the upper sections of the Yangtze River 長江 where it flows north of Kökenuur. Jürungγ-a, *Erdeni tunumal neretü sudur orosiba* (Beijing: Ündüsüten-ü keblel-ün qoriy-a, 1984), 49 n. 1.

11. Begtse Mahakala, known colloquially and iconographically as the Red Mahakala, is the main protector of the Hayagriva cycle of practice and was thus an important deity in the Sakya pantheon. Begtse Mahakala was later adopted by the Gelukpa and became an important protector deity in Mongolia.
12. Hayagriva is the fearful manifestation of Bodhisattva Avalokitesvara. In the sixth century Hayagriva was incorporated into the Buddhist tantric pantheon as a protector king, *vidhyaraja*, who was called upon for protection and the expulsion of demons. Later, in such works as the *Mahavairocana Sutra*, Hayagriva was co-opted into the sphere of Avalokitesvara and incorporated among the deities that emanated from Amitabha. In the twelfth century this union was again amplified by the great reformer of Tibetan Buddhism, Atisa, who placed Avalokitesvara and Hayagriva at the center of the mandala in the important work the *Guhyasamaja Tantra*. Consequently, Hayagriva developed into an important tutelary deity within the Tibetan traditions, particularly the Nyingma, who associated Hayagriva closely with Padmasambhava. Patricia Berger and Terese Tse Bartholomew, *Mongolia: The Legacy of Chinggis Khan* (San Francisco: Asian Art Museum, 1995), 234.
13. Gün Ergi, "Steep Bank," is the Haerji Range 哈爾吉領 on the north side of the Qushian River 曲什安河 in Qinghai 清海. Jürungγ-a, *Erdeni tunumal*, 114 n. 2.
14. The tripartite division of the welcoming parties found in the *Precious Summary* is also recorded in the two other major sources for these events, the *Jewel Translucent Sutra* and the *Biography of the Third Dalai Lama*. In these two sources the groups consisted of the following:

JTS	*DL3*
#1 Ordos' Sechen Khung Taiji	Bar-khu Tha'i-ji
Sechen Daiching	Ba-thur of the Yong-sha-bu
Üijeng Jongtulai	Kha-tan Ba-dur
#2 Namudai Sechen Khung Taiji	Se-chen Hong Tha'i-ji of the Ur-bsdus
Lord Dayan	Da-yan No-yon of the Mthu-mid
Lord Bayuud	
Daiching Ejei	
#3 Sechen Daiching	Jo-rug-thu Tha'i-ji
	Ching Ba-dur

It is clear that all three sources are in disagreement, and therefore uncertain as to how these parties were actually organized. Jun'ichi Yoshida, *Altan Qagan-u Tuyuji* (Tokyo: Kazama-shobo, 1998), 348.

15. *Sing sing dai güüshi* is a truncated form of the Chinese title based on the Tibetan: national preceptor, great prince of the three provinces (Ch. *sansheng daiwang guoshi* 三省太王國師).
16. Dromton Gyelwa Jungne (1004–1064) was the main disciple of Atisa and the founder of both the Kadampa school of Tibetan Buddhism and Reting monastery. https://treasuryoflives.org/biographies/ view/Dromton-Gyelwa-Jungne/4267 (accessed November 8, 2020).
17. Queen Jönggen (1551–1612) was the third wife of Altan Khan. Previously she had been promised to an Ordos prince in marriage, but Altan Khan kept her for himself and instead gave the prince a woman who was to marry Daiching Ejei (these events precipitated his surrender to the Chinese in 1570). After Altan Khan's death, Jönggen became an important figure in contemporary Mongol and Sino-Mongol political life. At first she planned on remaining independent from the other rulers, which could have been feasible, since she had in her possession the khan's official seal and controlled the tribute relations. However, the Chinese, having received a petition from seventy-nine Mongol noblemen to bestow the rank of *shunyi wang* 順義王 on Sengge Düüreng and to maintain the status quo of previous policy, pressured her to marry him. They married in October–November 1582. Taking advantage of Sengge Düüreng's ineptitude as a result of his drunkenness, Jönggen took his best troops and installed herself independent of him. To consolidate her power she wanted her son, Budashiri, to marry Baga Beiji, who had inherited control of Bayising (settlements built in Mongol territory by Chinese refugees) after Daiching Ejei's death. Dayan Kiya (the adopted son of Altan Khan), who was the true power in Bayising, opposed the marriage, so Baga Beiji married Namudai Sechen (Sengge Düüreng's son). Nevertheless, after Jönggen's plans had been thwarted, Sengge Düüreng died, and the Chinese promoted her marriage to Namudai Sechen. After Namudai Sechen died in 1607, there was again a dispute as to who would receive the rank of *shunyi wang*. The contenders were Boshogtu Jinong, Namudai Sechen's eldest son; Chogtu's son; and Sodnam, the son of Budashiri and Baga Beiji (who had married each other after Namudai Sechen divorced Baga Beiji and married Jönggen). This dispute lasted several years; however, under the direction of Urad Taiji, Boshogtu was selected and Jönggen was requested to marry him to ensure the bestowal of the rank from the Chinese. She complied and was married to her fourth husband on June 21, 1611. She died the following year. Henry Serruys, "Two Remarkable Women in Mongolia: The Third Lady Erketü Qatun and Dayicing-Beyiji," *Asia Major* New Series 19, 2 (1974–75): 191–245.
18. Most sources mention the seven jewels as consisting of gold, silver, lapis lazuli, crystal, agate, rubies, and red pearls; however, a Mongolian text describing Sukhavati describes the seven jewels as gold, silver, lapis lazuli, crystal, white

coral, red pearls, and cornelian. Henry Serruys, "The Seven Jewels in Mongolian Literature," *Mongolian Studies* 2 (1975): 133–140.

19. The eight offerings, which are symbolically represented by bowls of water on Tibetan Buddhist altars, are 1) water for drinking, 2) water for bathing, 3) flowers, 4) incense, 5) perfume, 6) food, 7) music, and 8) light.
20. On ideals and realities of vegetarianism in Tibetan Buddhism see Geoffery Barstow, *Food of Sinful Demons: Meat, Vegetarianism, and the Limits of Buddhism in Tibet* (New York: Columbia University Press, 2017).
21. The eight-part fast (< Ch. *baguanzhai* 八關齋) developed in medieval China and entailed lay Buddhists avoiding meat and fish (and following the Eight Precepts) for certain periods of time, such as three or six days. Over time, especially after vegetarianism was promoted by Emperor Wu of the Liang dynasty (r. 502–549), it became popular for the laity to observe this fast during Buddhist holidays.
22. This system of coordinating the hierarchies of secular and religious titles is drawn from the late sixteenth-century *White History*. Thus the highest-ranking religious title, *chöjé* (T. *chos rje*, Dharma lord) is paralleled with *khung taiji* (Ch. *huang taizi* 皇太子, crown prince); while rabjamba (T. *rab 'byams pa*) and Kachu (T. *bka' bcu*)— ranks of monastic eduation in the Gelukpa system—parallel *taiji* (Ch. *taizi* 太子, prince); and *gelong* (T. *dge slong*, a fully ordained monk) is equivalent to lesser noble ranks: *tabunang* (son-in-law), *khonjin* (< Ch. *guanren* 官人, lord), *taishi* (< Ch. *taishi* 太師, grand preceptor), and *jaisang* (< Ch. *zaixiang* 宰相, chancellor). On the importance of ranks and titles in Mongol society during this period, and especially in the *White History*, see Kai-lung Ho, "The Office and Noble Titles of the Mongols from the 14th to 16th Century, and the Study of the 'White History' *Čaγan Teüke*," *Central Asiatic Journal* 59, 1–2 (2016): 133–177.
23. *The Laws of the Ten Meritorious Deeds* refers to the *White History*, which was attributed to Khubilai Khan but was actually a creation of the late sixteenth century. It presents an idealized vision of Buddhist rule that is premised not only on the Two Realms but also on "assigning proper titles to monks and officials, who are to perform tasks grouped in numbered categories (three great deeds, four great principles, six great examples, etc.) and to receive prescribed rewards and punishments for meditative and governmental accomplishments or moral demerits." Christopher P. Atwood, *Encyclopedia of Mongolia and the Mongol Empire* (New York: Facts on File, 2004), 82.
24. On the dispensations granted to recognized religious groups during the Yuan period—such as not having to pay taxes or provide corvée labor—see Christopher P. Atwood, "Validated by Holiness or Sovereignty: Religious Toleration as Political Theology in the Mongol World Empire of the Thirteenth Century," *International History Review* 26, 2 (2004): 237–256.

25. "Heart of Aggregate" is the Mongolian translation of Bimbisara, the name of the ruler of Magadha who was a great supporter of the Buddha.
26. Why this title was not supposed to be translated into Mongolian is unclear; however, it accordingly was not, and thus Sagang Sechen recorded it as *gsarjal*, which presumably derives from the Tibetan *gsar gyal*, "new lord."
27. Father Lama (M. Ečige Lama) is how Asing Lama is identified in Chinese: Ai-qi-gai 哀氣蓋. Jürungγ-a, *Erdeni tunumal*, 99 n. 1.
28. Ayushi Güüshi (d. 1630?) is well known as the creator of the *Ali kali* alphabet and a translator of Buddhist works. The *Ali kali* alphabet, which was produced in consultation with the Dalai Lama during his visit to the Kharchins in 1587, arose out of the realization that the original Mongolian script could not accurately represent the Sanskrit sounds needed for dharanis to be effective. To remedy this problem Ayushi Güüshi invented many new graphs that could accurately transcribe all the Sanskrit and Tibetan phonemes. In the colophons of the St. Petersburg manuscript Kanjur, he is idenitifed as the translator of eleven sutras. Walther Heissig has also identified him as the translator of the *Sitapatra Sutra*, *Qutuγtu caγan sikürtei orusiba*, and *Qara kelen neretü sudur*, "*Disputation Sutra*," a work intended to take care of curses and fraud. Elverskog, *Jewel Translucent*, 162 n. 300.
29. Blue City (Kökeqota/Hohhot) is now the capital of the Inner Mongolia Autonomous Region. It was originally the largest of the Bayising settlements, and after the 1571 peace accord between Altan Khan and the Ming court it became the obvious metropole where relations between the Mongols and the Ming were conducted. In 1572 Altan Khan had a palace constructed there and gave it the name Kökeqota. Later, upon his request the Ming court gave it the name Guihua Cheng 歸化城, Town Returning to Civilization, on November 13, 1575. After meeting with the Dalai Lama in 1578 Altan Khan initiated the building of Yeke Juu, Great Monastery, constructed during 1579–80. Thereupon the city continued to expand, especially during the Qing formation when it functioned as an important staging area for Manchu campaigns against both the Chinese and later the Zunghars. In 1739 the Qianlong 乾隆 emperor ordered the construction of Suiyuan 綏遠 three kilometers to the east of Kökeqota; it became the bureaucratic center and residence of Banner families for the rest of the dynasty. Isabelle Charleux, "De la ville bleue à la métropole grise: Fondation, protection et destruction de Kökeqota (Huhehaote)," *Études Mongoles et Sibériennes, centralasiatiques et tibétaines* 35 (2004): 69–116.
30. Altan Khan not only had a Jowo statue made but also built a temple to house it: the Jowo Sakyamuni Temple. In 1581 the Ming granted it the title Hongci Si 弘慈寺. At the time it was the center of intensive translation activity, as evidenced in the colophon of the *Ocean of Tales* (*Üliger-ün dalai*): "(he translated, while

peacefully and for a long time residing in) the incomparable precious temple of the Lord [Juu: Buddha], perfected with all the symbols of the world, renowned in all directions, constructed with feelings of pure devotion, in the region east of the Yellow River, in the region South of the Lord of the Terrain [misreading for Khurugan Khan, the mountains north of Hohhot], and in the middle of the Vast and Great Mongol People" (quoted in Serruys, "Two Remarkable Women," 228 n. 163). In 1640 this temple was refurbished and expanded, at which time it became known as the Yeke Juu, Great Temple, and received the imperial title Immeasurable Temple (M. *Caglasi ügei süme*, Ch. *Wuliang Si* 無量寺). Altan'orgil, *Kökeqota-yin süm-e keyed* (Kökeqota: Öbör Mongγol-un arad-un keblel-ün qoriy-a, 1981), 98–126.

31. The Kanjur (T. *bka' 'gyur*) was first compiled during the Yuan dynasty and is the Tibetan compilation in 108 volumes of the Buddha's teachings, composed of three main sections: Sutra, Tantra, and Vinaya. The Tanjur (T. *bstan-'gyur*) is a collection of commentaries and treatises on the Buddha's teachings written mainly by Indian scholars, organized primarily by the great Tibetan scholar Buton Rinchen Drub (1290–1364). The oldest extant redaction of the Mongolian Kanjur is from the time of Ligdan Khan, who commissioned thirty-five persons headed by the Sakya monk Kungga Özer to translate the entire Kanjur in 1628–1629. At that time six manuscript copies were prepared, one written in gold (which may actually be older; now housed in the Library of the Academy of Social Sciences in Hohhot) and five in black ink (one of which is housed at St. Petersburg University). However, as evidenced in this work and in several colophons, the idea and possibly even the work of translating the entire Kanjur was begun and completed at the time of Altan Khan and his descendants. The *Jewel Translucent Sutra* claims that the entire Kanjur was translated in 1602–1607. It is therefore possible that when Ligdan Khan was engaged in his failed campaign against the Ordos in 1627, he acquired a copy while he was residing in Hohhot. He returned east and began the retranslation project of 1628–1929, which included altering colophons to erase the evidence of Altan Khan's initial work and reorganizing the contents. A similar phenomenon also occurred when the Kangxi 康熙 emperor ordered a Mongolian Kanjur to be prepared in Beijing in 1718–1720. Although it is not recorded in the *Precious Summary*, it is evident that parts of the Tanjur were also translated at this time. Elverskog, *Jewel Translucent*, 138 n. 226, 211 n. 76.

32. The Third Dalai Lama's meeting with Sadam, the King of Jang (< T. *Jang sa tham*), and the construction and consecration of a monastery in 1580 is recounted in his biography written by the Fifth Dalai Lama.

33. The Tibetan consecration ritual of an image involves the invitation of the "holy," called Enlightened Awareness Being (T. *ye shes sems dpa* < Skt. *jñanasattva*),

to reside in the object, whereby it is then worthy of worship. Yael Bentor, *Consecration of Images and Stupas in Indo-Tibetan Buddhism* (Leiden: E. J. Brill. 1996).

34. The three evil rebirths are being born as an animal, as a hungry ghost, or in the hell realm.
35. Altan Khan returned to Mongolia in the summer of 1580.
36. Tongkor Manjusri Khutugtu is Yönten Gyatso (1557–1587), who was the second reincarnated lama at Tongkhor monastery in the vicinity of Xining 西寧 in Qinghai 青海 and was recognized as an incarnation of Manjusri. He was appointed by the Third Dalai Lama to be a representative, or liaison officer, between Drepung and Altan Khan's court during the Dalai Lama's absence.
37. The Lungching emperor is the Longqing 隆慶 emperor (1537–1572, r. 1567–1572).
38. In 1579 the Ming court bestowed on Khutugtai Sechen Khung Taiji the honorary rank general of dragon and tiger (*longhu jiangjun* 龍虎將軍).
39. Irgai is Zhencheng 鎮城 in Ningxia 寧夏 (modern-day Yinchuan 銀) and Temeetü City is Yulin 榆林 in Shanxi 陝西; thus the twenty-one cities mentioned here are those found between the two along the southern edge of the Great Wall. For a map and study of these cities see Antoine Mostaert, *Erdeni-yin Tobči. Mongolian Chronicle by Sayang Secen* (Cambridge, MA: Harvard University Press, 1956), 103–105.
40. The spirit dolls (M. *onggud*) and fetishes (M. *čelig*) noted here are references to images used in pre-Buddhist Mongolian religious practices. These images were representations of sacred spirits of the earth (mountains, rivers, etc.) or humans (deceased shamans, ancestors, etc.) that needed to be ritualized in order to maintain social harmony, cure illness, etc. Magdalena Tatár, "Tragic and Stranger Ongons among the Altaic Peoples," in *Altaistic Studies*, ed. Gunnar Jarring and Staffan Rosén (Stockholm: Almqvist & Wiksell, 1985), 165–171.
41. Both the *Jewel Translucent Sutra* and Chinese sources confirm that this date is incorrect. Altan Khan died in the ninth year of Wanli 萬歷 on the 19th of the 12th month, which is January 13, 1582. Moreover, afterward, Queen Jönggen and his sons sent an official notification to the Chinese border officials, and the court accordingly prescribed memorial services. The *Ming shi lu* 明史錄 also notes that in the second month of 1582, the emperor made offerings of condolences for Altan Khan's death. It is also recorded that he gave 12 bolts of silk and 100 bolts of cotton plus "seven offerings," *qi tan* 七壇. What these offerings were is not clear. The Ming's compendium of the collected regulations, the *Da Ming Huidian* 大明會典, notes that there was a protocol of how many offerings were to be given based on the status of the deceased. Unfortunately, it does not clarify specifically who was to receive how many offerings; thus it is unclear whether the

seven given to Altan Khan meant a particularly high status or not. Yoshida, *Altan Qagan-u Tuγuji*, 380.

42. Although this work presents the enthronement of Sengge Düüreng as a fait accompli, there were actually many complications prior to his receiving his father's title. The main problem stemmed from the long-standing feud between Sengge and Queen Jönggen, who to Sengge's great disadvantage controlled the trade and tribute relations with the Chinese both before and after Altan Khan's death. Seventy-nine Mongol noblemen sent a petition to the court urging the Chinese to enfeoff Sengge as *shunyi wang*. Sengge himself also sent a messenger declaring that he, as the eldest son, should receive the title. He also requested that his son receive a higher rank and the imperial gifts for his mother be reinstated (they had been curtailed by Altan Khan in favor of Queen Jönggen). Yet the Ming was not ready to offer the title to Sengge; they wanted him to first marry Queen Jönggen, who had been consistently "pro-Chinese" and an avid supporter of peaceful relations. In response the Mongols again presented a petition in favor of Sengge, this time with 99 signatures; the queen flatly refused the marriage proposal and moved her residence away from the court. The governor-general Zheng Luo 鄭洛 then sent a letter to her saying she must marry Sengge in order to maintain her trade privileges, whereupon she accepted and they were married in November 1582. On April 3, 1583, Sengge Düüreng received the title *shunyi wang*. Serruys, "Two Remarkable Women" 204–207).

43. The transfer of merit is a standard component of Buddhist ritual practice, whereby one mentally or ritually directs the merit produced from a virtuous deed to a particular aim. "Merit may be dedicated to the benefit of all sentient beings or to the benefit of a specific person or persons (such as a family member) . . . Merit may also be dedicated toward the goal of rebirth in a specific realm (such as a Pure Land or the heavens) in the next lifetime" (Robert E. Buswell, Jr., and Donald S. Lopez, Jr., *The Princeton Dictionary of Buddhism* [Princeton, NJ: Princeton University Press, 2014], 628). "The transfer of merit is a practice found throughout the Buddhist world, based on the belief that the dead cannot directly receive offerings; instead, those offerings must be made to virtuous recipients, such as the Buddha or members of the samgha, with the merit of that deed then transferred to the departed" (637).

44. According to the Fifth Dalai Lama's biography of the Third Dalai Lama, he knew that Altan Khan had died on account of a vision he had during meditation. Karénina Kollmar-Paulenz, *Erdeni tunumal neretü sudur*: *Die Biographie des Altan qaγan der Tümed-Mongolen* (Wiesbaden: Harrassowitz, 2001), 323. Yet, as Leonard van der Kuijp and Gray Tuttle have noted: "this was a bit after the fact, for the Qaγan's passing appears to have taken place on January 13, 1582," and the Dalai Lama's versified obituary of the khan was only written ten months

later. "Altan Qaγan (1507–1582) of the Tümed Mongols and the Stag lung Abbot Kun dga' bkra shis rgyal mtshan (1575–1635)," in *Trails of the Tibetan Tradition: Papers for Elliott Sperling*, ed. Roberto Vitali (Dharamshala: Anmye Machen Institute, 2014), 467.

45. *Duutang* < Ch. 都堂 is military general, and here it refers to the governor of Gansu 甘肅 province. At the time the Ming was wary of Altan Khan's forces in Qinghai 清海; thus they urged the governor to invite the Dalai Lama in hope of convincing him to persuade Altan Khan to return to his territory. Ya Hanzhang, *The Biographies of the Dalai Lamas* (Beijing: Foreign Languages Press, 1991), 23.
46. Gamsu (< T. Gan cu) refers to Ganzhou 甘州 in Gansu 甘肃 province.
47. In Tibetan sources it is recorded that when the Dalai Lama went to China at this time he gave teachings to huge crowds of people who had come from Mongolia, China, and Eastern Turkestan. At first there was the problem that none of these people understood Tibetan; however, the governor offered him three interpreters who conveyed the teachings to the masses. Tsepon W.D. Shakabpa, *Tibet: A Political History* (New Haven, CT: Yale University Press, 1967), 95–96.
48. *Duutang* and *süngbing* are Chinese titles: *dutang* 都堂, a military general; *zongping* 總兵, a military regional commander. Charles O. Hucker, *A Dictionary of Official Titles in Imperial China* (Stanford, CA: Stanford University Press, 1985), 533, 543.
49. The Fifth Dalai Lama's *Biography of the Third Dalai Lama* confirms this visit, during which the Dalai Lama gave a teaching and performed an initiation; he was given a great deal of offerings including gold, silver, silk, horses, and animals. The text further notes that the Third Dalai Lama consecrated the Ordos monastery of Puntsog Dargyé Ling, which presumably relates to the temple sponsored by Boshogtu Jinong. Kollmar-Paulenz, *Erdeni tunumal*, 325 n. 632.
50. In the famous *Mahaparinirvana Sutra*, which recounts the Buddha's final teaching and his death, the Buddha explains how he is to be cremated like a cakravartin and his relics placed in a stupa: "The body of a cakravartin king is wrapped in new cotton cloth and cotton wool, five hundred layers of each, and once so wrapped, it is placed in an iron coffin filled with oil, which is then covered with another iron coffin. A funeral pyre of fragrant wood is piled up, set afire, and later extinguished with cow's milk. Then the bones are placed in a golden urn, which is carried on a golden palanquin to a great crossroads, where a stupa is built, on which umbrellas, flags, and banners are set up, . . . and to which homage and worship are paid with offerings of perfumes, garlands, flowers, incence and music." John S. Strong, *The Experience of Buddhism* (Belmont, CA: Wadsworth Publishing, 1995), 36.
51. The worship of these relics that remain after the cremation of a Buddhist holy personage has played a fundamental role in the Buddhist tradition across Asia. Kevin Trainor, *Relics, Ritual, and Representation in Buddhism: Rematerializing*

the Sri lankan Theravåda Tradition (New York: Cambridge University Press, 1997); Brian D. Rupert, *Jewel in the Ashes: Buddha Relics and Power in Early Medieval Japan* (Cambridge, MA: Harvard University Press, 2000).

52. Erlig is the Mongolian name of King Yama (Tib. *gshin rje*), the Lord of Death, who is the ruler of beings born in the hell realms in order to expiate bad karma (Nebesky-Wojkowitz 1996: 82–87). King Yama "may be traced to the beginnings of Indo-European civilization, where he appears with a twin sister. In the earliest hymns of the *Rg Veda*, he is a benign god who cares for the dead. In Indian Buddhism he is often portrayed as a judge of the dead." Stephen F. Teiser, *The Scripture of the Ten Kings and the Making of Purgatory in Medieval Buddhism* (Honolulu: University of Hawai'i Press, 1994), 175.
53. Abatai Sechen Khan (1554–1588) was the son of Lord No'onukuu Üijeng, the third son of Geresenje. During his youth he campaigned successfully against the Oirat, thereby acquiring dominance on the central Mongolian plateau. In the early 1580s he became interested in Buddhism, and in 1585 he founded the monastery of Erdeni Juu, which was built using stones from the ruins of the old capital city of Qaraqorum. In 1587 he visited the Dalai Lama in Hohhot and received the title of Vajra Khan. E. Alexandre, "Erdeni-zuu, un monastère de XVI siecle en Mongolie," *Études mongoles* 10 (1979): 7–34.
54. This prophecy is a commentary on the situation in the mid-seventeenth century, during which there was a four-way Buddhist civil war among the Qing, the Khalkha, the Oirat, and Tibet. On this conflict and the subsequent submission of the Khalkha to the Qing to ward off Oirat attacks, see Johan Elverskog, "Maitreya, Shambhala, and the End of Buddhist Empire," in *Faith and Empire: The Art of Politics in Tibetan Buddhism*, ed. Karl Debreczeny (New York: Rubin Museum of Art, 2019), 212–227.

11. HISTORY OF THE DALAI LAMAS AND ORDOS

1. These are three Chinese titles: *süngbing* is *zongping* 總兵, a military regional commander; *buujang* is *buchang* 部長, a minister; and *sanjang* is *sanguan* 三官, "a prestige title." Charles O. Hucker, *A Dictionary of Official Titles in Imperial China* (Stanford, CA: Stanford University Press, 1985), # 4765, 4868, 7146.
2. Although this invitation is not recorded in Chinese sources, the biography of the Third Dalai Lama records that the Wanli emperor did send envoys, who presented him with a new title (*guanding da guoshi* 灌頂大國師) and invited him to Beijing. L. Carrington Goodrich and Chaoyang Fang, *Dictionary of Ming Biography 1368–1644* (New York: Columbia University Press, 1976), 23.
3. Emperor Taisung is Taizong 太宗 (598–649, r. 626–649), the second emperor of the Tang dynasty.

4. Emperor Yunglo is the Yongle 永樂 emperor (1360–1424, r. 1402–1424).
5. Emperor Suvandi is the Xuande 宣德 emperor (1399–1435, r. 1425–1435).
6. On this title (< Ch. *sansheng daiwang guoshi* 三省太王國師) see page 243, note 27.
7. On the Hoopoe Moon (M. *ögeljin sara*), the third month, see Brian G. Baumann, *Divine Knowledge: Buddhist Mathematics According to the Anonymous Manual of Mongolian Astrology and Divination* (Leiden: Brill, 2008), 78.
8. The Third Dalai Lama died on April 22, 1588.
9. Where the Third Dalai Lama passed away is not identified in the *Biography of the Third Dalai Lama.* In the colophon of Ayushi Güüshi's translation of the *Mahamantranudhari Sutra*, however, it is noted that it occurred on the banks of Ja'asuti Lake. Louis Ligeti, *Catalogue du kanjur mongol imprimé* (Budapest: Socièté Korosi Csoma, 1942–44), 57.
10. A *kapala* is a cup "made from the cranium of a human skull, [which] is often elaborately carved and inlaid with precious metals. The symbolism of the skull cup is variously explained; most generally, it is yet another antinomian aspect of Buddhist tantra, in which things that would be regarded as polluting in Indian society (in this case the skull of a corpse) are put to use to overcome dualities. It is also said that the skull cup is a constant reminder of death." Robert E. Buswell, Jr., and Donald S. Lopez, Jr., *The Princeton Dictionary of Buddhism* (Princeton, NJ: Princeton University Press, 2014), 417–418.
11. Namudai Sechen Khan and Queen Jönggen took the Dalai Lama's ashes to Tibet in 1589, and in 1590, his remains and gifts from the Ming court were brought to Kumbum monastery and enshrined in a 430 cm.-high wooden stupa, inside which was also placed a portrait statue of him. Afterward a temple was built and the stupa placed in the center; it became known as Temple of the Omniscient. Another stupa at Drepung was also erected in memory of the Third Dalai Lama.
12. Sümer Daiching was the fifth son of Sengge Düüreng. He lived northwest of Xuanfu 宣府 and had a market at Xinping 新平. Henry Serruys, *Genealogical Tables of the Descendants of Dayan-Qan* ('S-Gravenhage: Mouton, 1958), 68, 96–97.
13. Yönten Gyatso (1589–1617) was born to Altan Khan's grandson, and people in Mongolia immediately recognized him as the incarnation of the Third Dalai Lama. On their advice the Tri Rinpoche of Ganden initially recognized him, but he was not officially confirmed until a group of Tibetans came to Mongolia in 1601. In the following year he was brought back to Tibet and enthroned at Drepung. Whereas the different factions in Tibet had held a truce, awaiting the arrival of the Fourth Dalai Lama, shortly after his return problems ensued. In 1605 the Pakmo Drupa attacked Lhasa, and in 1607 in trying to aid the Gelukpa, the Mongols attacked central Tibet; they were repelled by the Tsang troops of

the Rinpung, who simultaneously defeated the Pakmo Drupa. The Dalai Lama fled Lhasa and returned in 1611; during that time Lhasa was under the control of the Rinpung, whose leader Puntsok Namgyal also visited in 1611. While there, on account of his support for the Karmapa, he as a Gelukpa was denied access to the important New Year Monlam festival, yet he requested an initiation from the Dalai Lama. Upon the advice of his ministers the Dalai Lama refused, and tensions escalated, causing the Dalai Lama to flee to Samyé monastery; the affairs of state were taken over by the treasurer, Konchog Chöpel. While the situation was rapidly deteriorating, the Fourth Dalai Lama died at the age of twenty-eight. Goodrich and Fang, *Dictionary of Ming Biography*, 1604–1606.

14. This Ordos invasion of China was part of a much larger conflagration known as the Ningxia Mutiny of 1592, which initially involved the uprising of disgruntled Chinese troops against their superiors, who in turn were supported by the forces of Pubai 哱拜, a Mongol who had entered the service of the Ming government but recently lost power. It was he who requested Boshogtu Jinong to invade China so as to support the mutiny, which had begun in April and was incredibly successful. The Ming court sent troops from all over to China to suppress it, and this campaign began by expelling the Ordos Mongols from the area in July and August. The Ming forces were then able to focus directly on the mutineers, who were finally defeated in October. John W. Dardess, *More Than the Great Wall: The Northern Frontier and Ming National Security, 1368–1644* (Lanham, MD: Rowman & Littlefield, 2020), 451–456.
15. On account of Boshogtu's involvement with the Ningxia Mutiny the Ming court had not only closed his border markets but also launched punitive raids into the steppe. During one of these campaigns a Mongol nobleman was killed, which infuriated Boshogtu, and he "spent a month ravaging China's interior in the fall of 1594." The next year Boshogtu "broke through the defenses at Yan-Sui and for ten days corralled and made off with 'countless' males, females, oxen and horses." Dardess, *More Than the Great Wall*, 458.
16. Black City is Ningsai 寧塞.
17. The Fourth Dalai Lama was supposed to have been initiated into monkhood by Tri Rinpoche Peljor Gyatso, the head of Ganden monastery, but he died before the Dalai Lama arrived in Lhasa. Thus, the ceremony was done by his successor, Sanggye Rinchen, in front of the Jowo statue in the Jokhang. Günter Schulemann, *Geschichte der Dalai-Lamas* (Leipzig: Otto Harrassowitz. 1958), 216.
18. Tsongkhapa (1357–1419) was the founder of the Gelukpa tradition, which became the dominant Tibetan sect among the Mongols during the Qing dynasty. He was born in Amdo and became a monk at an early age. After a decade he traveled to central Tibet to study in different monasteries. In 1380 he was ordained

as a monk at Namgyal monastery in Yarlung. During the next twelve years he taught and wrote extensively, and as his followers and frequency of visions increased, began to organize his own school. This school was a reaction against the perceived laxity in the other traditions and prescribed a celibate and rigid curriculum within his reformulated philosophical system. In 1392 with eight disciples he preached his doctrine to the powerful Holkha family of central Tibet, who became his patrons. With this support and an increasing number of students, Tsongkhapa's renown spread, and he was eventually invited to the Ming court, although he declined and instead sent his disciple. A few years later, without having formed any relations with the Chinese, he died. Goodrich and Fang, *Dictionary of Ming Biography*, 1308–1309; Rudolf Kaschewsky, *Das Leben des Lamaistischen Heiligen Tsongkhapa Blo-bzang-grags-pa (1357–1419) dargestellt und erlautet anhand seiner Vita "Quellort allen Glückes."* 2 vols. (Wiesbaden: Otto Harrassowitz, 1971).

19. Queen Togtai Machig Buyantu Dalai, better known as Baga Beiji (1546–1625), was initially the wife of Daiching Ejei; when he passed away, she first married Altan Khan's grandson, Namudai Sechen, who divorced her when in 1587 he was required to marry Queen Jönggen to secure the *shunyi wang* title from the Ming court. At that time Baga Beiji married Budashiri (d. 1597), the son of Altan Khan and Queen Jönggen. In turn, after Namudai Sechen's death in 1607 another battle over the *shunyi wang* title ensued between his grandson, Boshugtu, and Sodnam, the son of Budashiri and Baga Beiji. This continued for five years until eventually the Ming recognized Boshugtu as the new *shunyi wang*, and for her role in resolving this dispute Baga Beiji was given the title loyal and righteous lady (*zhongyi furen* 忠義夫人). Throughout these events Baga Beiji lavishly supported the Dharma. Henry Serruys, "Two Remarkable Women in Mongolia: The Third Lady Erketü Qatun and Dayicing-Beyiji," *Asia Major* New Series 19, 2 (1974–75): 191–245.

20. Daiching Ejei Taiji was the son of Altan Khan's third son, Töbed Taiji. When Töbed Taiji died as a young man and Altan Khan had his wife executed after a quarrel, the three-year-old orphan Daiching Ejei was brought into Altan Khan's household and raised by his first wife. He is most famous for submitting to the Ming in 1570, which set in motion the peace accord finalized the following year. When Altan Khan died in 1582, the organization of the Twelve Tümed was divided into two wings. Daiching Ejei was the leader of the Western Wing and controlled it from Altan Khan's city of Bayising. Sengge Düüreng controlled the Eastern Wing, from an area north of Xuanfu 宣府. Daiching Ejei died June 19, 1583. Henry Serruys, "Notes on a Chinese Inscription of 1606 in a Lamaist Temple in Mai-ta-chao, Suiyüan," *Journal of the American Oriental Society* 78 (1958): 101–113.

21. As Serruys has pointed out, the ritual performed at this time was not simply the consecration of a Maitreya statue but rather the founding of Maitreya monastery, to the west of Hohhot in Inner Mongolia. Baga Beiji had a gate constructed and a Chinese inscription placed in the wall to commemorate the event. Isabelle Charleux, "Recent Research on the Maitreya Monastery in Inner Mongolia (China)," *Études Asiatiques/Asiatische Studien* 68 (2014): 1–64.
22. The "month of the great magical transformation" refers to the first month of the year. Baumann, *Divine Knowledge*, 436.
23. *Gunding dai wang güüshi* is the Chinese title *guanding daiwang guoshi* 灌頂太王國師, which the Wanli emperor gave to the Third Dalai Lama.
24. Sagang Taiji is Sagang Sechen, the author of the *Precious Summary*.
25. *Sulang* and *duutang* are Chinese titles: *sulang* is *silang* 廝郎, "staff supervisor;" and *duutang* is *dutang* 都堂, a general title of respect.
26. Since tea was one of the most highly priced commodities in Inner Asia—as well evidenced in the tea-for-horse trading system—the offering of tea to Buddhist monks was a meritorious deed in both Tibet and Mongolia.
27. Ganden monastery is "one of the three chief monasteries (known as the Gdan sag sum or 'three seats') of the Dge lugs pa sect of Tibetan Buddhism and one of the sect's principal monasteries, located twenty-eight miles (forty-five kilometers) east of Lhasa. Named after the Tusita heaven, the monastery was founded by Tsong kha pa in 1409 near a hill originally associated with the consecration rituals performed after the birth of the king Srong btsan sgam po." Buswell and Lopez, *Dictionary*, 236.
28. The Fourth Panchen Lama, Lozang Chökyi Gyeltsen (1570–1662), was a major figure in seventeenth-century Tibetan history. Having earned a reputation as a scholar and abbot of Wensa monastery, in 1601 he was appointed abbot of Tashilhunpo monastery, where he established a great prayer festival and a tantric college. On account of his stature he played an important role in recognizing the legitimacy of the Fourth Dalai Lama and in helping shore up the Gelukpa during the fighting with the rulers of Tsang. Only with the consolidation of the Fifth Dalai Lama's power in 1641 was he given the title Panchen Lama. https://treasuryoflives.org/biographies/view/Lobzang-Chokyi-Gyeltsen/9839 (accessed November 12, 2020).
29. Subhuti was "foremost among the Buddha's disciples in dwelling at peace in remote places and in worthiness to receive gifts. He was the younger brother of Anāthapiṇḍada and took ordination on the day the Jetavana grove was dedicated . . . Subhūti also plays a prominent role in a number of Mahāyāna sutras. The most famous of these is as the Buddha's chief interlocutor in the Prajñāpāramitā sutras like the *Vajracchedikāprajñāpāramitāsūtra*." Buswell and Lopez, *Dictionary*, 862.

30. Shambhala is the mythical hidden kingdom that preserves the teachings of the *Kalacakratantra*, which predicts an apocalyptic war in 2425 CE between the barbarians (usually identified as Muslims) and the twenty-fifth king of Shambhala, Raudracakrin. He and his Buddhist army will ride out of Shambhala, destroy the barbarians, and usher in a new golden age of the Dharma. Prior to that time, as noted herein, the Gelukpa tradition claims that the Panchen Lamas are reborn as kings of Shambhala. Buswell and Lopez, *Dictionary*, 748–749.
31. On the development of the narratives about the Panchen Lama's connections with Shambhala see Charles R. Bawden, "The Wish-Prayer for Shambhala Again," *Monumenta Serica* 36 (1984–85): 455–457.
32. "He Who Opens Well in Perfection" refers to Aryadeva (c. 170–270 CE), who renounced the Sri Lankan throne to become Nagarjuna's disciple. "After his teacher's death, Aryadeva became active at the monastic university of Nalanda, where he is said to have debated and defeated numerous brahmanic adherents, eventually converting them to Buddhism." Buswell and Lopez, *Dictionary*, 64–65.
33. Nagarjuna is "traditionally regarded as the founder of the Madhyamaka school of Mahāyāna Buddhist philosophy. Very little can be said concerning his life; scholars generally place him in South India during the second century CE." Buswell and Lopez, *Dictionary*, 561.
34. The two levels are better known as the two truths of Mahayana Buddhism: conventional truth and ultimate truth. Buswell and Lopez, *Dictionary*, 1066.
35. The three things to be studied are morality, concentration, and wisdom. Buswell and Lopez, *Dictionary*, 1068.
36. "The Victorious Good-Minded Accomplisher of Benefice" refers to Bensa Lozang Dondup (1505–1568), who according to a biography written by the Panchen Lama was the first king of Shambhala. Bensa Lozang Dondup was also later recognized as an earlier incarnation of the Panchen Lama, which played a role in connecting the Panchen Lama to Shambhala. Bawden, "The Wish-Prayer," 455.
37. Jangba Khan refers to the ruler of Tsang, Phuntsog Namgyel (1587–1620), who was a staunch supporter of the Karmapa and thus fought hard to limit the power of the Dalai Lama and the Gelukpa order.
38. Chagpo Mountain is the sacred mountain that lies southeast of the Potala Palace in Lhasa.
39. On this episode, the so-called Peace of Chagpo Mountain, during which the Fourth Panchen Lama played a crucial role in mediating the ongoing fighting between the Gelukpa and the rulers of Tsang and their Kagyu supporters, see Zahiruddin Ahmad, *Sino-Tibetan Relations in the Seventeenth Century* (Roma: Istituto Italiano per il Medio ed Estremo Oriente, 1970), 102–108.

40. It is unclear where the name Diba Guruba comes from, since the Fifth Dalai Lama's father was Miwang Dundel Rapten; nevertheless, the following section relates the early years of Ngawang Lozang Gyatso's life. For his subsequent consolidation of Gelukpa rule over Tibet during the seventeenth century, he is known simply as the Great Fifth (1617–1682).
41. Drepung monastery outside of Lhasa was at this time the religiopolitical center of the Gelukpa.
42. Contrary to how it is presented in the *Precious Summary*, the recognition of the Fifth Dalai was far more fraught, amid the ongoing political struggles between the rulers of Tsang in Shigatse and the Gelukpa headquartered in Lhasa. The Tsang ruler believed the Fourth Dalai Lama had cursed him with an illness and thus forbade his reincarnation to be recognized. Thus it was only after the Fourth Panchen Lama cured the king in 1622 that he allowed him to recognize Lozang Gyatso as the reincarnated Dalai Lama. Before being recognized as a Gelukpa incarnation, he had unsuccessfully been claimed as the reincarnation of a Kagyu hierarch, the Fourth Tsurpu Gyeltsap Drakpa Dondrub, and "at Drepung, he was in competition for the position of Dalai Lama with another candidate, Drakpa Gyeltsen (grags pa rgyal mtshan, 1619–1656), who was later identified as the fourth incarnation of Panchen Sonam Drakpa (pan chen bsod nams grags pa, 1478–1554, the Fifteenth Ganden Tripa (dga' ldan khri pa)" (https://treasuryoflives.org/9 [accessed November 29, 2020]).
43. On the relationship between the Fifth Dalai Lama and Tuba Taiji, especially how it tried to re-create the relations between Altan Khan and the Third Dalai Lama, see Ahmad, *Sino-Tibetan Relations*, 109–110.
44. "The One Who Laughs with a Lotus Horse Voice" (< T. Rta dbyangs) refers to Asvaghosa (ca. second century), who is renowned for his epic poem, the *Buddhacarita*, which is the first complete biography of the Buddha. Buswell and Lopez, *Dictionary*, 76.
45. The middle cakravartin khan refers to Trisong Detsen (r. 755–797).
46. As noted in the introduction, one of the key developments among the Mongols after the reign of Altan Khan was the devolution of royal power: various noblemen claiming the title khan in opposition to the rightful Chinggisid ruler of the Chakhar. Thus, as evidenced in this passage, both a Boshogtu Khan and a Kharchin Khan had been named.

12. HISTORY OF THE MING AND QING DYNASTIES

1. Nurhaci Baatur Taisui (1559–1621) is the ruler who began the consolidation of the Jurchens of northeast China into what would become the Manchus and subsequently the Qing dynasty.

2. The Altan Khan of the Manchus of old refers to the Jurchen rulers of the Jin dynasty (1115–1234), whom the Manchus claimed as their ancestors.
3. In the late Ming period there were three main Jurchen groups: the Jianzhou 建州, the Haixi 海西, and the Yeren 野人. The Jianzhou, so called because they lived near a Ming commandery of that name on the edges of the Liao River basin, was the group to which Nurhaci belonged. The Haixi, who are here called the Three Water Jürchid, comprised the Hada, Ula, and Hoifa, who lived to the north and west of the Jianzhou along the Sungari, Mudan, and Ussuri rivers south of the Amur. Mark C. Elliott, *The Manchu Way: The Eight Banners and Ethnic Identity in Late Imperial China* (Stanford, CA: Stanford University Press, 2001), 48. On Nurhaci's rise to power and his conquest of the Hada in 1599, the Hoifa in 1607, and the Ula the 1613, see Frederic Wakeman, Jr., *The Great Enterprise: The Manchu Reconstruction of Imperial Order in Seventeenth-Century China* (Berkeley: University of California Press, 1985), 23–58.
4. Although it is not certain, the Great White Jürchid presumably refer to the third Jürchen group, called in Chinese either the Yeren 野人 or Donghai 東海 Jurchen, who inhabited the far eastern and northern areas of Manchuria, two groups of which were conquered by Nurhaci in 1619.
5. Loudung is Liaodong 遼東 province in northeast China. In 1618 Nurhaci proclaimed to the Ming court his so-called Seven Grievances, which included their murder of his father and grandfather, the lack of respect given to his envoys, and other border violations. Under the pretext of holding a large trade fair, Nurhaci sent 3,000 merchants to Fushun 撫順, and when the Chinese merchants came out he attacked and took the city. Nurhaci then took the strategic chokepoint city of Qinghe 清河. In response the Ming sent four armies of 250,000 troops each to push back the Manchus. Yet all four armies were roundly defeated, and Nurhaci captured the garrisons of Kaiyuan 開原 and Tieling 鐵嶺, and then the city of Yehe 葉赫. By 1621 the Manchus controlled all of Liaodong except for the southern border regions. Gertraude Roth-Li, "State Building before 1644," in *The Cambridge History of China, vol. 9, Part One: The Ch'ing Empire to 1800*, ed. Denis Twitchett and John K. Fairbank (New York: Cambridge University Press, 2002), 41–42.
6. During the first two decades of the seventeenth century the night skies across the world were more active than usual. In Europe, for example, it was a period of spectacular northern lights, and in China there were unusual lights in the sky in 1612, 1614, and 1615. "During 1618, an overwhelming number of such heavenly signs allowed Manchus and Chinese to become used to the idea that a dynastic change might be nearing. Lines of light in the sky appeared nearly every month, once staying for the length of an entire month." Roth-Li, "State Building," 38.

7. Taisui (< Ch. Taisui 太歲) means literally "great year," yet here refers to Jupiter and signals the astral conjunctions signifying the greatness of Nurhaci. Brian G. Baumann, *Divine Knowledge: Buddhist Mathematics According to the Anonymous Manual of Mongolian Astrology and Divination* (Leiden: Brill, 2008), 137.
8. In Mongolian the term "destiny" (*jayayatu*), which is also translated as "fortune," is used exclusively in regard to rulers blessed by Heaven in the Chinggisid mold. In the early Ming period this term and its ideology were adopted by Zhu Yuanzhang in his imperial rhetoric to confirm his legitimacy as the rightful heir of the Mongol legacy. Here, as in Qing sources, it is made clear that after the chaos of Ligdan Khan's reign the Manchus were the proper rulers in the Buddhist and Chinggisid lineage of the "holy ones." They were the ones who through their state could once again create peace and order.
9. Hong Taiji (1592–1643, r. 1627–1643) was the eighth son of Nurhaci, who in 1636 declared the creation of the Manchus and the founding of the Qing dynasty. Arthur W. Hummel, *Eminent Chinese of the Ch'ing Period (1644–1912)* (Washington, DC: The Library of Congress, 1943), 1–3.
10. The Geng Tiger year, which is 1650, is a mistake for the Geng Monkey year, 1620.
11. The Five-Banner Khalkha were led by the descendants of Alchu Bolod and comprised the Jarud, Baarin, Qonggirad, Bayud, and Üjiyed, who had settled in the area that is now the Jirim League when Altan Khan expelled Daraisun Khan to the east of the Khingan mountains in 1547.
12. Although this episode is herein attributed to the reign of Hong Taiji, it more likely refers to events that unfolded in 1616. In that year Nurhaci had declared the formation of the Latter Jin 後金, which consolidated and confirmed his control of the Jurchens and several Mongol groups that had sided with this new rising power. Doing so, however, threatened the Ming, so the court sent an invasion to quash the confederation. Yet Nurhaci roundly defeated this Ming invasion and in so doing took the frontier cities of Kaiyuan 開原 and Tieling 鐵嶺, which resulted in the Five-Banner Khalkha and Khorchin losing their rights to trade with the Ming that had been conducted through these cities. In order to restore these rights the leader of the Khalkha Qonggirad, Jayisai, attacked Nurhaci's troops stationed at Tieling; he was defeated and captured. The Khalkha asked Nurhaci to spare Jayisai, which he did, and some of the Five-Banner Khalkha made an alliance with Nurhaci. Others, however, sided with Ligdan Khan, who at this time was being supported financially by the Ming in order to defeat Nurhaci. In 1621 this Chakhar-Khalkha alliance received 300,000 taels of silver, and 360,000 taels in 1622–23. But in 1625 when Nurhaci went on the offensive against these Mongols, the Five-Banner Khalkha abandoned the Chakhar. Moreover, in the following year when Nurhaci passed away the Khalkhas resumed their attacks on Manchu border posts. In 1627, however, both

the Manchus—now led by Hong Taiji—and the Chakhar attacked the Five-Banner Khalkha, whereby Ligdan conquered the Qonggirad, Bayud, and Üjiyed, while the Baarin and Jarud joined the Manchus. Disappointed with Ligdan, the following year the Qonggirad, Bayud, and Üjiyed—as well as the Ordos and Kharchin—allied with the Manchus and drove the Chakhars westward. Nicola Di Cosmo and Dalizhabu Bao, *Manchu-Mongol Relations on the Eve of the Qing Conquest: A Documentary History* (Leiden: Brill, 2003), 6–14.

13. After the majority of the Mongols of the Three Eastern Tümen had allied with the Manchus, Ligdan Khan hoped to find support among the Three Western Tümen in the Ordos region. After suffering under his rule and being attacked by the Manchus, however, they too abandoned Ligdan Khan and in 1635, "the forty-nine chiefs of the sixteen tribes of the southern Gobi desert gave Hong Taiji the title Boγod [*sic*] Qaγan, and the Manchus set up the Mongol Banners headed by *jasays* in what is today Inner Mongolia." Di Cosmo and Bao, *Manchu-Mongol Relations*, 14.
14. The Khorchin initiated political relations with Nurhaci in 1594; however, this alliance was only fully actualized in 1612 when the Khorchin leader, Minggan, gave his daughter in marriage to Nurhaci. The relationship was further cemented two years later when the Khorchin leaders Manggus and Khonggur married "their daughters respectively to Hong Taiji (Nurhaci's son and future successor) and Nurhaci." Di Cosmo and Bao, *Manchu-Mongol Relations*, 9.
15. After Ligdan Khan died of smallpox in 1634 in Gansu 甘肅, most of the Chakhar leaders deserted his heir, Erke Khonggor, and joined the Manchus. Erke Khonggur and his mother—Queen Mother Sutai—with the few remaining Chakhars continued to resist, and the following year Dorgon and his Manchu forces crossed the Yellow River and surrounded their camp at Tolitu. Erke Khonggur and Sutai Taikhu were then escorted back to the Manchu capital at Mukden.
16. After Dorgon and his forces had defeated the remaining Chakhar, he escorted Erke Khonggur and Queen Mother Sutai to Mukden and presented them to Hong Taiji. On account of earlier Mongol-Manchu intermarriage relations, Hong Taiji and Queen Mother Sutai were actually uncle and niece; thus mother and son were given back their original pasturage. Moreover, Hong Taiji not only gave his second daughter, Makata, in marriage to Erke Khonggur but also presented him with the highest Manchu rank, *hosoi qinwang*. He died at the age of twenty in 1641. Hidehiro Okada, "Origin of the Caqar Mongols," *Mongolian Studies* 14 (1991): 170–172.
17. "Peaceful holy one" (M. *nayiramdaqu boyda*) is part of the imperial title Hong Taiji gave himself in 1636. In that year he convened an assembly to which Erke Khonggur led a delegation of forty-nine princes representing sixteen Mongol groups. At the meeting Hong Taiji proclaimed himself emperor of a new dynasty,

the Great Qing (Da Qing 大清, M. Daičing), and took the Manchu title *gosin onco hewaliyasun enduringge han* (M. *ayuda örüsiyegci nayiramdaqu boyda qayan*). Okada, "Origin of the Caqar Mongols," 172.

18. Jingju is Jinzhou 錦州, which is today in the southwest of Liaoning 遼寧 province.

19. Khung Sulang Baatur Süngbing is Hong Chengchou 洪承疇 (1593–1665), a leading Ming official who in 1639 was appointed governor-general of Zhili 直隸 and Liaodong 遼東 and in 1642 surrendered to Hong Taiji, who ordered him to serve in the Chinese Bordered Yellow Banner. In 1644 when Beijing was conquered Hong was made a grand secretary, whereupon he became one of the most important Qing officials coordinating the Manchu conquest of south China. Hummel, *Eminent Chinese*, 358–360.

20. During six months in 1638–39 the Qing armies invaded China, ransacking areas south of Beijing and then turning toward Shandong 山東 before returning with over 400,000 captives and huge amounts of booty. While this was going on, Hong Taiji attacked Jinzhou 錦州 and Ningyuan 寧遠 to prevent Ming reinforcements from halting these Qing forays. At the time he did not capture these cities, nor did he in 1640, so in 1641 he again besieged Jinzhou. "Anxious to keep their northeastern defense line intact, the Ming ordered Hung Ch'eng-ch'ou (1593–1665), who had been fighting the peasant armies on the western front, to rescue Chin-chou. But Hung's force of nearly 200,000 men was defeated by the Ch'ing. Some of his generals fled and nearly 50,000 soldiers were killed. Hung Ch'eng-ch'ou, with a remaining force of 20,000, retreated into nearby Sung-shan (six miles south of Chin Hsien). After a siege that lasted several months, a Ming general from within betrayed the town. This allowed the Ch'ing to capture Hung Ch'eng-ch'ou, the highest ranking Ming official to fall into their hands thus far, and to carry off over two thousand large and small cannons." Roth-Li, "State Building," 57.

21. Contrary to the *Precious Summary*, it was actually Hong Taiji who in 1639 first sent envoys to Tibet to request the Dalai Lama to visit the Manchu court, whereupon the Tibetans sent Victorious Khutugtu to Mukden (Zahiruddin Ahmad, *Sino-Tibetan Relations in the Seventeenth Century* [Roma: Istituto Italiano per il Medio ed Estremo Oriente, 1970], 154–162). On the Manchu court's early relations with Tibetan Buddhists in the 1620s, especially the Gelukpa, see Tak-Sing Kam, "The dGe-lugs-pa Breakthrough: The Uluk Darxan Nangsu Lama's Mission to the Manchus," *Central Asiatic Journal* 44, 2 (2000): 161–176; Martin Gimm, "Zum mongolischen Mahakala-Kult und zum Beginn der *Qing*-Dynastie—die Inschrift *Shisheng beiji* von 1638," *Oriens Extremus* 42 (2000/01): 69–103.

22. The Nine-Gated One is the Mongolian name for Shanhai Pass 山海關. Henry Serruys, "The Mongol Name of Shan-hai-kuan in the *Erdeni-yin-Tobči*," *Études mongoles* 16 (1985): 37–40.
23. Chuvang Wang is the epithet Chuang Qiang 闖將, "Dashing General," assumed by Li Zicheng 李自成, who in spring 1644 dethroned the Chinese Ming emperor Chongzhen 崇禎 (who then hanged himself) and founded the Shun 順 dynasty. Shortly thereafter Li Zicheng was himself chased out of Beijing and defeated by the Manchus.
24. The Great Ming Chongjing emperor is the Chongzhen 崇禎 emperor (1611–1644, r. 1627–1644).
25. Qaratai City is most likely Ningyuan 寧遠 (today's Xingcheng 興城), where Wu Sangui 吳三桂 resided before being ordered to defend Shanhai Pass 山海關.
26. Commander Wu is Wu Sangui 吳三桂 (1612–1678), who in 1644 allied with the Manchus and then for the next thirty years helped the Qing conquer south China. Most notably he marched his army all the way to Burma and killed the last emperor of the Southern Ming. In 1674, however, with his army in control of the south, he rebelled against the Qing and demanded that they return to Manchuria. The subsequent War of the Three Feudatories, which lasted until 1681, resulted in not only in the death of Wu Sangui but also the incorporation of all south China into the Qing. Hummel, *Eminent Chinese*, 877–880.
27. The Juu Khunggu emperor is the Hongwu 洪武 emperor (1328–1398, r. 1368–1398).
28. On the legendary story of the Yongle 永樂 emperor actually being Mongolian see Henry Serruys, "A Mongolian Version of the Legend of the Mongol Ancestry of the Yung-lo Emperor," in *Analecta Mongolica: Dedicated to the Seventieth Birthday of Professor Owen Lattimore*, ed. John G. Hangin and Urgunge Onon (Bloomington: Indiana University Press, 1972), 19–61.
29. Juu Dagaya is presumably the Jianwen 建文 emperor (1377–1402, r. 1398–1402).
30. Lord Yunglo is the Yongle 永樂 emperor (1360–1424, r. 1402–1424).
31. Rolpé Dorjé was the Fourth Karmapa (1340–1383), and he was not invited to China by the Yongle 永樂 emperor. Rather, it was the Hongwu 洪武 emperor who already in 1375 sent a letter of praise to Rolpé Dorjé, who had held one of the highest positions at the Yuan court. In 1407 the Yongle emperor did invite the Fifth Karmapa, Dezhin Shegpa (1384–1415), to Nanjing to perform the Mass of Universal Salvation in honor of his late father, the Hongwu emperor, and his late mother, Empress Ma. This event was subsequently commemorated in a famous 163-foot-long scroll painting that depicts 49 miracles that are also described in Persian, Chinese, Mongolian, Tibetan, and Uyghur. Patricia Berger, "Miracles in Nanjing: An Imperial Record of the Fifth Karmapa's Visit to the

Chinese Capital," in *Cultural Intersections in Later Chinese Buddhism*, ed. Marsha Weidner (Honolulu: University of Hawai'i Press, 2001), 145–169.

32. Tegchen Chöje refers to Kungga Trashi of the Sakya, who was recommended to the Yongle 永樂 emperor as an important Buddhist teacher by the Fifth Karmapa and therefore was invited to Nanjing 南京 in 1410. Kungga Trashi arrived at the Ming court in 1413, where he resided in a newly built temple in Beijing 北京, gave teachings to the emperor about Mahakala, and also initiated him into the mandala of Hevajra. He was bestowed with the title great vehicle prince of the Dharma (*Dacheng fawang* 大乘法王). He returned to Tibet in 1414 laden down with imperial gifts, including volumes of the 1410 Ming dynasty printing of the Kanjur. Elliot Sperling, "Early Ming Policy Toward Tibet: An Examination of the Proposition that the Early Ming Emperors Adopted a 'Divide and Rule' Policy Toward Tibet" (PhD diss., Indiana University, Bloomington, 1983), 136–146.

33. Semchen Chöjé refers to Shakya Yeshe (d. 1435), who was sent to the Ming court by his teacher, Tsongkhapa (1357–1419). He arrived at Nanjing in 1415 and was given the title great state preceptor (*daguo shi* 大國師); when he returned to Tibet the following year he was accompanied by Chinese envoys carrying gifts, such as a set of sixteen arhat statues made of white sandalwood and a set of the 1410 printing of the Tibetan canon. Karl Debreczeny, "In the Shadow of the Khan: Tibetan Buddhist Art and Political Legitimation in the Ming Dynasty," in *Faith and Empire: The Art of Politics in Tibetan Buddhism*, ed. K. Debreczeny (New York: Rubin Museum of Art, 2019), 131.

34. On the Ming court's broader engagement with Tibetan Buddhism see Karl Debreczeny, "The Early Ming Imperial Atelier on the Tibetan Frontier," in *Ming China: Courts and Contacts*, ed. C. Clunas et al. (London: British Museum, 2016), 152–162; Peter Schweiger, "A Document of Chinese Diplomatic Relations with East Tibet during the Ming Dynasty," in *Tibetstudien: Festschrift für Dieter Schuh zum 65. Geburtstag*, ed. P. Maurer and P. Schwieger (Bonn: Bier'sche Verlaganstallt, 2007), 209–226; Shen Weirong, "On the History of Gling tshang Principality of mDo khams During the Yuan and Ming Dynasties: Studies on Sources Concerning Tibet in *Ming Shilu* (I)," in *Tibetstudien: Festschrift für Dieter Schuh zum 65. Geburtstag*, ed. P. Maurer and P. Schwieger (Bonn: Bier'sche Verlaganstallt, 2007), 227–265; Ching, "Tibetan Buddhism and the Creation of the Imperial Image," in *Culture, Courtiers, and Competition: The Ming Court (1368–1644)*, ed. D. M. Robinson (Cambridge, MA: Harvard University Asia Center, 2008), 321–364; Marsha Haufler, "Faces of Transnational Buddhism at the Early Ming Court," in *Ming China: Courts and Contacts*, ed. C. Clunas et al. (London: British Museum, 2016), 143–151.

35. Emperor Suvandi is the Xuande emperor 宣德 (1399–1435, r. 1425–1435).

36. Semchen Chöjé refers again to Shakya Yeshe, who was invited to the Ming court in 1434 by the Xuande 宣德 emperor, who gave him the prestigious title great compassionate king of the Dharma 大慈法王. Debreczeny, "In the Shadow of the Khan," 131.
37. Although chronologically the order of these two emperors is reversed, Emperor Khungki refers to the Hongxi 洪熙 emperor (1378–1425, r. 1424–1425).
38. As with the earlier history of Esen Khan and the capture of the Ming emperor at Tumu Fort, Jingtai 景泰 (1428–1457, r. 1449–1457) is a mistake for the Zhengtong 正統 emperor (1427–1464, r. 1435–1449 and 1457–1464).
39. Emperor Jingtung (Zhengtong 正統) is a mistake for the Jingtai 景泰 emperor (1428–1457, r. 1449–1457), who was put on the throne when the Zhengtong 正統 emperor was captured at Tumu Fort in 1449.
40. Teshün is Tianshun 天順, the Zhengtong 正統 emperor's reign name during his second time on the throne (1457–1464).
41. Emperor Chingkhua is the Chenghua 成化 emperor (1447–1487, r. 1464–1487).
42. Emperor Khungji is the Hongzhi 弘治 emperor (1470–1505, 1487–1505).
43. Emperor Jingden is the Zhengde 正德 emperor (1491–1521, r. 1505–1521).
44. Emperor Ji'ajing is the Jiajing 嘉靖 emperor (1507–1567, r. 1521–1567).
45. Emperor Lungching is the Longqing 隆慶 emperor (1537–1572, r. 1567–1572).
46. Emperor Wanli is the Wanli 萬曆 emperor (1563–1620, r. 1572–1620).
47. Emperor Taichang is the Taichang 泰昌 emperor (1582–1620, r. 1620).
48. Emperor Tenchi is the Tianqi 天啟 emperor (1605–1627, r. 1620–1627).
49. Emperor Chongjing is the Chongzhen 崇禎 emperor (1611–1644, r. 1627–1644).
50. The "ruling peacefully emperor" is the Mongolian reign title (*ey-e-ber jasayci qayan*) of the Shunzhi 順治 emperor (1638–1661, r. 1644–1661).
51. These ranks—*wang* 王 "prince," *beile* 貝勒 "lord," *beizi* 貝子 "imperial clansman," *gong* 公 "duke"—were used in the early years of Manchu rule, after which they were replaced with the far more elaborate Qing dynasty system of ranks and titles.
52. The Western Yellow Temple 西黃寺 was built in the northern part of Beijing in 1652 to house the Fifth Dalai Lama and his retinue when they visited the capital the following year. It "was composed of Dalaimiao 達賴廟 and Qingjinghuachengmiao. The Anglo-French armies destroyed Dalaimiao in 1860, and only Qingjinghuachengmiao, including the pagoda, has been preserved. Dalaimiao consisted of an entrance pavilion, a Great Hall (Dadian or Daxiongbaodian, containing the statue offered by Zanabazar), a *dugang* (assembly hall that could house 250 monks), two lateral pavilions for two stone inscriptions, a Dalailou 達賴樓, and the monks' dwellings in the rear part. The axis of these buildings was aligned with the one of the Forbidden City (particularly Taihedian 太和殿), with the monastery acting as a protective geomantic barrier for the palace." Isabelle Charleux, "Qing Imperial Mandalic Architecture for

Gelugpa Pontiffs Between Beijing, Inner Mongolia, and Amdo," in *Along the Great Wall: Architecture and Identity in China and Mongolia*, ed. Eric Lehner, Alexandra Harrer, and Hildegard Sint (Vienna: IVEA-ICRA, 2010), 108–109.

53. On the Qing dynasty's concept of imperial grace and the loyalty it fostered, see Christopher P. Atwood, "'Worshipping Grace': Guilt and Striving in the Mongolian Language of Loyalty," *Late Imperial China* 21 (2000): 86–139.

54. Emperor Peace and Tranquility is the Mongolian reign title (*engke amuγulang qaγan*) of the Kangxi 康熙 emperor (1654–1722, r. 1661–1722).

55. On the importance of fur—especially fur coats as a sign of status—in Qing dynasty rule see Jonathan Schlesinger, *A World Trimmed with Fur: Wild Things, Pristine Places, and the Natural Fringes of Qing Rule* (Stanford, CA: Stanford University Press, 2017), 27–45.

56. At this time, the "Lord of the Tibetan people" was Dayan Khan (d. 1688), the son of Güüshi Khan (d. 1655) who had brought the Fifth Dalai Lama to power in Tibet. In recognition of this the Dalai Lama had made him the "king of Tibet," a title that Güüshi's descendants would retain until the Manchus invaded Tibet in 1720. The "Vajra Khan of the Oirat" was Sengge (d. 1670), the son of the Oirat ruler Baatur Khung Taiji (d. 1653). To explain these burgeoning ties between Tibet and the Oirat it is important to note that Sengge's brother was Galdan (b. 1644, r. 1678–1697), who had been recognized as a reincarnated lama and was therefore sent to study in Tibet. When Galdan returned home in 1666, his brother was facing opposition from two half-brothers, who assassinated Sengge. To avenge his death Galdan renounced his vows and married Sengge's widow. She was the granddaughter of Ochirtu Tsetsen Khan, the Khoshud ruler and most powerful Oirat. With his backing Galdan was successful in defeating his two half-brothers, then began consolidating his own power, so much so that in 1676 he overthrew his grandfather-in-law, becoming the ruler of the Oirat. In recognition of these developments the Dalai Lama gave him the title Boshugtu Khan ("khan with the mandate") in 1678. Galdan Boshugtu Khan and the Oirat Zünghars were set to become a major force in both Buddhist and East Asian history. On the history of the Zünghars see Peter C. Perdue, *China Marches West: The Qing Conquest of Central Eurasia* (Cambridge, MA: Belknap Press, 2005); Lhamsuren Munkh-Erdene, "The 1640 Great Code: An Inner Asian Parallel to the Treaty of Westphalia," *Central Asian Survey* 29, 3 (2010): 269–288.

57. This reincarnation, the Fifth Panchen Lama, Lozang Yeshe (1663–1737), was to become a major figure in Tibetan history during the turbulent late seventeenth and early eighteenth century, including the cover-up of the Fifth Dalai Lama's death, the invasion by Lhazang Khan, and the struggle over the recognition of the Sixth Dalai Lama (https://treasuryoflives.org/biographies/view/Lobzang-Yeshe/2180 [accessed October 23, 2020]).

13. EPILOGUE

1. *The Meaningful and Important Necessity* is Shireetü Güüshi Chöjé's late sixteenth-century revised and expanded version of Pakpa Lama's *What Is to Be Known* of 1278. Agata Bareja-Starzynska, "Siregetü Güüsi Čorji's *Treatise that Contains the Complete Meanings of the Most Important [Buddhist Concepts] to be Used* (The Last Chapter)," in *Sources of Mongolian Buddhism*, ed. Vesna A. Wallace (New York: Oxford University Press, 2020), 6–42.
2. Although this work is cited here and in later Mongolian sources, it is no longer extant and thus little is known about it; however, *The Flower Bouquet Marvelous to Behold* was presumably a historical work of some sort. Walther Heissig, *Die Familien- und Kirchengeschichts-schreibung der Mongolen. Teil I: 16.–18. Jahrhundert* (Wiesbaden: Otto Harrassowitz, 1959), 101.
3. The *Red Book* is Kungga Dorjé's (1309–1364) *Deb-ther dmar-po* (ca. 1346–1363). Dan Martin, *Tibetan Histories: A Bibliography of Tibetan-Language Historical Works* (London: Serindia, 1997), #78.
4. Sharba Khutugtu (fl. 1617–1629) was the leading Sakya monk at the court of Ligdan Khan; it is therefore presumed that this was written to promote Ligdan Khan's legitimacy. Since the work is no longer extant, what it actually entailed is unknown. Nevertheless, Heissig conjectures that Sharba Khutugtu's history was subsequently used by both Sagang Sechen and Lubsangdanjin when he wrote the *Golden Summary*. Heissig, *Die Familien*, 48–50.
5. It is unclear what Chinese source this title refers to; Heissig believes that it may have been a reference work of some kind. Heissig, *Die Familien*, 103.
6. The *White History*, which is attributed to Khubilai Khan, was actually a creation of the late sixteenth century and presumed to be the work of Khutugtai Sechen Khung Taiji.
7. Although there is a well-known Mongolian chronicle with this same title, *The Yellow History*, the extant version of the work was actually completed after the *Precious Summary*. In order to account for this temporal problem it has been suggested that there was an earlier work with the same title in circulation during the early seventeenth century, which is now lost but was used by several Mongol authors; this may explain the many parallel passages found across these works. Heissig, *Die Familien*, 103–107.

14. COLOPHON

1. (30 x 10) + (4 x 4) = 316.
2. (7 x 10) + (3 x 3) = 79. The colophon consists of seventy-nine verses of four lines each; 316 ÷ 4 = 79.
3. The star wood planet day is Thursday.

Bibliography

Abramowski, Waltraut. "Die chinesischen Annalen von Ögedei und Güyük: Übersetzung des 2. Kapitels des Yüan-shih." *Zentralasiatische Studien* 10 (1975): 117–167.

Ahmad, Zahiruddin. *Sino-Tibetan Relations in the Seventeenth Century*. Roma: Istituto Italiano per il Medio ed Estremo Oriente, 1970.

——. *The Song of the Queen of Spring or A History of Tibet: Nag-dBan Blo-bZan rGya-mTSHo Fifth Dalai Lama of Tibet*. New Delhi: Aditya Prakashan, 2008.

Alexandre, E. "Erdeni-zuu, un monastère de XVI siècle en Mongolie." *Etudes mongoles* 10 (1979): 7–34.

Allsen, Thomas T. *Commodity and Exchange in the Mongol Empire: A Cultural History of Islamic Textiles*. Cambridge: Cambridge University Press, 1997.

——. *Culture and Conquest in Mongol Eurasia*. Cambridge: Cambridge University Press, 2001.

——. "Ögedei and Alcohol." *Mongolian Studies* 29 (2007): 3–12.

——. *The Steppe and the Sea: Pearls in the Mongol Empire*. Philadelphia: University of Pennsylvania Press, 2019.

Altan'orgil. *Kökeqota-yin süm-e keyid*. Kökeqota: Öbör Mongyol-un arad-un keblel-ün qoriy-a, 1981.

Atwood, Christopher P. "Banner, Otog, Thousand: Appanage Communities as the Basic Unit of Traditional Mongolian Society." *Mongolian Studies* 34 (2012): 1–76.

——. *Encyclopedia of Mongolia and the Mongol Empire*. New York: Facts on File, 2004.

——. "The First Mongol Contacts with the Tibetans." In *Trails of the Tibetan Tradition: Papers for Elliot Sperling*, ed. Roberto Vitali, 21–46. Dharamsala: Amnye Machen Institute, 2014.

——. "*The History of the Yuan*, chapter 1." *Mongolian Studies* 34 (2017–2018): 2–80.
——. *The Rise of the Mongols: Five Chinese Sources*. Indianapolis: Hackett Publishing, 2021.
——. "Six Pre-Chinggisid Geneaologies in the Mongol Empire." *Archivum Eurasiae Medii Aevi* 19 (2012): 5–57.
——. "Validated by Holiness or Sovereignty: Religious Toleration as Political Theology in the Mongol World Empire of the Thirteenth Century." *International History Review* 26, 2 (2004): 237–256.
——. "'Worshipping Grace': Guilt and Striving in the Mongolian Language of Loyalty." *Late Imperial China* 21 (2000): 86–139.
Badai, Altan'orgil and Erdeni. *Oyirad teüken surbulji bičig*. Qayilar: Öbör Mongγol-un soyul-un keblel-ün qoriy-a, 1985.
Bagchi, Jhunu. *The History and Culture of the Palas of Bengal and Bihar (cir. 750 A.D.–Cir. 1200 A.D.)*. New Delhi: Abhinav Publications, 1993.
Bareja-Starzynska, Agata. "Siregetü Güüsi Čorji's *Treatise that Contains the Complete Meanings of the Most Important [Buddhist Concepts] to be Used* (The Last Chapter)." In *Sources of Mongolian Buddhism*, ed. Vesna A. Wallace, 6–42. New York: Oxford University Press, 2020.
Barnett, Robert. *Lhasa: Streets with Memories*. New York: Columbia University Press, 2006.
Barstow, Geoffrey. *Food of Sinful Demons: Meat, Vegetarianism, and the Limits of Buddhism in Tibet*. New York: Columbia University Press, 2017.
Baumann, Brian G. *Divine Knowledge: Buddhist Mathematics According to the Anonymous Manual of Mongolian Astrology and Divination*. Leiden: Brill, 2008.
Bawden, Charles R. *The Modern History of Mongolia*. London: Kegan Paul International, 1989.
——. *The Mongol Chronicle Altan Tobči*. Wiesbaden: Otto Harrassowitz, 1955.
——. "The Wish-Prayer for Shambhala Again." *Monumenta Serica* 36 (1984–85): 453–510.
Bechert, Heinz. *The Dating of the Historical Buddha*. Göttingen: Vandenhoeck und Ruprecht, 1991–97.
Becker, Eva. *Die altmongolische Hauptstadt Karakorum: Forschungsgeschichte nach Aussagen und archäologischen Quellen*. Rahden: Verlag Marie Ledorf, 2007.
Becker, Jasper. *City of Heavenly Tranquility: Beijing in the History of China*. New York: Oxford University Press, 2008.
Bell, Christopher. "Worldly Protector Deities in Tibet." In *The Brill Encyclopedia of Buddhism*, ed. Jonathan A. Silk et al., 1254–1266. Leiden: Brill, 2019.
Bentor, Yael. *Consecration of Images and Stupas in Indo-Tibetan Buddhism*. Leiden: E. J. Brill, 1996.

Berger, Patricia. "Miracles in Nanjing: An Imperial Record of the Fifth Karmapa's Visit to the Chinese Capital." In *Cultural Intersections in Later Chinese Buddhism*, ed. Marsha Weidner, 145–169. Honolulu: University of Hawai'i Press, 2001.

Berger, Patricia and Terese Tse Bartholomew. *Mongolia: The Legacy of Chinggis Khan*. San Francisco: Asian Art Museum, 1995.

Bira, Shagdaryn. *Mongolian Historical Writing from 1200 to 1700*. Trans. John R. Krueger. Bellingham: Center for East Asian Studies, Western Washington University, 2002.

Biran, Michal. *Chinggis Khan*. Oxford: Oneworld, 2007.

Bivar, A. D. H. "Coins." In *The Oxford Encyclopedia of Archaeology in the Near East*, ed. Eric M. Meyers. New York: Oxford University Press, 1997.

Bosson, James. *A Treasury of Aphoristic Jewels: The Subhasitaratnanidhi of Sa Skya Pandita in Tibetan and Mongolian*. Bloomington: Indiana University Publications, 1969.

Brook, John and Monica Green. "Thinking Big About the Plague." *Inference* 4, 2 (2018). https://inference-review.com/letter/thinking-big-about-the-plague.

Brook, Timothy. "Commerce: The Ming in the World." In *Ming: 50 Years That Changed China*, ed. Craig Clunas and Jessica Harrison-Hall, 254–295. Seattle: University of Washington Press, 2014.

——. *Great State: China and the World*. New York: Harper, 2020.

——. "Great States." *The Journal of Asian Studies* 75, 4 (2016): 957–972.

Brophy, David. *Uyghur Nation: Reform and Revolution on the Russia-China Frontier*. Cambridge, MA: Harvard University Press, 2016.

Buswell, Robert E., Jr. *Encyclopedia of Buddhism*. New York: Macmillan Reference, 2004.

Buswell, Robert E., Jr. and Donald S. Lopez, Jr. *The Princeton Dictionary of Buddhism*. Princeton, NJ: Princeton University Press, 2014.

Chan, Hok-lam. "Exorcising the Dragon: A Legend about the Building of the Mongolian Upper Capital (Shangdu)." *Central Asiatic Journal* 55, 1 (2011): 1–32.

Charleux, Isabelle. "De la ville bleue à la métropole grise: Fondation, protection et destruction de Kökeqota (Huhehaote)." *Études Mongoles et Sibériennes, centralasiatiques et tibétaines* 35 (2004): 69–116.

——. "From North India to Buryatia: The 'Sandalwood Buddha' from the Mongols' Perspective." In *Studies on Sino-Tibetan Buddhist Art: Proceedings of the Fourth International Conference on Tibetan Archaeology and Art*, ed. Xie Jisheng, Luo Wenhua, and Shi Yangang, 539–558. Shanghai: Shanghai Classics Publishing, 2014.

——. "Qing Imperial Mandalic Architecture for Gelugpa Pontiffs Between Beijing, Inner Mongolia, and Amdo." In *Along the Great Wall: Architecture and Identity in China and Mongolia*, ed. Eric Lehner, Alexandra Harrer, and Hildegard Sint, 107–118. Vienna: IVEA-ICRA, 2010.

——. "Recent Research on the Maitreya Monastery in Inner Mongolia (China)." *Etudes Asiatiques/Asiatische Studien* 68 (2014): 1–64.

Ching, Dora C.Y. "Tibetan Buddhism and the Creation of the Imperial Image." In *Culture, Courtiers, and Competition: The Ming Court (1368–1644)*, ed. David M. Robinson, 321–364. Cambridge, MA: Harvard University Asia Center, 2008.

Chiodo, Elisabetta. "History and Legend: The Nine Paladins of Činggis (Yisün Örlüg) According to the Great Prayer (*Yeke öčig*)." *Ural-Altaische Jahrbücher* 13 (1994): 175–225.

——. *Sayang Sečen. Erdeni-yin Tobči: A Manuscript from Kentei Ayimay.* Wiesbaden: Harrassowitz Verlag, 1996.

Chu Hung-lam. "Intellectual Trends in the Fifteenth Century." *Ming Studies* 27 (1989): 1–33.

Čigči. "Asing Lama-yin udum üile-yi tobči tanilčaγulqu ni." *Öbör Mongγol-un neyigem-ün sinjilekü uqagan* 3 (1983): 177–181.

Clunas, Craig, J. Harrison-Hall, and Y. P. Luk. *Ming China: Courts and Contacts.* London: British Museum, 2016.

Dabringhaus, Sabine. "Chinese Emperors and Tibetan Monks: Religion as an Instrument of Rule." In *China and Her Neighbours: Borders, Visions of the Other, Foreign Policy 10th to 19th Century China*, ed. Sabine Dabringhaus and Roderich Ptak, 119–134. Wiesbaden: Harrassowitz, 1997.

Dalton, Jacob P. *The Taming of the Demons: Violence and Liberation in Tibetan Buddhism.* New Haven, CT: Yale University Press, 2011.

Damdinsüren, Ts. "Two Mongolian Colophons of the Suvarnaprabhasottama-Sutra." *Acta Orientalia Academiae Scientiarum Hungaricae* 33, 1 (1979): 39–58.

Dardess, John W. *Conquerors and Confucians: Aspects of Political Change in Late Yüan China.* New York: Columbia University Press, 1973.

——. *More Than the Great Wall: The Northern Frontier and Ming National Security, 1368–1644.* Lanham: Rowman & Littlefield, 2020.

Davidson, Ronald M. *Indian Esoteric Buddhism: A Social History of the Tantric Movement.* New York: Columbia University Press, 2002.

——. *Tibetan Renaissance: Tantric Buddhism in the Rebirth of Tibetan Culture.* New York: Columbia University Press, 2005.

Debreczeny, Karl. "The Early Ming Imperial Atelier on the Tibetan Frontier." In *Ming China: Courts and Contacts*, ed. C. Clunas et al., 152–162. London: British Museum, 2016.

——. "Faith and Empire: An Overview." In *Faith and Empire: The Art of Politics in Tibetan Buddhism*, ed. K. Debreczeny, 19–51. New York: Rubin Museum of Art, 2019.

——. "In the Shadow of the Khan: Tibetan Buddhist Art and Political Legitimation in the Ming Dynasty." In *Faith and Empire: The Art of Politics in Tibetan Buddhism*, ed. K. Debreczeny, 125–150. New York: Rubin Museum of Art, 2019.

Dharma. *Altan kürdün mingγan kegesütü*. Ed. Čoyiji. Kökeqota: Öbör Mongγol-un arad-un keblel-ün qoriy-a, 1987.

Di Cosmo, Nicola. "Military Aspects of the Manchu Wars against the Caqars." In *Warfare in Inner Asian History (500–1800)*, ed. Nicola Di Cosmo, 337–367. Leiden: Brill, 2002.

——. "Qing Colonial Administration in Inner Asia." *The International History Review* 20 (1998): 287–309.

Di Cosmo, Nicola and Dalizhabu Bao. *Manchu-Mongol Relations on the Eve of the Qing Conquest: A Documentary History*. Leiden: Brill, 2003.

Diemberger, Hildegard. *When a Woman Becomes a Religious Dynasty: The Samding Dorje Phagmo of Tibet*. New York: Columbia University Press, 2007.

Dotson, Brandon. *The Old Tibetan Annals: An Annotated Translation of Tibet's First History, with an Annotated Cartographical Documentation by Guntram Hazod*. Vienna: Verlag der Österreichischen Akademie der Wissenschaften, 2009.

Elliott, Mark C. "The Limits of Tartary: Manchuria in Imperial and National Geographies." *The Journal of Asian Studies* 59, 3 (2000): 603–646.

——. "Manchu Historical Consciousness in the Early Qing." In *Temporalities of the Ming-Qing Transition*, ed. Lynn Struve, 31–72. Honolulu: University of Hawai'i Press, 2004.

——. *The Manchu Way: The Eight Banners and Ethnic Identity in Late Imperial China*. Stanford, CA: Stanford University Press, 2001.

Elverskog, Johan. *The Jewel Translucent Sutra: Altan Khan and the Mongols in the Sixteenth Century*. Leiden: Brill, 2003.

——. "The Legend of Muna Mountain." *Inner Asia* 8, 1 (2006): 99–122.

——. "Maitreya, Shambhala, and the End of Buddhist Empire." In *Faith and Empire: The Art of Politics in Tibetan Buddhism*, ed. Karl Debreczeny, 212–227. New York: Rubin Museum of Art, 2019.

——. *Our Great Qing: The Mongols, Buddhism and the State in Late Imperial China*. Honolulu: University of Hawai'i Press, 2006.

——. "The Story of Zhu and the Mongols of the 17th century." *Ming Studies* 50 (2004): 39–76.

——. "Sagang Sechen on the Qing Conquest." In *The Black Master: Essays on Central Eurasia in Honor of Professor György Kara on his 70th Birthday*, ed. Stéphane Grivelet, Ruth Meserve, Àgnes Birtalan, and Giovanni Stary, 43–56. Wiesbaden: Harrassowitz Verlag, 2005.

——. "The Story of Zhu and the Mongols of the Seventeenth Century." In *Long Live the Emperor: Uses of the Ming Founder Across Six Centuries of East Asian History*, ed. Sarah Schneewind, 211–243. Minneapolis: Society for Ming Studies, 2007.

——. "The Tumu Incident and the Chinggisid Legacy in Inner Asia." *The Silk Road Journal* 15 (2017): 142–152.

Emmerick, R. E. *The Sūtra of Golden Light: Being a Translation of the Suvarnabhṡottamasūtra*. London: Luzac & Company, 1970.

The Encyclopaedia of Islam. Leiden: E. J. Brill, 1960–.

Favereau, Marie. *The Horde: How the Mongols Changed the World*. Cambridge, MA: Belknap Press, 2021.

Franke, Herbert. "Tibetans in Yuan China." In *China under Mongol Rule*, ed. John D. Langlois, Jr., 296–328. Princeton, NJ: Princeton University Press, 1981.

Franke, Herbert and Denis Twitchett. *The Cambridge History of China: Alien Regimes and Border States, 97–1368*. New York: Cambridge University Press, 1994.

Franken, Christina. *Die "Grosse Halle" von Karakorum: Zur archäologischen Untersuchung des ersten buddhistischen Tempels der alten mongolischen Haupstadt*. Wiesbaden: Reichert Verlag, 2015.

Geiss, James. "The Chia-ching reign, 1522–1566." In *The Cambridge History of China*, ed. F. W. Mote, vol. 8: 1, 440–510. New York: Cambridge University Press, 1998.

Gethin, Rupert. *The Foundations of Buddhism*. New York: Oxford University Press, 1998.

Gimm, Martin. "Zum mongolischen Mahakala-Kult und zum Beginn der *Qing*-Dynastie—die Inschrift *Shisheng beiji* von 1638." *Oriens Extremus* 42 (2000/01): 69–103.

Goodrich, L. Carrington and Chaoyang Fang. *Dictionary of Ming Biography 1368–1644*. New York: Columbia University Press, 1976.

Grupper, Samuel. "Manchu Patronage and Tibetan Buddhism During the First Half of the Ch'ing Dynasty." *The Journal of the Tibet Society* 4 (1984): 47–75.

Gyatso, Janet. "Down with the Demoness: Reflections on a Feminine Ground in Tibet." In *Feminine Ground: Essays on Women and Tibet*, ed. Janice Dean Willis, 33–51. Ithaca, NY: Snow Lion, 1987.

Hambis, Louis. "Note sur l'installation des Mongols dans la Boucle du Fleuve Jaune." In *Mongolian Studies*, ed. Louis Ligeti, 167–179. Amsterdam: B. R. Grüner, 1970.

Harris, Clare E. *The Museum on the Roof of the World: Art, Politics, and the Representation of Tibet*. Chicago: University of Chicago Press, 2012.

Haufler, Marsha. "Faces of Transnational Buddhism at the Early Ming Court." In *Ming China: Courts and Contacts*, ed. C. Clunas et al. 143–151. London: British Museum, 2016.

Heissig, Walther. *Die Familien- und Kirchengeschichts-schreibung der Mongolen. Teil I: 16.-18. Jahrhundert*. Wiesbaden: Otto Harrassowitz, 1959.

——. "Eine kleine mongolische Klosterbibliothek aus Tsakhar." *Jahrbuch des Bernischen Historischen Museums in Bern* 41 (1963): 557–590.
——. "Zur Entstehungsgeschichte der Mongolischen Kandjur-Redaktion der Ligdan Khan-Zeit (1628–1629)." In *Studia Altaica. Festschrift für Nikolaus Poppe zm 60. Geburtstag am 8. August 1957*, ed. Omeljan Pritsak, 71–87. Wiesbaden: Otto Harrassowitz, 1957.
Henthorn, William E. *Korea: The Mongol Invasions*. Leiden: E. J. Brill, 1963.
Hirshberg, Daniel A. *Remembering the Lotus-Born: Padmasambhava in the History of Tibet's Golden Age*. Cambridge, MA: Wisdom, 2016.
Ho, Kai-lung. "The Office and Noble Titles of the Mongols from the 14th to 16th Century, and the Study of the 'White History' *Čayan Teüke*." *Central Asiatic Journal* 59, 1–2 (2016): 133–177.
Hoog, Constance. *Prince Jin-gim's Textbook of Tibetan Buddhism*. Leiden: E. J. Brill, 1983.
Horlemann, Biana. "The Relations of the Eleventh-Century Tsong Kha Tribal Confederation to Its Neighbour States on the Silk Road." In *Contributions to the Early History of Tibet*, ed. M. T. Kapstein and B. Dotson, 83–106. Leiden: Brill, 2007.
Hucker, Charles O. *A Dictionary of Official Titles in Imperial China*. Stanford, CA: Stanford University Press, 1985.
Hummel, Arthur W. *Eminent Chinese of the Ch'ing Period (1644–1912)*. Washington, DC: The Library of Congress, 1943.
Huth, Georg. *Die Inschriften von Tsaghan Baišin. Tibetisch-Mongolischer Text*. Leipzig: F. A. Brockhaus, 1894.
Inaba, Shoju. "The Lineage of the Sa skya pa: A Chapter of the Red Annals." *Memoirs of the Research Department of the Toyo Bunko* 22 (1963): 107–123.
Jackson, David. *The Entrance Gate for the Wise (Section III). Sa-skya Pandita on Indian and Tibetan Traditions of Pramana and Philosophical Debate. 2 vols.* Wien: Arbeitskreis für Tibetische und Buddhistische Studien Universität Wien, 1989.
Jackson, Peter. *The Mongols and the Islamic World: From Conquest to Conversion*. New Haven, CT: Yale University Press, 2017.
Jürungγ-a. *Erdeni tunumal neretü sudur orosiba*. Beijing: Ündüsüten-ü keblel-ün qoriy-a, 1984.
Kam, Tak-Sing. "The dGe-lugs-pa Breakthrough: The Uluk Darxan Nangsu Lama's Mission to the Manchus." *Central Asiatic Journal* 44, 2 (2000): 161–176.
Kapstein, Matthew T. "Remarks on the Maṇi Bka'-'bum and the Cult of Āvalokiteśvara in Tibet." In *Tibetan Buddhism: Reason and Revelation*, ed. Steven Goodman and Ronald Davidson, 79–93. Albany: State University of New York Press, 1992.
——. *The Tibetan Assimilation of Buddhism. Conversion, Contestation, and Memory*. New York: Oxford University Press, 2000.

——. *The Tibetans*. London: Wiley-Blackwell, 2006.

Kara, György. "On Some Sources of Sagang Sechen's Teachings (1662)." *Acta Orientalia Academiae Scientiarum Hungaricae* 73, 4 (2020): 603–615.

——. "Sagang Sechen's Teachings Reconsidered." *Acta Orientalia Academiae Scientiarum Hungaricae* 74, 2 (2021): 267–324.

Karmay, Samten G. and Jeff Watt. *Bon: The Magic Word. The Indigenous Religion of Tibet.* New York: Rubin Museum of Art, 2007.

Kaschewsky, Rudolf. *Das Leben des Lamaistischen Heiligen Tsongkhapa Blo-bzang-grags-pa (1357–1419) dargestellt und erlautet anhand seiner Vita "Quellort allen Glückes." 2 vols*. Wiesbaden: Otto Harrassowitz, 1971.

King, Matthew W. *Ocean of Blood, Ocean of Milk: A Mongolian Monk in the Ruins of the Qing Empire*. New York: Columbia University Press, 2019.

Kollmar-Paulenz, Karénina. *Erdeni tunumal neretü sudur: Die Biographie des Altan qagan der Tümed-Mongolen*. Wiesbaden: Harrassowitz, 2001.

Krueger, John R. *Poetical Passages in the Erdeni-yin Tobči. A Mongolian Chronicle of the Year 1662 by Sayang Sečen*. The Hague: Mouton, 1961.

Kuijp, Leonard van der. "From *Chongzhen lishu* 崇禎曆書 to *Tengri-yin udq-a* and *Rgya rtsis chen mo*." In *Tibetan Printing: Comparison, Continuities and Change*, ed. H. Diemberger, F. Ehrhard, and P. Kornicki, 51–71. Leiden: Brill, 2016.

——. *The Kalacakra and the Patronage of Tibetan Buddhism by the Mongol Imperial Family*. The Central Eurasian Studies Lectures. Bloomington: Department of Central Eurasian Studies, Indiana University, 2004.

Kuijp, Leonard van der and Gray Tuttle. "Altan Qayan (1507–1582) of the Tümed Mongols and the Stag lung Abbot Kun dga' bkra shis rgyal mtshan (1575–1635)." In *Trails of the Tibetan Tradition: Papers for Elliott Sperling*, ed. Roberto Vitali, 461–482. Dharamshala: Anmye Machen Institute, 2014,

Lhamsuren Munkh-Erdene. "The 1640 Great Code: An Inner Asian Parallel to the Treaty of Westphalia." *Central Asian Survey* 29, 3 (2010): 269–288.

Li Baowen. *Arban doloduyar jayun-u emün-e qayas-tu qolbuydayu Mongyol üsüg-ün bičig debter. Shiqi shiji menggu wen wenshu dang'an (1600–1650)*. Tongliao: Obör Mongyol-un bayacud keüked-ün keblel-ün qoriy-a, 1997.

Ligeti, Louis. *Catalogue du kanjur mongol imprimé*. Budapest: Socièté Korosi Csoma, 1942–44.

Loewanthal, Rudolf. *The Mongol Chronicles of the Seventeenth Century*. Wiesbaden: Otto Harrassowitz, 1955.

Lubsangdanjin. *Altan Tobči*. Ed. Čoyiji. Kökeqota: Öbör Mong ol-un arad-un keblel-ün qoriy-a, 1983.

Martin, Dan. *Tibetan Histories: A Bibliography of Tibetan-Language Historical Works*. London: Serindia, 1997.

May, Timothy. *The Mongol Conquests in World History*. London: Reaktion, 2012.

——. *The Mongol Empire*. Edinburgh: Edinburgh University Press, 2018.
Miyawaki, Junko. "The Birth of Oyirad Khanship." *Central Asiatic Journal* 41 (1997): 38–75.
Morikawa Tetsuo. "Manuscripts of Erdeni-yin Tobci and Their Connections." *Journal of Asian and African Studies* 50 (1995): 1–41.
——. "The Manuscripts and Manuscript Families of the *Erdeni-yin tobči*." *Memoirs of the Research Department of the Toyo Bunko* 59 (2001): 49–86.
Mostaert, Antoine. *Dictionnaire ordos*. New York: Johnson Reprint Corporation, 1968.
——. *Erdeni-yin Tobči. Mongolian Chronicle by Sayang Sečen*. Cambridge, MA: Harvard University Press, 1956.
——. "Sur le culte de Sayang Sečen et de son bisaieul Qutuγtai Sečen chez les Ordos." *Harvard Journal of Asiatic Studies* 20 (1957): 534–566.
Mote, F. W. "The T'u-mu Incident of 1449." In *Chinese Ways in Warfare*, ed. Frank Kierman Jr. and John K. Fairbank, 243–272. Cambridge, MA: Harvard University Press, 1974.
Na-ta. *Altan Erike*. Ed. Čoyiji. Kökeqota: Öbör Mongγol-un arad-un keblel-ün qoriy-a, 1989.
Obermiller, Eugene. *The History of Buddhism*. Heidelberg: Otto Harrassowitz, 1931–32.
Okada, Hidehiro. "An Analysis of the Lament of Togon Temür." *Zentralasiatische Studien* 1 (1967): 55–78.
——. "The Chakhar Shrine of Eshi Khatun." In *Aspects of Altaic Civilization III*, ed. Denis Sinor, 176–186. Bloomington, IN: Research Institute for Inner Asian Studies, 1990.
——. "Dayan Khan in the Battle of Dalan Terigün." In *Gedanke und Wirkung. Festschrift zum 90. Geburtstag von Nikolaus Poppe*, ed. Walther Heissig and Klaus Sagaster, 262–270. Wiesbaden: Harrassowitz Verlag, 1989.
——. "The Fall of the Uriyangqan Mongols." *Mongolian Studies* 10 (1986–87): 49–57.
——. "Life of Dayan Khan." *Acta Asiatica* 11 (1966): 46–55.
——. "The Mongolian Literary Tradition in Early Manchu Culture." In *Proceedings of the 35th Permanent International Altaistic Conference*, ed. Chieh-hsien Ch'en, 377–386. Taipei: National Taiwan University and Center for Chinese Studies Materials, 1992.
——. "The Ordos Jinong in *Erdeni-yin Tobči*." *Journal of Asian and African Studies* 27 (1984): 155–162.
——. "Origin of the Caqar Mongols." *Mongolian Studies* 14 (1991): 155–179.
——. "Origins of the Dörben Oyirad." *Ural-Altaische Jahrbücher* Neue Folge 7 (1987): 181–211.

——. "Outer Mongolia in the Sixteenth and Seventeenth Centuries." *Journal of Asian and African Studies* 5 (1972): 69–85.

——. "The Third Dalai Lama and Altan Khan of the Tümed." In *Tibetan Studies. Proceedings of the 5th Seminar of the International Association of Tibetan Studies*, ed. Ihara Shoren and Yamaguchi Zuiho, 645–652. Narita: Naritasan Shinshoji, 1992.

Pelliot, Paul. "Les systèmes d'ecriture en usage chez les anciens Mongols." *Asia Major* 2 (1925): 284–289.

Pelliot, Paul and Louis Hambis. *Histoire des campagnes de Gengis Khan. Cheng-wou ts'in-tcheng lou*. Vol I. Leiden: E. J. Brill, 1951.

Perdue, Peter C. *China Marches West: The Qing Conquest of Central Eurasia*. Cambridge, MA: Belknap Press, 2005.

Petech, Luciano. *Central Tibet and the Mongols. The Yüan-Sa-skya Period of Tibetan History*. Rome: Istituto Italiano per il Medio Estremo Oriente, 1990.

——. "Tibetan Relations with Sung China and with the Mongols." In *China Among Equals: The Middle Kingdom and Its Neighbors, 10th–14th Centuries*, ed. Morris Rossabi, 173–201. Berkeley: University of California Press, 1983.

Powers, John. *A Bull of a Man: Images of Masculinity, Sex, and the Body in Indian Buddhism*. Cambridge, MA: Harvard University Press, 2009.

Prazniak, Roxann. *Sudden Appearances: The Mongol Turn in Commerce, Belief, and Art*. Honolulu: University of Hawai'i Press, 2019.

Qu Jiusi 瞿九思. *Wanli Wugong Lu* 萬曆武功錄. 1612 ; reprint, Taipei: Yiwen, 1978.

Rachewiltz, Igor de. *In the Service of the Khan: Eminent Personalities of the Early Mongol-Yüan Period (1200–1300)*. Wiesbaden: Harrassowitz, 1993.

——. *The Secret History of the Mongols: A Mongolian Epic Chronicle of the Thirteenth Century*. Leiden: Brill, 2004.

Rachewiltz, Igor de, Hok-lam Chan, Hsiao Ch'i-ch'ing, and Peter W. Geier. *In the Service of the Khan: Eminent Personalities of the Early Mongol-Yüan Period*. Wiesbaden: Otto Harrassowitz, 1993.

Richardson, Hugh. "The Mgar Family in Seventh-Century Tibet." In *High Peaks, Pure Earth: Collected Writings on Tibetan History and Culture*, ed. Michael Aris, 114–123. London: Serindia, 1988.

——. "The sKar-Cung Inscription." *The Journal of the Royal Asiatic Society of Great Britain and Ireland* 1 (1973): 12–20.

Robinson, David M. *In the Shadow of the Mongol Empire: Ming China and Eurasia*. New York: Cambridge University Press, 2020.

——. *Ming China and Its Allies: Imperial Rule in Eurasia*. New York: Cambridge University Press, 2019.

Rogers, Leland Liu. *The Golden Summary of Činggis Qaγan: Činggis Qaγan-u Altan Tobči*. Wiesbaden: Harrassowitz Verlag, 2009.

Rossabi, Morris. *Khubilai Khan. His Life and Times.* Berkeley: University of California Press, 1988.

——. "Ming Foreign Policy: The Case of Hami." In *China and Her Neighbours: Borders, Visions of the Other, Foreign Policy 10th to 19th Century*, ed. Sabine Dabringhaus and Roderich Ptak, 79–97. Wiesbaden: Harrassowitz, 1997.

——. *The Mongols and Global History.* New York: Norton, 2010.

Roth-Li, Gertraude. "State Building before 1644." In *The Cambridge History of China, vol. 9, Part One: The Ch'ing Empire to 1800*, ed. Denis Twitchett and John K. Fairbank, 9–72. New York: Cambridge University Press, 2002.

Rupert, Brian D. *Jewel in the Ashes: Buddha Relics and Power in Early Medieval Japan.* Cambridge, MA: Harvard University Press, 2000.

Sayang Sečen. *Erdeni-yin Tobči. ('Precious Summary') A Mongolian Chronicle of 1662. Vol. I.* Ed. M. GØ, I. de Rachewiltz, J. R. Krueger, and B. Ulaan. Canberra: The Australian National University, 1990.

Sagang Sechen. *Geschichte der Mongolen und ihres Fürstenhauses, Herausgegeben und mit einem Nachwort con Walther Heissig.* Zürich: Manesse Verlag, 1985.

Sagaster, Klaus. *Die Weisse Geschicte. Eine mongolische Quelle zur Lehre von den Beiden Ordnungen Religion und Staat in Tibet und der Mongolei.* Wiesbaden: Harrassowitz, 1976.

Saguchi, Toru. "Historical Development of the Sarïgh Uyghurs." *Memoirs of the Research Department of the Toyo Bunko* 44 (1986): 1–26.

Schaik, Sam van. "Dharma from the Sky: The Pangkong Prayer." *Central Asiatic Journal* 61, 1 (2018): 61–70.

——. *Tibet: A History.* New Haven, CT: Yale University Press, 2011.

Schaik, Sam van and Imre Galambos. *Manucripts and Travellers: The Sino-Tibetan Documents of a Tenth-Century Buddhist Pilgrim.* Berlin: de Gruyter, 2012.

Schlesinger, Jonathan. *A World Trimmed with Fur: Wild Things, Pristine Places, and the Natural Fringes of Qing Rule.* Stanford, CA: Stanford University Press, 2017.

Schuh, Dieter. *Erlasse und Sendschreiben mongolischer Herrscher für tibetische Geistliche.* St. Augustin: VGH-Wissenschaftsverlag, 1977.

Schulemann, Günter. *Geschichte der Dalai-Lamas.* Leipzig: Otto Harrassowitz, 1958.

Schwieger, Peter. "A Document of Chinese Diplomatic Relations with East Tibet during the Ming Dynasty." In *Tibetstudien: Festschrift für Dieter Schuh zum 65. Geburtstag*, ed. P. Maurer and P. Schwieger, 209–226. Bonn: Bier'sche Verlaganstallt, 2007.

Serruys, Henry. "Four Documents Relating to the Sino-Mongol Peace of 1570–1571." *Monumenta Serica* 19 (1960): 1–66.

——. *Genealogical Tables of the Descendants of Dayan-Qan.* 'S-Gravenhage: Mouton, 1958.

——. "The Mongol Name of Shan-hai-kuan in the *Erdeni-yin-Tobči.*" *Etudes mongoles* 16 (1985): 37–40.

——. "A Mongol Settlement in North China at the End of the 16th Century." *Central Asiatic Journal* 4 (1959): 237–278.

——. "A Mongolian Version of the Legend of the Mongol Ancestry of the Yung-lo Emperor." In *Analecta Mongolica: Dedicated to the Seventieth Birthday of Professor Owen Lattimore*, ed. John G. Hangin and Urgunge Onon, 19–61. Bloomington: Indiana University Press, 1972.

——. "A Note on Two Place Names in Mongolia." In *Documenta Barbarorum. Festschrift für Walther Heissig zum 70. Geburtstag*, ed. Annemarie von Gabain and Wolfgang Veenker, 370–381.Wiesbaden: Otto Harrassowitz, 1983.

——. "Notes on a Chinese Inscription of 1606 in a Lamaist Temple in Mai-ta-chao, Suiyüan." *Journal of the American Oriental Society* 78 (1958): 101–113.

——. "The Office of Tayisi in Mongolia in the Fifteenth Century." *Harvard Journal of Asiatic Studies* 37, 2 (1977): 353–380.

——. "The Seven Jewels in Mongolian Literature." *Mongolian Studies* 2 (1975): 133–140.

——. *Sino-Mongol Relations During the Ming II. The Tribute System and Diplomatic Missions (1400–1600).* Bruxelles: Institut Belge des Hautes Études Chinoises, 1967.

——. *Sino-Mongol Relations During the Ming III. Trade Relations: The Horse Fairs (1400–1600).* Bruxelles: Institut Belge des Hautes Études Chinoises, 1975.

——. "Two Remarkable Women in Mongolia: The Third Lady Erketü Qatun and Dayičing-Beyiji." *Asia Major* New Series 19, 2 (1974–75): 191–245.

Shakabpa, Tsepon W.D. *Tibet: A Political History.* New Haven, CT: Yale University Press, 1967.

Shen, Weirong. "On the History of Gling tshang Principality of mDo khams During the Yuan and Ming Dynasties: Studies on Sources Concerning Tibet in *Ming Shilu* (I)." In *Tibetstudien: Festschrift für Dieter Schuh zum 65. Geburtstag*, ed. P. Maurer and P. Schwieger, 227–265. Bonn: Bier'sche Verlaganstallt, 2007.

Si-tu Pan-chen Chos-kyi-'byung-gnas and Be-lo Tshe-dbang kun-khyab. *Sgrub brgyud karma kam tshang brgyud pa rin po che'i rnam par thar pa rab 'byam nor bu zla ba chu shel gyi phreng ba vol. 1.* New Delhi: N.p., 1972.

Smith, Paul J. *Taxing Heaven's Storehouse: Horses, Bureaucrats, and the Destruction of the Sichuan Tea Trade, 1074–1224.* Cambridge, MA: Council on East Asian Studies, 1991.

Sneath, David. *The Headless State: Aristocratic Orders, Kinship Society, and Misrepresentations of Nomadic Inner Asia.* New York: Columbia University Press, 2008.

Snellgrove, David L. *Indo-Tibetan Buddhism.* Boston: Shambhala, 1987.

Sørensen, Per K. *Tibetan Buddhist Historiography. The Mirror Illuminating the Royal Genealogies. An Annotated Translation of the XIVth Century Tibetan Chronicle: rGyal-rabs gsal-ba'i me-long.* Wiesbaden: Harrassowitz Verlag, 1994.
Sperling, Elliot. "Early Ming Policy Toward Tibet: An Examination of the Proposition that the Early Ming Emperors Adopted a 'Divide and Rule' Policy Toward Tibet." Ph.D. diss., Indiana University, 1983.
——. "Rtsa-mi Lo-tsa-ba Sangs-rgyas grags-pa and the Tangut Background to Early Mongol-Tibetan Relations." In *Tibetan Studies: Proceedings of the 6th Seminar of the International Association of Tibetan Studies*, ed. Per Kvaerne, 801–824. Oslo: The Institute for Comparative Research in Human Culture, 1994.
——. "The Szechwan-Tibet Frontier in the Fifteenth Century." *Ming Studies* 26 (1988): 37–55.
Stein, Rolf A. *Tibetan Civilization*. Stanford, CA: Stanford University Press, 1972.
Strong, John S. *The Experience of Buddhism*. Belmont, CA: Wadsworth, 1995.
——. *The Legend of King Aśoka*. Princeton, CA: Princeton University Press, 1983.
Szerb, János. "Glosses on the Oeuvre of Bla-ma 'Phags-pa: II. Some Notes on the Events of the Years 1251–1254." *Acta Orientalia Hungarica* 34 (1980): 263–285.
——. "Glosses on the Oeuvre of Bla-ma 'Phags-pa: III. The 'Patron-Patronized' Relationship." In *Soundings in Tibetan Civilization*, ed. Barbara Nimri Aziz and Matthew Kapstein, 165–173. New Delhi: Manohar, 1985.
Tatár, Magdalena. "Tragic and Stranger Ongons among the Altaic Peoples." In *Altaistic Studies*, ed. Gunnar Jarring and Staffan Rosén, 165–171. Stockholm: Almqvist & Wiksell, 1985.
Teiser, Stephen F. *The Scripture of the Ten Kings and the Making of Purgatory in Medieval Buddhism*. Honolulu: University of Hawai'i Press, 1994.
Togan, Isenbike. "Otchigin's Place in the Transformation from Family to Dynasty." In *Interpreting the Turkic Runiform Sources and the Position of the Altai Corpus*, ed. Marcel Erdal, 403–421. Berlin: Klaus Schwarz Verlag, 2020.
Trainor, Kevin. *Relics, Ritual, and Representation in Buddhism. Rematerializing the Sri Lankan Theravåda Tradition*. New York: Cambridge University Press, 1997.
'Tshal-pa Kun-dga' rdo-rje. *Deb-ther dmar-po*. Beijing: Mi-rigs dpe-skrun khang, 1981.
Tuttle, Gray. "A Tibetan Buddhist Mission to the East: The Fifth Dalai Lama's Journey to Beijing, 1652–1653." In *Power, Politics, and the Reinvention of Tradition: Tibet in the Seventeenth and Eighteenth Centuries*, ed. B. J. Cuevas and K. R. Schaeffer, 65–90. Leiden: Brill, 2006.
Vinkovics, Judit. "Name-Giving Among the Mongols: An Ethnographico-Bibliographical Survey." *Acta Orientalia Academiae Scientiarum Hungaricae* 39, 1 (1985): 25–37.

Vitali, Roberto. *The Kingdoms of Gu.ge Pu.hrang: According to the mkhan.chen Ngag. dbang grags.pa*. Chicago: Serindia, 1997.

——. *Records of Tho.ling: A Literary and Visual Reconstruction of the "Mother" Monastery in Gu.ge*. Delhi: Marg Publishing, 1999.

Wakeman, Frederic, Jr. *The Great Enterprise: The Manchu Reconstruction of Imperial Order in Seventeenth-Century China*. Berkeley: University of California Press, 1985.

Walravens, Hartmut. *Isaak Jacob Schmidt (1779–1847)—Leben und Werk des Pioneers der mongolischen und tibetischen Studien: Eine Dokumentation*. Wiesbaden: Harrassowitz Verlag, 2005.

Weiers, Michael. "Die historische Dimension des Jade-siegels zur Zeit des mandschuherrschers Hongtaiji." *Zentralasiatische Studien* 24 (1994): 119–145.

Ya, Hanzhang. *The Biographies of the Dalai Lamas*. Beijing: Foreign Languages Press, 1991.

Yoshida, Jun'ichi 吉田順一. *Altan Qagan-u Tuyuji*. Tokyo: Kazama-shobo, 1998.

You, Wenpeng, Francesco M. Galassi, Elena Varotto, and Maciej Henneberg. "Genghis Khan's Death (AD 1227): An Unsolvable Riddle or Simply a Pandemic Disease?" *International Journal of Infectious Diseases* 104 (2021): 347–348.

Yuan Shi 元史. Beijing: Zhonghua Shuju Chubanshe, 1995.

Yule, Henry. *The Book of Ser Marco Polo the Venetian concerning the Kingdoms and Marvels of the East, Translated and Edited, with Notes, by Colonel Sir Henry Yule, R.E., C.B., K.C.S.I., Corr. Inst. France, Third Edition, Revised Throughout in the Light of Recent Discoveries by Henri Cordier (of Paris)*. New York: Charles Scribner, 1929.

Zhu-rong-ga 珠榮嘎. *A-la-tan Han Zhuan* 阿勒坦汗傳. Hohhot: Nei Menggu Renmin Chubanshe, 1990.

Zürcher, Erik. *The Buddhist Conquest of China: The Spread and Adaptation of Buddhism in Early Medieval China*. Leiden: Brill, 1959.

Index

GPSR Authorized Representative: Easy Access System Europe, Mustamäe tee 50, 10621 Tallinn, Estonia, gpsr.requests@easproject.com

www.ingramcontent.com/pod-product-compliance
Lightning Source LLC
Chambersburg PA
CBHW030831110726
47900CB00006B/1834